HISTORY
AND WARFARE IN
RENAISSANCE
EPIC

HISTORY
AND WARFARE IN
RENAISSANCE
EPIC

MICHAEL MURRIN

THE UNIVERSITY OF CHICAGO PRESS
Chicago and London

MICHAEL MURRIN is professor of English, comparative
literature, and divinity at the University of Chicago.

The University of Chicago Press, Chicago 60637
The University of Chicago Press, Ltd., London
© 1994 by The University of Chicago
All rights reserved. Published 1994
Printed in the United States of America

03 02 01 00 99 98 97 96 95 94   5 4 3 2 1

ISBN (cloth): 0-226-55403-1

Grateful acknowledgment is made to the Program for Cultural Cooperation between Spain's Ministry of Culture and
United States' Universities and to the Division of the Humani-
ties of the University of Chicago for their generous contributions toward the publication of this book.

Library of Congress Cataloging-in-Publication Data

Murrin, Michael.
    History and warfare in Renaissance epic / Michael Murrin.
        p.   cm.
    Includes bibliographical references and index.
    ISBN 0-226-55403-1
    1. Epic Literature—History and criticism.   2. European
literature—Renaissance, 1450–1600—History and criticism.
3. History in literature.   4. War in literature.   I. Title.
PN56.E65M87   1994   94-20498
809'.93358—dc20   CIP

To my teachers and to the scholars,
some of whom I have never met and never could,
who have helped me in my work

CONTENTS

FIVE
The Problems History Makes for the Poet
Torquato Tasso

——*Part Three*——
THE GUN, OR THE NEW TECHNOLOGY

SIX
Negative Critiques
Ludovico Ariosto and John Milton

SEVEN
Positive Evaluations
Alonso de Ercilla y Zuñiga and Luís Vaz de Camões

EIGHT
The Heroic Few
Alonso de Ercilla y Zuñiga and Gaspar Pérez de Villagrá

NINE
The Officers Take Over
Juan Rufo and Pedro de Oña

——*Part Four*——
VIOLENCE

TEN
Are There Limits to Violence?
Matteo Maria Boiardo, Torquato Tasso, and Alonso de Ercilla y Zuñiga

ELEVEN
Ácoma
Gaspar Pérez de Villagrá

——*Part Five*——
THE EPIC WITHOUT WAR

ILLUSTRATIONS

ACKNOWLEDGMENTS

I OWE MUCH TO THE HELPFUL CRITIQUES OF INDIVIDUAL chapters I received from colleagues at my university: Janel Mueller, Joshua Scodel, and Richard Strier in English; Peter Dembowski and Elissa Weaver in Romance Languages; and Robert Dankoff in Near Eastern Languages and Civilizations. Outside the University of Chicago, Charles Ross at Purdue University, Michael Salda at the University of Southern Mississippi, Peter DeSa Wiggins at the College of William and Mary, J. R. Hale at the University of London, and Dave Henderson in Sonoma, California, have offered both advice and bibliographical help for particular chapters and topics. I also am grateful to the readers for the University of Chicago Press, who guided my final revisions.

I read an early draft of chapters 6 and 7 to the Davis Seminar (then presided over by Lawrence Stone) at Princeton University in 1983, and the members gave me encouragement and useful suggestions. I also thank those who attended oral presentations of chapter 6 at conferences held in Tempe, Arizona, and at Ball State University, especially Constance Jordan, who gave me an extended verbal critique after I read my paper at Tempe.

I also wish to thank the members of the Ariosto and Tasso Seminar, organized by Albert Ascoli and David Quint at Northwestern University, and the faculty and students of the Divinity School at the University of Chicago, assembled for the Nuveen Lecture, to whom I read a version of chapter 10.

Most of all, I owe a profound debt to David Quint, who first suggested I look at the Spanish poets, read all my chapters as I wrote them, and encouraged me to persevere in an enterprise that ultimately took more than a decade to complete.

I have published two sections of this book previously: chapter 3 on Boiardo appeared in *Annali d'Italianistica* 1 (1983), and the first half of chapter 4 appeared in *Modern Language Notes* 103 (1988). They are reprinted here by permission of the publishers.

ABBREVIATIONS

AD	Pedro de Oña, *Arauco domado*
Araucana	Alonso de Ercilla y Zuñiga, *La Araucana*
Arte	Niccolò Machiavelli, *Arte della guerra*
Austriada	Juan Rufo, *La Austriada*
Austriadis libri duo	Juan Latino, *Austriadis libri duo*
BW	Michael Drayton, *The Barons Warres*
CW	Samuel Daniel, *The Civile Wars between the Two Houses of Lancaster and Yorke*
Defence	Sir Philip Sidney, *The Defence of Poesie, or An Apologie for Poetrie*
Dragontea	Lope de Vega, *Dragontea*
Fayttes	Christine de Pisan, *The Book of Fayttes of Armes and of Chyvalrye,* trans. William Caxton
FQ	Edmund Spenser, *The Faerie Queene*
FV	Hierónimo Corte Real, *Felicissima victoria concedida del cielo al señor don Juan d'Austria, en el golfo de Lepánto . . .*
GL	Torquato Tasso, *Gerusalemme liberata*
HR	William of Tyre, *Historia rerum in partibus transmarinis gestarum*
Huth *Merlin*	*Merlin,* ed. Gaston Paris and Jacob Ulrich, 2 vols. Paris: Firmin Didot, 1886.
Lusiadas	Luis de Camões, *Os Lusiadas*
M	Luigi Pulci, *Morgante*
Morte	Sir Thomas Malory, *La Morte Darthur*
NA	Sir Philip Sidney, *New Arcadia*
NM	Gaspar Pérez de Villagrá, *Historia de la Nueva Mexico*
OD	*Don Juan de Oñate, Colonizer of New Mexico, 1595–*

	1628, ed. George P. Hammond and Agapito Rey. Albuquerque: University of New Mexico Press, 1953.
OF	Ludovico Ariosto, *Orlando furioso*
OI	Matteo Maria Boiardo, *Orlando innamorato*
PL	John Milton, *Paradise Lost*
PR	John Milton, *Paradise Regained*
Suite	*Suite du Merlin.* Cambridge University Library, Additional MS 7071, fols. 202v–343v.
Tirant	Joanot Martorell and Martí Joan de Galba, *Tirant lo blanc*
UT	Thomas Nashe, *The Unfortunate Traveller*
Vulgate *Merlin*	*L'Estoire de Merlin.* Vol. 2 of *The Vulgate Version of the Arthurian Romances.* Ed. H. Oskar Sommer. Washington, D.C.: Carnegie Institution of Washington, 1908.

INTRODUCTION

LITERATURE IN THE SIXTEENTH CENTURY UNDERWENT A profound change, and we still live with its consequences. The change occurred within heroic narrative, the socially and critically privileged form of the period, and involved an exclusion that was also a contradiction. By the end of the century heroic narrative had begun to drop war as its subject matter, even though military strife, actual or threatened, was present throughout the period. The contradiction of such writing avoiding its proper subject matter may have led eventually to the demise of the form in the following century. At the same time this change determined the parameters of the genre that replaced it. Despite efforts by writers like Tolstoy and Hemingway, warfare has never been a standard subject for major novelists; modern literary culture tacitly assumes an exclusion made four to five centuries ago.

Yet the shift, while in process, gave rise to a fascinating series of experiments in heroic poetry and prose. A critic who takes a long view of the tradition (all the way back to the Gilgamesh epic and to Homer) would find many of these efforts strange, although artistically excellent. Yet many of these experiments are considered classics in the various vernacular traditions. *Paradise Lost* is a good example: a poem in which all the wrong people glorify heroic activity. Compared to the *Iliad* or *Gerusalemme liberata,* Milton's epic seems almost a generic contradiction. Even intelligent students, however, often do not see its peculiarity, since they have grown up in a different literary culture and generally do not read the older languages. As a result, they are unable to appreciate the rich eccentricity of their own tradition. I hope my book helps to remedy this accidental blindness.

To understand this shift in sixteenth-century literature, one must examine many epics and romances, now largely forgotten. One must also study the warfare that ultimately caused these changes. Military art itself

went through a slow revolution, one determined in large part by technological changes. I begin here.

THE JANISSARIES held part of the Aragon bastion (fig. 1),[1] and the
Greek population of Rhodes refused to support further fighting. The
weather intensified the war-weariness. December 1522 had been wet and
cold, and the Carian Mountains across the channel had snow. On Christmas Eve the sultan made an offer, and two days later the grand master of
the Knights Hospitallers, Philippe Villiers de l'Isle Adam, surrendered.
On New Year's Day the last of the Knights sailed away from Rhodes,
never to return.[2]

Yet they had almost won. They had defended the city of Rhodes successfully for five months, resisting many cannonades in which the Ottomans used bombards that were able to shoot balls nearly three meters
in circumference.[3] The Ottomans had concentrated on the English and
Aragonese sectors using guns and exploding mines, and they had tried
thirteen assaults in that area of the walls (fig. 2). On 4 September 1522 a
stretch of wall twelve meters wide fell by the Tower of the Virgin, and
the troops who attacked managed to plant seven banners on the walls
before they were repulsed. Five days later a mine blew open another
breach, two to three meters wide, and two assaults followed, the first of
which set nine banners on the walls; the Knights repulsed them both. On
24 September the Janissaries struck again at the breach in the Aragonese
sector and took its tower temporarily, but cannon fire from the neighboring walls cut off reinforcements, and the Ottomans suffered severe
losses.[4] By the end of the month the many tunnels and counter tunnels
under the bulwark of the English sector caused it to fall down. Worse
followed. In October the Turks had earthworks that protected them from
flank fire, so they could approach the wall in relative safety. They began
pulling down stones from the walls by ropes. They made seven assaults
that month, yet still none succeeded. In November the Knights had to
evacuate the bastion of Aragon, and its tower fell as a result of mining on
the fourteenth. Then another mine brought down part of the fortification and widened the old breach, and on 29 November the Ottomans
tried another assault. Heavy rain washed away their earthworks, leaving
them once again open to flank fire, and they left behind in the mud three
thousand of their dead. At this point Christopher Waldner, chief of the
German-speaking Knights, wrote home saying that the city had been besieged for five months and had endured twenty-five assaults made in three
different places, two of the attacks terrible, one of them lasting seventeen

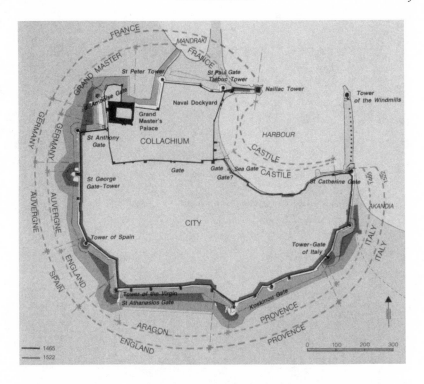

Figure 1. Map of the siege of Rhodes. Courtesy Ekdotike Athenon S.A. Copyright © 1991.

hours. The last try, that of 17 December, at last won the Ottomans a toehold on the Aragonese bastion and led to the surrender. So ended a drama not of five months but of seventy years. It was a technological race between the Hospitallers and the Ottomans, with the Knights winning most of the time until that fateful December.[5]

By the mid-fifteenth century the Knights, following the best medieval thinking, had rebuilt or mostly built anew the whole defense system of Rhodes.[6] Cannon, however, had just become effective in sieges. The French pioneered the new technology, and the Knights, most of whom were French, understood the danger it posed. The Mamluks in their last siege of the city, in 1444, had already used cannon, but the danger really came from the expanding Ottoman Empire.[7] In 1453 the Turks blew their way into Constantinople, and Mehmed II began systematically conquering all the Greek and Latin principalities in the area. He ended his reign with a massive attack on Rhodes in 1480. The modern tourist still sees cannonballs everywhere in the city, now mostly used for decoration or

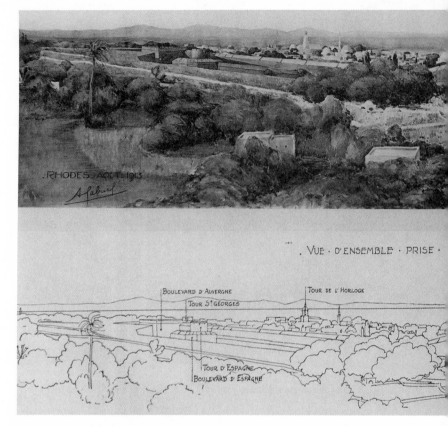

Figure 2. View of the England-Aragon sector of the walls of Rhodes. Courtesy De Boccard Editi Diffusion, Paris.

kept in orderly piles: the results of this and the last siege in 1522.[8] The siege of 1480 still showed the marks of a transitional phase in warfare because the Ottomans used old siege engines alongside their cannon: the mangonel, which shot jars of "wild fire" that was the medieval equivalent of napalm, and the trebuchet, which lobbed rocks.[9] The Knights withstood the assault, but the city and fortifications sustained terrible damage. An earthquake the next year completed what the Ottomans had begun, and the Hospitallers had to rebuild everything, both the walls and their buildings. In the next forty years they redid almost their entire land defenses. They were still working on the bastion of Auvergne when the Ottomans returned in June 1522.[10]

The Knights tried to adapt a traditional style of defense to a completely new kind of threat. Cannon had changed all the rules. Gone were

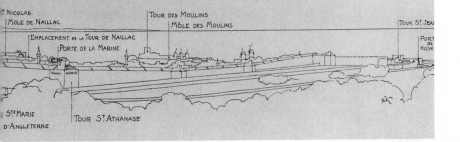

· DES · SAINTS –ANARGYRES .

NICOLAS.
MÔLE DE NAILLAC

EMPLACEMENT DE LA TOUR DE NAILLAC
PORTE DE LA MARINE

Ste MARIE
D'ANGLETERRE

TOUR DES MOULINS
MÔLE DES MOULINS

TOUR St JEAN

PORT
DE
KOSK

TOUR St ATHANASE

the old scaling ladders and movable towers. Cannons simply knocked
down portions of a wall, opening a breach that made possible an assault.
The high thin walls of the medieval enceinte were especially vulnerable
to cannon, so the Hospitallers frantically worked to make the old walls
into something quite different. They began with a rampart more than
two meters thick and a parapet of nearly half a meter but ended with a
rampart of more than twelve meters and a parapet four meters across.
Great mass and low towers could better resist direct hits by cannonballs.
The Towers of Aragon and the Virgin show the new system. Polygonal
bastions with low loopholes through which cannon could shoot into the
dry moat transformed the old towers; the Knights constructed a network
of galleries under them to ward off mining. Soon after the Knights added
ravelins within the moat itself: these were freestanding walls that paral-

Figure 3. The Tower of Spain. Courtesy De Boccard Edition-diffusion, Paris.

Figure 4. The Ramparts of Spain with ravelins (view from the Tower of Spain). Courtesy De Boccard Edition-Diffusion, Paris.

leled the main wall and would make a direct assault difficult, since they flanked the approaches to the gates and blocked the way to the curtain (figs. 3–6).[11]

The French thinking that governed these alterations was well expressed by Robert de Balsac in his *Nef des princes* (ca. 1500).[12] He stressed flank fire along the moat, and the Knights put ravelins in front of the curtain to get at attackers who might assemble at the salient or blind

Figure 5. The Ramparts of Spain (view from the Tower of the Virgin). Courtesy De Boccard Edition-Diffusion, Paris.

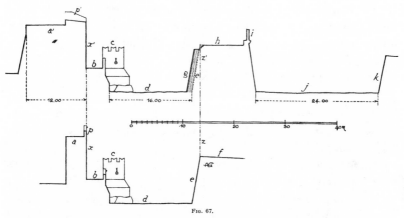

FIG. 67.

Figure 6. Diagram of the comparative widths of the walls of Rhodes, before and after gunpowder. Courtesy De Boccard Edition-Diffusion, Paris.

angles of the bastion. Medieval ideas, unfortunately, still governed this modernization. The Knights wanted to annihilate the enemy at the walls, but the Ottomans nullified the flank fire by constructing earthworks to protect their approaches.[13] It was precisely the modernized sectors of the walls, the southwest section with the Towers of the Virgin and of Aragon, that the Ottomans penetrated in 1522. De Balsac and the Knights had not yet found the proper use of cannon in a modern defense system.

The Italians, however, were developing a new and effective defensive system that became standard during the 1530s. The Knights themselves used this new thinking when they successfully defended Malta against their old enemy Süleyman, forty years after the fall of Rhodes.[14]

IN THIS BOOK I study a literary response to the same crisis the Knights faced, one less dramatic but no less significant culturally. The old medieval order, which had produced the Knights of Saint John, had a fully developed literary genre through which it expressed military engagements: the romance. This genre, particularly when it was composed in or represented actions in the Mediterranean zone, normally imagined the same kind of war the story of Rhodes illustrates: the clash between Christian and Muslim. The majority of the authors covered in this book came from this zone and specialized in such stories, even though later they might transplant the scene to the Americas, where Indians replaced Muslims as the enemy. In all cases these writers had to adjust their narratives to the Gunpowder Revolution. Some tinkered with the old genres, as the Knights did with their medieval walls; others opted for a different form, that of classical epic, which came into Italy along with the star-shaped forts of the new military system. This period of experimentation and reaction to the gun is half of my story.

On the military side the art of war underwent a slow but complete revolution, mostly but by no means solely through the development of firearms. The new technology made war first offensive and then defensive. Initially, it led to a century of expansion from the 1440s to the 1530s and produced the so-called gunpowder empires. The Ottomans conquered the Balkans and united the Arabs under their rule, the Portuguese sailed east and west, and the Spaniards occupied much of Mexico and Central and South America. During this period the gun gradually became effective in all kinds of warfare, from sieges to open field engagements. The same technology determined the defensive posture of the later sixteenth century. Once the Italians turned forts into gun platforms, the defense could accumulate more guns and destroy an attacker.[15] War then returned to the traditional methods of siege and attrition, which had dominated the Middle Ages and quattrocento Italy. Since the gun ultimately generated opposite effects, I had to study both phases, the offensive and the defensive periods. This explains the time span under study, roughly the sixteenth century or, more precisely, 1483–1610.

I have, however, left the boundaries elastic. The first romancers, Martorell and Malory, really bring us back to the mid-fifteenth century. Martorell, who composed most of *Tirant lo blanc,* died in 1468, although the romance was not published until 1490,[16] and Malory dates his book to

1469–70, though Caxton published it many years later.[17] Similarly, at the other end I include Milton with Ariosto in chapter 6 to show the tenacity of the conservative rejection of firearms. The sixteenth century, nevertheless, remains my focus, and I do not deal with *Perceforest* and other romances written before 1450 or with the *L'Adone* and other seventeenth-century epics.

Both aspects of the Gunpowder Revolution, the offensive and the defensive, affected heroic narrative and require the kind of informed reading a student of literature often lacks. In my teaching of comparative epic I have found that literary students frequently shy away from military narrative, even when it determined a text or gave authors one of their principal topics. Sometimes this reluctance seems to manifest a post-Vietnam distaste for war and stories of war, yet such moral revulsion, however highly principled, can lead to a serious misunderstanding of the past. It could be said that war was the main activity in the West during the early modern period. The sixteenth century, for example, enjoyed less than ten years of complete peace.[18] On the other hand, students and critics who try to work with military narrative often lack the necessary background. They may not know how to read maps or assess fortifications, armor, and weapons, or they may read the past in light of the present. Often they try to interpret a story before they understand what they have read. For these reasons I have tried to cover most aspects of early modern warfare in this book, including regular field battles (chapter 1), strategy (chapter 2), sieges (chapter 4), guerrilla tactics (chapter 8), and the two kinds of naval war, involving galleys and sailing ships (chapter 9).

The following passage from the *Arauco domado* illustrates the need for an informed reading of military poetry. Pedro de Oña is here describing the guns and shot that the viceroy, Garcia Hurtado de Mendoza, provided in 1594 for the flotilla he had put together to fight Richard Hawkins's *Daintie*, which had just appeared in the sea off Peru:

> La máquina artillada fué tan buena
> Que deshiciera torres diamantinas:
> Pedreros, esmeriles, culebrinas,
> Con balas de navaja y de cadena;
> El salitrado povo más que arena.
> (*AD* 18.97, p. 642)[19]

The artillery was so good that it could unmake towers of adamant: *pedreros*, esmerils, culverins with sharpened balls and chain shot, more gunpowder than sand.

A reader would probably wonder first whether Oña in this octave gives anything more than a list of names. In an age of nonstandardized equipment people did not always use terms precisely, and of course poets tended to be even less precise than most.[20] Oña himself had an academic and legal training, rather than a military education.[21] Yet other information indicates that the reader should take the poet's details seriously. He came from a military family stationed on the Chilean frontier, a zone of permanent war, and lived there long enough to learn the local natives' language.[22] He certainly would have known about guns, and for his description of the Hawkins affair he used the military report of the incident, provided by Balaguer de Salcedo (*AD* 18.48, p. 626n). As a result, precision marks all aspects of this episode in the *Arauco domado,* even to phrases borrowed from Salcedo's *Relación,* a precision not always evident elsewhere in the poem.[23]

Precision characterizes the rest of the information the poet gives us concerning the little fleet. The two lead galleons shared sixty bronze guns, and the poet specifies their maker, the "famous Tejeda."[24] The third galleon, the *San Juan,* had fourteen large pieces.[25] Finally, each of the three packet boats or *pátajes* had four *versos* in front (*AD* 18.69, 71, pp. 632, 633). In such a narrative as this, then, we can trust the poet's list of guns and shot and see what it tells us.

Oña specifies culverins, *pedreros,* esmerils, and *versos.* Culverins used light iron shot, and the poet later shows us an old man pushing one across the deck of the second ship.[26] The *pedreros* were short-barreled rock throwers. The esmerils shot iron or lead balls and were also carried in the *patajes* (fig. 7).[27] Like the *versos,* which shot iron balls, they were small pieces. For the shot Oña specifies "balas de navaja y de cadena."[28] The former were sharpened or pointed balls; the latter, two half-balls connected by a small chain.

These specifics tell us two important things about the fleet. First of all, *versos* were obsolete by the late sixteenth century.[29] One might expect the colonies to use such weapons, but their presence also might reveal the desperation felt over Hawkins's arrival. His was the third English break into the Pacific zone, an area as yet almost undefended.[30] The viceroy collected what he could, including old as well as new guns.

More significant, Oña mentions no really large guns. Esmerils were intended to kill men, not to sink ships,[31] and chain shot was designed to sweep a deck. The armament presupposes the standard Spanish tactic of grapple and board—something Philip II specifically told the Armada

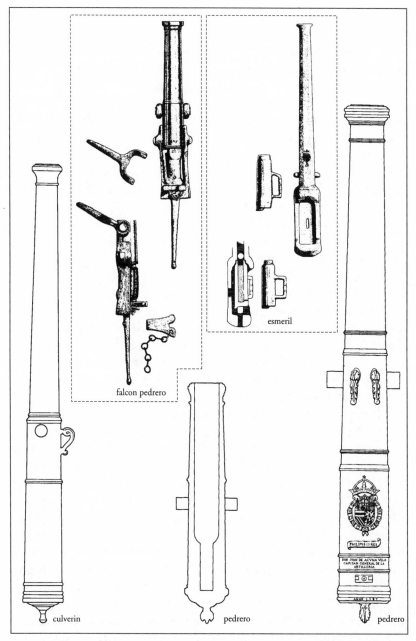

Figure 7. Drawings of pedreros, culverins, and esmerils. Reprinted from Martin and Parker, *Spanish Armada*, with the permission of W. W. Norton and Company, Inc., and Hamish Hamilton, Ltd. Copyright © 1988 by Colin Martin and Geoffrey Parker.

commanders to do[32]—and the Spaniards were still using this method as late as 1639.[33]

As I argue in chapter 9, this tactical attitude had important consequences for poetry and, in fact, made Oña's narrative possible. If he had shared Hawkins's view of naval fighting, he might not have written up the battle at all. An old-style conflict like Lepanto produced much narrative poetry; a new-style engagement like that of the English with the Armada, none.[34] A list of guns, thus, can tell us much and actually imply a sort of gunpowder poetics.

The core of this book, chapters 6 and 7, treats the poets' own reactions to the Gunpowder Revolution. The improvement of firearms led to a crisis, which Ariosto signaled in the last version of his *Furioso*—a crisis made more intense by the movement into history. Of course, other factors also contributed to it. The Swiss, for example, won battles with infantry, not cavalry, and by the time Ariosto wrote, something closer to the modern army already existed, with infantry, artillery, and heavy and light cavalry, all in their own units. The whole practice of war had drifted far from traditional narrative modes. The poets, however, focused on the gun, which stood for all these changes by synecdoche. They understood that they faced a crisis that called into question the future of heroic narrative as well as the heroic code such stories express. Some tried to accommodate the new warfare and worked out a "modernist" position, which anticipated Charles Perrault by a century.[35]

I begin back in the period of the Knights of Rhodes, in the late fifteenth century, to show how traditional romance ignored or adapted to the earlier stages of the technological revolution. Poets like Luigi Pulci, for example, could afford to ignore guns as they affected regular battles. Handgunners fought like crossbowmen, and large guns, although they were used, had not yet produced new tactics. Moreover, the Italians, unlike the Swiss, still favored cavalry. I discuss this matter in chapter 1. More dangerous was the (perhaps willful) ignorance writers showed of the modern Muslim enemy, who bore no resemblance to the Saracen warriors commemorated in medieval romance. I analyze this blindness in chapter 3, where I discuss Matteo Maria Boiardo and the traditional view of Muslim enemies in Western narratives. But quattrocento writers sometimes tried to incorporate some aspects of contemporary warfare. In chapter 2 I focus on Malory's attempt to work out a new military strategy appropriate to his period and his realization that his romance sources resisted modernization. In all these chapters, I also talk about history and the written forms of history.

FIFTEENTH- AND SIXTEENTH-CENTURY WRITERS were obsessed
with history, a literary preoccupation that both parallels and interacts
with their attempts to cope with the Gunpowder Revolution. A literary
change, for example, paralleled the shift from offense to defense in the
waging of war, as the writers of romance and epic switched from the fictional use of historical forms to something resembling actual history.
Malory and Boiardo assumed the role of historians and spoke of their
narratives as history, but Boiardo at least understood that he was composing fiction. The Iberian poets of the later sixteenth century, however,
wrote something more like actual history. The poets of Lepanto and Luíz
Vaz de Camões chose the recent past, but Alonso de Ercilla and others
like Gaspar Pérez de Villagrá who imitated him, went further and composed eyewitness history. Ercilla fought in the war he narrated, and historians as well as literary critics still study his *Araucana* as a primary source.

I am pleased to draw attention to these Iberian poets in my book and
to expand the canon normally studied by scholars of comparative epic.[36]
The typical scholar travels north from Italy to England by way of France,
bypassing Spain and Portugal. In this book I have attempted to remedy
this omission. I treat the changeover from the pretence of history to the
use of actual historical sources most explicitly in chapters 3–5, but this
theme runs throughout the book.[37]

With eyes on Italy, scholars have usually explained this transformation
generically, as a move from romance to epic. Such a thesis ignores two
central issues discussed in this book. The first concerns the Gunpowder
Revolution. To my knowledge, critics so far have not recognized or acknowledged that the two genres present different kinds of war. The warrior in romance usually fights on horseback, while in classical epic Achilles and Aeneas chase their enemies about the field on foot.[38] Romance
thus fits the old cavalry battles of the Middle Ages, while classical epic
better accommodates the new styles of infantry fighting adopted by the
English, Swiss, and Spanish. Tasso's heroes, accordingly, do most of their
fighting on foot.

More telling for us, however, are the Iberian poets who composed heroic narratives of colonial enterprise. They clearly show the military significance behind this generic change. Spanish poets like Ercilla stuck to
the old romance form, imitating Ariosto not just in specific passages but
in their chronological order, varied with inset stories. Ercilla could do so
because the Spaniards, though they pioneered infantry tactics in Italy,
continued to fight on horseback in America. The genre fit the style of
fighting. Camões, however, celebrating Portuguese achievements in the

Indian Ocean, opted for epic. The Portuguese troops there were mostly naval and amphibious forces, who regularly fought on foot when they had land battles, so once more the choice of genre fit the mode of combat. Of course, it is unlikely that poets thought through the matter in the way I have just described it. I speak of a tendency and not a developed, self-conscious theory of generic choice.

The second issue concerns the poets' long flirtation with history, which the traditional or generic argument does not fully explain. Ercilla, who stayed within the old romance genre, was probably closer to the historical facts of his story than either Tasso or Camões, who opted for classical epic. In this respect the change in military practice refines the old theory and explains issues it does not cover. Heroic narrative and modern warfare were diverging in the sixteenth century. Outside the Iberian colonies the old representations of warfare by heavy cavalry no longer related to current practice. The move to the classics helped forge a new link with an audience trained in those same classics, and thus we find classical formulas and echoes in Ercilla as well as in Camões.

Aristotle's *Poetics,* which spurred the revival of classical epic around mid-century, could theoretically have led poets in one of two *opposite* directions, since Aristotle located poetry between history and philosophy. Nonetheless, both the poets who followed his theory and those who did not looked toward history. Indeed, Aristotle's famous ladder of history, poetry, and philosophy encouraged scholars of Italian neoclassicism to look for differences between these disciplines, to create dichotomies. In the early 1960s Bernard Weinberg and Baxter Hathaway opposed fiction and history,[39] a dichotomy adopted by later critics who were not especially concerned with Aristotle, such as William Nelson and Ronald Levao.[40] The writers of heroic poetry, however, moved in the opposite direction and tended to blur the distinction between their own and historical narratives.[41] Rhetoric suggests a possible explanation for this trend. The Renaissance tended to conceive of art rhetorically; theorists spoke of audience and worried about the relation between word and object, narrative and fact. Tasso, the only writer who theorized the poets' preference for history over philosophy, appealed to rhetoric and not to poetics to explain the choice. Writers want to deceive readers with a semblance of truth, he said, a purpose they can best attain if they use documents that readers can check.[42] Here Tasso tacitly assumes that he can no longer take his audience for granted. History makes the poet's stories plausible. To preserve heroic narrative the poet must establish a bond with the audience, one taken from history. In fact, to continue to exist heroic narrative underwent a radical change irrespective of generic choice. Both Tasso and Ercilla, who wrote no theory and preferred romance, adopted a historical approach.

The question of history invites comparison between historical texts and those of the poets, and at the same time it leads us back to the Gunpowder Revolution. As the poets concentrated more and more on recent or even contemporary history, they had to respond directly to military developments. Juxtaposition is one of the most effective and economical ways to show this double issue of the relation of heroic poetry to war and to history. In my analyses, therefore, I switch back and forth between historical and poetic battles. With the Iberian poets the difference between the two sometimes approaches the vanishing point, since they give us poetic versions of real battles. Aristotle would probably have dismissed eyewitness narrators like Ercilla and Villagrá as historians, but he might finally have passed the same judgment on Camões and the Lepanto poets as well.

If I were a New Historicist, such juxtapositions would contextualize a literary work as one more product of its historical culture. Following that movement's lead, Beverly Kennedy in her *Knighthood in the "Morte Darthur"* (1985) has tried to do this with Malory. Like her, I owe a profound debt to the New Historicists, particularly to Stephen Greenblatt, Richard Helgerson, and Frank Whigham. Thanks to their work, literature departments for the first time in decades have become more tolerant of historical work. I am really an "Old Historicist," however, since I still privilege the poets and their compositions and worry about how they struggled to accommodate or deny the new military reality and how they thought their poetry related to history writing. This concern has led me closer to the methods of empirical history than to the anthropological approaches favored by the New Historicists.[43] I not only juxtapose documents of differing provenance or genres or disciplines, I also use historical and legal documents to reconstruct a practice or a battle, or else I follow historians who have already done so.

My goal of understanding the relation between a poetic and a real war has involved much travel. I tried to visit the sites of the various battles, fictional or real, and test my impressions against those given by the poet. I have looked at many battlefields and at many towns and forts that were once besieged, from the Levant to Chile. Occasionally my attempts proved frustrating. The opportunity to visit Chile, for example, came before I knew exactly which battles from the *Araucana* I would study. I visited as many places in the old war zone as I could, but road repairs and time did not allow me to see Purén and Tucapel (Cañete), and I was able to determine the sites of two battles only long after my visit. Yet the trips taught me much about the texts I was studying. Ariosto clearly describes Paris, though he never visited the city, but Villagrá, who wrote an eyewitness account of the killings at Ácoma Pueblo, presents a town quite different from the one the Indians rebuilt afterward and that tourists now visit in New Mexico.

The preceding summary of my argument involves considerable simplification. The chapters that follow provide the nuances and suggest the complications. The move to history, for example, initially created many problems, even though it ultimately helped heroic narrative to survive for as long as it did. Poets now had to worry about verisimilitude, an issue exacerbated by the imitation of Roman poets like Virgil and Ovid, who favored an illusionist realism in their descriptions. Verisimilitude as well as the new warfare made Ariosto try to describe a Paris he had never seen, a topic I explore in chapter 4. Later poets like Camões and Tasso, who worked directly with chronicles, had to decide how a poet should give an artistic arrangement to such material. This is an issue I discuss in chapter 5.

No single explanation can rationalize a complex series of changes. Throughout this book I have argued a double, not single, hypothesis. One involves the Gunpowder Revolution, while the other concerns the poets' fascination with written history and with history in the making. Even a double hypothesis, however, oversimplifies reality. This investigation supplements other more strictly literary studies of romance and epic; it does not replace them.

Ultimately, the poets, like the Knights of Rhodes, had to give up their attempt. Neither effort can simply be dismissed as a failure. By their feverish efforts to modernize the defenses of Rhodes, the Knights won another seventy years for themselves (1453–1523). Moreover, their heroic defense in 1522 cost the Ottomans untold numbers of soldiers[44] and elicited this praise from the young emperor Charles V: "Nothing in the world was ever so well lost as Rhodes." They won more than praise: Charles gave them a new home to the west, the island of Malta. When the Knights left Rhodes on that wintry morning, they had in their ranks a young Provençal, Jean Parisot de la Valette, who lived to defeat Süleyman in their new island home.[45]

Poets, responding to the same crisis—the new warfare—prolonged the life of heroic narrative for another century and made possible a kind of afterlife in the seventeenth century. Their efforts preserved not only a kind of story telling but the old chivalric code implied in it. Intense ethical debate informed heroic poetry in the sixteenth century. Writers argued how or whether the new warfare fit the military code—a subject I analyze in chapters 6 and 7—and whether ethical limits existed for violence committed in wartime, the topic of chapters 10 and 11. As so often happens in such circumstances, continuity masked an important change. Poets shifted their emphasis from the individualistic, rampaging heroes of medieval romance to officers or to a group seen as a heroic unit, an issue I explore in chapters 8 and 9. This development anticipates the way we conceive of war today.

By the end of the sixteenth century signs of surrender were clear. The English tradition, from Spenser to Milton, reveals this situation, as its writers developed what one might call the peaceful epic. Although precedents could be found in Ovid or in some medieval Arthurian romances, such works were something of an anomaly. This was in no way an ethical evolution away from the militarism of the Western past. Instead, the transformation signaled the death of the genre, as Milton indicates in the Proem to book 9 of *Paradise Lost* (27–31), saying that he was

> Not sedulous by Nature to indite
> Wars, hitherto the only Argument
> Heroic deem'd, chief maistry to dissect
> With long and tedious havoc fabl'd Knights
> In Battles feign'd . . .

Such an attitude requires a new genre altogether, and in fact the novel soon replaced the epic as the major narrative mode in the West. I consider the beginnings of this new development in chapter 12, but I do not go far into the seventeenth century.

.·❧ PART ONE ❧·.

War
without
the
Gun

The Romance Tradition

ONE

The Tactics of Roncesvalles

Luigi Pulci

IN THE SECOND HALF OF THE FIFTEENTH CENTURY CHIVAL-
ric romance determined the literary representations of war, just as it had
for the whole later Middle Ages. Five authors, writing in three languages,
illustrate this point: Luigi Pulci and Matteo Maria Boiardo in Italy, Sir
Thomas Malory in England, and Joanot Martorell and Martí Joan de
Galba on the Catalan-speaking coast of Aragon. Taken together, these
five writers offer a reasonably complete picture of the kind of warfare that
romances normally presented. In part I of this book I discuss romance
military tactics and strategy, and the writers' conception of the men who
did the fighting. I begin with tactics, since field encounters posed the
most severe test of skill for both commander and writer. The poet had to
create a plausible narrative for a battle, that most complicated of military
actions, involving simultaneous movements of masses of troops and re-
quiring a chain of command. For this purpose I have chosen to focus
upon Pulci, since the poet devotes several cantari, or cantos, of his *Morgante* to the battle of Roncesvalles, which he describes in detail, including
an elaborate tactical plan for the Saracen attack. His narrative also most
clearly attests to the longevity of the romance tradition.

In *Morgante* Pulci reworked two fairly recent texts, the *Spagna in rima*
and the *Rotta di Roncisvalle*, but these two in turn had reworked the *Entrée d'Espagne*, itself a *rifacimento* of the *Chanson de Roland*.[1] If one juxtaposes the poems at either end of this line, the *Roland* and the *Morgante*,
one can easily see that the essentials of the story did not change through
all the intermediate versions. That a story composed about 1100, re-
counting an event of the eighth century, could be redone without major
changes in the late fifteenth century shows the continued viability of traditional vernacular forms.[2] The same observation applies to the authors

who used Arthurian romance, though the time span is shorter. Malory abbreviated texts of the thirteenth and fourteenth centuries.[3] Boiardo mixed Arthurian and Carolingian materials. The battle narratives in both Malory and Boiardo resemble Pulci's because Arthurian romance originally modeled its military sequences on those in the chansons de geste. They all go back to the same sources, the oldest of which is the *Chanson de Roland*. In my discussion of the *Morgante* and of these related texts, I emphasize continuity, Pulci's debt to traditional methods, and the impact of contemporary warfare upon his narrative.

Pulci may or may not have had direct experience of war, but he certainly completed the last five cantari, or cantos, of the *Morgante* in wartime. His employer, the condottiere Roberto da San Severino, served against the poet's native Florence during the War of the Pazzi Conspiracy, leading raids out of Serazzano during the winter and spring of 1479. That August and September San Severino helped Ludovico Sforza capture Milan and take power there, and he then went into Venetian service, fighting in the Ferrara War (1482–84).[4] Pulci published the final version of the *Morgante,* including the new cantari, in 1483, the same year that Boiardo (whose patron, the condottiere Ercole d'Este, fought as San Severino's opponent in both wars) came out with the first two parts of his *Orlando innamorato*.[5] Both poets were connected with the same set of wars.

Four condottieri tracts illustrate the tactical thinking of the commanders involved in these wars and thus help us to see how romance battles relate to contemporary warfare. Chiereghino Chiericati published his "Trattatello della milizia" in 1471 and dedicated it to Cardinal Orsini.[6] A professional soldier, Chiericati had recently served as "revisore generale," or military inspector, for the papacy (1465–71).[7] Pulci's patron San Severino had himself collaborated with other captains over the Christmas holidays of 1472–73 to produce the bulk of the documents that Filippo degli Eustachi compiled for Galeazzo Maria Sforza in Milan and called the "Ordine dell' esercito ducale."[8] Sforza had asked the captains to estimate the size and kind of army needed for a possible war with Venice, now distracted by the Long War against the Ottoman Empire. Soon after, on 2 January 1477, Orso degli Orsini completed the "Governo et exercitio de la militia" for King Ferrante in Naples, who then sent him as an adviser to Alfonso, duke of Calabria, who commanded the troops of the Regno during the Pazzi War.[9] Finally, in 1478 and 1479 Diomede Carafa sent two memorials to Alfonso that were intended to guide his conduct for the same war.[10] Together these treatises represent the views of an older generation of condottieri, who still controlled the conduct of war.[11] They adhered to the Sforza school of military theory, then dominant in the peninsula[12] and as yet unaffected by contemporary developments in the north.[13]

THE SARACEN PLAN FOR RONCESVALLES

Gano (Ganelon) sets the tactics for Roncesvalles (*M* 25.102–7). He would have the Spanish Saracen army attack in three waves, on an ascending scale: the vanguard with 100,000, the second group with 200,000, the third with 300,000. He assumes that the French rear guard will repel the first two attacks but fail before the third. Thus, the Saracens will first tire out their enemies and then overwhelm them. The Saracen king, Marsilio, carefully follows these instructions with a twist that fits Gano's intention (*M* 25.175–80). He surrounds the valley, intending to annihilate the French (*M* 26.72). All this corresponds to the arrangements in the *Chanson de Roland*. There Guenes (Ganelon) again wants 100,000 men to deliver the first attack, but he thinks the second group will guarantee Roland's death (*Chanson de Roland*, 44).[14] On the battlefield, as in Pulci, the Saracens actually come in three groups (*Chanson de Roland*, 93, 113, 143). The two poems thus present the same tactics.

Both poets assume a series of wave attacks, delivered by battles. In the later Middle Ages the term designated a continuous shallow line of cavalry, three or four ranks deep, which charged in close order but normally engaged section by section, often starting at the right.[15] Pulci translates the term by *schiera*.[16] Malory has *batayle* (*Morte*, 1.14), and Martorell and Galba in their Catalan romance *Tirant lo blanc* use *batalla* (*Tirant*, 387.1031). The continuity in terms reflects a continuity in tactical thinking.

Condottieri thinking uses a sophisticated form of medieval tactics; it did not envisage a new order of things.[17] The Sforza school in some respects stood closer than that of Braccio da Montone[18] to these medieval modes, with its emphasis on large masses, used cautiously—a characteristic of Gano's plans in both poems. Like Gano the Sforzeschi worked with prearranged battle plans. Carafa, for example, provides Duke Alfonso with a detailed blueprint, for use if a battle—as opposed to skirmishes—should occur during the Pazzi War.[19] He assumes a straight frontal clash, as does Gano. The wings protect the center but have no autonomous function, no massive maneuvers. Carafa similarly limits the reserve to reinforcement of the front ranks. The battle of Fornovo (1495) well illustrates this approach. Philippe de Commynes, who was an eyewitness, complained that the Italians fought squadron after squadron and that, as a result, the fighting could continue all day with neither side winning.[20] Any Italian who read Pulci would have understood Gano's arrangements for Roncesvalles because contemporary commanders thought in a similar, if more complex, way.

The other romancers likewise assume wave tactics. Such tactics characterize every engagement in Boiardo's *Orlando innamorato,* and the arrangements are often elaborate. At Barcelona, for example, both sides prepare six battles (*OI* 1.4.27–35).[21] In *Tirant* Galba imagines a still larger series for Caramèn, the last battle of his African war. The Christians have seven battles, the Moslems, nine (384.1025–387.1034).[22] Malory, when he describes an engagement, likewise has waves of cavalry clash in succession. At Bedgrayne the French ambush comes in the standard three battles (*Morte,* 1.15–16).[23] The number of battles varies from writer to writer, but the tactical thinking remains the same.

The historian Francesco Guicciardini, discussing the battle of Fornovo, revealed the logic behind these tactics. A commander tried to wear down the enemy, reinforcing his fighting groups only as they tired and massing them at the end for a final blow. The side that still had fresh troops won. This assumption governed the thinking of both condottieri schools. Montone, for example, divided his men into small companies for the battle of San Egidio (1416) and committed them piecemeal, using a rotation system. Soldiers would fight hard for a brief interval and then fall back. Since it was a hot day, Montone kept water barrels behind the lines. After he had worn down the army of Carlo Malatesta and saw it becoming somewhat disorganized, he threw in the reserves and routed his opponent.[24]

The romancers imagined similar situations. In the *Morgante* the Saracens oppose their main army to the French rear guard. Gano would have them attack in three ascending waves, because the French would have to commit all they had at once. Tired by a battle growing increasingly unequal, the French should collapse at the third wave. In the two battles with Gradasso, Boiardo has the French side break through all the ranks of the enemy but the last, where the pagan king has his own troops.[25] This reserve then sweeps back the French (*OI* 1.4.38–5.8, 6.62–7.36). In Malory's work Merlin achieves the same result for Bedgrayne, when he conceals the French allies in a wood. They enter battle only after the troops of Arthur and the northern kings have worn each other down. The opposing commander, King Lot, meanwhile, tries to initiate a platoon system, somewhat like the one Braccio da Montone used for San

Egidio (*Morte*, 1.15–16).[26] Plans vary in detail, but their objectives do not change.

In such engagements the king normally commanded the last battle. Marsilio leads the third, or the reserves, in the *Morgante*. Boiardo similarly has Gradasso preside over the last rank of horsemen at Barcelona and Paris.[27] This positioning fit some contemporary practice. Carafa would have the general stand above his men, as eagles do above their prey. The men would then perform well because they would know that their commander was watching them.[28] Pulci's Marsilio indeed watches Roncesvalles from a high mountain (*M* 26.72). Robert de Balsac in *La nef des princes et des batailles de noblesse* (1502) recommended much the same. The commander should sit on horseback with his advisers so that he can see everything. The French, in fact, tried not to risk their king or prince after Poitiers, so he did not appear with the first battle.[29] Again, romance narrative and military practice coincide.

THE BATTLE ITSELF

Caught off guard by the Saracen surprise attack, Orlando orders a seeming anarchy for the French (*M* 26.50). He tells everyone to act on their own, saying that they are all accomplished knights. He counts on his veteran troops knowing what to do—and condottieri mercenaries certainly did, since they stayed together over long periods of time. The French government had an equivalent situation, once Charles VII instituted the nucleus of a standing army with his Ordonnance Companies (1439, 1445).[30] Pulci knew about this innovation and used its technical terminology. At Paris Orlando summons the "franchi arcier" (*M* 24.55), or crossbowmen who served in the Ordonnance Companies. In his "Governo" Orsini argued in favor of a similar institution for Naples, claiming that a good small army serves the state more effectively than masses raised suddenly during a crisis.[31] Pulci's Roncesvalles would illustrate his thesis, since the tiny veteran French rear guard repels the attacks of a huge enemy host.

Orlando follows his own advice. He does not try to direct the battle but fights in front, enacting an older and competing theory of the commander, whose example animates his men. In the earlier battle of Saint-Denis, in fact, his action turned around the fighting. Carlo had fallen, and the pagan Sicumoro had seized the royal standard. Warned by Baldwin, Orlando charged. He cut off Sicumoro's hand, which held the banner, and the Saracens fell back. Then Orlando found horses for Carlo and other paladins, and soon the Saracens began to flee (*M* 24.133–44).

This scenario presupposes the older medieval situation that underlay the chansons de geste and romances. A medieval army was a grouping of soldiers of diverse training, so it could not execute complex and coordinated tactics.[32] Nervous and unequal troops like these could easily swing between enthusiastic attack and panic.[33] The warriors looked to their leaders and responded accordingly. At Bouvines (1214), where the rulers on both sides fought, the French won, in part because Emperor Otto and his ally, the duke of Brabant, fled.[34] The romances present similar cases. The *Suite du Merlin,* a direct source for Malory, has King Lot animate the men of Orkney, fighting Arthur. Once Pellinor kills Lot, Lot's men flee at a gallop and are slaughtered on the road or captured by the English.[35] Just as a leader's death could sow panic, his prowess and courage could win battles; individuals who showed those characteristics could gain the right to lead men.[36]

Fifteenth-century romancers kept alive this idea of the leader. Malory might be expected to do so because he abbreviates older material. In the civil war the English army looks to Gawain and their opponents to Lancelot. At Joyous Garde Lancelot's men claim that he does not fight hard enough (*Morte,* 20.13). On the second day he exerts himself, and they win. When Gawain is wounded at Benwick, the English lose confidence (*Morte,* 20.22). Malory has Merlin explain to a bedridden Uther, "[Y]e may not lye so as ye doo, for ye must to the feld, though ye ryde on an hors-lyttar. For ye shall never have the better of your enemyes but yf your persone be there, and thenne shall ye have the vyctory" (*Morte,* 1.3–5). Uther goes, and his army wins a great victory at St. Albans.[37] Martorell and Galba stress the same point for their invented romance. Tirant regularly leads the fighting, and his men win only when he is present. In one action the Greek emperor is assaulting a town (*Tirant,* 161.504, 508–9). The Saracens knock down Tirant's ladder, but he merely gets another, explaining to the emperor that he encourages his troops by such deeds. And at the next assault the town falls.

Even seasoned troops need leaders to follow. It was the better trained armies of the fifteenth century and not the medieval levy that provoked Machiavelli's sarcastic remark that the turning of a horse's head or rump meant victory or defeat.[38] Carafa accordingly wants his officers to set an example (first "Memoriale," 2.182). They must go first in their units, so that their actions can substitute for commands and their valor can win a battle (second "Memoriale," 3.202–3, 5.205). Carafa develops a compromise between the two conceptions of the leader, Pulci's Marsilio directing events from his hilltop and Orlando fighting out in front. He would have the king or general adopt Marsilio's role and would assign Orlando's part to subordinate officers. At Pulci's Roncesvalles, Orlando is just such an officer, presiding over the rear guard while Carlo holds supreme command.

A commander who fights in the front rank cannot direct tactics, nor does Orlando try. His approach, however, and not the plan of Gano and Marsilio, determines the fighting.[39] A series of duels heralds both stages of the conflict, as the Saracens commit their battles, the second two at the same time. In the melee that follows each set of duels, Pulci describes only the actions of the leaders and principal knights, so the whole battle seems an affair of individual encounters, much like a tournament. Pulci emphasizes the initial duels: Orlando himself climaxes the first series, when he kills Falserone (M 26.64–72). The Saracen wanted to avenge his son Ferraù, though he had publicly made peace with Orlando over the issue. Seeing Orlando come, Falserone loses heart and prays to his god. Orlando calls him traitor and then kills him with a lance thrust through shield, mail shirt, and breast. Not realizing he has killed his enemy, who still sits on his horse, Orlando taunts him and, of course, gets no response. He then touches Falserone with his sword, and the body of the Saracen falls to the ground. Orlando's men, however, find nothing inside the armor: his corpse has disappeared. Such duels form little vignettes, made memorable here by the demonic marvelous and always by concrete details (for example, Pulci informs us that Falserone's shield is made of the bone of a certain fish).

All this fits the pattern set initially by the *Chanson de Roland,* which ritualized the process. Before the battle twelve Saracens vow to kill Roland, and they meet the twelve peers in the opening duels. Roland begins, killing Aelroth, a nephew of Marsilie, with a thrust through the breast that simultaneously overturns and kills his horse (*Chanson de Roland,* 69–70, 93). Like his counterpart in Pulci, Roland follows his victory with a vaunt, a variant of his famous claim that Christians are right and pagans wrong. The French poet stresses the ritual character of these duels by keeping the same order in a double series, the first when the pagan champions make their vows (69–78), and the second when they come to joust (93–103). Duels likewise initiate the second wave of fighting and signal an increasing difficulty for the Franks. In the first round the peers killed eleven of the twelve Saracen champions. Now a Saracen kills a Frank before he dies (112–24). The whole is an affair between heroes. In this sense Pulci, though he did not follow a ritual mode of presentation, remained true to the spirit of the *Chanson.*

The other quattrocento romancers kept the same formula but sometimes stressed different stages of the combat. For Bedgrayne Malory preferred the melee, when waves of cavalry swirl about after the initial duels. Malory's narrative follows the leaders, who want to unhorse the enemy and get their friends on horseback again. First the northerners must remount their kings, then it is Arthur's coterie (*Morte,* 1.14–15). In contrast, Boiardo emphasized the end of every wave. The Spanish phase of Montealbano concludes with five combats: Carlo and Marsilio, Ogier and Serpentino, Oliviero and Grandonio, Orlando and Rodamonte, Ranaldo and Feraguto (*OI* 2.25.2). The African eruption then sets up a new series (2.30.52–54). Wherever the stress falls, the manner does not change. All the romancers resolve battles into duels between leaders and heroes.

Battles generate the same descriptive pattern whether someone plans them or not. So far I have discussed conflicts where leaders had time to prepare and arrange their army, but Malory includes for his Roman wars three clashes that occur suddenly, with no or little planning, and yet follow the same pattern. The battle of the Embassy provides an example (*Morte,* 5.6).[40] Gawain, who leads an embassy to Emperor Lucius, resents a remark made by a certain Gaius and beheads him. The ambassadors flee, pursued by Roman foot and horse troops. Duels start the skirmish, as Bors kills a knight in gold who left his companions behind and then a knight in purple who overturned many knights. Meanwhile Gawain cuts down Felderake, who wanted to avenge Gaius. The Romans try to retreat, but Gawain has an ambush ready, the only plan made by anyone before the skirmish. Eventually more troops coming from the Roman camp capture Bors and Borel, but then Idres, Yvain's son, shows up with 500 men. Gawain and Idres rescue the prisoners, and the English manage to reach their own camp, keeping all their prisoners. Everything in this engagement is improvised except the ambush, but the pattern holds: initial duels followed by a melee in which knights kill or capture each other. In this respect battles follow the same pattern, planned or not.

This descriptive procedure both fits and has helped to create the modern notion of medieval warfare. Piero Pieri, for example, describes real engagements succinctly. Armies in two or three groups charge each other successively, the first wave against the first, the second against the second. The cavalry attack fractions at contact, some knights ahead, others behind. Or as one historian put it, "the battle was a collection of individual combats in which the commander of the army participated as a simple combatant." Philippe Contamine tries to modify this view but must allow that it accurately characterizes many a battle.[41] These analyses resemble my characterization of romance representations of battle, which either indicates how close romance was to reality in the high Middle Ages or, more likely, shows that romance narrative technique affected the historical records. In any case, the two corresponded closely during the generative period of the chanson de geste and romance.

ROMANCE AND CONTEMPORARY WARFARE

Parallels

Many readers and critics forget that although the Franks lost the real battle of Roncesvalles, they won the fictive versions. Pulci's Orlando turns the tide of the conflict when he finally blows his horn (*M* 27.69–72). The sound causes the enemy to panic.[42] Marsilio, Bianciardin, and Balugante flee immediately, and the Franks slaughter the masses as they try to follow their leaders (*M* 27.73–76, 81–94). In the *Chanson de Roland* the pagan collapse occurs in two stages. When Roland reaches Marsilie, cutting off his right hand and killing his son, Jurfaleu the Blond, the main army flees, leaving behind the Algalife and his blacks to eliminate the few surviving Franks (*Chanson de Roland,* 142–44). The arrival of Charlemagne chases off these Saracens, most of whom drown in the River Sebre (180). In either version the French win a technical victory because they occupy the battlefield afterward. This scenario illustrates a major point in medieval and condottieri tactics, the assumption that the attacker will lose. French experience in the Hundred Years War provides the historical analogue: at Crécy, Poitiers, and Agincourt, the French attacked.[43]

The would-be victor in a battle had to lure the enemy into making an attack. Carafa says that it is better to have the enemy come and find you. Pieri interprets this advice to mean that the commander should begin with light troops to draw the enemy into an unfavorable position and then commit his main force.[44] *Tirant* provides an exact equivalent (157.485–87). At Malveí Tirant uses a cavalry screen to draw the Saracens into a charge. Once their pursuit has lost formation and the cavalry has left the infantry behind, Tirant has his horse wheel about and attack.[45] Agincourt illustrates the historical basis for such thinking. The English took up a defensive position, making a narrow front on land made slippery by fall rains. Tall stakes protected the archers, whom Henry V projected forward on the flanks of his three battles. Yet to provoke the French attack, Henry had to advance, putting his archers in an unprotected position.[46] At the same time the French commander, Constable d'Albret, would have found it difficult not to attack, since the odds favored him at three or four to one.[47] The English victory despite these odds explains why Carafa prefers defensive tactics.

Such thinking does not encourage battle, and there were but two regular field engagements in the Pazzi War. Prudence ruled the military manuals. The "Ordine" advises Duke Galeazzo Maria always to choose the more secure alternative in dubious matters.[48] Carafa gives the most extreme expression of this approach. He tells the duke of Calabria never to offer or accept battle unless he has all the advantages in the world.[49]

Commanders wished to avoid battle for two reasons, both of which Roncesvalles illustrates. They did not wish to risk so many lives, and they wanted to avoid the political consequences of a defeat. Machiavelli's famous remark that the condottieri fought battles without deaths seems to contradict the first reason, since commanders need not have feared heavy losses in a field engagement.[50] Two facts, however, qualify Machiavelli's generalization. First, his remark applies only to intra-Italian conflicts. When outsiders were involved, casualty rates rose. Thus, at Genoa in 1461 the French lost 2,500 of 6,000 knights when they attacked a prepared position.[51] Second, gunpowder caused the death ratio to rise in the fifteenth century. For example, Pieri argues that the Pazzi War was bloody.[52]

High casualty figures mark especially the conflicts between Christian and Muslim, and Roncesvalles is just such a battle. After the battle Pulci's Carlo looks at the dead knights, piled one on top of the other, some under horses, others overturned in muddy ditches. He sees so many bodies cut to pieces or mutilated, so many intestines or brains outside that the bodies seem splinters and stumps. Shields and broken lances cover the bloody ground; round about are scorched trees and rocks dripping blood (*M* 27.198–200). Pulci's recurring epithet is *bloody* Roncesvalles.[53] At the end Orlando's squire finds himself stuck in blood, kicking about like a cooking lamprey (*M* 27.99).

The *Chanson de Roland* indicates the reason for the high number of casualties in interfaith conflicts. After the capture of Zaragoza Charlemagne sends 1,000 Franks through its streets to the synagogues and mosques. Pagans must either accept baptism or die by hanging, burning, and slaughtering (*Chanson de Roland,* 266). Similarly, we learn that earlier the population of Cordres were told they must either convert or die (*Chanson de Roland,* 8). The other romancers show the same lack of mercy. In the battle of Sessoyne Malory, who turns Romans into Sara

cens, has Arthur, angry over Sir Kay's injury, order that his knights take
no prisoners.[54] The Roman Saracens lose 100,000 slain (*Morte*, 5.8). In
Tirant the Christians capture a fleet of sleeping Saracens, who surrender
but are beheaded anyway (*Tirant*, 418.1091–92).

Reality supports the romancers. At Negroponte (1470) the victorious
Turks enslaved the Greeks but killed the Italians. They sawed in half those
who surrendered, including Paolo Erizzo, who had been guaranteed his
head.[55] Christians and Muslims both valued mercy, but they did not often extend it to enemies outside their own religion.

In all battles the loser could expect to sustain many more casualties
than the victor. Contamine observes that the defeated generally lost 20–
50 percent of the army.[56] At Poitiers (1356) and Agincourt (1415), the
French lost 40 percent of their cavalry, while the English in the latter
battle lost only 100 out of around 10,000 men, or 1 percent. During the
Wars of the Roses the victors generally killed all defeated knights.[57] Roncesvalles falls into line with these examples. In the *Chanson de Roland*
only 20,000 survive of 400,000 Saracens (*Chanson de Roland*, 68, 187),
the same number as the whole French rear guard (41–42, 63). Pulci gives
no figures but has Carlo destroy the Saracen survivors on the third day
after the battle, so the Saracens lose virtually their whole army. The other
romances provide analogies. In *Tirant* the Saracens at Malveí lose
103,700, and their dead make the road to the next town impassable (*Tirant*, 159.497–99). The Christians have only 1,234 casualties.

Such figures suggest the political risks involved in a battle. The
condottieri theorists assumed that the state could gamble its existence on
a single battle. Orsini, for example, argues that the army is the basis of
the state, so a defeated army is a ruined state.[58] Carafa tacitly understands
that a major military defeat would cause a revolt.[59] Both theorists had
experience in Naples and had fought through one of its many wars of
succession (1460–62). They knew the insecurity of its central government
in relation to the barons. Other states, though better organized, had rulers who lacked tradition and legitimacy, like the Medici in Florence and
the Sforza in Milan. The condottieri rightly argued, therefore, that a ruler
or his commander ought to avoid the hazards of battle.

Roncesvalles again bears out this thinking. The *Chanson de Roland* emphasizes its dangers for the French; the *Morgante*, its results for the Spanish Saracens. The Guenes of the *Chanson* argues that Charlemagne, losing Roland, loses his right arm (*Chanson de Roland*, 44–45) and will never
collect such an army again. The *Chanson* constantly associates 20,000
men with Roland. These knights follow the leader who favors continued

war (*Chanson de Roland,* 14, 41–42) and fight at Roncesvalles (63–64). They make up Charlemagne's strike force, which Marsilie annihilates. Pulci shows the price Marsilio pays. Having lost his army, he has nothing left to defend Zaragoza, nor will any of the other peninsular powers, shocked at his treason, support him (*M* 27.237). For Roncesvalles Marsilio pays with his capital, his kingdom, and ultimately with his life.[60]

Old Disjunctions

Although romance reflects current military practice in many matters, it also keeps a certain distance from that practice. Some of the disjunctions between romance and reality are traditional, and some are new. Among the traditional differences are the romancers' use of hyperbole and the aristocratic viewpoint.

Hyperbole in the romances concerns both time and numbers. At Roncesvalles noon has passed before Orlando sounds his horn, and Carlo must ask God to stop the sun so that he can reach the battlefield that same day (*M* 27.171–74). In the *Chanson de Roland* the sun stops so Charlemagne can finish the battle (*Chanson de Roland,* 180). In contrast the real engagement there probably was quite short;[61] most cavalry battles took only one to three hours.[62] The poets lengthen the time to indicate the importance of the event. The battle of Salisbury, which destroys Arthur's chivalry, lasts all day (*Morte,* 21.4). Such a long battle was uncommon, but it could occur. I noted earlier Commynes's complaint that condottieri armies could fight indecisively all day. Galba, in his part of *Tirant,* stretches even these possibilities. The battles that turn the tide of the African war precede and follow a truce. Five days of fighting precede it, the first lasting from dawn to dusk (*Tirant,* 339.938–340.944). A two-day battle follows the truce, both fights lasting most of the day (*Tirant,* 343.949–349.964).

Hyperbole strains temporal probability, but when applied to the size of armies, it far exceeds any possibility. The romancers especially exaggerate the size of Saracen armies (see chapter 3), but even the much lower totals for Christian armies are excessive. The French rear guard at Roncesvalles numbers 20,000 in both the *Chanson de Roland* (41–42, 63–64) and the *Morgante* (27.78). This total equals Orsini's suggested number for the whole Neapolitan army.[63] Milan under Galeazzo Maria projected a giant army by Italian standards—43,000 men—yet Carlo's main army at Paris numbers more than twice as many (100,000).[64] No French army ever reached anywhere near this size in the Middle Ages, and in any case a round number like 100,000 inspires skepticism. Mordred brings 100,000 to Salisbury Field (*Morte*, 21.3), and 100,000 die there (21.4, 8). One suspects that the repeated round number merely means "many." Pulci himself throws doubt on his statistics (*M* 27.76,113). *Tirant*, as usual, exceeds even these numbers. The tiny Greek Empire, fighting Turks near Constantinople, is said to have 60,000 soldiers on the frontier, 80,000 in the city, and 25,000 on its ships (*Tirant*, 123.327). Time and size both grow with the tactical importance of a battle and can reach beyond the medieval and early modern imagination in the poet's attempt to convey the tragedy of a Salisbury or a Roncesvalles.

Although one cannot construe them literally, hyperbolic numbers do have meaning. As we have seen, they can indicate the importance of a battle. Sometimes they are used to convey a sense of odds. At Bedgrayne the army of the northern kings outnumbers Arthur's two to one (*Morte*, 1.11–12). We might expect a greater disproportion at Roncesvalles, where the Saracen main army attacks the French rear guard, but odds of twenty to one (*Chanson de Roland*, 43, 55, 68) and thirty to one (*M* 27.78) clearly exceed the possible, at least when we recall that the Franks won the battle. To take a more modern example, Davout's brilliant action at Auerstädt in 1807, where a French advance guard defeated the bulk of a retreating Prussian army, had odds of less than one to three.[65] The exaggerated numbers of Roncesvalles communicate rather the emotional sense of the battle, the feeling that the enemy had far too many men, the sense that prompted Oliver to ask Roland to blow his horn.

As customary as the poets' use of hyperbole is their portrayal of events through an aristocratic bias that controls what we see of these battles. With the exception of Orlando's squire, Pulci shows us only men-at-arms, fighting on horseback.[66] He mentions no bowmen or infantrymen of any kind, though such fighters were rarely absent from battles, whether in the quattrocento or in earlier periods.[67] The poet inherited this bias from his sources. The *Chanson de Roland* likewise ignores all but knights.[68] Yet this aristocratic mode bore a different relation to military practice in the quattrocento than in the twelfth century. To properly appraise Pulci's descriptive technique, we must see precisely what he excludes from his account.

The man-at-arms in the fifteenth century never fought alone but functioned as the officer of a lance or platoon. His heavy armor caused him to have to change mounts frequently, so he needed extra horses as well as attendants, some of whom participated in the fighting.[69] The number of attendants per man-at-arms rose gradually during the quattrocento. Orsini assumes that a man-at-arms needs three horses, so he also has two

servants or a servant and a boy. The man-at-arms and the servant both
have a crossbow and ride horseback, while the boy looks after the supply
wagon, where he keeps his own crossbow.[70] Orsini thus assumes earlier
practice, when a lance included three persons: a *capo-lancia,* or man-at-
arms, a page, and a *piatto,* or boy.[71] Orsini does not include a squire, who
reappears, however, once the lance reaches four, as it did in Florence at
least by 1483.[72] Pulci reflects this stage when he assigns the squire, Terigi,
to Orlando, but in fact the lance had already reached six in Milan, as it
had long since done in France.[73]

At times, amid all the individual heroics, Pulci lets us glimpse this late
medieval knight, the commander of a lance. Orlando in particular has an
entourage and moves with a group. Normally his companions are other
heroes like Anselmo (*M* 26.76, 134) or Sansonetto (26.134), but sometimes the poet mentions Terigi, who functions as synecdoche for the rest
of the lance. Normally Terigi fights, following his lord through the press,
"stinging" in his relief (26.134), but he also performs other services.[74] He
takes Sansonetto's corpse to Orlando's pavilion (*M* 27.16) and carries the
news of the battle to Carlo (27.160, 177–85).[75]

Just as Terigi stands for the other subordinates in a lance, it is logical
to see in Orlando, who commands the group, the symbol of its deeds.
Vico made just such an analysis, talking of the Homeric heroes but drawing parallels to Norman crusaders. The *socii* or *plebs* defend their lord but
give him the glory, so an Ajax or Orlando masks the exploits of his house
or in this case of a lance.[76]

This narrative mode of aristocratic bias possesses a certain justice beyond the rhetorical rationale usually assigned to it.[77] Other soldiers,
shooters of various kinds and infantry, still lacked an independent existence. Orsini, for example, mixes the infantry with the lances. His columns combine men-at-arms, crossbowmen, and foot soldiers.[78] Carafa's
armies *ride,* they do not *march,* even though they included many infantrymen.[79] The romancers found it more efficient to narrate the deeds of
the men-at-arms, since their actions automatically involved those of
others and ultimately the deeds of the whole army.

New Disjunctions

In addition to the disjunctions traditional to romance, two other depar-
tures from actual practice set the *Morgante* securely in its fifteenth-
century context. The first, which Pulci himself discusses, concerns fortified camps. The second, which Pulci never mentions, has deeper implica-

tions: the fact that condottieri armies fought in a coordinated fashion and not in the old manner through individual duels.

At Roncesvalles Orlando allows the men of his old brigade to scatter themselves as they camp (*M* 25.181–82). The old Burgundian Guottibuoffi says that they should set up a fortified camp, and Olivieri wants one too (in fact, he tries to strengthen their position on his own; *M* 26.5, 22). The two men recommend what had become standard practice by the mid-fifteenth century. Every army fortified its camp, especially in hostile territory.[80] The condottieri all advised field fortifications, though they recommended different means. Those in Milan wanted a *Wagenburg* on the Hussite model, with the wagons of the small artillery chained together.[81] Carafa thought the commander should know ahead of time where to camp but need strengthen the place artificially only if it lacked natural defenses.[82] Orsini, influenced by classical precept and practice, had the most elaborate model.[83] He wanted a deep ditch with bastions, *rivellini* (ravelins) to protect the gates, palisades, and the small artillery set up at the ditch. Everyone talked of fortified camps, everyone built them, and they determined much of the fighting in the later fifteenth century.[84] Castillon (1453), which ended English rule in France and killed John Talbot, earl of Shrewsbury, provides the most famous example. French cannon decimated the small English force, massed together and charging the French defenses.[85] Twenty-six years later the storming of the Florentine camp at Poggio Imperiale decided the Pazzi War.[86]

Orlando might have averted his own death and the terrible losses the French suffered if he had fortified his encampment. Orsini, for example, makes a long list of battles determined by the presence or adequacy of field fortifications.[87] Maclodio (1427) stands out as the most disastrous. At that battle Filippo Maria Visconti, seeing that Francesco Bussone, called Carmagnola, had a smaller army, did not fortify his position and so lost the battle. He was never afterward able to overcome the Venetians and Florentines because of the disparity in numbers, and Venice annexed Brescia and Bergamo. Pulci himself cannot make sense of Orlando's carelessness. He suggests that the hero realized his end was near and argues that a person in great peril has difficulty making proper decisions (*M* 26.7). Such an argument, however, merely turns Orlando into a bad general. Orlando himself says that he had trusted Marsilio and did not expect him to attack (*M* 26.24). In fact, the day before the battle Bianciardin had come to Roncesvalles, bringing camels laden with food, a gesture that encouraged Orlando in his mistake (*M* 25.183–84). Neither explanation would have convinced a quattrocento reader, since the French were camping in hostile territory after a long war. No argument can excuse Orlando's mistake, and Olivieri cannot resist reminding his friend of his error, as the Saracen army draws near. Orlando does not answer, and Pulci remarks that the truth has no reply (*M* 26.20–23).

This issue shows well how some parts of an old story can clash with current practice and defy rationalization. According to Leo the Wise, writing ca. 900, Frankish troops did not make fortified camps.[88] The *Chanson de Roland* has them camp throughout the country (*Chanson de Roland*, 55), and so it ultimately forces Pulci to say the same. The issue does not, however, point to any problems in romance as such. In the invented tale of Tirant, Martorell and Galba, unlike Pulci, are free to emphasize the importance of such camps. William, count of Warwick, defends his camp near the enemy with a trench and a stockade (*Tirant*, 24.56). Tirant himself sets up elaborate patrols so no one can surprise his encampment (*Tirant*, 133.369–70, 145.429). The day guard consists of 2,000 horse and 1,000 foot, the cavalry serving in twelve-hour rotation. At night he has 2,000 horse and 2,000 foot with a guard change at midnight.

The question of the fortified camp, although it created difficulties for Pulci, did not challenge his chosen literary form. The change in the manner of fighting did. Fifteenth-century theory and practice emphasized coordination and timing for an army rather than a series of duels between individuals. Of course, earlier commanders also sought coordinated movement—there was a clear tradition of communal valor—but the background and training of their warriors made such an objective difficult. The Italian mercenary groups, in contrast, were professionals, and the North had already developed the predecessor of the standing army in the Ordonnance Companies.[89] The quattrocento commander could expect a certain coordination from his troops, and he developed his tactics accordingly. The Sforzeschi used battle plans that required carefully disciplined troops. Federigo of Urbino, who led the allies against Florence during the Pazzi War, followed this school.[90] Tirant has the romance analogue at the battle of Malveí. Tirant explains to his men that victory depends on their keeping formation (*Tirant*, 156.484), and later he harshly criticizes his close friend and subordinate, Diaphebus, for disobeying orders (157.493).[91] The other school of thought, that of the Bracceschi, advocated coordination through many small battle units, and this emphasis also had its effect.[92] Pulci, for example, mentions *schiere* or battles, terms that designate large numbers of men, but he also speaks of squadrons and columns, quattrocento terms for much smaller units (*M* 24.143–44). In the earlier part of the century Micheletto had set up his mercenaries for battle in squadrons of 25 lances each, or about 150 people.[93] At the same time the French were organizing their men into companies of equal size. This trend continued, and the condottieri who compiled the "Ordine" assumed Micheletto's number for a squadron and added the post of *colonello* for the commander of a column. Orsini assumes 10 columns to 100 squadrons.[94] Smaller units of uniform size permit coordinated tactics of a complexity not possible to earlier armies and not envisaged in medieval romance. The authors of the Vulgate Cycle would have found the battle plans of Charles the Bold or Ridolfo Gonzaga complicated, and a thirteenth-century commander could not have executed them.[95]

This new situation challenged traditional story telling. Romance presupposed simpler tactics, and the narrator related the activities of several heroes—not just Orlando and Rinaldo, but also many other secondary persons, such as Anselmo and Astolfo. The new tactics emphasized the commander instead. The change is evident in the condotte. The fourteenth-century contract mentioned corporals as well as the commander, recognizing that the condottiere governed by aid of "caporales et consiliarii." Companies at that time were a union of smaller companies that elected their leaders. Quattrocento contracts, however, name only the captain.[96] Tirant once again documents the change for romance. At Malveí Tirant alone has the traditional series of heroic duels (*Tirant,* 157.487–90). Others appear only to assist him when he falls or to get him a horse.[97]

In *Tirant* Martorell and Galba really present the biography of a commander, one who fights like a quattrocento condottiere. The authors had read Frontinus's *Stratagems,* then the second classical manual in popularity and a study in deceptions.[98] Tirant and William, count of Warwick, win battles by surprise and by clever devices. For example, William coordinates a midnight attack with an explosion of Greek fire set up in the enemy camp (*Tirant,* 10.27–28, 12.31–32). At Fairdale Tirant greases the enemy bombards with an ointment that causes them to crack at their next firing (*Tirant,* 302.853–55). Under siege he fills a countermine with brass bowls that rattle at every blow of a pickax and reveal the enemy's tunneling activity (*Tirant,* 339.937–38). Tactically, both William and Tirant bluff effectively, using women disguised as soldiers so that the enemy will overestimate their numbers (*Tirant,* 14.34; 343.948–49, 951; 344.953–54; 349.962). Tirant also knows how stampedes can disrupt an opponent.[99] Martorell and Galba thus anticipate later developments in their own peninsula, when Iberian poets would limit heroism to officers (see chapter 10).

For a time the tournaments and duels of contemporary life masked this growing rift between romance narrative and military practice. Martín de Riquer and Larry Benson have shown that quattrocento nobles patterned their lives on romance models (see chapter 2). Martorell exemplifies both sides, since he involved himself in two lengthy challenges and wanted others to learn chivalry from *Tirant*.[100] Like the author, Tirant has difficulty extricating himself from a cycle of challenges, as he proves himself initially in the duels and tourneys that celebrate the English monarch's coronation and marriage.[101] The place held in life by individual heroics allowed contemporary audiences to enjoy this feature of traditional romance, even though such deeds no longer played a major role in military practice.

The writers of romance may have further smoothed over the rift by means of an effective literary device, abbreviation. Pulci abridges two of the three battles he presents in the five cantari added later to the *Morgante*. He shortens the battle of Saint-Denis so much that a reader can get no sense of its tactics (*M* 24.123–44).[102] The battle with Balugante is recounted in only twelve ottave (*M* 27.223–34). Together these battles add up to a tiny portion of the ottave devoted to Roncesvalles (34 as opposed to 219). Malory shows the same trend over time. Early in his work of translation and abridgment, he presented in reasonably full detail the battles that brought Arthur to power and won him an empire.[103] Later he practically eliminates such descriptions. Four field encounters mark Arthur's fall: Joyous Garde, Dover, Barren Down, and Salisbury. Only Joyous Garde and Salisbury receive any attention, and that very little. Salisbury in particular dramatically demonstrates abbreviation. The Vulgate author presented an elaborate engagement. He enumerated the battles, had readers follow five successive waves of attack, described the make-up of particular battles, highlighted certain commanders, and even recounted what the lookout boy said.[104] Malory reduces this narrative of many pages to a few small paragraphs, and he has no word about tactics, dispositions, or troop movements (*Morte*, 21.4). Most extreme are Martorell and Galba, who narrate numerous battles and abbreviate *all* of them.[105] The hero, moreover, wins his eastern war in condottieri fashion, by maneuver and not by battle. Having destroyed the Saracen fleet, he blockades the army and forces a capitulation (*Tirant*, 418.1091–94, 422.1101–2, 448.1150–51).

Only Boiardo does not participate in this trend toward abbreviation, for he narrates in full all his battles: Barcelona, Paris, those around Albraca, and Montealbano. One could, of course, argue that artistic necessity determined much of this abbreviation and that Boiardo did not require it because he alternated his battle descriptions with blocks of narrative about the wanderings of his characters and their magical adventures. Pulci, in contrast, had to abbreviate to avoid tedium, since the battles with Antea and Balugante flank Roncesvalles.[106] Martorell and Galba similarly have sequences of battles, which they must abridge. But this explanation of artistic necessity does not account for the abbreviation of *all* battles by Martorell and Galba, and it does not apply to Malory, who either presents in detail the different battles in a series or shortens them all.

The social and military hypothesis can account for all these examples. The romancer of the later fifteenth century abbreviated when he could because he sensed a rift between his traditional manner of narration and current military practice. He probably felt that such descriptions were less relevant to his audience and to his own circumstances than other parts of his story, so he tended to drop them. At the same time one must not overemphasize this trend. None of the romancers expresses discomfort with the current conduct of war, and we have seen that condottieri tactics, however elaborate, still had the man-at-arms on horseback like the medieval knight. Similarly, condottieri tactics allowed for the officer to fight in front of his men, encouraging them by his example, not unlike the medieval hero. Tactical complexity alone did not provoke a crisis in romance. Heavy cavalry had to decline further (see chapter 3), and the new technology of firearms had to change field tactics. Another forty years passed before Ariosto sounded the warning bell.[107]

—TWO—

Arthur's Rise to Power

Sir Thomas Malory

WHEN ROMANCERS TURNED FROM TACTICS TO STRATEGY, from battles to the plan of a campaign, they found little direct assistance in the military manuals and histories.[1] Among the classical writers they really had only Frontinus, whom they could read either directly or through extracts in Vegetius and his many vernacular adaptations.[2] Yet even Frontinus sketches not strategy but stratagems, or specific applications of strategy. The reader must infer the plan of campaign. Frontinus did offer many hints, and one modern historian has characterized the *Stratagems* as a casebook of deceptions and psychological warfare. His work was especially popular in the fifteenth century with the other writers of military manuals, such as Christine de Pisan, and with romancers, such as Martorell and Galba.[3] Frontinus's work also illuminates the war plan Malory presents when he narrates Arthur's struggle to establish himself as a ruler.

The romancers also turned to other romancers for assistance with military strategy. Malory, for example, found in his source, the Cambridge version of the *Suite du Merlin,* a coherent strategy behind Arthur's early wars inherited from the Vulgate *Merlin.*[4] The magician works out for Arthur what we would call today a strategy of the inner lines, the kind familiar to modern readers from the plans devised by the German general staff during the two world wars. What a Schlieffen or Manstein devised was implemented, however, while Merlin's strategy fits rather the fantasy world invented for Britain by the French romancers. It had no practical applications.

This situation changed in the book-based culture of the fifteenth century, when people, north and south, began to design their lives according to their reading. Some southerners might prefer classical texts, and northerners, the vernacular literature of the high Middle Ages, but the impulse was the same.[5] For the North Jacques de Lalaing provides a good example of the tendency. In 1450 he defended the Pas de la Fontaine aux Pleurs near Chalon-sur-Saône in Burgundy for a year, just as Alexander the Orphan had defended the grounds of a ruined castle in the Prose *Tristan* and would do again in Malory.[6] Jacques was just one of those who made romance fiction real.

This trend brought the writing and reading of romance and history close to each other. Most people at that time still considered Arthur a real person, however wildly imaginative the romances might be.[7] The English chroniclers might have questioned the authenticity of Geoffrey of Monmouth, but they never doubted Arthur's historicity.[8] Malory, though a romancer, can thus pose as a historian. He has a chronicler's style and handles his source materials in such a way as to enhance the historical status of his story.[9] He also speaks of his sources as a historian would. For example, he notes that they disagree on the identification of Joyous Garde, and he prefers the French to the English authorities when he discusses the after-history of Lancelot's kin (*Morte,* 21.12.1257, 21.13.1260).[10]

The same process also worked in reverse. It allowed Jean de Bueil to disguise his military manual, *Le jouvencel,* as a romance. A respected captain under Charles VII, he designed a guide to the military education of a young gentleman, which he based partly on his own wartime experiences. His romance thus had a certain historical status, besides its technical nature, and modern historians regularly cite it in discussions of the later fifteenth century.[11] De Bueil composed *Le jouvencel* in the 1460s, at the same time that Malory was abridging his set of Arthurian romances. The work of both men shows that clear generic distinctions between fiction and fact, romance and history, did not exist for them.

In fact, the Catalan scholar, Martín de Riquer, remarks that at times one cannot distinguish formally between the romance and the history written in this period. He cites the example of *Jehan de Saintré* by Antoine de la Sale. A reader unfamiliar with French history could not tell the difference between this fictional romance and histories like the *Livre des faits de Jacques de Lalaing.* Antoine actually borrowed an episode from the *Livre.*[12] In this case the literary presentation is identical, and only external criteria can separate history from romance.

This rapprochement between romance and history had serious implications for a writer like Malory. He had to treat the strategic problems of Arthur's early wars with the same seriousness Jean de Bueil devoted to contemporary warfare. Therefore, Malory had to bring strategy out of the realm of fairy tale into something resembling the real world. In this endeavor he encountered problems he did not meet when he realistically recounted the peacetime activities of Arthur's knights, their duels, tournaments, and journeys. The very closeness between romance and history helped reveal a rift that might have remained concealed longer, if romance had stayed safely in the fantastic realm.

STRATEGY IN THE VULGATE *MERLIN*

Romancers followed a conventional format in describing a campaign. Typically, a campaign description begins with the siege of a castle or fortified town: Bedgrayne,[13] Castle Terrable in the *Suite du Merlin*, Albraca in the *Orlando innamorato,* and Paris in the *Innamorato* and the *Furioso*. The opposed armies resolve the siege by one or more battles. When the siege involves a castle, as it normally did in Arthurian romance, a single battle suffices: Bedgrayne, Castle Terrable. When a city is besieged, as at Albraca or Paris, a series of battles follows.[14] The side with the larger army normally starts the war and begins the siege, as in all the cases just mentioned. The writer and reader or hearer, however, usually view the aggressor as the enemy and sympathize with the defender. Thus, our sympathy lies with Arthur rather than the kings, with Charlemagne rather than King Agramante and his Saracens.[15] As a consequence, the strategy we follow is that of the defense, which grows out of weakness. Strategic defense is especially characteristic of Arthur's rise to power.

This blueprint for a campaign involved issues that had dominated warfare in its high and later medieval phases and still concerned commanders in the years when Malory was growing up.[16] At the same time it provided a critique of the way generals preferred to fight, since those in the north were as reluctant to risk battle as the condottieri in the south.[17] Actual sieges normally dragged on through the campaign season. Castles and towns fell not to assault but to mining or starvation. Conversely, the besieging army might melt away or return home with the onset of winter. Romance commanders, unlike their real counterparts, resolved a siege quickly and decisively, risking battle.

Even with battle the romance formula reversed the chronological pattern that had marked the two major English invasions of France. Victory in the field, at Crécy and Agincourt, gave the English army freedom to besiege Calais or to reduce the fortified places in Normandy. Where the romancer assumed that a battle could decide a war, for Edward III and

Henry V victory in the field started the war in earnest, which was an affair of sieges.

By the 1450s and 1460s, however, the romance formula had gained new relevance. A single field engagement decided the English fate in Aquitaine, and battles regularly determined the many campaigns of the Wars of the Roses. A strategist could no longer assume that castles would resist the new siege artillery; instead, he had to plan for battle. Accordingly, for Malory, the old romance blueprint seemed to apply more exactly than perhaps it ever had before.

In the Vulgate *Merlin* the enemy kings initiate both phases of the campaign, trusting to odds. At Caerleon, where they defy the new High King, they outnumber Arthur's knights seven to one, a ratio Malory reduces to the more probable three to one.[18] When they later invade Arthur's territory at Bedgrayne, the kings have a two-to-one advantage, which Malory raises to three to one. Merlin, nevertheless, has Arthur attack them in both places, and both decisions, although risky, follow sound strategic thinking. At Caerleon Merlin's logic corresponds to what Jean de Bueil outlines in his guide, based on the French campaign against the Swiss in 1444 (*Jouvencel*, 3.1.197.n). The inferior force, having a friendly town at its back, can risk an attack and count on its shock value, because the larger enemy army does not anticipate an engagement and has not prepared for one (*Jouvencel* 3.1.197–202). At Caerleon, moreover, the townsfolk, emboldened by Arthur's daring, come out with axes, maces, and clubs to help him. They probably would not have intervened if Arthur's knights had not first shown their will to fight and their ability to hold the field.[19]

For the second and decisive encounter, that at Bedgrayne, Merlin arranges a double ambush. The royal army attacks the enemy camp by night. The kings, confident in their superiority, have not posted guards; warned too late, they are attacked while arming.[20] Next morning Merlin stations Arthur's Breton allies in a wood and lures the enemy once more into battle with a supposedly inferior force. Since the kings do not know the Bretons have come to England, the ambush has maximum effect.[21]

Malory could take over the ambushes with only light revision, because romancers and commanders in the field still relied on such arrangements.[22] In *Tirant lo blanc* both Christian and Saracen armies constantly stage ambushes.[23] Martorell has William of Warwick defeat Saracen invaders much as Merlin in the Vulgate works to defeat Arthur's enemies (*Tirant*, 10.27–28).[24] Frontinus sketches an ambush tactically similar to the day battle Merlin directs at Bedgrayne (*Stratagems*, 1.6.2), but he also indicates the difficulties such maneuvers involved.[25] In two places he discusses Claudius Nero's movement of a relief army into a camp facing the Carthaginian Hasdrubal (*Stratagems*, 1.1.9, 2.9). Nero would not let the camp be enlarged, lest Hasdrubal suspect something, but when the Carthaginian saw horses lean from travel and men somewhat sunburned, as happens during a march, he knew reinforcements had arrived. Such operations absolutely depend upon secrecy and deception.

Night maneuvers best achieve this goal, but they carry their own risks. In the Vulgate the night attack essentially wins the campaign.[26] Tirant likewise favors night operations. He breaks the Saracen siege of Pelidas by a night attack (*Tirant*, 133.373–75), and his great victory at Malveí requires crossing a bridge by night (155.481). The military manuals encourage such operations. Christine de Pisan prefers ambushes and skirmishes to open battle (*Fayttes*, 1.18.64). She shows how the Romans defeated a tired enemy by a night attack (*Fayttes*, 1.18.63–64) and recommends that one ambush a sleeping enemy (1.15.51). Jean de Bueil gives the logic behind this: in the dark a small force can defeat a large one (*Jouvencel*, 2.2.71). Night maneuvers, however, also encourage confusion. Drawing on his experiences fighting Gilles de Rais in 1430, Jean shows two armies passing each other by night. His hero, the Jouvencel, must turn his own about and rushes ahead of it to warn his castle. He is captured in the process (*Jouvencel*, 2.2.63–70).

Surprise requires an intelligence network. In the Vulgate, Arthur forbids all road travel, once he has his army in Bedgrayne Wood and his supplies delivered.[27] A battle of scouts follows, and Arthur's men overpower those of the enemy, so that Merlin and the king know where the enemy camp is and can prepare their trap accordingly.[28] In *Tirant lo blanc*, Tirant has a spy in the enemy council, who informs him of their plans.[29] Similarly, the manuals constantly stress the importance of espionage. Christine de Pisan, drawing on Vegetius, recommends that a commander have informers in the enemy army and take precautions against enemy spies (*Fayttes*, 1.15.52–53). The commander should send agents ahead, disguised as pilgrims or laborers, who can look for ambushes. If they do not return, he should choose another route, since captured spies talk (*Fayttes*, 1.16.56). Christine would have faulted Arthur's enemies, who took no precautions even after their scouts failed to return. Jean de Bueil favors a combination of scouts and spies. Scouts regularly precede his army (for example, *Jouvencel*, 3.1.192), and spies inform them of the enemy's moves during the night operations in which the Jouvencel is captured (2.2.67). Jean would in fact allot one-third of his expenses for an intelligence service.[30] Carafa in the south gives the most elaborate set of instructions. The commander must pay informers well, but he must beware of double agents (first "Memoriale," 7.184–85). Would-be deserters should stay in the enemy camp and become informers (second "Memoriale," 9–10.211). At the same time the general should not rely too much on spies, should use his own officers if possible, and should multiply spies and make certain one does not know the other (first "Memoriale," 10.187). In one way the medieval commander needed an intelligence service even more than his sixteenth-century counterpart did: the medieval commander lacked maps.[31]

The logic behind Merlin's strategy is that of the inner lines. He has Arthur summon the Breton rulers Ban and Bors to aid him against the enemy kings. Arthur needs the support of the Breton rulers, and they more than double the size of his army.[32] Even so he goes to Bedgrayne outnumbered two to one, because the enemy kings have likewise increased their alliance, from five to eight rulers.[33] At the same time the Breton monarchs have a dangerous enemy in Claudas, whom they have just defeated; they assume he will attack again. Together Arthur and the Bretons will defeat first Arthur's enemies and later King Claudas. Malory makes the situation more dramatic. Arthur must face eleven kings at Bedgrayne, and the situation in France is more perilous.[34] Ban and Bors are losing their war with Claudas (*Morte,* 1.10.20), and they must return home after the Camylarde expedition because Claudas has once more invaded their lands (1.18.39). The drama clarifies the logic behind Merlin's strategy. The weak must ally against the strong, but united action involves a risk. The allies must leave one frontier without an army, while they concentrate on the other opponent.

In his anecdote about Claudius Nero, Frontinus provides an exact parallel to this strategy, drawn from the Second Carthaginian War (207 B.C.E.). Hasdrubal is bringing a relief army through northern Italy to link up with Hannibal in the south, so the Romans have armies on two fronts. Claudius Nero wishes to join with Livius Salinator in the north, so that together they can crush Hasdrubal before he reaches Hannibal. Nero leaves a screen of elite troops facing Hannibal, who maintain the usual number of patrols and sentries and light the same number of fires. He then goes to Umbria by secret marches, and the combined Roman army destroys Hasdrubal. Nero has his troops back in the south before Hannibal learns of the battle (*Stratagems,* 1.1.9).

The strategy of the inner lines, though based on weakness, encourages expansionism. Christine de Pisan warns a commander not to let an enemy invade his country: better to hurt the enemy land than to let your own suffer harm (*Fayttes*, 1.18.61). Arthur meets the hostile kings at his frontier in Bedgrayne, protecting his zone, as Christine advises. At the same time Merlin has already planned an extension of Arthur's rule. When Arthur summons Kings Ban and Bors, Merlin lectures the council on an expedition to Camylarde, a foreign venture to follow this year's defensive campaign (Vulgate *Merlin*, 167). Merlin explains to King Ban, who fears what Claudas might do while he stays in England, that a man must draw back to make a great jump (Vulgate *Merlin*, 107–8). He is justifying the expedition to Camylarde, which has the same strategic basis.

The district of Camylarde separates Arthur's lands from those of King Ryons, a man who has subdued many kings already, is currently fighting King Lodegreaunce of Camylarde, and, if victorious, would attack Arthur (Vulgate *Merlin*, 92, 107). The Knights of the Round Table, who left England after Uther's death, defend Camylarde. Arthur must help Lodegreaunce defeat Ryons and must marry the king's daughter and heir, Guinevere. The expedition and marriage together will rid Arthur of a dangerous neighbor,[35] increase the royal domain, and bring back to his family the fellowship of the Round Table.[36] Both here and at Bedgrayne an alliance defeats an otherwise superior enemy and secures the realm. At the same time such alliances expand the realm. Arthur inherits Camylarde through marriage, and Ban and Bors do him homage.[37] The great kingdom is the secure one.

The financing of the war likewise presupposes expansion. Arthur begins the war with an empty treasury. As Merlin explains in council, the king is young, the nobles disdainful, and the lesser people would have been suspicious but for the great gifts he has distributed (Vulgate *Merlin*, 111–12). With no money, Arthur must somehow finance a war. He does so partly by use of a great treasure, buried near Bedgrayne and known only to Merlin (Vulgate *Merlin*, 112), but mostly by plunder. At Caerleon Arthur pays his soldiers with the horses and apparel won at the battle, and with the gold, silver, and money left by the kings in their camp (Vulgate *Merlin*, 95–96). He thus wins the love of poor soldiers, who were his army at Caerleon, and makes new knights the following September, to whom he gives rents and gifts. After Bedgrayne the three kings distribute all the booty (Vulgate *Merlin*, 122). Malory varies the distribution but makes the same point. Arthur gives the spoils to Ban and Bors, who can use the wealth to finance their war with Claudas. Arthur presumably can use the hidden treasure to pay the English (*Morte*, 1.17.37).

This seemingly reckless spending is prudent. If Arthur had been cautious and tried to build up his treasury, he would have had no political and military support. His generosity wins an army. When the enemy kings later are fighting the Saxons, they can attract no soldiers from Arthur's land because his men are too well paid (Vulgate *Merlin*, 126). At the same time the policy presupposes victory. Arthur pays his men not from what he has but from what he will win. His security thus depends on warfare, which in turn expands the kingdom. The logic is typical. The *Beowulf* prologue gives it in its clearest form: Scyld began defending his house. His success frightened others, and the tribes of the neighboring seacoasts sent tribute. Scyld thus built up a treasury, which his son Beowulf used to win trustworthy friends, who would support him in time of war. And he too prospered (*Beowulf*, 4–25).[38]

The thinking of the Vulgate author still applied in the fifteenth century, though appropriately modernized. Kennedy shows how Malory models the Round Table, which Arthur acquires in Camylarde, on the royal retinues maintained by Lancastrian and Yorkist monarchs.[39] Such arrangements involved money as well as land. In *Tirant lo blanc,* Martorell emphasizes the need for money, especially for war. His hero states flatly that war requires troops, money, and provisions (*Tirant*, 123.327).[40] Martorell shows the recruiting tables in Sicily and gives the pay scales for soldiers (*Tirant*, 116.303).[41] The feudal warrior has become the soldier in the root sense of the word, a person fighting for pay. Condottieri theory emphasized the need for regular pay, and the inspector, Chiericati, wanted them well paid, like Arthur's men.[42] A Venetian himself, Chiericati cites Venetian examples. Well-paid troops conquered Verona and Padua, but badly paid soldiers failed at Trieste. In other words a well-paid army expands the realm.[43]

The logic is really the same in the old and the new romances and manuals, only the fifteenth-century author adopts the specifics of the mercenary armies in Italy and of "bastard feudalism" in the north.[44] Exploding war costs in the fifteenth century made the whole question more acute. Mallett gives some figures for Italy. In the late 1440s Venice spent its entire state revenue on the army, and the Papal States for one siege in 1469 spent twice their annual revenue.[45] In this respect finance determined strategy. The romance Arthur had no alternative but to pursue an expansionist policy. His actions would resemble well enough the building of large states that occurred in the fifteenth century: the expansion of the Ottoman Empire, the conquest of the terra firma by Venice, the union of Castile and Aragon, and the failed English attempt on the Continent, which led instead to a greater France.

It still remains true that Merlin set up a very risky plan for the young
Arthur. Malory, taking up the old story, might have thought of John Talbot, earl of Shrewsbury. Much outnumbered at Bordeaux, with three armies approaching from different directions, he followed a daring offensive strategy that ended in the disaster of Castillon (1453). He began it
with a night march and a surprise attack at dawn.[46] The parallel between
the fictional and the real campaign is sufficient to show what else Merlin
and Arthur needed for victory. Martorell provides a hint in his prologue
to *Tirant:* "Fortitud corporal e ardiment se vol exercir ab saviesa: com per
la prudència e indústria dels batallants, diverses vegades los pocs han ob-
tesa victòria dels molts, la saviesa e astúcia dels cavallers ha bastat aterrar
les forces dels enemics" ("Physical strength and courage should be employed with wisdom, for through prudence and strategy, the few at times
have vanquished the many, laying low their enemies through astuteness
and cunning"; *Tirant,* prol.9).[47] Merlin had the time to plan with prudence, something Talbot did not have, and careful calculation marks
Merlin's war aims. Malory had to revise these aims, but to understand
what he did, we must first look at the Vulgate solution to Arthur's first
war, for its ghost haunts Malory's version.

In the Vulgate, Merlin's political and military strategy exactly fits Arthur's needs and achieves its ends in every detail. The Vulgate author
establishes a situation in which plot and theory correlate precisely. Its
precondition is the fantastic geography of Britain, where the dilemma of
the enemy kings and Merlin's policy of military audacity and political
restraint make sense. Fantasy then does not exclude the political and the
military, nor does it idealize the real, at least in this case. Rather its imagined setting encourages the play of theory, allowing the author to develop
the detailed implications of a particular military or political strategy.

The authors of both the Vulgate and the *Suite du Merlin* inherited
from Robert de Boron a fanciful geography for England. Robert took
place names from English chronicle but fit them to his own map. Logres,
for example, becomes a town, and Winchester a seaport.[48] The Vulgate
author makes this fantasy into a clear schema (fig. 8). All the places
named are near each other. Logres is close enough to Bedgrayne that Arthur's army can return there after the battle (Vulgate *Merlin,* 122). The
enemy city of Sorhaut, to which the kings withdraw, is a similar distance
from the battlefield, and the kings themselves live near each other, despite
their titles.[49] An enemy force can simultaneously threaten Cornwall and
Orcanie (Vulgate *Merlin,* 124).

Recognition of this smallness is essential to understand Merlin's military strategy and hence his war aims. Arthur rules an inner area. Beyond are petty but independent principalities that separate his kingdom from some potentially dangerous enemies, who are not far distant from Arthur's capital. Ryons, for example, is making a mantle from the beards of conquered kings, which he has carried before him on the days when he holds court. He rules over a land of giants and shepherds, a land uncultivated because no farmer dares live there (Vulgate *Merlin*, 92, 107). He himself is of giant lineage and has corresponding ambitions. On the other side are the infidel Saxons, who wish to occupy and settle the land and who are Arthur's traditional enemies in the chronicle tradition.

Such a situation explains Merlin's aggressive policies. A larger, unified kingdom would overawe the enemies beyond the borders. Merlin partially secures this aim in Camylarde by military aid and a political marriage. Arthur inherits the kingdom and integrates its army with his own. The other kings, however, must be persuaded that submission to Arthur will serve their interests better than independence. Here the Saxons provide the necessary pressure.

Defeated by Arthur, the kings find the Saxons threatening all their lands at once. The Saxons raid, devastate zones, burn towns, and kill many of their subjects. Currently, they are besieging Vandaliors in "Cornwall" (Vulgate *Merlin*, 113). The expanded version of the Vulgate makes the threat plainer. King Brangoires says they must chase the Saxons out or lose everything, for the Saxons have come to occupy the land and to expel the natives. The enemy already has a fortified base, the Roche as Sesnes, well supplied and defended by magic. The British kings do what they can and fight a defensive guerrilla-style war, which forces them to turn their own area into a wasteland (Vulgate *Merlin*, 125, 131). They do not have the strength to expel the enemy.

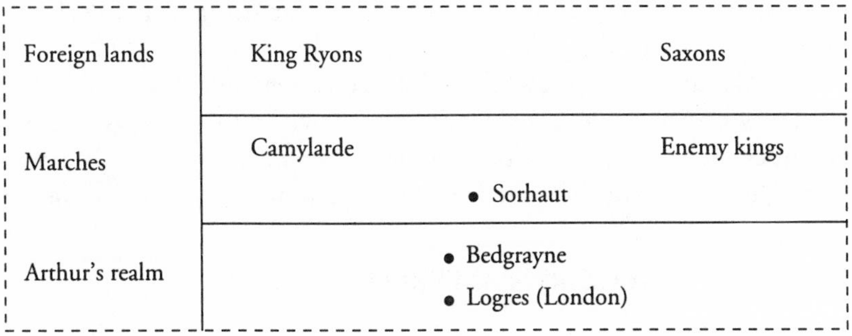

Figure 8. Map of the fictional England of the Vulgate *Merlin* and the *Suite du Merlin*.

This threat eventually converts the kings into loyal subjects. The author shows the logic through a conversation between Lot's wife and sons (Vulgate *Merlin*, 130–31). She tells Gawain that he should serve Arthur and win peace for his father. Then together the two kings could expel the Saxons. Agravain adds that the Saxons, who are only a day away, could otherwise trap them like birds. The family decides that the sons shall serve Arthur. The assumed situation is circular. The kings need Arthur's help against the Saxon invader, while Arthur needs their armies to create the great realm envisaged by Merlin, a realm so strong that the enemies beyond the frontier will no longer trouble it.

This process can occur only if Arthur treats the other kings with restraint. Merlin accordingly does not allow Arthur to exploit the victory of Bedgrayne. There is no invasion of enemy territory, not even a pursuit.[50] Merlin here follows a standard strategy. Frontinus cites the example of Pyrrhus, who advises a commander never to press relentlessly after a fleeing enemy. Such leniency avoids driving the enemy to desperation and makes him more inclined to withdraw another time, knowing that the victor would not try to destroy him in flight (*Stratagems*, 2.6.10).[51] By this strategy Merlin allows the kings to escape with an army and so defend themselves against the Saxons. He sends Arthur to Camylarde and waits for events to bring the enemy kings around. The children of the enemy, impressed by Arthur's heroic victory against odds, turn to him for knighthood. Their leaders are Gawain and Galescins, themselves nephews of the king.[52] The political marriages arranged earlier by Uther thus work for Arthur. The sons choose the Arthurian not the paternal side of the family, the great not the petty king. Merlin predicts that they will draw the other sons after them and that Gawain and Yvain will be Arthur's strongest support (Vulgate *Merlin*, 96–97). At the same time the barons from the inner realm now do homage voluntarily, lest Arthur take away their lands (Vulgate *Merlin*, 124). Military dynamism and political patience make Arthur the great ruler.

The Merlin of the Vulgate followed a consistent and successful strategy. He wished to defeat but not wreck the army of the rival kings because he anticipated eventual political union rather than conquest. Malory, writing more than two hundred years later, had no such clear option.

MALORY'S ALTERED STRATEGY

For Malory, Arthur's enemies exist in a real, not a fantasy, England. This change in the legend had mostly already occurred before Malory composed his one-volume abridgment. English authors had done much of the work, reinterpreting the geography of the French romancers. The process began, however, with the author or scribe of the Cambridge *Suite*.[53] He checked the chronicles against the Vulgate *Merlin* and so reintroduced Aurelius Ambrosius and corrected the spelling of the usurper's name to *Vortiger* (*Suite*, 207r). Such details fit into the later tendency to historicize all the Arthurian place names, a tendency well developed in the fourteenth century. For example, Dover had its Arthurian relics, and a traveler could assume that the King of the Hundred Knights had ruled the Isle of Man.[54] The Stanzaic *Morte Arthur* (ca. 1350), which was Malory's source for the fall of Arthur, turns a tendency into a method.[55] Winchester, Rochester, Carlisle, and Glastonbury now appear on the map.[56] The process was simple and logical; it united the Arthurs of fantasy and chronicle and assumed for England what the Vulgate author had already assumed for France, a real geography. It restored to Arthur the historicity he had lost when he left the chronicles for the romances.

Malory accordingly gives the royal opposition a precise geographical location (fig. 9). The kings come from the north and the Celtic west, and Uther and Arthur have to fight on both frontiers.[57] Westward, Uther wages war in Cornwall, and Arthur later meets all his enemies there in a single battle.[58] The north, however, is our immediate concern because it is there that Arthur fights the battle of Bedgrayne. Lot has his lands in Scotland, and the king of Northumberland is one of the enemy monarchs. The area of Arthur's secure control stops, therefore, at the River Trent, and Malory identifies Bedgrayne with Sherwood Forest.[59] This realistic geography automatically changes the strategy behind Arthur's first campaign.

On the new historical map Arthur's enemies do not form a coherent group. Some are widely separated from each other, such as Cornwall and Lothian; hence, the chances of unified action are limited and would not be of long duration. As a result, the kings act quickly and fight in midwinter. Armies normally avoided conflict in winter, but desperation could force one.[60] The Lancastrians took over northern castles in October 1462, and the Yorkists had to fight a winter war there, much as the enemy kings forced Arthur into Sherwood sometime between November 1 and February 3.[61] Merlin's strategy of patience here takes on a new meaning. Arthur need only survive their attack, and his power will grow, while theirs declines. At Caerleon 300 of the best knights desert to Arthur (*Morte*, 1.9.18–19). Later Arthur's barons think they are already a match for the

Figure 9. Malory's England.

kings (*Morte,* 1.10.19). After Bedgrayne the kings must fight Saracens, while other lords submit to the new monarch.

Survival, however, does not end the war or conclude the story. Merlin's advice not to pursue the defeated now has a different strategic meaning, geared not to war aims but to the immediate needs of the campaign. In his speech to Arthur he makes two points: "Thou has never done. Hast thou nat done inow? Of three score thousande thys day hast thou leffte on lyve but fyftene thousand! Therefore hit ys tyme to sey 'Who!' for

God ys wroth with the for thou woll never have done. For yondir a eleven
kynges at thys tyme woll nat be overthrowyn, but and thou tary on them
ony lenger thy fortune woll turne and they shall encres" (*Morte*, 1.17.36).
The spectacular triumph of the Vulgate dwindles to a Pyrrhic victory in
Malory. After 45,000 casualties the enemy kings, though defeated, have
kept their army intact. To pursue them is dangerous, and Merlin argues
out of Vegetius. To leave no avenue of escape encourages desperate fighting and could turn around the battle.[62] At Bedgrayne Arthur repels an
invasion but accomplishes no more. Malory shows nothing of the greater
realm glimpsed through Merlin's plans in the Vulgate. The reader, therefore, does not see an end to the state of war between Arthur and his rivals,
and the story thus lacks closure. This problem was exaggerated by another aspect of the same trend that gave Arthur a realistic geography.

Romancers normally modernized their stories, bringing them closer to
their audience. Critics have shown how Malory adds contemporary details to the tournaments and other peacetime activities of his knights, and
he does the same for war, when possible.[63] To protect against spies the
Vulgate Arthur had ordered that all travelers be sent to him (Vulgate *Mer-*
lin, 109). In Malory, Merlin merely requires that all men of arms who
travel in Arthur's zone carry royal passports (*Morte*, 1.11.25). More to the
point, Malory modernizes the Saxons, who become Saracens, the only
known infidels of the fifteenth century.

Saracens, however, live far away.[64] They do not occasion the fear
caused by the old pagan Saxons, who had crossed the North Sea to conquer England and settle down. In Malory the Saracen attack distracts the
enemy kings for three years, but the Saracens are not threatening enough
to cause the kings to reconcile their differences with Arthur. Malory instead has the kings plan a renewed war. They draw Ryons into their alliance: "All thys whyle they furnysshed and garnysshed hem of good men
of armys and vitayle and of all maner of ablemente that pretendith to
warre, to avenge hem for the batayle of Bedgrayne" (*Morte*, 1.18.41). The
kings, not the Saxons, are the problem.

This reinterpretation destroys the logic of the old story.[65] The Vulgate
kings had to join Arthur eventually or be conquered by the Saxons. Malory imagines a very different situation. The kings of the north and west,
who reject Arthur's claim to the throne, had fought his father as well.
Uther warred with the duke of Cornwall and ended his reign defeating a
northern host at Saint Albans.[66] Nor does their enmity cease after Bedgrayne. When Arthur faces and defeats a foreign invasion, his victory
makes the kings unhappy: "And all the kynge Arthurs enemyes, as the

kynge of North Wals and the kynges of the Northe, knewe of this batayle; they were passynge hevy" (*Morte*, 4.4.130). These kings would oppose *any* member of Uther's family, and the Bedgrayne campaign becomes just one in a series of conflicts, part of the long attempt by Uther and Arthur to bring order to the realm.

Unending hostilities of the sort Malory imagines befit his period. Medieval wars generally had resisted closure,[67] but the giant conflict we call the Hundred Years War far exceeded anyone's nightmares. The English could win battles and capture towns but could not stop the struggle. Then came the Wars of the Roses, which continued throughout the time Malory composed the *Morte Darthur*. Nor were the English alone; Venice was currently mired in its Long War with the Ottomans, which lasted from 1463 to 1479.

Yet Malory needed an end to the young Arthur's wars because the bulk of his stories occurred in peacetime and presupposed a powerful and stable system in England. Unable to use the Vulgate blueprint, Malory opted for a contemporary solution, that of annihilation, the normal practice in the Wars of the Roses.[68] His immediate source, the *Suite du Merlin,* had Arthur win a great double battle by Castle Terrable against King Nero and eleven lesser monarchs. Lot also brings an army to the battle, and the kings die there. Arthur has them buried in Camelot and erects a victory memorial. The king stands with drawn sword over the portrait statues of his enemies (Huth *Merlin,* 245–63).

Malory carefully adapts this battle to the Vulgate war. At Bedgrayne he changes the number of the enemy kings from eight to eleven, and he adds a prediction by Merlin, who anticipates the battle at Castle Terrable and the deaths of the kings (*Morte,* 1.18.40, 2.10.77). Malory later notes the fulfillment of this prediction. Moreover, he makes Castle Terrable the property of the duke of Cornwall and has Uther besiege this castle when he makes war for Igrayne. In fact, Malory did all he could to integrate the battle at Castle Terrable with the Vulgate war. It, not Bedgrayne, concludes the fighting and brings a kind of peace to Arthur's England.

Unfortunately, this solution, although it made strategic sense, wrecked his story, for the author of the *Suite* did not connect Nero and his kings with those who opposed Arthur at Bedgrayne.[69] He continued to envisage the old Vulgate solution to the war, the eventual voluntary union between Arthur and his enemies. Malory, following his lead, also preserves this assumption. We see the sons of the enemy at Arthur's court. The king knights Gawain (*Morte,* 3.2.99) and makes King Uriens a Knight of the Round Table (4.4.130–31).[70] Malory gives the theory its most elaborate presentation later, when he returns to Vulgate material in the Book of Sir Lancelot and Queen Guinevere. The enemy kings now cosponsor the tournaments, where Lancelot wins glory for the queen. Sides change from one tournament to another, and chivalric play replaces war.[71] The kings are by now all members of the Round Table. Malory concludes the book with an invented episode in which Sir Urry comes to Arthur's court for healing. One hundred ten Knights of the Round Table are present, and Malory gives the list. It begins with the kings of the north and the west.[72]

The solutions by the authors of the earlier *Merlin* books and by Malory mutually exclude each other. Kings killed at Castle Terrable reappear in later episodes. But more important, the logic of one solution contradicts the other. In the one a weak monarch and his adviser preside over a formidable army made by the voluntary union of French and English forces and those of the kings of the north and west. In the other the monarch with French allies first defeats and then destroys the enemy kings. He assures his own power, but how or whether he creates a larger realm is unclear. Here we have one of those discrepancies in Malory—or rather a whole set of them—which scholars have debated in a different context. They have argued over whether Malory wrote one work or compiled an anthology. That dispute does not concern us here because the contradictions we have found exist within the limits of a single tale. Nor would an appeal to multiple and conflicting sources help. Here Malory worked from a single source, the Cambridge manuscript, and he is responsible for the discrepancies, not the Cambridge scribe.

THE RIFT

The rapprochement between romance and history, which worked so well in other areas of aristocratic life, such as tournaments and duels, created unexpected strains when it concerned military campaigns.[73] It forced Malory first to reinterpret and then to rework the old story he was abridging. Yet he still could not make it fit. The threads of the tapestry crossed in the wrong places, and the edges tore. Pulci in the south provides a contrasting example. Although a considerable distance separated his story, likewise rooted in traditional romances, from contemporary warfare, the distance was not so great that he had to discard his narrative, and contemporary warfare did not ruin the plot.

Malory was less fortunate. Modern warfare messed up his story of Arthur's early wars, and he also maintained the old narrative of Arthur's fall at a price. He had to know that Lancelot's whole strategy of passive resistance—staying in his castles and refusing to fight—no longer corresponded to contemporary practice. Malory identifies Joyous Garde either with Alnwick or with Bamborough Castle (*Morte*, 21.12.1257), but neither place effectively resisted Yorkist armies. Alnwick held out for a cold winter month in 1462–63 but did not resist a second time (1464). Bamborough fell quickly to cannon and assault that same year.[74] The strategy involved was the opposite of that used by Lancelot, who holds off Arthur's forces fifteen weeks into harvest time (*Morte*, 20.10–11.1187). The Lancastrians would seize border castles, which they could not hold but which would force the Yorkists to considerable expense, bringing cannon up from London, and would then make them destroy their own national defenses.[75] Lancelot's strategy against Arthur must have appeared archaic to both Malory and his readers. And in fact, in this section of his work he stresses the distance between the Arthurian world and contemporary reality. An example is his apostrophe to Guinevere (*Morte*, 18.25.1119–20) or his observations on the law of treason (20.7.1174). This stress on historical separation contradicts his efforts to modernize his sources elsewhere.[76] Thus, two of the three military sequences that Malory presents, those of Arthur's initial and final wars, show signs of strain, though in different ways. The first disturbs the story line, while the second cannot be connected to the fifteenth-century present.[77]

—THREE—

Agramante's War
Matteo Maria Boiardo

IN ONE RESPECT MATTEO MARIA BOIARDO DIFFERS FROM other writers of romance in the late fifteenth century, for he invented a purely fictional world. He did not abbreviate or rework older stories, as did Malory and Pulci, nor did he model the career of his fictional hero on that of a historical person, as Martorell did to some extent in modeling his Tirant after Roger de Flor.[1] Both Pulci and Boiardo wrote about Charlemagne, but where Pulci ended at least with a historical event, the battle of Roncesvalles, Boiardo told a story without precedent in the old chronicles.[2] It is doubtful that anyone in his audience would have believed that Agramante had ever existed or led a huge African army into France.[3]

Yet Boiardo too imitated history, its formal devices rather than its content. He discusses his romance as if it were history, exploiting the ambiguity of the term *storia* or *istoria,* which can mean simply "a narrative" or "a history." He begins his *Orlando innamorato* by saying that a "bella istoria" moves his song, and he repeats the phrase often throughout the romance. He develops this claim when he introduces his first catalogue (*OI* 2.22.1–3).[4] He cannot climb Parnassus for the laurel, he says, but rather will sing at the bottom of the hill "questa istoria." Although humble, his song too serves a purpose, for no one would remember the valor of Alexander or Caesar without history. The poet's patron Ercole preferred history, and Boiardo adjusts his form accordingly.[5] His style is "low," like the prose of a historian; his order is chronological; and when he presents catalogues and councils, which are common to the epic poet and to the classical historian, he follows the historian rather than the poet.[6]

Formal imitation lent a certain verisimilitude to this, the most fantastic of the late fifteenth-century romances. Boiardo has the leaders of a

Saracen army debate the pros and cons of a possible invasion of France, and his catalogues give precise details about the soldiers and their lands of origin. This trend to historical verisimilitude grew in the years after Boiardo composed his work.[7] It affected Ariosto's presentation of the siege of Paris and reached its Italian climax with Tasso, who encouraged the use of historical chronicles for verisimilitude, though he carefully avoided the vanishing point himself. He never let the *Gerusalemme liberata* become indistinguishable from history. The conventions of historical writing helped make romance more probable, even believable.

The kind of history Boiardo imitated signals the Renaissance and separates him from his quattrocento contemporaries north and south. True to his humanist education, the poet looked to Livy and Herodotus rather than to medieval chronicles, thus lending dignity to his romance.[8] More especially he used Herodotus when he tried to assess the goals and the power of King Agramante, whose invasion of France is the public focus for books 2 and 3 of the *Innamorato*.[9] Boiardo constructed his analysis through the same means the Greek historian had used for Xerxes's invasion. Giovanni Ponte has already sketched briefly the extent of this debt.[10] Here, I wish to flesh it out and suggest the relationship between this classical vision of war and military practice in the quattrocento. Historical form came easily to the man who had already translated Herodotus.[11] (For a discussion of the translation, see appendix 2.) Certain peculiarities of geographical reference link the translation to the poem. For example, in his translation he calls the Ethiopians whom Cambyses fights Macrobii (*Hist.* 7.18; Boiardo, 119v), and they reappear as troops who serve Gradasso when he invades Spain (*OI* 1.4.34).[12] Next the poet puts a wood with serpents and lions on the south slope of the Atlas range or Mount Carena (*Hist.* 7.191; Boiardo, 154r), the kind of area in which Rugiero grows up (*OI* 2.1.74, 3.5.35–37). More important than borrowed words or phrases, however, is the understanding Boiardo gained from his work on Herodotus, one possible only to a translator. This understanding helped him compose his original variations when he turned to the *Innamorato*.

Herodotus gave Boiardo his conception of the Saracen enemy, and it is the Saracens on whom I focus in this chapter: both the leaders and the soldiers who followed them to war. The price of this classical imitation came perhaps too high. It reinforced old stereotypes of the Saracen and thus promoted a dangerous military illusion, one Italians could not afford in the 1480s. The imitation of history, in fact, allowed Boiardo to evade contemporary reality.

The poet's use of Herodotus necessitates a literary discussion, for the details of the imitation reveal the poet's attitude to the enemy. I will focus on the councils of war that begin book 7 of Herodotus and book 2 of the *Innamorato* and the military catalogues given later in the same books, which define the empires and war potential of the invaders (*Hist.* 7.61–99; *OI* 2.22.4–18). Throughout, however, one must remember that Boiardo used many sources, even for single scenes. Rodamonte may take Mardonius's place at the first council, but he hardly resembles the Persian general.[13]

THE COUNCILS OF WAR

Although Boiardo does use Herodotus elsewhere in his romance, he concentrates on the parallel between Agramante and Xerxes, their war deliberations and army.[14] The two monarchs deliver similar speeches before a council of advisers. Each gives two speeches, which open and close the debate. Both rulers appear as young men, eager to act in a manner worthy of their ancestors and to surpass them, for they dream of world conquest.

Herodotus has Xerxes constantly talk like a young man, though in fact he has grown children. He treats his elders with a mixture of respect and short temper.[15] Agramante similarly begins speaking with great politeness to his advisers, but can only end the debate by a fiat. Boiardo makes his king twenty-two years old, so he was a boy of seven when his father died fighting Charlemagne in Burgundy (*OI* 2.1.14–16).[16] Neither ruler has experienced warfare with his European enemy. Both dwell on family precedent. Xerxes sees the Achaemenid past as a pattern of expansion that he projects on his own future. He must make a conquest worthy of Cyrus, Cambyses, and Darius (*Hist.* 7.8.1). For Agramante the family past is more distant and yet more visible. He appeals to the founder of his family, Alexander the Great, whose story appears sculpted on the walls of the hall where the Africans deliberate (*OI* 2.1.22–30).[17] It is the romance story of Alexander, which surpasses in extravagance the historical record, for he concludes his conquests with a tour of the sky, flying behind two griffons, and descends in a glass compartment to view the whales and great fishes of the sea. Balas rubies and sapphires decorate the frieze and make this past even more splendid.

Both kings misunderstand their past. Persian expansion, at least in the West, had stopped with Darius, who faced rebellion in Babylon, Egypt, and Ionia, and whose campaign beyond the frontiers ended unsuccessfully.[18] Where Xerxes misreads, Agramante ignores the immediate past, for three previous kings have died fighting Charlemagne (*OI* 2.1.14). Both kings would reopen wars with enemies who have previously defeated their armies.

Applied to the future, this family pattern causes hubris.[19] After his conquest of Greece, Xerxes intends to march throughout Europe, so the sun will not look upon any land beyond the Persian borders (*Hist.* 7.8.g.2). Certainly his preparations suggest that he wishes for a permanent conquest: the new royal road through Thrace (*Hist.* 115.3), the bridges of boats at the Hellespont and the Strymon, the canal at Athos. Agramante, as befits a romance hero, has a still wilder vision: first France, next the world, finally Paradise (*OI* 2.1.64).[20]

The kings provoke a battle of youth and age. In Herodotus the ruler and his cousin Mardonius speak for the young and argue for war, while Xerxes's uncle Artabanus opposes them. In Boiardo it is Agramante and the young Rodamonte against Sobrino, a veteran of the previous war; Branzardo who carried the baby Agramante in his arms and regards him as a son (*OI* 2.1.43); and especially the king of Garamanta, now over ninety, who dies during the second council (2.1.57, 62). The young speak first.

Mardonius has supplied Xerxes with some of his arguments and dreams of ruling Hellas.[21] His speech in council, however, is contradictory. On the one hand, he argues that the Persians need not fear the Greeks in battle, thus ignoring the defeat at Marathon; on the other, tacitly admitting the defeat, he recommends that Xerxes bring a large army and navy (*Hist.* 7.9). Agramante will similarly go to France with a huge land army, by which arrangement he recognizes the European tactical superiority demonstrated in the previous wars, though he never refers to it. His own supporter in council is the giant Rodamonte, who hopes to be crowned king in France (*OI* 2.3.35). Otherwise he resembles Mardonius not at all and presents no practical arguments for the war. Instead he argues for royal authority (*OI* 2.1.53–56): whoever contradicts the royal mandate is a traitor. At the oath taking he reinforces this appeal, saying that he will follow or even go before Agramante wherever he leads, even to heaven or hell (*OI* 2.1.65). In fact, it is not clear that he follows his own precepts. Later, dissatisfied with the postponement of the war, Rodamonte leaves the second council without a goodbye (*OI* 2.3.36) and leads his own expedition to France. Perhaps this constitutes "going before" the monarch, but it hardly fits the royal politics he argued at the first council. His actions seem as contradictory as Mardonius's speeches.

Artabanus opposes the war against Greece, both at the council and at Abydos, using three arguments that Boiardo in his poem assigns to several speakers. Artabanus warns of divine anger, explains the geographic problem, and begins an assessment of Hellene military power, which Demaratus continues at Doriscus and Thermopylae. Boiardo has the king of Garamanta argue the first, Sobrino of Garbo the second, and Branzardo of Bugia the third.

Both authors express the first point in contemporary terms. Artabanus sees God as a Greek tyrant who does not bother with little lives but thunders against the high, hurling his "arrows" at great houses and trees. When the envious deity, like Zeus in the *Iliad* (8.66–77), throws panic or thunder, a large army can be destroyed by a small one. God allows great thoughts only to himself and does not tolerate fantasizing (*Hist.* 7.10.e).[22] Artabanus directs this argument at the hubris he perceives in his royal nephew, who wishes to conquer all of Europe. Mardonius, he warns, will feed the birds and dogs, either in Greece or on the way there (*Hist.* 7.10.e).

The king of Garamanta takes up these points but modernizes them. Rodamonte will indeed feed the crows in France, but for the rest the king replaces an envious deity with an unfavorable disposition of the stars (*OI* 2.1.57–59). The king is an astrologer and a priest of Apollo, the sun god, and his desert kingdom has clear skies by night.[23] Saturn is in the ascendant and will destroy the Africans. The army, large or small, will not return. At best, if Rugiero joins the Africans, they will win honor and some victories (*OI* 2.1.70). Agramante accepts the practical suggestion for reasons that reinforce the astrologer's authority: the old man has always correctly forecast the future (*OI* 2.1.76–77). Agramante thus unwittingly grants the old man his major premise, that the Africans will lose the war.

The argument from geography concerns the enemy land and is clearer in Herodotus, since he works with real and not romance landscapes. At Abydos Artabanus argues that the great size of Xerxes's forces does not fit Greece (*Hist.* 7.49). The coast does not afford the navy a port capable of saving the ships in a storm. A storm ruined Mardonius's previous expedition, and another one will hit at Cape Sepias. The land presents a different problem: the farther the army advances, the more hostile the land becomes. Artabanus presumably alludes both to the military opposition and to supplies.

Sobrino likewise speaks of sea and land, but the application is purely tactical (*OI* 2.1.44–51). The Africans could sail directly to France and land at Aquamorta (Aigues-Mortes), a swampy district southwest of Arles. There, however, ten Christians would be worth a hundred Saracens, presumably because the latter would be struggling out of the water. Rodamonte proves Sobrino's point, at least partially. A four-day storm forces him to sail directly on the rocks at Monaco, and he loses two-thirds of his men (*OI* 2.6.41) and more than two-thirds of his 190 ships with their supplies and horses (2.6.48–49). This total does not include casualties from the battle that follows. Sobrino thinks the land route by Spain would be easier initially but would end up being even more difficult than the naval route. The Africans would have to confront first Ranaldo at Montealbano and then Orlando. In the event, by good luck Agramante's forces win at Montealbano, and Orlando is diverted from the war, but the Saracens fail at Paris. The main invasion supports Sobrino's analysis. Sobrino emphasizes the quality of the Christian soldiers, which improves as the Africans advance, a point parallel to Artabanus's and one that leads logically to an analysis of the enemy army.

In council Artabanus states that the Hellenes are best on land or sea (*Hist.* 7.10). He warns that a naval defeat could leave the Persians stranded in Europe and reminds the councilors that the Athenians by themselves destroyed the army of Datis and Artaphrenes on land. Demaratus, the exiled Spartan, later continues this second argument. Among other points he says that although a single Spartan does not surpass another soldier in strength, as a group the Spartans fight more effectively than any other company of soldiers. He attributes this group coordination to the rule of law and contrasts it implicitly with Xerxes's mass levies, driven into battle by whips (*Hist.* 7.102–4). At Thermopylae the Spartans illustrate his point. By keeping a tight organization they can simulate flight. When the enemy pursues and presumably loses order, the Spartans turn and cut down great numbers (*Hist.* 7.211.3).

In Boiardo's work King Branzardo demonstrates the same point in a triple manner: by reason, example, and experience (*OI* 2.1.39–43). By reason Agramante should not attack France because he would have to use untrained masses against veterans who stand by each other in battle. Branzardo's example turns around one of the young king's own claims. Agramante does not resemble another Alexander, setting off to conquer the world, but the Darius whom Alexander defeated. The Greek had old and seasoned troops, but in the Persian army one soldier did not know another. Experience reinforces the point, for the Africans failed in their last attack, fifteen years previously. Tactically, neither of the invading armies, the Persian or the African, has the requisite skill to win a war against professional soldiers.

Through the council scenes both writers show young people who plan badly through inexperience. This explains why they misread the past and

think that a large enough army will remedy the failures of earlier campaigns. Inexperience likewise explains their willingness to begin aggressive wars and their unrealistic dreams of world conquest. On the other
side, the older men have all the caution that experience of defeat can
produce. They know the enemy, his army and his land, and they construct an array of practical arguments against this new enterprise. Finally,
they fear the supernatural and wish to rest with what they have. The
young, however, win the meetings, for the kings are young and desire
glory. Nevertheless, the military catalogues that follow the councils show
that in this case the old men are right.

THE CATALOGUES

Boiardo indicates two of the three sources for his catalogues when he
claims that Agramante had collected together the largest army ever (*OI*
2.29.1–2).[24] Not Hannibal when he brought all Africa and Spain to Italy,
not Xerxes who took Scythians and Ethiopians to Thermopylae, had an
army of this size. Livy and Herodotus, the classical historians of a Europe
invaded by foreigners, provide his model. Boiardo's third source comes
from the romancers' practice of modernization. Charlemagne's enemies
had to be Saracens, not the old pagan Persians and Carthaginians, and
the towns and districts of Islamic Africa had to be given their current
names. Boiardo thus had to use portulans, contemporary nautical maps,[25]
rather than that of Ptolemy, which copyists also continued to reproduce
(figs. 10, 11). The conception is classical, but many of the details are
modern.

Livy gave Boiardo his notion of political Africa and the grand outlines
of the war. Agramante's family comes from Tarabulus, or Tripoli (Livy,
2.1.9), and he has his own capital at Bizerte (Biserta). The two towns
define roughly the coastal limits of the old Carthaginian homeland, and
half of Agramante's elect troops come from this area: Bizerte, Tunis, and
Tarabulus, not to mention others from Jerba (Alzerbe).[26] Westward Agramante's control extends at least as far as that of the old Punic colonial
system: on the Mediterranean coast Bejaïa (Bugia), Algiers, Bellamarina,[27] and Oran; Ceuta (Septa, Sette) and Alcazar el-Saghir (Alghezera) at
the Pillars of Hercules; then down the Atlantic coast with Asilah (Arzila),
Larache (Alvaracchie),[28] and Azemmour (Azumara, Zumara). The campaign resembles the Second Punic War, for Agramante joins a Spanish
army, and together they win a great initial victory and occupy most of
the enemy's territory. The outcome, however, will resemble the last Punic

War, for it is predicted that Orlando will level Bizerte and leave it in ruins, as the second Scipio demolished Carthage (*OI* 2.1.19).

Herodotus's influence can be seen in the catalogues by the inclusion of a naval as well as an army catalogue. Similarly, the poet's emphasis on the exotic in his presentation of the diverse contingents reveals the historian's influence. More important, however, the Greek gave Boiardo his sense of the oasis kingdoms (fig. 12).

Boiardo includes an unnecessary catalogue of ships (*OI* 2.29.3–20), unnecessary because the ships serve only as troop transport, from Bizerte to Malaga (Maliga). Herodotus had described both land and sea forces because Persian strategy required their cooperation.[29] The Persians fought simultaneously on both, as the battles of Thermopylae and Artemisium indicate. Boiardo imagines only a land war but includes the naval catalogue for two purposes: he wants to remind his audience of the enemy leaders, just before they take part in the battle of Montealbano, and he

Figure 10. Mauro's map of North Africa (1459). Courtesy the University of Chicago Libraries.

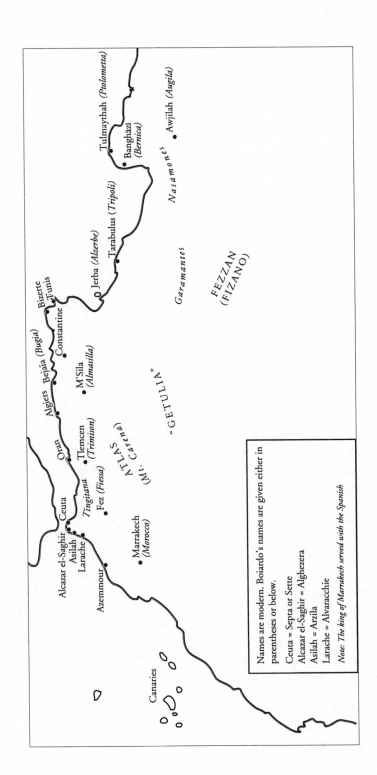

Figure 11. Places in Agramante's empire that can be exactly located on a modern map.

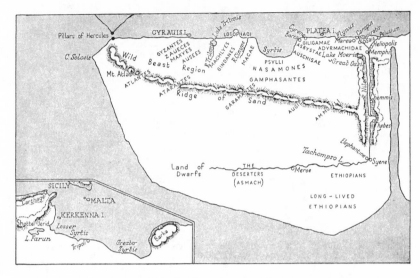

Figure 12. Herodotus's map of North Africa. Reprinted from How and Wells, *Commentary,* 1:160, by permission of Oxford University Press.

likes color and exotic detail, so he enumerates all the ensigns of the Saracen leaders.[30] This color becomes traditional in the first catalogue (*OI* 2.22.4–28), where Boiardo imitates Herodotus's descriptions of exotic peoples.[31] The people from Alcazar el-Saghir (Alghezera), for example, use dragon bones for iron and substitute lion heads for helmets (*OI* 2.22.17–19).[32] So far Herodotus influenced the poet's form, but the Greek also influenced Boiardo's content.

Boiardo turned to Herodotus for material when he needed information on the desert oases in "Getulia."[33] The portulans gave few precise locations for places in the African interior, and Boiardo had to look elsewhere for the information. This situation explains some peculiarities in Boiardo's catalogues, for the Renaissance text of Herodotus had doublets that required interpretation. Farthest east was Siwa (Amonia), the place where Zeus Ammon had his temple, followed by Awjilah (Augila), the oasis where the Nasamones harvested dates (*Hist.* 4.172). Next came the Garamantes, listed twice but only once for the oasis, which, however, Herodotus located too far west.[34] In between, Boiardo put Fizano (the modern Fezzan in western Libya). Now the Garamantes of Herodotus hunt the Ethiopian troglodytes, who live on serpents and lizards. They become Boiardo's people of Bulga, a place in the deep desert (*OI* 2.22.10).[35] Next Herodotus has the Atlantes, listed twice (*Hist.* 4.184).[36]

Boiardo took the description of the first but the location of the second, farthest west under Mount Atlas. Herodotus says that they are blameless but curse and revile the sun while it is high, because its burning wears out their land and them. The Italian poet keeps the detail but reverses the judgment: there is no group worse (*OI* 2.22.11). He also incorrectly modernizes their name, for they become the people of Fez (Fiessa).[37]

The rest of Agramante's kingdom can be briefly told. Boiardo has some sense of the cities of the Tell (Constantine, Tlemcen or Tremison)[38] and of the Atlas district (Mount Carena),[39] and he adds the Canaries and the black kingdoms of West Africa, which the Portuguese were exploring.[40] He thus conveys a sense that Agramante brings all of Africa west of Egypt—all of it that Europeans knew about—to the great war (*OI* 2.22.28). Agramante's realm thus equals in extent the earlier empires in the area. Its center and policies are Carthaginian, but the king controls the whole of North Africa, as had the Almohads, and his rule extends as far south as that of the Almoravids.[41] In this fashion Boiardo creates an imaginary rival of the historical Persian empire that invaded Greece.

Militarily, both Herodotus's and Boiardo's catalogues describe armies that consist mostly of light troops and must fight heavily armored soldiers: the phalanx of the Greeks and the mailed cavalry of medieval Europe. Xerxes has hardly any hoplites or heavy infantry in his army.[42] The Persians themselves set the standard: armored archers who could serve as infantry.[43] Otherwise the king has archers who wear no armor, and javelin throwers from Anatolia.[44] The Persian tribes likewise provide the heavy cavalry.[45] Agramante's army shows the same pattern exaggerated. Nine of his contingents are well armed.[46] Of the rest, where Boiardo gives information, none has any value militarily.[47] There are the nomads and oasis dwellers, who wear no armor (nine contingents);[48] the people of the Atlantic seaboard, whom Boiardo imagines living in Stone Age conditions;[49] and the black troops.[50] Finally, he dismisses those from Normandia as deaf, lame, and cross-eyed (*OI* 2.22.19).

Few of these troops could face heavily armed Europeans. Both kings, the real and the fictive, discover this fact quickly. Xerxes sends Medes and Cissians (Elamites) to capture the diminutive force at Thermopylae *alive*. The Asiatics, of course, cannot advance in the narrow pass, and the Persian Immortals who replace them fare no better. Courage cannot compensate for shorter spears (*Hist.* 7.210–12).[51] At Montealbano Boiardo constructs a variation on this scene. Agramante tells Pinadoro of Constantine to get information on the battle below. He is to go where the battle is fiercest and capture one to six prisoners alive and bring them back for interrogation. Instead Orlando unhorses him, leans over, *picks him up,* and does his own interrogating (*OI* 2.29.32–36). He sends the shaken youth back to Agramante, and Pinadoro now argues against the battle, saying that, if the other warriors resemble the one he met, their own fate will be terrible.

The invaders of necessity must rely on numbers. Xerxes regularly assumes that the size of his army obviates combat and brings to Thermopylae a land army that Herodotus estimates at 2.1 million (*Hist.* 7.184).[52] Boiardo gives few numbers, but one is telling: 100,000 ships bring the army to Spain (*OI* 2.29.22). This total does not include King Marsilio's army, which Agramante finds fighting at Montealbano. Both rulers intend to overwhelm their opponents.

The two authors have the same military analysis of this strategy. At Thermopylae Xerxes learns that he has many people but few men (*Hist.* 7.210.2). The judgment is harsh because the king has used only his best troops that day. Boiardo is, as usual, more explicit. Contempt marks his first catalogue. At one place he says that he does not give numbers because Orlando could easily chase such a rabble (*OI* 2.22.7), and in the battle the Africans are simply canaille.[53]

Good fortune accounts for the initial victories won by the invaders. Xerxes finds a way around Thermopylae, and the Africans arrive late in the day at Montealbano, while the French have been fighting for many hours. In both cases numbers win, but the military future remains uncertain.[54] Victory allows the invaders to occupy much enemy territory, but they lose the next battle. Hardly any Persian who fought at Plataea survived the battle.[55] In Boiardo's work, Agramante fails in his initial assault on Paris, but he keeps his army intact. The poet has told us, however, that this army will perish in France. The many may win the first battle, but they will inevitably lose the war.

SIGNIFICANCE OF BOIARDO'S IMITATION
OF HERODOTUS

Boiardo's classicizing analysis has a double focus and requires a double evaluation. Its explicit concern is Africa, but its real application and the force of the Herodotean model apply to the Turks, the new threat to Europe from the East.

The threat from Barbary was fictional in the quattrocento. The weak sultanates of North Africa threatened no one, and serious piracy had not yet begun.[56] Boiardo imagined for his background the matter of the *As-*

premont, in which Saracens from Africa invade southern Italy. It recalled the last period during which Islam threatened Italy, the long-ago days of coastal raids and the Muslim occupation of Sicily. Andrea da Barberino had recently put the story into Italian prose, and Boiardo made his Agramante the successor of its African leaders, the young king who would avenge the previous defeat.[57]

Herodotus helped Boiardo to evaluate such a kingdom correctly, not just for details of geography but also for a sense of its military potential. Herodotus had known a land where the cities on or near the coast had Greek hoplites, while the interior had nomadic tribes with little or no armor. Despite all the changes of the intervening two millennia—the introduction of the camel, the coming of the Arabs—the model still had a certain validity. Boiardo turned the hoplites into the elite troops around Agramante, coming from the coastal cities of modern Tunisia and Libya, and he kept Herodotus's nomads for inner Africa. In fact, the sultans of fifteenth-century Barbary ruled from towns, such as Fez, Tlemcen, and Tunis, and surrounded themselves with a core of mercenaries. However, they themselves were tribal and depended ultimately on the nomadic light cavalry of the countryside, the Arab and the Berber tribesmen who fought with short lances and used a dagger and a sword for close fighting. These nomads wore no real armor and so invited Boiardo's negative presentation. The tribes simply came together for war in spring and summer, without a fixed command system or strategy, and were no match for the Iberian troops that were beginning to seize the coastal cities.[58]

This use of Herodotus, though valuable, cannot by itself account for the historian's importance to Boiardo's narrative. The poet could have found similar material on Africa in other classical writers and geographers, whose works were available in the ducal library.[59] Moreover, Boiardo imagines a Muslim threat to Europe, not merely to Italy, and Africa had never so menaced Europe, at least not since the days of Hannibal. The Almoravids and Almohads had fought defensive actions in Spain, but the great cavalry charge that stopped only at Tours had emanated from Asia and the Umayyad administration in Damascus. Boiardo turned to Herodotus primarily because he and his contemporaries worried about a new threat from the East that concerned many kingdoms besides the Italian states and seemed invincible in the 1470s: the Turkish armies of Mehmed II Fatih, the Conqueror.[60]

Ottoman troops had already reached the Danube before Mehmed II came to power. He began his reign by the capture of Constantinople in 1453 and soon had occupied the other Greek states (1453–61). With Bosnia

(1463) he began his approach to Italy. Albanians fled there in 1467, and
their state began to collapse in the following year. The Turks were now
on the Adriatic and raiding Venetian territory in Dalmatia (1467, 1469).[61]
They were in Istria in 1471, and Turkish cavalry raided the Friuli several
times in the 1470s. Venetians could climb their campanile and glimpse
the smoke of burning villages.[62] Finally, the Turks reached Otranto in the
south, which Gedik Ahmed Paşa captured in 1480. This threat to Italy
coincided with the years when Boiardo wrote most of his poem. Venice
was the great neighboring power, and its misfortunes would not pass un-
noticed in Ferrara, since the Friuli was less than 300 kilometers away.
Otranto concerned the house of Aragon, which Boiardo had praised in
his poem and which had given Ferrara its duchess. The concern and the
fear that were felt during the 1470s recalled for a classically trained poet
the original East-West conflict chronicled by Herodotus, when the mere
appearance of a Persian army could cause panic (*Hist.* 6.112.3) and the
enemy zone of control ultimately included all the cities of the Asiatic
Greeks, those of the Aegean islands, and most of the European homeland.
Boiardo's use of Herodotus is an indication of his sense of a threat to the
very existence of his culture, quite as fundamental as that of the Persian
to the Hellene, and perhaps without parallel in the intervening millennia.
For a century the clash of Muslim and Christian dominated Italian epic.

There is a further, more precise reason for Boiardo's use of Herodotus.
Certain actions in the Long War between Venice and Turkey (1463–79)
paralleled closely some events in Xerxes's invasion of Greece. Like the
Spartans and their allies before them, the Venetians and insurgent forces
of the Morea in 1463 thought to prevent an enemy invasion by the construction of the Hexamilion, a wall across the Isthmus of Corinth. In
both cases the defenders labored feverishly.[63] In a mere fifteen days Venetian sailors as well as soldiers—about 30,000 men altogether—managed
to reerect the whole wall. They made it three and a half meters high and
more than a meter thick, with 136 towers and a moat on both sides. Herodotus points out the futility of such a defense, though the Persians
never tested it.[64] The Turks did, and, at the approach of the main army,
the Venetian admiral Alvise Loredano ordered a withdrawal to Navplion,
and the whole defense of the Morea collapsed. With the failure went
Venice's one serious chance of victory in the war.[65] This parallel alone
need not have recalled Herodotus, because military thinking in any age
would suggest a wall at the isthmus, and the Turks had already crossed the
Hexamilion when they first conquered the Morea. However, the parallel
supports another, which is striking enough to make a classically trained

writer think about historical repetition. This is the crucial action of the war that destroyed Venice's status as a great power: the siege of Chalkis or Negroponte (1470).

The year before, the Venetian admiral Niccolò da Canale had raided in the northern Aegean and provoked Mehmed II sufficiently that he personally led a massive counterattack the following year. Galley warfare requires nearby bases, and the Venetian port for the central and northern Aegean was Negroponte, on the island of Euboea. To take it, Mehmed led a combined land and sea offensive, the size of which recalled the old Persian invasion. In both cases exaggerated numbers given by the European historians indicate the panic it caused. Mehmed II led an army overland of 120,000 men, but it was the size of his fleet that shocked the West. Venice had counted on its naval superiority, but what could Canale with 55 galleys do against 300 ships and 70,000 men?[66] Eyewitnesses called it a forest at sea, stretching across nearly twelve kilometers of water. The Persians had assumed that an overwhelming force would make combat unnecessary. They guessed wrong for the Greeks, but the same policy worked against the Venetians. Although the garrison defended Negroponte brilliantly, the Venetian fleet achieved nothing and failed to relieve the town in time.[67] Venice continued to fight for another nine years, but it had lost the war and no longer ruled the sea.

The actions at the Hexamilion and Negroponte seemed to be a repetition of Herodotus—with the wrong ending. Nevertheless, the warfare had not ended, and the action involved Italy and the Balkans as well as Greece. The Herodotean scenario might still apply, and that is the emphasis of Boiardo's fantasy war. However many battles the Europeans might lose initially, however much territory the enemy might occupy, the elite soldiers of Europe would finally win and expel the invader. The pattern forecasts the failure of the enemy even in his successes. Catalogues of the hostile forces at the battles of Thermopylae, Roncesvalles, and Montealbano all showed his weakness.

This pattern, though comforting, was false. It had been true for Herodotus and for the writers of the chansons de geste, who signaled the Christian offensive in Spain, but by the fifteenth century it no longer applied, at least not for the Italians and eastern Europeans. Yet this thinking persisted in people's minds, and not only in their fantasies. Machiavelli, drawing on the Roman historians, still assumed the pattern in the generation after Boiardo's. It is well, then, to clarify its assumptions so as to see more clearly the illusions involved.

Herodotus and Boiardo present variations on a single theme: the clash of foreigner and European. The foreigner can be Asiatic and eastern or African and southern, but he is invariably alien and aggressive. He practices another religion and initiates the war. Young people, dreamers of impractical dreams, lead this attack. They rule vast but polyglot empires that produce a mass of untrained light troops that depend upon a core of elite soldiers and commanders. They attack smaller but more racially homogeneous areas.[68] While the Greeks consist of independent and often warring city states, the Franks serve a single ruler, though the lords are feudal and can act on their own. The army, though small, consists in both cases of heavily mailed troops, soldiers with extensive military experience.

Machiavelli, thinking of the classical and contemporary worlds, gives political reasons for the superiority of European soldiers. Although his argument would not apply directly to the real or fictional empire of Charlemagne, it shares illusions with Boiardo's fantasy. Machiavelli assumes that the more states there are in an area, the more valiant the men will be. Europe is the best because it has many kingdoms and states to cultivate virtue. Africa has fewer good soldiers, and those in the past mostly came from the republic of Carthage. Asia, a single vast kingdom, has even fewer. The constitution of a state also makes a difference. A republic encourages virtue, but kings fear virtue. Asia, since it has only one kingdom and one ruler, has the least active men.[69]

This thinking rests on three illusions. The first concerns the kind of soldier involved. Like Pulci and the other romancers, Boiardo portrays clashes of heavy cavalry between Christian and Saracen, whether in Central Asia or in France. In fact, war with the Saracen did not resemble this paradigm very closely. Cavalry was important, but not the heavy cavalry of the West, as the French knights discovered at Nicopolis. In that battle the knights were annihilated by the Janissaries and Spahis, the infantry and light horsemen of the Turks. The latter conducted the great Ottoman raids in Yugoslavia and Albania, and Venice had its own version, the Stradiots, whom it brought to Italy for the Ferrara War (1482–84).[70] These were mostly Greek-speaking Albanians from the Morea who wore breastplates, had shields, and carried light lances pointed at both ends and sometimes a crossbow. Their horses, lacking armor, moved swiftly.[71]

Italian writers were quick to see the parallels between these light horsemen and the Eastern enemies of Rome. Machiavelli, speaking of the Parthians, at the same time envisaged for contemporary cavalry essentially the role of the Stradiots. Horsemen were to scout, raid, cut off enemy supplies, and pursue the enemy after a battle (*Arte*, 2.368–69). Writing after the Ferrara War, Boiardo likewise introduced Parthian tactics in book 3 of the *Innamorato*. He invented an episode that portrayed the frustrations of the heavily mailed cavalry soldier before the fast light raiders of the enemy (*OI* 3.6.16–27). Old Daniforte of Tunis draws Bradamante away from an ambush by a feigned flight. Daniforte goes at a trot, complaining and pretending exhaustion. He slows, letting her approach, gallops ahead, slows again, till he has lost her in the wild, far from Rugiero. Bradamante forces her tired horse over a mountain ridge and down to a plain, only to lose it in a ditch. Daniforte now circles around her, attacking at unexpected points. Bradamante finally wins by a ruse. She plays dead, and even then the old man spears her experimentally before he dismounts. The episode demonstrates the difficulties of Roman versus Parthian, medieval knight versus Mongol or Turk. The enemy keeps out of range and draws the Westerner into a trap.[72]

The critique does not go far enough because Boiardo still ignores infantry, and this, the despised class of the romances, dominated the colonial wars of Venice. The sultan's Janissaries were infantry, and like any Western commander he especially needed infantry for an attack on fortified positions and for mountain warfare.[73] Infantry won the Albanian passes and fought the Venetians at the Isthmus of Corinth. Naval warfare likewise required infantry. Venice used foot soldiers for its naval raids, and the force it sent to conquer the Morea was predominantly infantry.[74] The Venetian troops were bowmen, drawn mostly from Venice itself, where any citizen had to learn to use the crossbow and many had fought on the galleys.[75] Bowmen and light cavalry determined the war in the East.[76]

Between his catalogues and battle narratives Boiardo does address this situation indirectly.[77] Herodotus again provides the model. Soldiers tend to wear clothing and adopt modes of fighting suitable to the climate and topography of their home areas. Oasis dwellers and African nomads, for example, would not wear armor, since they operate in the Sahara. Now, modes of fighting that fit one zone may not work in another. The Persians, who won Asia on horseback, had to fight the Spartans on foot. The mountains of Greece, although they allowed for the use of light cavalry, favored infantry. The Italians of Boiardo's day preferred heavy cavalry, but they had to adapt to these same conditions. The Venetians hired local light horsemen and brought their own infantry with them. Technology in this case reinforced topography. Galleys were not good horse transports, and Venetian overseas troops had to be prepared to fight on land or sea.[78] The colonial from across the sea can hardly avoid fighting like the local.

Boiardo imagines a series of battles fought, not overseas in Africa, but within France, where Africans become the invading would-be colonials and must fight like Franks. In France, Saharan nomads or the light armed troops of the Tell and of the Atlantic coasts could not cope with Frankish heavy cavalry. Agramante must depend upon his elite troops to do the fighting, as Xerxes had had to do in Greece. Following this logic Boiardo shows only cavalry duels because the other soldiers took a negligible part in combat. By the same token, the Ottomans if they invaded Italy would suffer defeat—as happened at Otranto (1480–81)—because they would have to adopt Italian modes of fighting. This argument does have force, but it still does not escape other misconceptions.

A second illusion involves a special use of numerical hyperbole. Pulci had assumed that Marsilio, trying to expel the invading Franks from Spain, mobilized all the forces of his realm, which he brought to Roncesvalles. Boiardo and his model, Herodotus, imagine much less plausible scenarios. Herodotus assumes that Xerxes brought the whole army of the empire against Hellas, and this is what he catalogues rather than the actual invading force.[79] He thus gives enormous figures, which conform to earlier opinion. Aeschylus had made the same assumption, and Simonides estimated the army at 3 million.[80] The Greeks forgot that the Persians would need troops to protect a very extended frontier, particularly in the northeast, and others to control restless provinces.[81] Boiardo thinks in the same erroneous fashion. He has King Agramante bring the forces of his entire empire to Europe, and he explains the French defeat at Montealbano by numbers. Numbers are finally necessary because they allow the defeated Europeans to continue to assume that they were qualitatively superior.

This is the third illusion.[82] Herodotus had described a military revolution; with Xerxes's defeat the military advantage shifted to Europe and remained there for eleven centuries. By the fifteenth century, however, Europeans were losing more often than they won. Victory in the West—the recovery of the Iberian peninsula, the Balearics, and Sicily—did not balance the loss of Anatolia, Greece, and the Balkans. The Turks had demonstrated their military superiority at Nicopolis (1396) and Varna (1444), and Constantinople now belonged to them.[83] Venice's defeat in the Long War confirmed a long-term trend in the East. Europeans could not rely on quality.

The reasons are clear. The enemy had not a rabble but an army as well trained and experienced as any that Italy or Europe could field. The Janissaries, for example, were professional soldiers, removed from civilian life and material cares, who won advancement through merit. They were only the largest and most famous contingent among the sultan's slave soldiers.[84] Moreover, in the colonial wars they faced mostly Venetian militia and conscripts, not the condottieri companies of Italy. A well-trained few can defeat a mob but not an army equal in training and superior in numbers. In fact, Western leaders and soldiers had become so demoralized by constant defeat that Scanderberg, the famous guerrilla leader in Albania, asked for an escape galley and a guaranteed pension from Venice before he would participate in the Long War.[85]

Such misconceptions and illusions, especially the last, were comforting, but they were particularly dangerous in the crisis Italians thought they were facing. Circumstances, however, spared them disillusionment. Bâyezîd, the next sultan, did not pursue an expansionist policy; Selim turned east and south; and Süleyman looked north to Hungary. The Habsburgs fought the Western defense at Vienna, and the Ottomans never seriously attacked Italy.

Undispelled, these illusions had a strange afterlife. The fiction that Westerners with small armies could defeat alien multitudes became a reality once more shortly after Boiardo's death, though in a transformed situation. Small bands of Spaniards succeeded in conquering much of America, their victories made possible by a technological superiority that negated the need to fight like the locals. The old paradigm, wrongly applied in Europe, worked quite well on the other side of the Atlantic.

PART TWO

The Movement into Realism and History

——FOUR——

The Siege of Paris

Ludovico Ariosto, Torquato Tasso, and Alonso de Ercilla y Zuñiga

MOST MODERN CRITICS HAVE STRESSED THE FANTASY IN THE *Orlando furioso,* but it was rather the realism of certain scenes that affected, perhaps even generated, a new approach to heroic poetry in the later sixteenth century.[1] An outstanding example of Ariosto's realism is Agramante's assault on Paris, which Ariosto presented with a plasticity unprecedented in previous romance.[2] Tasso, Ercilla, and Ercilla's imitators pushed this new realism ever further but never quite to the point where the distinction between poetry and history disappears.[3] They too depicted sieges—Tasso of Jerusalem, Ercilla of a fort at Penco in Chile, where he had his own first experience of war. Sieges, in fact, were a literary specialty of the Renaissance; medieval romancers, although they presupposed sieges, did not describe them.

I have arranged this material in a logical rather than in a chronological order. Ercilla and Tasso developed Ariosto's innovations independently of each other.[4] The second installment of the *Araucana,* in which Ercilla describes the siege of Penco, appeared in 1578, several years before Tasso's *Gerusalemme liberata* (1580–81), but it brings poetry closer to history than does Tasso's work. Ercilla, therefore, comes last. I have not, however, ignored chronology where it is crucial to my analysis. In the case of Ariosto, the critical date is 1515, the year he sent the first edition of the *Furioso* to the printer,[5] and not 1532, the year of the third edition. Throughout his later revisions the poet left his scenes of siege as they had been in the first edition, limiting himself to stylistic changes. The date thus makes a difference for any historical analysis, most especially because technological development was so rapid but also because the military and political scenes differed profoundly from 1515 to 1532. My historical argument is based on the situation that prevailed in 1515.

ARIOSTO

Boiardo began a siege of Paris that Ariosto had to complete. He had models elsewhere in *Orlando innamorato* for such a sequence: an earlier siege by Gradasso and more especially the warfare around Albraca, which he used for the later parts of his own story (*OF* 27, 30–31).[6] Boiardo did not provide a model for the kind of literary art Ariosto used to transform the poetry of war, but the earlier poet did find the sources that made Ariosto's achievement possible.

Boiardo tended to use Statius and Virgil for scenes of siege. For example, Turnus's rampage in the Trojan camp set the pattern for Agricane's in Albraca, but Boiardo cut most of the details. He strove for economy and swiftness of presentation and limited his particulars to the duel of the Tatar king that begins the sequence. Agricane slices through the mace and chain of King Bordacco. Virgil in contrast had filled his scene with precisely described kills, such as Antiphates, hit by a javelin that goes through his belly into his lungs (*Ae.* 9.696–701), or young Pandarus, who wants revenge and first talks with Turnus, before the Latin warrior lands a downward blow that slices his head in half so that the Trojan falls, staining his armor with his own brains (9.735–55).

When he had Rodomonte rage down a Paris street, Ariosto used both the Latin poets and Boiardo as models.[7] His classical sources clearly had the greater impact on him, for he made a mosaic imitation of Virgil and Statius, line by line, image by image.[8] He followed Virgil in his precision violence but then sketched in everything else. He states the width of the ditch at the city walls, knows just where Rodomonte runs in Paris, and mentions the building materials used for the houses.[9] As a result, Ariosto creates a complete picture, more detailed and comprehensive than anything in his sources, Latin or Italian.

Angelo Poliziano with his *Stanze* had pioneered this shift to realism. His classical imitation produced the illusion in his readers that they saw what he described.[10] Giraldi Cinzio, Ariosto's great apologist, later discussed the technique at length and gave numerous examples, one of which glances at Virgil:

> Queste ci fanno vedere le città andare a ruba, ci pongono innanzi agli occhi le fiamme sparse per gli tempj, per le torri, per le case private, ci fanno udire le ruine dei tetti, udir le grida degli impauriti e malmenati popoli, vedere le madri stringersi i figliuoli al seno con suono di amaro pianto; i rubatori pel contrario allegri spogliare i tempj degli iddj immor-

tali, e le case dei cittadini, e cacciarsi tuttavia gli incatenati prigioni innanzi.

They make us see cities sacked, put before our eyes flames spread through temples, towers, and private houses. They make us hear the collapse of roofs, hear the screams of terrified and ill-used people, see mothers press children to their breasts with the sound of bitter lament; the looters, on the contrary, joyfully spoil the temples of the immortals and the houses of citizens, and chained prisoners, nevertheless, press ahead.[11]

Ariosto's predecessor, Boiardo, toward the end of his life had also experimented with this new style,[12] but he shied away from it for scenes of warfare. Here it was Ariosto who followed through on Poliziano's experiments.[13]

Ariosto made a threefold contribution to military poetry. First, with classical clarity he described war in all its diverse aspects. Some brief examples will suffice. A single ottava effectively evokes panic (OF 18.159). The broken Saracens do not hear trumpet, drum, or signal for retreat: terrified, many drown themselves in the Seine. On a humorous note, the king of Oran wishes to joust with Rinaldo (OF 16.47) but though strongboned, he is small of stature and so has to aim at Rinaldo's shield. Finally, Ariosto conveys the horror of battle. The night after the great assault, Cloridano and Medoro come to the army where amid swords, arrows, shields, and lances the poor and rich, king and vassals, lie in a red lake, horses on top of men (OF 18.182). So vivid were his descriptions that critics quickly noticed parallels between Ariosto's poetry and painting. Ludovico Dolce said that one seems to see more than read the poem, and critics of the present century continue to make the same point.[14] Ariosto makes his audience feel that they have been spectators at a war in progress.[15]

The poet extends this realism to the way the seasons set the rhythm of a war. He describes spring (OF 12.72) because it introduces a new campaign, and troops that had gone into winter quarters are returning to Agramante's camp.[16] Similarly, the heavy rain that saved Paris the year before, suddenly turning the plain into a lake and putting out fires that were beyond control (OF 8.69–70), probably signaled the onset of winter and the end of the previous campaign.[17] The poets who followed him took this insistence on weather and developed it much further for their own presentations of war.

Second, this revived classical technique enabled Ariosto to represent an assault on a fortified town. Virgil had shown the Greeks sacking Troy

Figure 13. Porte Saint-Michel, Paris. Photograph: Roger-Viollet, Paris. Lithograph of Nouveaux and Fourquemin (1839), after Pernot.

and Latins attacking a fort, and Ariosto now did the same for Paris. His romance predecessors had avoided such scenes, despite the importance of sieges to warfare in the high and late Middle Ages, the period that generated the literary form of romance. They did not have the old classical means to describe such scenes, and they may have passed over sieges for social reasons as well. Romance was an aristocratic form, but knights had little to do in a siege. In sieges, pioneers and infantry, drawn from the lower classes, did the essential work.[18] Romancers normally presupposed a siege but assumed that a battle or duel resolved it. Boiardo so handled both the earlier attack on Paris by Gradasso and the long drawn-out siege of Albraca.

Finally, Ariosto described the war at Paris without the element of the marvelous. Aside from Rodomonte's prowess and the personification comedy of Discord, none of the wonders for which the *Furioso* is famous appears here. Although his plastic style could heighten the marvelous—as it does, for example, in the knights' fight with the hippogrif (2.48–53)—here it accentuates the realism of war instead.

The result of these innovations was a series of stunning scenes, mostly involving Rodomonte.[19] Two will suffice to show what Ariosto achieved at Paris. In the first (*OF* 14.126–34, 15.3–5) Rodomonte leaps the ditch to the inner wall, landing silently, as if he were wearing felt on his feet (fig. 13).[20] Meanwhile his men, numbered precisely at 11,028, suffocate in a fire trap below. The dying make a horrible harmony of screams with the devouring flames, and Rodomonte, looking back, blasphemes heaven with terrifying cries.[21] In the second (*OF* 16.21–28), Rodomonte goes berserk, rushes down a street, and slaughters all he meets. The old, who had been waiting for news, now raise a loud cry. People try to flee to houses and churches, but few succeed. Rodomonte kills them all from behind, as they run. One leaves half his legs; another's head flies from his body; one is cut crosswise and another vertically from head to flanks. The Saracen kills without distinction of age or social position: servant and lord, saint and sinner, priest, boy, lady, old man. Not content with murdering people, he also attacks buildings, setting fire to the wooden houses and churches, shaking pieces out of roofs. Ariosto concludes with a contemporary illustration: no bombard—which his patron Cardinal Ippolito d'Este saw at Padua, so large that it could make a wall fall—could do as much.

These scenes spoke directly to the experience of Ariosto and his audience and marked the difference between the cinquecento and quattrocento. Virgil's Turnus and Boiardo's Agricane, the heroes in the scenes that served as models for Ariosto, fight other soldiers.[22] Rodomonte slaughters civilians. The French had shocked the Italians in 1494, when they killed all their prisoners.[23] These executions were mere preludes to the agonies of cities they took, while Ariosto was writing his poem. Guicciardini says that after 1509 civilians "saw nothing but scenes of infinite slaughter, plunder and destruction of multitudes of towns and cities, attended with the licentiousness of soldiers no less destructive to friends than foes."[24] The poet himself criticized the French for their treatment of Brescia and Ravenna, where the soldiers robbed and raped indiscriminately (*OF* 14.8–9). Rodomonte merely did more spectacularly what soldiers in the sixteenth century did as a matter of course.[25] The power of the scenes involving Rodomonte comes not only from Ariosto's plastic style but also from the reality of contemporary warfare. These two factors also explain the special difficulties Ariosto faced.

The relationship of romance to contemporary warfare was already difficult in the fifteenth century, and the realism of Ariosto's chosen style made it a critical issue. He had to keep his fiction reasonably close to the experience of his audience, which had an intimate knowledge of war. Ariosto himself casually refers to his own military experience (*OF* 19.83) when he says that he has seen a bombard open squadrons the way Marfisa did.[26] Normally the romance poet discreetly updated his fiction. Under

the pretense that it happened long ago, he described a more or less contemporary form of fighting. Ariosto had the same intent but experienced
serious difficulties in its execution.

Contemporary warfare varied from one region to another. Ariosto's
fiction presupposed the war of Christian and Saracen, but this was a false
model for at least two reasons. First, the Ottomans did not at present
menace Europe. The new sultan had turned east, attacking Persians and
Mamluks. Ariosto accordingly represents the Levant benignly, as a Damascus of tournaments and chivalric enterprise.[27] Second, actual warfare
in the Levant differed from the persistent fighting that convulsed Italy at
that time. Venice, for example, did not campaign in the Levant in the
same way as in Italy. The quick attacks and fast sieges of an amphibious
strategy had marked the previous war between Venice and the Ottoman
Empire (1499–1503).[28] Nor did the colonial wars fought by Venice resemble those in North Africa, where the Spaniards enjoyed a technological superiority they did not have in Italy.[29] In such wars cities like Modon,
and even great ones like Constantinople and Granada, could not resist a
determined siege, yet Ariosto's fiction required just that for Paris.[30]

In Italy, however, a good-sized town could still survive a siege, and the
attackers could not assume that their cannon would blow up the walls.
Padua, for example, successfully withstood Maximilian's forces. The Este
served there under the emperor, and Ariosto refers to the bombards used
(*OF* 16.27), tacitly paralleling the efforts of unsuccessful besiegers,
whether Imperials or Saracens.[31] The Italian wars made sense out of Ariosto's plot, and in any case they were the background required by the
poet's rhetorical situation. The Italian style of warfare had determined
the expectations both of the poet[32] and of most of his audience.

Although the Italian wars fit Ariosto's plot, they involved him in further difficulties, since Italy served as the proving ground for all the latest
experiments in offense and defense. Ariosto tried to make his warfare as
modern as possible, but he could only go so far with technology.[33] Still,
he did what he could. Armies had used fortified camps since the mid-
fifteenth century; Agramante has one at Paris with an embankment and
a ditch (*OF* 18.157), and his defeated troops spend the night digging more
ditches and shelters and molding bastions (18.163).[34] All this fits contemporary procedure. Piero Pieri cites the condottieri Orso Orsini and Diomede Carafa, who would use the earth dug out for the trench to make
the walls, often with stakes. Machiavelli was soon calling a camp a mobile
fortress city and advising that the bastions provide cross fire into the
ditch.[35]

Ariosto extends his references to other technological developments. Rinaldo takes the British across the Seine on a pontoon bridge, which he then breaks up afterwards (*OF* 16.31).[36] The poet alludes to the new exploding mines (*OF* 27.24):

> Come quando si dà fuoco alla mina,
> pel lungo solco de la negra polve
> licenziosa fiamma arde e camina
> sì ch'occhio a dietro a pena se le volve;
> e qual si sente poi l'alta ruina
> che 'l duro sasso o il grosso muro solve . . .

As when they set fire to a mine, the impetuous flame burns through the long furrow of the black powder and travels so that the eye can barely follow it, and as one then feels the high ruin that unlooses hard rock and a thick wall . . .

Castel Nuovo in Naples had fallen to an exploding mine (1503), and Pedro Navarro and Antonello da Trani won Cephalonia from the Turks in the same way.[37] Mobile forts, special bridges, modern explosives—Ariosto puts them all into his poem.

But all his efforts were not enough. The siege of Padua illustrates the difficulty. The key issue here is not cannons (see chapter 6) but rather the military architecture that artillery warfare generated. When Emperor Maximilian finally collected enough heavy guns to mount a serious attack on the city, he failed in three assaults on the Porta Codalunga. All three faltered at an advance bastion and were destroyed by fire and a counterattack of pikes. The Venetians had better artillery and Fra Giocondo to direct repairs on the walls. The building and use of the bastion help to explain the victory of the defense. A bastion was a platform for heavy guns, designed to break up concentrations of the besiegers and dismount the artillery.[38] If it functioned properly, the attacker never approached the city walls, and the Venetians so used it at Padua.[39] Pedro Navarro explained its principle to Machiavelli, when the two inspected the walls of Florence: "A city can expect to have more guns than an army can carry with it; whenever you can present more guns to the enemy than he can range against you, it is impossible for him to defeat you."[40] In its mature form the enceinte became a continuous gun platform, and the Este—already leaders in cannonry—had Biagio Rossetti put round bastions on the walls of Ferrara (ca. 1500–1506). They then added three angle bastions (1512–18), the form that dominated military architecture for centuries.[41]

Such developments were beyond the limits of Ariosto's art. The prob-

lem was not just anachronism—the concern that cannons and gun platforms would not fit a fiction about Charlemagne—for Malory had not
hesitated to give Mordred what might have been cannon, when he besieged Guinevere in the Tower of London (*Morte,* 21.1).[42] It was also that
Ariosto's classical models could not help him here. The revived realistic
style presupposed massed action close by the walls of the kind cannon
made impossible. Boiardo, however, had pointed out a way to disguise,
if not eliminate, the rift between the poet's fiction and contemporary
reality.

In describing Paris Ariosto departed from his common practice, a
practice that Simon Fornari claimed the poet followed elsewhere. He did
not describe an Italian town and call it Paris, the way he described Florence and called it Damascus.[43] Instead, he assumed the real Paris of his
own day. Boiardo had made gestures in this direction. His idea was to
increase the apparent realism of the scene by including mention of specific, real places. For example, in presenting the second siege of Paris he
mentioned the Seine (*OI* 3.8.11), and for both sieges he named a real gate,
that of Saint-Denis, as well as a series of fictional ones.[44]

The mixture of real and fictional places would not have troubled
Boiardo's audience. Although the Ferrarese of his day might read chansons de geste and French romances, these literary sources would not have
given them a precise sense of French geography, and guidebooks for Paris
were not yet available.[45] A few famous names sufficed for the poet, who
invented the rest. All this had changed by the time Ariosto wrote the
Furioso. During the long French occupation of northern Italy, the Ferrarese had developed close connections with them, cultural as well as political and military.[46] Ariosto himself tried to learn French and had met
Louis XII and Chevalier Bayard.[47] Probably through such contacts, oral
rather than literary, Ariosto learned enough to produce what Bertoni considered an exact description of Paris, sufficient to make one think he had
visited the place.[48]

In two stanzas Ariosto sets up the topography of Paris and with it
establishes the military logic of his plot (*OF* 14.104–5):[49]

> Siede Parigi in una gran pianura,
> ne l'ombilico a Francia, anzi nel core;
> gli passa la riviera entro le mura,
> e corre, et esce in altra parte fuore.
> Ma fa un'isola prima, e v'assicura
> de la città una parte, e la migliore;

l'altre due (ch'in tre parti è la gran terra)
di fuor la fossa, e dentro il fiume serra.

Alla città, che molte miglia gira,
da molte parti si può dar battaglia;
ma perché sol da un canto assalir mira,
né volentier l'esercito sbarraglia,
oltre il fiume Agramante si ritira
verso ponente, acciò che quindi assaglia:
però che né cittade né campagna
ha dietro, se non sua, fin alla Spagna.

Paris sits on a great plain, in the navel of France, or rather in its heart. The river passes between its walls and runs and comes out on the other side, but first makes an island, and there secures one part of the city, and the better [part]. The other two, for the great city is in three parts, are enclosed by a fosse outside and the river inside.

One could assault the city, which circles around for many miles, from many directions, but because he intends to attack from one side only and would not voluntarily close off his army, Agramante retires across the river toward the west, so that he might attack from there, since he has behind [him] neither city nor land, except his own, as far as Spain.

Such stanzas became standard for later historical epic. They were the poet's equivalent of the maps the French used for their campaigns and introduced to Italy.[50] At the same time Ariosto reflected the visual illustrations of battles, which became detailed and meticulous with Pavia a decade later.[51]

With these stanzas Ariosto establishes two factors that make a military action believable, and at the same time he tacitly corrects Boiardo's presentation. First of all, Paris is a huge city, far larger than any in northern Italy, and no army could surround it, as Boiardo imagines for both his sieges, much less assault it from all sides.[52] Second, the Seine is too deep west of the city. Rinaldo needs a bridge to cross it, Rodomonte must swim that way out of Paris, and the defeated regularly drown there.[53] Agramante, therefore, must attack the Latin Quarter. As Ariosto explains, a defeat on the Right Bank could leave his army cut off from its zone of occupation to the south.[54]

Clear topographical description like this makes it possible to diagram the battle of Paris on a map, stage by stage, and Barbara Reynolds has done this. Although I disagree with her on details, she has made the essential point (fig. 14).[55] Ariosto gave his fictional war not just visual realism but the details that mark a history or military report. A reader can still trace, for example, Rodomonte's route across Paris. He followed the old Rue de la Harpe, which still exists in part, and crossed over to the Ile de la Cité by the Pont Saint-Michel.[56] This kind of methodical realism helped Ariosto bring his fiction closer to his audience, despite the differences between his inherited chivalric warfare and contemporary military practice.

Paris did even more for Ariosto, for the city still fit perfectly the old-style war Ariosto had to present. Its architecture was still as medieval as Ariosto's romance plot.[57] The vistas of the late medieval city given by Hugo and Stevenson in the nineteenth century apply as well to the Paris of Ariosto's time. Here is Hugo's summary:

> Refaites le Paris du quinzième siècle, reconstruisez-le dans votre pensée, regardez le jour à travers cette haie surprenante d'aiguilles, de tours et de clochers, répandez au milieu de l'immense ville, déchirez à la pointe des îles, plissez aux arches des ponts la Seine avec ses larges flaques vertes et jaunes, plus changeante qu'une robe de serpent, détachez nettement sur un horizon d'azur le profil gothique de ce vieux Paris, faites-en flotter le contour dans une brume d'hiver qui s'accroche à ses nombreuses chemi-

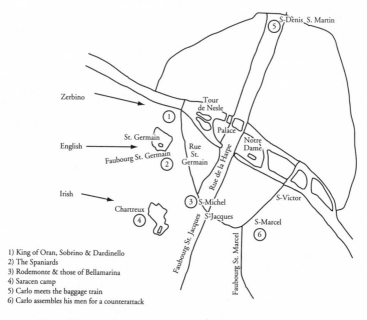

1) King of Oran, Sobrino & Dardinello
2) The Spaniards
3) Rodomonte & those of Bellamarina
4) Saracen camp
5) Carlo meets the baggage train
6) Carlo assembles his men for a counterattack

Figure 14. Map of Paris in the early sixteenth century.

nées, noyez-le dans une nuit profonde, et regardez le jeu bizarre des té-
nèbres et des lumières dans ce sombre labyrinthe d'édifices; jetez-y un
rayon de lune qui le dessine vaguement, et fasse sortir du brouillard les
grandes têtes des tours; ou reprenez cette noire silhouette, ravivez d'ombre
les mille angles aigus des flèches et des pignons, et faites-la saillir, plus
dentelée qu'une mâchoire de requin, sur le ciel de cuivre du couchant.[58]

Remake the Paris of the fifteenth century, reconstruct it in your thought,
look at the day across that surprising hedge of spires, of towers and belfries;
spread out amid the immense city; tear at the point of the isles; at the
arches of the bridges fold the Seine with its large pools, green and yellow,
more changing than a snakeskin; render clearly on the blue horizon the
Gothic profile of this old Paris; make its contours float in a winter mist
that clings to its many chimneys, plunge it in deep night and watch the
strange play of darkness and light in the somber labyrinth of structures;
throw there a ray of moonlight that vaguely outlines it and makes the great
tops of the towers rise from the mist; or return to that black silhouette,
revive with shadow the thousand sharp angles of the spires and gables, and
make it project, more indented than the jaw of a shark, under a coppery
sunset sky.

The public buildings erected early in the sixteenth century did not alter
this Gothic appearance, even when the architect was Italian. Giovanni
Giocondo designed the Cour des Comptes in the Gothic style to harmo-
nize with Sainte-Chapelle and the east wing of the old palace in which
Ariosto has the Parisians take refuge and resist Rodomonte's attack.[59] All
new churches, furthermore, followed Gothic models throughout the sixteenth century.[60]

Private houses as much as public buildings gave Paris its characteristic
medieval appearance. Ariosto remarks that Paris formerly had almost all
wooden houses and that at present the proportion is still six out of ten
(*OF* 16.26). He alludes three times to the fire hazard they might pose
during a siege. The city might have burned down after one assault, if rain
had not come (*OF* 8.69–70). Rodomonte threatens to burn Paris (*OF*
14.65) and later runs through the city, setting fires (16.26–27). The houses
were mostly, in fact, what Americans would call Tudor: they had wood
beams and frame, with stone or loam between, covered with plaster, and
saw-toothed roofs.[61] We must then imagine Rodomonte on a narrow,
unpaved street, trying to tear down the narrow houses of two to four
stories on either side.[62] He would have had little difficulty, not only because he was a giant but also because the upper stories projected over the
street, with timbered overhanging roofs blocking out the sky.[63]

The city walls, however, determined the military pattern. Ariosto correctly describes those with which Etienne Marcel and Charles V ringed Paris in the later fourteenth century (fig. 13).[64] Rodomonte first wades through a moat of mud and water up to his neck (*OF* 14.119) and reaches the *bertresche* (14.121), or overhang of the wall.[65] This outer wall has crenelations, and the Saracen throws two men from its *merli*, or battlements, into the water moat (*OF* 14.124). His own soldiers mount this wall behind him by ladders (*OF* 14.126), only to find a deep dry moat beyond, between them and the main wall. Rodomonte leaps this ditch, where his men die by fire. The inner wall likewise has an overhang (*OF* 14.132). Such a system was designed to repel direct assaults of the sort that Ariosto describes. The walls were wide enough so that the defenders could move about on top. They had crenelations so the men could safely shoot at the attackers, machicolations to allow them to drop things, and high, unscalable towers so they could provide flank fire.[66] Ariosto vividly evokes this kind of assault in canto 14. Agramante has collected from the area round about innumerable ladders, axes, logs, and matting, plus bridges and boats.[67] Carlo, on the other hand, has had communication trenches run to the water moat, chains fastened at the river entrances, and matting prepared to dull the impact of missiles and rams (*OF* 106). The French throw down on the Saracens rocks, the crenelations themselves, boiling water, lime, burning oil, sulfur, turpentine, pitch, and fire balls (*OF* 111–12). It is all very medieval and could have occurred at any time in the centuries before the 1440s, when large cannon finally began to blow the old castles to pieces.[68]

Paris, still so very Gothic, made Ariosto's fictional war plausible and softened the tension between romance and contemporary siege warfare. The contrast might have been glaring if he had assumed for Paris a modern city wall like that of his own Ferrara.

Ariosto's achievement also had limits that were unconnected to technology. First, he made mistakes about Paris. His oral sources did not warn him of all the buildings and enclosures outside the walls. Much of the fighting takes place within the gardens, buildings, and property of Saint-Germain-des-Prés, and Carlo assembles his men outside the Gate of Saint-Marcel or Bordelles, where Ariosto says there is open space (*OF* 18.39) but where the Faubourg Saint-Marcel then spread out along the road.[69] One could imagine that Carlo would have had such structures removed, but one would still have to explain why Ariosto depicts a typical romance landscape outside town and not the devastated zone regularly created by a siege.[70]

Figure 15. The old palace on the Ile de la Cité. Photograph: Roger-Viollet, Paris. Lithograph of Nouveaux and Fourquemin (1839), after Pernot.

Ariosto makes other mistakes as well, of the sort already noticed by critics, such as the internal inconsistencies that make the dead rise again.[71] On the way to the Ile de la Cité Carlo sees the evidences of Rodomonte's rampage: men cut up, palaces burned, churches ruined, much of the city desolate (*OF* 17.6–7). He could have seen none of this, of course, since he has crossed over to the Right Bank to welcome the English at the Gates of Saint-Denis and Saint-Martin (*OF* 16.30, 85), and Rodomonte never reached that side of the river.[72] Then there is the bridge (*OF* 27.32). During a later battle many French, fleeing outside Paris, drown in the Seine, since the bridge cannot allow so many. Now Ariosto regularly has the defeated drown in the Seine, but all bridges are inside the city walls, unless we take him to mean the water moat and a gate bridge.[73]

Literary imitation causes other mistakes, mostly in the scene at the palace. Ariosto here follows two scenes in Virgil, that of Pyrrhus before Priam's palace (*Ae.* 2) and that of Turnus's escape from the Trojan camp (9).[74] As Rodomonte cuts away at the palace gate, the people in the palace courtyard all lament. Women run through the house, embracing the doors and beds they will have to leave (*OF* 17.9, 12–13). This picture fits Priam's palace, which had fifty bedrooms for his children (*Ae.* 2.503), but hardly fits the Palais de Justice, even when the royal family lived there (fig. 15).[75] Rodomonte next swims downstream to safety, as had Turnus on the Tiber (*OF* 18.21–24; *Ae.* 9.815–18). Unfortunately, the Ile de la Cité then ended in the palace wall and had two islets at its tip,[76] plus a great chain across the river, which Ariosto remembered earlier (*OF* 14.106). None of these mistakes is serious, but taken together, they reduce the poet's realism more than he would have wished.

The second major limit was self-imposed. Ariosto confines his realism to an episode, which he interweaves with Eastern stories (cantos 14–18). Afterward he reverts to standard romance technique and follows the model of Albraca. The arrival of six heroes suffices to defeat the French and drive them back into Paris (*OF* 27.18–34), as nine had convulsed the Tatar armies in Boiardo (*OI* 1.14.56–15.39).[77] One group, then another, reverses the military situation, and the siege ends in a series of open battles, briefly narrated, and in duels between heroes.

Boiardo determined the third limit for Ariosto. Though he might pretend he was versifying Turpin's history and use many historical techniques, Boiardo wrote fiction. Ariosto, as his continuator, could not alter this fact, however close he might bring his story to life in the early cinquecento. Yet his insistence on a real Paris and on a war that could be diagramed led his followers in a very different direction, as they tried to transcend all three limits. They wanted to remove errors, extend the realism, and minimize the fictional element. For both Ercilla and Tasso, this meant insisting on history.

TASSO

Tasso inherited from Ariosto both a realistic visual style and methodical attention to the topography and architecture that determined the nature of the military action he wished to represent. He developed the first, but with regard to the second he found himself in difficulties similar to those Ariosto had experienced when he chose to represent a real Paris.[78]

Stylistically, Tasso greatly developed Ariosto's concern for the seasons. In the *Furioso* the seasons determined the rhythm of the campaign. Now they affect tactics. Tasso would have writers carefully attend to the meteorological circumstances of an action:[79] "Simile avvertimento potrebbe mostrare ove descrive la fame, la sete, la peste, il nascer de l'aurora, il cader del sole, il mezzo giorno, la mezza notte, le stagioni de l'anno, la qualità de' mesi o de' giorni, o piovosi o sereni o tranquilli o tempestosi" ("He should show similar care where he describes hunger, thirst, disease, dawn, sunset, midday, midnight, the seasons of the year, the quality of the months or of the days, whether rainy or clear or calm or stormy"; *Discorsi del poema eroico* 2.555). In canto 7, for example, the Crusaders lose a skirmish. A sudden

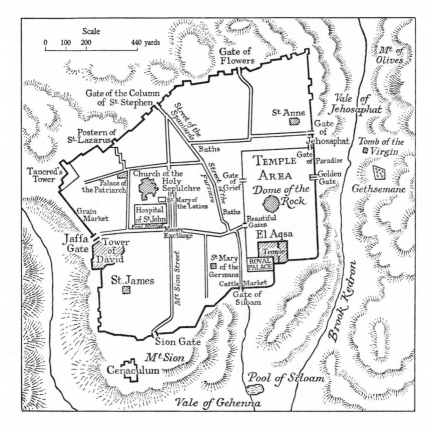

Figure 16. Jerusalem under the Latin kings. From Sir Steven Runciman, *A History of the Crusades,* vol. 2 (Cambridge: Cambridge University Press, 1952). Reprinted with the Permission of the Syndics of Cambridge University Press.

hailstorm blows into their faces, blinding them, as Clorinda charges down-hill and breaks their attack (*GL* 7.114–20). At the same time the wind causes much damage to the Crusader camp, ripping canvas, breaking tent poles, and even blowing away whole tents (*GL* 7.122).[80]

Like Ariosto, Tasso gives just enough topography to explain the strategy and tactics of the siege (*GL* 3.55–56). The two hills of Jerusalem make the city impregnable on all but one side, the north, where Goffredo sets his camp and where most of the action occurs (fig. 16).[81] Then there is the problem of water. The city has water from fountains and reservoirs, but outside there is nothing.[82] Tasso later describes the terrible thirst during the heat wave that follows the first assault (*GL* 13.58–60). Like Paris, Jerusalem had not changed significantly over the years. The Mamluks and Turks had worked on the walls, but they still followed the old lines, and their crenelations and square towers presupposed an old style of attack.[83] Modern notices would have confirmed what Tasso read in the Crusader chronicles for all but the "torre angolare," from which Clorinda shoots so many leaders in the first assault (*GL* 11.27–28) and which no longer existed. Tasso's descriptions thus fit reasonably well both contemporary and Crusader Jerusalem.

Nevertheless, Tasso experienced the same problems Ariosto had. Discrepancies came about either through his sources or through literary imitation. For example, Tasso assumes Aladino lived in the old Fortress Antonia, which Herod had built (*GL* 10.30–31) and which he himself read about in Josephus.[84] This structure vanished long before the Crusaders arrived in Palestine.[85] Tasso's sources mentioned the Aqsā Mosque in the southwest corner of the Temple area, which the Christian rulers made into their palace, but the Fortress Antonia stood north of the Temple. Yet Tasso tried to make his presentation accurate, even after he had completed the poem; he asked Luca Scalabrino in Rome to find him a map of Jerusalem, since he could get none in Venice.[86]

Literary imitation accounts for the other mistakes. Galileo complained that Erminia on the walls could not possibly distinguish individual Christian knights during a dusty skirmish.[87] Tasso, of course, had a passage from the *Iliad* (*Il.* 3.161–244) in mind, where Helen from the walls of Troy points out to Priam the Achaean chiefs. Basically, Tasso erred whenever he wanted women to watch chivalric action. Erminia stands on the tower of the Fortress Antonia and sees the whole battlefield north of the city (*GL* 6.62), and Clorinda watches Tancredi and Argante duel from a hillock (6.26).[88] None of these vantage points exists.

Tasso nevertheless succeeded well enough to convince Chateaubriand, who walked about Jerusalem and checked Tasso's references.[89] The poem assumes a specific city, with its walls, its surroundings, and weather conditions, which together exist nowhere else and determine the military narrative.[90]

Tasso made two specific contributions to the poetry of war. Looking to the *Iliad*, he made a siege his plot,[91] and he based his narrative on written history. In canto 3 he has the Crusaders begin a formal siege of Jerusalem, which ends only with the last canto, when Tancredi captures the Tower of David.[92] The poet thus risked his whole epic on the presentation of a military situation that Ariosto himself had confined to a few cantos. This innovation alone indicates the stature of the later poet and differentiates the *Gerusalemme* from previous epic and romance. Yet the poet took less of a chance than it might seem to one looking solely at literary traditions.

By Tasso's day military defense once more prevailed over offense. Already in the late 1520s engineers had begun to surpass the achievements of the artillerists, and sieges grew longer and longer every year, culminating in the three-year siege of Ostend (1601–4). The Dutch War, which set the pattern for the late cinquecento, consisted mostly of sieges.[93] Through the siege of Jerusalem Tasso could reflect many problems familiar to contemporary soldiers: famine, weather conditions, desertion, supplies, and technology. He developed the last in a particularly striking manner.

Tasso puts much emphasis on technical paraphernalia. Siege towers in particular dominate the second half of his plot. In the first assault Goffredo's tower and a battering ram below start cracking the north wall, but the tower breaks two wheels near town (*GL* 11.83–86), enabling Clorinda and Argante to burn it that night. Demons then possess the only wood that can supply the needed lumber,[94] and the Christians must wait for Rinaldo before they can make new engines some weeks later. For the second and successful assault, Guglielmo, a Genoese sailor, constructs three iron-plated towers, which move on a hundred wheels and have rams at the bottom, a bridge at the middle, and a tower above, and which can shoot up higher than the city wall (*GL* 18.41–45). A war of machines follows. The enemy has canvas out to deaden missile blows and a giant ram, which can swing out and smash Goffredo's tower (*GL* 18.68–72, 80–101). The Crusaders cut its cords with scythes. Then comes fire; the Christians have almost used up the little water they have, and the steel covering of the tower is beginning to curl, when the wind blows the fire back against the canvas protection of the walls and starts a conflagration that scatters the defenders. Now the bridge goes down; the tower goes up, overawing the Saracens (*GL* 90–91, 97–101); and the Crusaders gain the wall and the city. When he presents the fighting around Paris, Ariosto has nothing like this and never even mentions anything so unchivalric as a siege tower. Tasso, in contrast, had to emphasize them because the chronicles did, and he was determined to follow the historical record.[95]

Tasso believed that writers must base their plots on documented history.[96] True events, lost in legend, are not enough; the poet needs the authority of written records. For the *Gerusalemme* Tasso indeed went back to primary sources, in particular to William of Tyre, the best of the Crusader historians.[97] The poet thus had highly accurate chronicles to draw on, and these all required a battle of machines. Tasso has Argante spell out the moral for Tancredi: you come with all your men not as warriors but as inventors of machines (*GL* 19.2–3).

Written records also served to limit the prowess of his heroes. Tasso says to Scalabrino, "Io non ricevo affatto nel mio poema quell'eccesso di bravura che ricevono i romanzi; cioè, che alcuno sia tanto superiore a tutti gli altri, che possa sostener solo un campo: e se pure il ricevo, è solo ne la persona di Rinaldo" ("I do not indeed allow in my poem that excess of valor which the romances allow; i.e., that someone is so superior to all the others, that he alone can sustain a field. And if I do, nevertheless, allow it, it is only in the person of Rinaldo").[98] History does not allow for the nine in Boiardo, who convulsed a million soldiers at Albraca (*OI* 1.14.56–15.39), or for Ariosto's six, who chased the French back to Paris (*OF* 27.18–34). Even Tasso's dynastic hero, the one exception to his rule, at times merely exaggerates the brilliant fighting of the historical Tancredi.[99]

With Tasso the poetry of war comes very close to versified history. The reader can compare his poem with the Crusader chronicles, and his heroes do not surpass the efforts of ordinary mortals. His plot concerns a siege with all its mechanical details, and it is the technology, specifically the siege towers, that raises a new issue in the relationship of epic to reality.

The Crusaders used no more than ladders for their first assault on Jerusalem, a venture made quickly and without adequate equipment. On the other hand, the successful second assault took two days, divided by a night of anxious waiting, with the siege towers close to the walls.[100] Tasso moved the events of this first day back to the first assault and so gave it epic stature. At the same time, by making this change he further accentuated the importance of siege towers, and the towers themselves indicate a limit to his war poetry that he himself does not discuss.

Tasso had to describe the towers as carefully as he did because no one used such devices any more and had not done so for more than a century. In fact, the more the poet emphasized technology, the more he revealed how much the age of the Crusaders differed from his own. Nor could the anachronisms required to put Italian (as opposed to Norman) characters in his poem counteract this sense of long ago.[101] Ariosto tried to preserve a sense of contemporaneity by his talk of current wars, his use of similes involving guns and mines, and his inclusion of the story of Cimosco. Tasso, however, could not use his methods. Classicism did not allow the author speeches in his own right, and the sources predated artillery.

Where Ariosto only pretended to write up past events, Tasso truly does and thereby anticipates the historical novel.

His audience probably would have expected as much. They themselves were becoming more and more civilian; the last tumults of the Hapsburg-Valois duel died out when Tasso was still a teen-ager.[102] The great battles with the Saracens occurred, as always, outside Italy (at Malta, Famagusta, Lepanto, and Tunis), though Tasso had reason to remember a pirate raid on his hometown (1558).[103] Ferrara in particular stayed quiet. When all the Italian princes followed Don Juan to Lepanto, Alfonso remained at home. Although the duke did mobilize a force to help the emperor in Hungary, Tasso did not travel with the army, and in the event the soldiers did not see any fighting.[104] Tasso's audience lacked that sense of war all around, which Ariosto's readers had possessed. The absence of a modern technology, the sense that the warriors fought in an older world—all this would have come to them naturally.

Iberian poets like Ercilla, on the other hand, experienced none of these cultural limitations. Unaffected by neoclassicism, Ercilla still wrote in the romance form, and he had direct experience of warfare from fighting in Spain's colonial wars. He had no need of the past as a basis for his story.

ERCILLA

Ercilla narrates how 130 select youths,[105] unprotected but landed by night, hurriedly constructed a fort on a small hill by the Bay of Concepción (*Araucana*, 2.17.18–28, pp. 285–87). Within a single day they had made the essentials with whatever tools they could find.[106] Some dug deep defensive trenches with bars, hoes, and pickaxes, while others cut logs for a curtain wall, using long knives, hatchets, and saws. The Spaniards soon had eight pieces of artillery mounted and had raised the standard of Philip II.[107]

One morning the Indians came in three squadrons (*Araucana*, 19.4, p. 312) but attacked from all sides (19.25–29, pp. 316–17), trying every point, however strong or rugged.[108] Some filled up the fosse with earth and logs, but it filled more quickly with those who fell or were shot by harquebus. Some leaped over it, others climbed by pikes. The Spaniards repelled them with fire and lance, but the Indians persisted. Meanwhile a parallel action developed on the beach, as Spanish sailors tried to land and help the beleaguered garrison. The Indians attacked them as well (*Araucana*, 19.37–39, p. 319), but soon they had to give way, both at the fort (19.51, p. 321) and on the beach (20.14, p. 326), where they had heavy losses.[109] They retreated in order, however, and the Spaniards followed them at a moderate pace. The victors soon returned, fearing ambush. By this time it was noon (*Araucana*, 20.18–19, p. 327). And so Ercilla closed his account of the action at Penco Fort, which began Mendoza's campaign to reconquer Araucania (southern Chile).

In his story Ercilla shares with Tasso three developments of Ariosto's technique, which the Spanish poet worked out independently: the precise topography, the realistic style with its concern for weather, and the insistence on historical fact.

For the first, Ercilla describes the great Bay of Concepción economically (*Araucana*, 16.17–18, p. 267) and gives sufficient geographical details for the reader to understand the assault on the fort (fig. 17). But while we can still check Ariosto and Tasso on Paris and Jerusalem, it is more difficult to do so with Ercilla, since an earthquake in 1835 changed the landscape of the area.[110]

For the second, Ercilla inherited Ariosto's realistic style and developed a sense for seasons and weather much as did Tasso. A winter storm nearly destroys the flagship as it approaches the bay, and the very next night another flattens the encampment on Quiriquina Island (*Araucana*, 16.32–33, p. 270). Winds and rains then keep the Spaniards detained on this sterile island for two months (*Araucana*, 17.18, p. 285), during which period they must live on ship's rations and sleep on wet ground (20.23–34, p. 328).[111] Winter floods likewise delay the reinforcements that were to come by land (*Araucana*, 21.14, p. 344). The men finally construct the fort in August (early spring), when the days lengthen (*Araucana*, 17.23, p. 286).

Like Tasso, Ercilla insists on historical truth, and contemporary chronicles confirm his presentation of the battle.[112] This insistence on history has the same consequences for Ercilla as for Tasso. The poet keeps heroic action within probable bounds, and here he allows no exceptions. For example, in the episode of Julián de Valenzuela, who fights Fenistón by the ships (*Araucana*, 19.40–44, pp. 319–20), the whole action is probable. The Indian jumps suddenly, striking with his club, a move Julián parries by holding up his shield with both hands. Even so the club knocks the shield on his head and stuns him. Valenzuela barely jumps to avoid a second blow, which sinks deep into the ground. Meanwhile Julián scores the Indian's breast with his sword, and a reverse gets the middle of the jaw. Fenistón waves his arms, but Julián stabs him three times with a

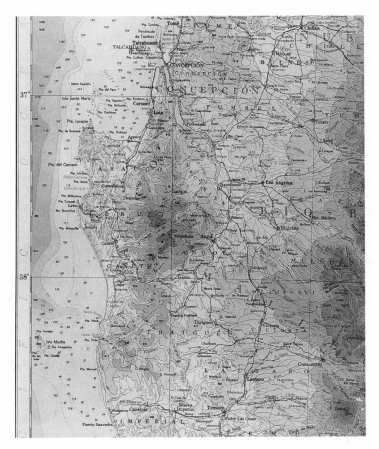

Figure 17. Map of the war zone in Chile (Carahue is the old Imperial, Penco is the old Concepción). Courtesy the University of Chicago Libraries.

dagger, killing him. Neither warrior has the prowess of an Orlando, yet the poet makes the encounter exciting by his clear visual style.

Ercilla's major contribution to the poetry of war also concerns history: he writes an eyewitness report of the battle at Penco. As far as I know, no other poet—at least no other poet of comparable reputation—had ever done this before. Where Tasso with his epic of a past war could look to the classical precedent of a Lucan or a Silius Italicus, not to mention Trissino and the tradition of the *poemetti bellici* among the Italians, Ercilla claims he had no model but his own experience. He tells us he helped build the fort (*Araucana,* 17.19, p. 285) and did sentry duty the night after

the battle (20.21, p. 327). He says elsewhere that he wrote up events at
night on whatever he could find: pieces of letters, even leather, some
pieces so small they hardly held six verses.[113] Of course, scholars have
qualified these claims. Like Tasso, Ercilla had his eye on Lucan.[114] Moreover, whatever versifying Ercilla may have done in Chile, he published
the *Araucana* in installments years later and so had time to elaborate on
his original material. The passage in which he claims to have written the
poem while on campaign, for example, came out two decades later.

These qualifications to the poet's claim do not diminish his achievement. Ercilla's narrative differs in kind from that of previous historical
epic, since he does not versify someone else's history. His epic itself functions as a primary source and has been used by historians, just as classi-
cists use Xenophon's *Anabasis* or Caesar's *Commentaries*. His efforts had
some influence, for other Spanish poets in their turn became wartime
correspondents. In his *Historia de la nueva Mexico,* for example, Captain
Gaspar de Villagrá composed an epic that was also the basic account of
Oñate's colonization of the upper Rio Grande. For these soldier-poets the
old debate between the sword and the pen ceases, for the two have become one.[115] This development alone makes Ercilla the most original epic
poet of his period, if not of the tradition.

Ercilla's innovation carried with it a far-reaching consequence, which
the duel of Valenzuela and Fenistón illustrates. The Spaniard's victory
lacks tactical significance, for the Indians do not fall back when they see
their hero fall.[116] Nor do the much more elaborate heroics of Gracolano
and Martin de Elvira affect the fighting at the fort (*Araucana,* 19.5–14,
19–24, pp. 312–14, 315–16). In the *Furioso,* by contrast, during the last
stages of the battle of Paris, Dardinello's heroics and speech alone restrain
his African troops from panic. When Rinaldo kills him, the Saracens flee
(*OF* 18.45–58, 155–64), and the whole army must fall back on its fortified
camp. Heroic actions have consequences in Ariosto's fiction, but not necessarily in Ercilla's history.

Technology provides a partial explanation for this difference, since artillery won the battle of Penco.[117] Ercilla acknowledges this in several
ways. Young Piñol seizes Martin de Elvira's pike from the ditch and tries
to escape but gets only four steps before two large balls cut him in two,
from shoulder to breast (*Araucana,* 19.15–17, pp. 314–15).[118] Guns quickly
fill the fosse with the dead. Old chief Peteguelén climbs to the highest
part of a bastion, only to have a ball take his head off and another kill the
four who follow him (*Araucana,* 19.35–36, p. 318).[119] Afterward Ercilla
patrols a connecting slope, one side of which is filled with the dead, shot

THE SIEGE OF PARIS

by harquebus and cannon (*Araucana*, 20.21, 25, 27, pp. 327–29). Spanish guns simply blow the enemy away, and yet, paradoxically, these same guns help explain the persistence of fiction in Ercilla's narrative, when we might have expected it to disappear altogether.

The poet invents a heroic rampage for Tucapel, one of the main characters on the Indian side (*Araucana*, 19.31–34, 51–52, 20.7–17, pp. 317–18, 321–22, 325–27). He runs with his club on the wall of the fort, breaking up men and arms. When the other Indians retire, he is rambling about inside the fort, then retreats to a precipice and jumps, followed by a cloud of missiles. Hit in ten places, he turns in rage, vainly tries five or six times to find a way back up, while the missiles rain down upon him, and finally rushes to the beach and breaks through to the Indians retreating there.

Ercilla models this scene on Ariosto as well as on Virgil, for it is Rodomonte and not Turnus who wants to return and who exits to a cloud of similes as well as missiles. Moreover, where Virgil gestured toward legendary history, Ariosto presented a purely fictional character, and so does Ercilla. I will argue later that Tucapel is a fictional character (see chapter 8). Certainly his action at Penco is fictional, whether the character is or not. And so we have come full circle. Virgilian imitation initially signaled a movement toward realism. It now indicates the persistence of the fictional even in this most historical of epics.

For an explanation one can appeal again to the problem of artillery. By this argument the poet wants heroes whose actions count, like those of romance. Ercilla finds such warriors on the Indian side, because they do not have firearms and prefer to fight at close quarters.[120] He can therefore project on them literary models. The fictional Tucapel, like Turnus or Rodomonte, has the prowess that might have turned around a battle. This argument by itself, however, does not account for the poet's literary imitation. The Indian victory games of cantos 10–11 and the dialogue between Lautaro and Gualcolda do not present warfare, and Ercilla does not use such inventions in all his narratives of battle.[121] Mareguano and Purén, for example, lack them. He does require fiction for Penco, and the example of Tasso points to a further reason.

Sieges as well as firearms require a certain amount of fiction from a poet. Like Ercilla, Tasso uses literary imitation to intimate that a hero's action can determine the outcome of an assault. He uses Clorinda and Rinaldo for this purpose and invents actions for his siege, even though it occurred long before the development of the gun. In the first assault on Jerusalem Clorinda determines its outcome. She wounds or kills a long list of Christian leaders (*GL* 11.41–45)[122] and eventually turns the assault back when she hits Goffredo in the leg (11.54–59). All see him leave, and the Crusaders lose heart. They recover somewhat when he returns, but not enough to reach the walls, and Clorinda instigates the burning of the siege tower that night. She is, of course, an invented character, and Tasso imitates both *Il.* 11.248–327 and *Ae.* 12.311–440 for the wounding of Goffredo. As with Ercilla, literary imitation indicates fiction.

For the second assault Tasso uses his dynastic hero and ascribes all decisive actions to him. Rinaldo leads his adventurers by ladder up the toughest part of the wall, clearing the way for the rest (*GL* 18.72–79) and then, rushing along that wall, breaks up Solimano's defense against the great siege tower so the historical Goffredo can reach the wall (99) and plant his banner.[123] The Crusades provide examples of heroism that made a tactical difference, and Tancredi is Rinaldo's historical model. Sieges, however, whether in the Middle Ages or the Renaissance, did not normally allow for spectacular acts by individuals, and Jerusalem was no exception. Tasso therefore resorts to fiction, just as Ercilla does at Penco.

Perhaps there was something quixotic in the whole Renaissance attempt to depict sieges realistically. Homer, some medieval romancers, Boiardo, and Ariosto had plots that presupposed sieges, but the poets avoided their representation.[124] Tasso and Ercilla, on the other hand, needed fiction to maintain epic heroism. Yet Virgil had sieges, and it is a strength of Roman epic that it did present such scenes. War, at least in the West, has more often been an affair of sieges than the fast-moving offense popular since Frederick the Great. And war was the principal subject of epic and of many Renaissance romances. These poets, Roman and Renaissance, tried to give a rounded picture of war, and sieges provided some of their most powerful scenes: the fall of Troy, Rodomonte in Paris. Chateaubriand's praise of Tasso indicates the goal these poets shared: "C'est surtout le poème des soldats; il respire la valeur et la gloire; et, comme je l'ai dit dans *Les martyres,* il semble écrit au milieu des camps sur un bouclier" ("It is above all the poem of soldiers. It breathes valor and glory; and, as I said in *The Martyrs,* it seems written in the midst of armies on a shield").[125]

——FIVE——

The Problems History
Makes for the Poet
Torquato Tasso

ALL THE POETS OF HISTORICAL EPIC AND ROMANCE HAD
problems with their plots. These difficulties came from the material, and
not from the possible ordering of that material, since all the poets faced
them, whether they began their plots at the beginning of the story, romance fashion, or started in the midst of things and presented only a
single set of interlocked events, after the classical manner. The success of
Tasso's *Gerusalemme liberata* and of Camões's *Lusiadas* might lead one to
associate the historical heroic poem with Renaissance neoclassicism, since
both poets began "in medias res" and generally followed the recommen-
dations of Aristotle and Horace for a tightly knit plot. The case of Ercilla,
however, who followed the romance model and arranged his plot chrono-
logically, starting at the historical beginning of the Araucanian wars,[1] indicates that neoclassicism cannot be held responsible for the difficulties
history posed for story telling.[2]

I have chosen Tasso rather than his contemporaries Ercilla or Camões
as my focus in this chapter, not because the Italian poet was an Aristotelian but because more is known about the composition of the *Liberata*
than about the writing of either the *Lusiadas* or the *Araucana*. I believe
that Tasso's Aristotelian theory, though it justifies what he did, masks the
radical nature of his experiment. In particular, his notion of transposition, which he developed in the *Discorsi dell' arte poetica,* concerns history
and provides a focus for this discussion.

One needs a context for such an analysis, and I will begin by comparing Tasso briefly with his two great contemporaries: Camões and Ercilla.
An Aristotelian frame befits an Aristotelian poet—in this case, the notion
of the mean and its extremes, deflected, however, from ethics to art.

Among the three major poets of historical heroic poetry during the Renaissance Camões maintains the mean. He kept fiction to a minimum in *Os Lusíadas,* mostly confined to his epic machinery,[4] and had the gods in turn allegorize aspects of his narrative, whether as planets,[5] elements,[6] or ethical qualities.[7] For his main plot Camões chose Vasco da Gama's great voyage of discovery, the journey to India. For the rest he covered the history of Portugal,[8] announcing this intent in his invocation (*Lusíadas,* 1.2) and presenting it through flashbacks and prophecies. The recall of medieval history takes up roughly one-third of the epic,[9] and prophecy of the imperial future occupies much of canto 10.[10] He thus produced a national epic in which plot and history blend almost without difficulty. I say "almost" because Camões does not provide rhetorically convincing situations for his medieval retrospectives. It is natural to have the Catual ask Paulo da Gama about the banners on his ship,[11] yet this is the same person who later takes bribes from the Muslim merchants in Calicut (Kozhikode) and tries to block the Portuguese return (*Lusíadas,* 8.56). He might make a curious but hardly a sympathetic listener. Much less plausible is the situation Camões imagines for Malindi. It is one thing for Dido, already falling in love, to ask Aeneas about his escape from Troy, quite another for a local African ruler to sit through a long recital of Portuguese history that continues across three cantos of the epic.[12] Camões thus shows, if only slightly, the strain history places on the narrative poet. This becomes much more evident in Ercilla and Tasso.

Don Alonso de Ercilla began his *Araucana* with the initial Indian revolt in Chile and followed a chronological order. He promised to sing how the Spaniards with their swords forced unconquered Arauco to bow its neck to a hard yoke (*Araucana,* 1.1.1, p. 1). Later, however, when he published part 2 of his poem (1578), he remarked that the Araucanians were still fighting and the war incomplete.[13] Nor had they stopped a decade later, at the time Ercilla published part 3 (1589). The young poet-soldier of the late 1550s could not have guessed that he had chosen one of the three wars that continued through the forty-year reign of Philip II.[14] The Araucanian war long outlasted both the poet and his king.

Ercilla died, leaving his poem unfinished, or so it is believed, because the *Araucana* promises more to come: the election of a new leader to replace Caupolicán and the battles that followed (*Araucana* 3.36.43, p. 586). In its present form the romance concludes with a canto justifying Philip's invasion of Portugal, an action that unfortunately has nothing to do with the Araucanian wars. One can only speculate where Ercilla himself would have ended his romance.[15] The assault on Quipeo and the poet's departure would have provided logical closure of sorts. Quipeo ended Don Garcia's campaign and put a temporary stop to hostilities, and Ercilla refers to it. But these events occurred after the poet's arrest and threatened execution, a painful matter to which he alludes in the same passage (*Araucana*, 3.36.34–36, p. 584).[16] Ercilla would have had to describe both Don Garcia's personal heroism at Quipeo and his own departure for trial in Lima, sent there by this same hero. The juxtaposition would have ended the romance in dissonance.

Whatever the conclusion he might have provided for the *Araucana*, Ercilla would still have been open to criticism by contemporaries for his choice of subject. Tasso, developing an Aristotelian point, argued that a writer should not choose a topic like a whole war, since it was too large even for epic.[17] His argument would apply doubly to the *Araucana*, since the war Ercilla chose to narrate had no natural closure.

Tasso himself faced the opposite problem. Where Ercilla struggled with too much material, Tasso did not have enough. He wanted to portray the First Crusade, but if he did so, he would have to cover the capture of Jerusalem, which was the goal of the First Crusade and the emotional appeal behind all later crusades as well. The earlier story of that expedition, the struggles and march across Anatolia and the long siege and battle at Antioch, while more varied and exciting in themselves than the action at Jerusalem, would not have compelled attention from an audience that still considered the recovery of Jerusalem a legitimate goal. The poet had to concentrate on the capture of the holy city.

Jerusalem did not offer Tasso much historical material. The siege had lasted only a month, and the Christians had spent most of that time building siege machines.[18] Tasso's friend, the Latin poet Pier Angeli da Barga, who wrote a competing epic on the First Crusade, the *Siriade*, reached the siege only in his last 143 verses.[19] This brevity reflected the sources available to both poets. The chroniclers Robert of Rheims and Paolo Emilio each devoted only one to two pages to the siege, and even William of Tyre, Tasso's principal source, had to expand his account artificially to give Jerusalem proper emphasis.[20] Rhetorical amplification, uncharacteristic for William, marks book 8 of his *Historia rerum in partibus transmarinis gestarum*, where he narrates the siege, and in book 9, which covers the battle of Ascalon, he adds biographical anecdotes about Goffredo. By careful use of these sources, Tasso found enough material for about five cantos (*GL* 1, 3, 11, 18–19), or a quarter of his epic—enough to make a brief narrative poem, but hardly enough for a major work that would make his reputation as a great artist. In contrast, the voyage of Vasco da Gama takes up more than half of *Os Lusiadas*.[21]

Tasso could not avail himself of the means Camões used to fill up the rest of his epic. Since the individual Crusaders came from all over western Europe, Tasso could not turn the expedition into a national epic.[22] He could not appeal to an Italian past or future; moreover, the First Crusade did not invite such a technique, even if conceived on an international scale. Prophecies would have revealed the long defeat that marked later crusades, a retreat before Mamluks and Ottomans that ultimately led to naval battles close to Italy itself. And of course the expedition of the 1090s, the first such venture attempted, had no prehistory. Tasso needed to look elsewhere for historical material.

Tasso solved his difficulty with historical material by a means I have called transposition. As he explained in the late 1560s, in his *Discorsi dell'arte poetica,* the poet can change the means and circumstances in the historical record and confound the times and order of events.[23] The Crusader assaults on Jerusalem provide an example. The army made two attacks, separated by a month. Since the first attack, in early June, ended quickly and lacked excitement, Tasso transposed to it details from the first day of the second assault, such as the elaborate struggle around Goffredo's siege tower and the end of that day's fighting, with the tower stalled near the walls and under guard.[24] Tasso thus kept the chronology of two assaults, separated by a month's time, but made the first one grander, more worthy of epic, by moving to it particulars from the second, successful attack. So explained, transposition seems a fairly straightforward procedure. This kind of transposition, however, involving only details from the historical siege of Jersulaem, could not have solved Tasso's problem of the lack of sufficient historical material for a long poem. In fact, Tasso went much further.

Canto 9, which presents Solimano's night attack on the Crusader camp, shows how far reaching and complicated transposition could be in Tasso's hands. In this respect the canto resembles an archaeological site where a grand superstructure masks a series of previous buildings that form its base and to an extent determine its shape. Patient digging reveals three levels of occupation below the present, going backwards in time, and four structures, two on the highest or most recent level. In other words, Tasso based his narrative on two actions that occurred during the siege of Jerusalem (the most recent level), on another that took place at Antioch, and finally (the lowest level, which determines the contours of the site), on the battle of Dorylaeum, in which the Crusaders fought Solimano, who tried to block their passage across Anatolia. I will follow the same procedure as the archaeologist, beginning with the superstructure, or Tasso's version of the military engagement.

Tasso assumes that the Crusaders' old enemy, Solimano, now leads a band of Arab irregulars in Palestine. The Egyptian caliph sent him there with much gold to draw Arab support and to organize raids for plunder (*GL* 9.6), and Solimano presents the attack on the Crusader camp in such terms, telling the Arabs that the Crusaders have the spoils of Asia (9.17). So far, Solimano has done well. Although the Arabs have mostly burned hovels and carried off cattle and sheep (*GL* 9.10), they have managed to cut Christian communications with the coast (9.7) and have stolen the supplies intended for the army, which a fleet had brought into Jaffa (5.87–88). The Crusaders now must worry about famine, and they have been sending foragers as far as Gaza (*GL* 8.51). Solimano, moreover, has destroyed the Danish party under Sveno that was coming to Jerusalem— an escalation of guerrilla activity that leads to the ambitious attempt in canto 9.

Tasso conveys the military logic behind the attack mostly through the devil's agent, the Fury Aletto. The demon acts out of desperation, for the Crusaders have finished constructing siege machines (*GL* 8.85) and will shortly attack Jerusalem. Because the Egyptian army has not yet assembled, Aletto uses the available means. Knowing that the Arabs have already arranged to run supplies into the city (*GL* 6.10–11), Aletto decides to turn this event into a surprise attack. The Arabs will assault the Crusader camp from the west,[25] at the same time as the Jerusalem garrison attacks it from the south. Such an assault would serve a double strategic objective. First of all, Aletto wants at all costs to upset the Crusader timetable and to delay the assault. Second, she hopes to drive them out of their fortified camp, north of the city. The invaders have surrounded this camp with a ditch and a wall (*GL* 3.66, 9.19, 9.54) to enable them to resist incursions from any direction. The Saracens must break up this defense, if they hope ever to dislodge the Crusaders from Jerusalem by force.

Such an attack has little chance of success. Although Solimano still has with him a band of Turks who wear proper armor, a thousand in all (*GL* 9.89), his Arabs lack armor (9.77) and the Crusaders regard them with contempt. Goffredo calls them a vile mob (*GL* 9.47), and Argillano dismisses them as an inept people, the dregs of the world (9.76). Only coordination with the city garrison and the element of surprise give them any chance whatever. Aletto and Solimano see to the latter. The audacity of the attack surprises Goffredo (*GL* 9.42), as Aletto guessed it would (9.11), and Solimano moves his force to Jerusalem with speed. They arrive ahead of any news of their coming (*GL* 9.13), and Solimano has them attack while it is still dark so as to minimize the difference between the armed and the unarmed, as Argillano remarks (9.77). Unfortunately for them, the sentinels give the alarm, so the Arabs do not really surprise their foes after all.

The double attack works to the extent that the Saracen troops on both sides manage to break through the Crusader defenses and get inside the camp. On the west Solimano puts to flight the camp guards, and Arab and Christian enter the camp together (*GL* 9.22–24). On the south Argante chases off the guard, leaps the ditch, and fills it with bodies, so the garrison troops have a level road into the camp (*GL* 9.54).[26] Goffredo, as soon as he hears of the fighting, sends Guelfo against Clorinda and Argante, and he stiffens the resistance there.[27] At the same time Goffredo takes men to face Solimano, since the Franks have not as yet offered effective resistance on the west. As he goes in that direction, he collects fugitives, so that he has a large troop when he confronts Solimano. The clash of leaders signals the turning point of the battle, and the Saracen attack breaks. The plight of his page, Lesbino,[28] distracts Solimano, who leaves his duel with Goffredo, allowing the enemy to attack his elite corps of a thousand Turks (*GL* 9.88). At this point the fifty champions, whom Armida had lured away from camp, arrive unexpectedly on the west and attack both the unwarlike Arabs and the warlike Turks (*GL* 9.91–92). They turn a probable defeat into a rout. Solimano exits anonymously, amid a cloud of arrows and lances (*GL* 10.1–3), and must later watch the corpses of his men burn (10.26–27). On the south Aladino has just come out of Jerusalem with more Saracens. When he sees his army, though larger, already bent, he orders Clorinda and Argante to collect their soldiers and withdraw. Since they are as yet undefeated, the two obey reluctantly, but it is not always easy to withdraw troops already in combat. The garrison soldiers panic, throwing away their shields and swords, and flee not to the city but into Hinnom, the steep valley west and south of Jerusalem (*GL* 9.95). Guelfo does not pursue them, however, since the king still has his uncommitted troops at the city above. And the brief battle ends.

The defeat gravely weakens the Saracen cause. Although the city has received supplies, its garrison has failed to break up the Crusader camp or slow down the enemy timetable. After the battle Goffredo sets the assault for the second day (*GL* 10.57). On the other side the force of Arab irregulars has disintegrated, and the Christians can reopen communications with Jaffa. The offensive has definitely passed to the Franks, and they now have most of their heroes back. Solimano must bear full responsibility for this debacle. He initiated the attack, and his love for Lesbino drew him away from his entourage just at the crisis.

Tasso used a variant of this pattern for the other and larger battle of the epic, that with the Egyptians in canto 20. In that battle, the Persians on the left, who have so far with difficulty held their own against the Lorrainers, collapse once their leader, Altamoro, deserts them to succor Armida (*GL* 20.69). For both battles, Tasso had in mind the pattern of Actium, and in both he contrasted Goffredo/Augustus with an opponent weakened by love.

In fact, Solimano and the Arabs never had much of a chance. Tasso admitted as much in a letter he wrote to Luca Scalabrino on 2 June 1575. The poet could not prolong the fighting much beyond nighttime because the Crusaders—an army of well-armed veterans that had never lost a battle—were fighting a rabble. Daylight would have revealed to the Crusaders their advantage, and they would have quickly scattered Solimano's irregulars. The poet, therefore, times the assault to a slow-motion dawn, which marks every stage of the battle and emphasizes the shift of fortune away from the Arabs and to the Christians.

Tasso dramatizes the dawn mostly through his epic machinery, the clash of demon and angel. At the beginning red vapor tinges the shadows and the dew looks bloody as hell empties its monsters into the air and ghosts scream (*GL* 9.15). At the crisis Michele descends and chases away the demons, making a path of light from the sky like a rainbow after a storm or a falling star. With his golden wings he shakes away the thick darkness, and his face scatters sparks (*GL* 9.62).[29] Argillano, who now leaves prison, taunts the Arabs, saying that they work by night but will now need arms and valor (*GL* 9.77). He is the one who kills Lesbino, drawing Solimano away from his duel with Goffredo, the action that helps turn around the battle. Finally, the fifty appear in silver armor, like lightning in a cloud, displaying the red cross of the French Crusaders (*GL* 9.91–92).[30] Tasso thus integrates the battle into one of his dominant image patterns, the war of light and darkness, and dawn as the place where light conquers the dark. The late Fredi Chiappelli has carefully studied this pattern.[31] Spenser later imitated it for book 1 of *The Faerie Queene*.

Tasso bases this elaborate action on very slender historical evidence, at least as far as he draws details from the actual siege of Jerusalem. Two unrelated skirmishes suggested material for canto 9. The first he found in Robert of Rheims and the mysterious Procoldo, count of Rochese.[32] I will give Robert's version of the first incident as related in his *Historia iherosolimitana* and use William of Tyre, always Tasso's first choice among his sources, for the second.

Robert tells how Raimundus Piletus, Raimundus de Taurina, and others left camp to reconnoiter the nearby area, lest some enemies come on the Crusaders unexpectedly.[33] They found 200 Arabs, whom they fought and defeated, killing many and taking thirty horses. Robert's account provides the indication that Crusader troops fought with Arab irregulars, but otherwise it has nothing to do with canto 9 of *Gerusalemme liberata.* Tasso could not have found here the topography of his battle—an action involving a city garrison as well as irregulars—the presence of the Crusaders' great foe, Solimano, or the fact that Goffredo's Lorrainers, and then still more Crusader troops, appearing unexpectedly, decided the battle.

Another skirmish, which also occurred near Jerusalem, did contribute something to Tasso's tactical presentation and may have suggested to the poet his whole practice of transposition. William of Tyre says that when Genoese ships came into Jaffa (Yafo) with supplies, Raimondo (of Toulouse) stingily sent only thirty horse and fifty foot to get the provisions. He was later persuaded to send an additional fifty cavalry. Six hundred Saracens ambushed the first group near Lydda (Lod) and Ramla, but the second group arrived just in time to rout the Saracens, who lost one-third of their force (*HR* 8.9.336–37). Tasso found in this story the fifty horsemen who come onto the battlefield at the last minute and provoke panic in the enemy. Perhaps more important, the incident suggested to the poet a similar episode that happened during the siege of Antioch, and he used that episode to set up the topography of his battle.

He found the story in William of Tyre, and also in Paolo Emilio, who wrote a history of the French arranged by monarchs.[34] A Genoese fleet had come with carpenters and smiths, and Boemondo and Raimondo led an armed group to bring back the supplies. Raimondo commanded the van, and Boemondo, the rear. Yaghi-Siyan sent out a force from Antioch, which successfully intercepted the Christian party, seized the supplies, and scattered the drovers and foot soldiers.[35] The knights, however, escaped, and Boemondo reached the camp, which had already been roused by Goffredo. The Crusaders then caught the Turks trying to get back to Antioch and slaughtered them, while the citizens, mobilized at the town above with the gates open, deterred their pursuit. The Turks nonetheless sustained heavy casualties, including Yaghi-Siyan's son, and the Crusaders recovered their supplies. They also regained their morale, which had been shaken by, among other things, the destruction of Sveno's party crossing Anatolia. They sent part of the spoils back to the fleet, and the local Syrian Christians began to help the Latins once again.

Antioch thus provided Tasso with a general model for his battle. It involved two enemy forces, one inside and one outside a city; was fought within view of the city, near the Crusader camp; and required the intervention of Goffredo. Furthermore, the presence of the city forces limited the Christian victory, which at the same time involved a moral reversal and the passing of the initiative to the invaders. Tasso simply substituted Arab irregulars for the Turks who attacked the supply train.

Although it provided a model, the Antioch episode does not explain the tactical development of the battle, stage by stage. In Tasso's version whole armies fought. Solimano attacked the Crusader camp itself, timing his assault for dawn. A series of late arrivals determined the Crusader victory: first Goffredo, then the fifty heroes. All this Tasso found at Dorylaeum rather than Antioch.[36]

After the capture of Nicaea (Iznik), the Crusaders divided their army into two parts for the march across Anatolia. In this fashion they would ease the supply problem. Boemondo led the van, which consisted of Normans from both southern Italy and northern France, plus the troops of the counts of Flanders and Blois, and the Byzantine escort led by Taticius (Tasso's Tatino). Behind came the men from Toulouse, Lorraine, and Vermandois, led by Raimondo. Meanwhile Kiliç Arslan ibn Süleyman ibn Kutlumísh (Solimano) had prepared a trap for them by Dorylaeum (near the modern Eskisehir). His army, screened by a line of hills, waited for the Crusaders to come over a pass to a plain, following the old Byzantine military road. Solimano did not realize, however, that another group was approaching behind the Normans. He thought he would trap the whole Crusader force, and this mistake explains the Turkish defeat.[37]

Like his namesake in the *Liberata*, Solimano hoped to surprise his enemy with a dawn attack, and as in the poem, he failed. Scouts picked up the Turkish presence the night before,[38] so Boemondo had the Normans camp by the Sari-su or River Bathys and sent a messenger to Raimondo for aid.[39] Emilio, assuming Renaissance procedure, claims that Boemondo tried to fortify the camp but had not completed the defenses when the Turks hit them.

The Turks used their normal tactics, shooting clouds of arrows at the Normans and attacking them from all sides.[40] A detachment crossed the river and broke into the Christian camp, killing the women and children who were there. Meanwhile the Crusader front line, half panicked, fell back on the camp. The mere mass of the troops relieved the enemy pressure there.[41] At the same time the Turks found to their dismay that their arrows could not harm those wearing armor, but they still kept up the arrow shower for some hours.

At this point the other part of the Crusader army, which Boemondo had summoned the night before, began to arrive. Goffredo and Ugo came first, appearing on the pass above, and charged, clearing away the Turks from the area by the camp. The other Crusaders heard the Lorrainers' battle cry and recovered confidence, while the surprised Turks lost their impetus. Now Raimondo showed up, while Ademaro, bishop of Le Puy, brought his army around *behind* the Turks.[42] The Franks charged, and the Turks, upset by Ademaro's group, fled eastward. They never challenged the Crusaders again.

Dorylaeum gave Tasso a tactical model for canto 9. Solimano leads a surprise attack, timed for dawn, on a fortified Crusader camp. Scouts pick up the advance, and word gets back to Goffredo. Meanwhile the Saracens hit the Crusaders from more than one direction and break into the camp, provoking a crisis in morale. The arrival of Goffredo reinvigorates the Christians, and the later appearance of still more Crusader troops panics the enemy troops, who now flee. Afterward Solimano can no longer lead his own troops against the invaders.

In addition to the tactics Tasso would have found in his sources a sizable Arab contingent serving under Solimano. Robert of Rheims gives lists of the enemy forces, which include Saracens, Arabs, and Agarenes, all terms for the same people.[43] Moreover, after the battle Solimano turns back a party of Arabs from Syria coming to his aid.[44] Dorylaeum thus probably suggested to Tasso the whole idea of making this Seljuk Turk the leader of an Arab force.

Dorylaeum further allowed Tasso to aggrandize the skirmishes by Jerusalem and make them worthy of epic.[45] One of five major military actions in the First Crusade, Dorylaeum probably so shocked everyone in the area—it involved the complete defeat of Seljuk Turks, who controlled much of the Near East and had recently conquered Anatolia—that no Muslim army put up a serious fight afterward. It is the equivalent in plot to what Virgilian imitation did for Tasso's style.[46] An example that unites both is the poet's remark that Solimano and Goffredo duel for the rule of Asia (*GL* 9.50), a grandiose statement that hardly fits a struggle in Palestine, where Solimano was not even a ruler, but would fit Asia Minor and Dorylaeum, at least as a pardonable exaggeration.

Idealization often follows from elevation in plot and style, but Tasso found this already in his sources. William of Tyre makes a hero of Goffredo not only at Dorylaeum but throughout his narrative of the First Crusade. He introduces the Lorrainer as a "vir quoque strenuus et insignis dominus" ("a man also active and a distinguished lord"; *HR* 1.17.45), stresses the honor he receives in Hungary (2.3.75) and his delicate role at Constantinople (2.6–12.90), and concludes his story with biographical anecdotes about the duke.[47] For the First Crusade William used Albert of Aix almost exclusively,[48] who in turn drew on an eyewitness account by one of Goffredo's soldiers for the march across Anatolia.[49] The idealization of Goffredo thus goes back ultimately to original oral testimony of the First Crusade. Tasso simply developed it. He had to make some adjustments, however, to fit this material to his epic.

Western epic and romance traditionally scorned missile shooters (see chapter 6), so the writers imagined the Eastern enemy fighting more or less in Western fashion. Tasso does the same in the *Liberata*, this time, however, with a basis in reality. Tasso assigns to Solimano an Arab not a Turkish army, and Arab horsemen, like the Frankish, fought at close quarters with lance and sword.[50]

Tasso also struggled to eliminate anachronisms. This is clear from a comparison of the earlier draft of canto 9 to the vulgate, or printed, text. Of the three manuscripts that preserve the earlier version, I cite from the Angelini manuscript *(An)*, since it alone has been frequently printed.[51] In it Tasso tends to think of Solimano and the Arabs as foot soldiers. The host marches to the Crusader camp (*An* 9 = vulg. 13), and Solimano *walks* quickly, getting near the camp (12 = 16). Twice the poet has the ambiguous term *corre* (runs), which could describe movement by either a foot soldier or a cavalryman. Solimano *runs* before the rest against the guards (18 = 22) and *runs* to Lesbino's aid (77 = 85). Tasso probably was thinking of the contemporary situation, both militarily and socially. Militarily most soldiers now fought on foot, and socially only aristocrats in Italy could afford a horse. The poet would have to remind himself that Arabs rode to battle and that Bedouin tribes, though poor by Western standards, regularly used horses and camels. Of these slips Tasso caught only the last, putting Solimano on a horse when he goes to Lesbino's aid.[52]

Canto 9 shows that transposition meant much more for Tasso than the brief description in his Academy lectures might indicate. He did not simply change the means and circumstances of some skirmishes by Jerusalem or confound their order in time. Rather, the poet superimposed one event on another, and in canto 9 he did so with several of them. As a result, a series of events originally separate in time blend together to form a new pattern identical to no single historical event, yet with all the particulars that give a story historical verisimilitude. If there were a single major source for canto 9, it would be the battle of Dorylaeum, itself involving a massive transposition. When Tasso said the poet could confound the time and sequence of events, who among his listeners in Ferrara would have realized that he meant the whole First Crusade, not just the siege of Jerusalem?

Solimano best exemplifies this larger sense of transposition.[53] Although he dominated events early in the Crusade, he disappeared after Antioch and had nothing to do with the invasion of Palestine. Tasso felt that some explanation was needed for his presence in the poem. He told Scipione Gonzaga that he here imitated Virgil and Homer, who united enemies—presumably alluding to the presence in the *Aeneid* of Dido, who lived centuries after Aeneas and whose curse on the hero Virgil connects to the Carthaginian Wars.[54] Again the reference, though correct, masks the exact nature of Tasso's transpositions and especially the way he superimposes events. Transposition or superimposition, in fact, marks much of his epic.

Mostly Tasso thinks of Antioch, that longer and more difficult siege in the north. We have already seen that it provided the poet with the topography for his battle in canto 9; it also determined the sequence he presupposes in cantos 8 and 9. News of Sveno's catastrophe dismayed the Crusaders before the Genoese fleet sailed in and Christian fought Saracen over its supplies.[55]

Tasso thought of Antioch in part because the two sieges had several parallel events. When two episodes, one at Jerusalem and one at Antioch, resembled each other, he tended to combine them. In both cities, for example, the Saracens considered massacring the Christian population and looked for provocation to do so. Tasso derived his novella of Sofronia and Olindo from an incident that occurred before the arrival of the Crusaders at Jerusalem. A Saracen, seeking to incite retaliation against Christians, took a dead dog and threw it into the Haram esh-Sharif by night. Next morning angry Muslims were ready to have the Christians executed, as a judgment for desecration, but instead a teenager offered himself and was killed for the people. In place of the dog, Tasso substitutes a statue, which Ismeno takes from the Church of the Dormition and tries to use for magical purposes (*GL* 2.5–7). Here, the poet is clearly thinking of

Turkish iconoclasm in the churches of Antioch, the violation and mutilation of the images of the saints.[56]

Tasso made use of Antioch especially to set up the climax of the *Liberata.* In the first place, the battle with the Egyptians did not qualify for
epic treatment, particularly as William of Tyre tells it. Late on the previous day the Crusaders met huge herds of domestic animals—cattle,
horses, and camels—belonging to the enemy, which followed them the
next day to battle. The Egyptians thought that the whole host approaching, both the men and the domestic herds, was one immense army,
and they mostly ran away (*HR* 9.12.380–82). Instead of this inglorious
tale, Tasso turned to the battle with Karbuqa (28 June 1098), the atabeg
of Mosul (Al Mawsil) who led the huge Muslim relief force to Antioch,
for much of his material.[57] Like the caliph (*GL* 17.8), Karbuqa ran the
battle through delegates. The Crusaders in both the history and the epic
used a hill on the left to anchor their line and make an outflanking maneuver by the much larger enemy force difficult (*GL* 20.8–9). In both
Solimano came from behind, just as the battle began to turn in favor of
the Christians (*GL* 20.92–107). And finally, Tasso made use of the dew
that fell before the battle, only he transferred it to Rinaldo on Olivet (*GL*
18.15–17). Dew fell gently on the Crusaders as they went out to battle,
and moved everyone, because they sensed the presence of the Holy Spirit
and now hoped for victory.[58]

Even more, the siege of Antioch set the strategy and timing of the last
three cantos and gave Tasso's epic an exciting climax. The actual battle
with the Egyptians occurred more than a month after the fall of Jerusalem
(12 August 1099) and in another place, near Ascalon. Vincenzo Vivaldi
long ago noted that Tasso here assumed the Antioch model instead,
where the siege and the battle followed each other closely.[59] In both the
siege of Antioch and the *Liberata,* the Crusaders have to capture the city
before the relief army arrives, and in both they barely do.[60] They must go
out to battle with the relief force, leaving Raimondo behind, watching an
uncaptured tower (which Robert of Rheims claimed he took by assault).[61]

The siege of Antioch was the crisis of the First Crusade; the whole
enterprise might have collapsed there. The Crusaders' success at Antioch
guaranteed the rest. At Jerusalem, however, the Egyptians lacked the
Turks' military skill and could not prevent the fall of the city once the
army moved south. By drawing so heavily on Antioch, Tasso thus came
as close as he could to imitating the *Iliad.*[62] Horace had defined it as a
historical epic, or the "res gestae regumque ducumque et tristia bella"

("the deeds of kings and leaders and the sad wars"), which began "in medias res."[63] Homer did not narrate the whole war or the fall of Troy, but
rather confined his tale to the crisis of the siege, when the Achaeans, frustrated over the long delay, were ready to go home, and quarreling had
deprived them of their greatest warrior.[64] The Trojan failure to expel the
Achaeans under these conditions led directly to the death of their own
greatest hero and forecast the fall of their city. Tasso imitates this pattern.
Though he must concentrate on Jerusalem and the end of the First Crusade, he presents it as if it were Antioch, the siege that determined the
success or failure of that campaign.

Critics have long noted Tasso's imitation of the *Iliad,* and the poet
himself said that the *Gerusalemme* resembles the Greek epic for the action
at Jerusalem.[65] Certainly both poems concentrate their main action in a
small area: Troy and its coastal zone, Jerusalem and the plain north of
town. Tasso further imitates the central plot of the *Iliad,* when he begins
"in medias res" and has Rinaldo withdraw from camp because of a quarrel.[66] Finally, the poems are about the same length, considerably longer
than other classical epics, such as the *Odyssey, Aeneid, Lusiadas,* and *Paradise Lost.*[67]

This massive transposition and the imitation of the *Iliad* had implications for Tasso's neoclassicism. Aristotle preferred the complex to the
simple plot, the *Odyssey* to the *Iliad.*[68] The complex plot often involved
flashbacks and prophecies. Odysseus, for example, narrates his previous
adventures at Phaiakia (*Od.* 9–12) and hears of the future from Teiresias
(11.90–151). Virgil also used retrospectives and views of the future for his
Aeneid, and his choice had great importance for Tasso, since the Italian
poet derived his notion of epic style from that work, which he often imitated, line by line, word by word. We have also seen that Camões used
the same technique to integrate Portuguese history with his epic,[69] yet
Tasso has no temporal excursus other than the obligatory dynastic prophecy connected to Rinaldo's shield. Instead he follows the *Iliad* and produces a plot that begins "in medias res" but thereafter follows a chronological order with only the briefest references to past or future.[70]

Tasso's own use of transposition prevented him from imitating the
backward and forward movement of an *Odyssey* or *Aeneid,* even if he had
desired to do so. How could he have composed a flashback, when he had
already crammed so much of the First Crusade, so many particulars of
the whole campaign, into that brief month at Jerusalem? The prehistory
had become part of the present.[71] The poet's whole procedure goes back
to the very beginnings of the composition of the *Liberata.*

When the sixteen-year-old Tasso composed the *abbozzo,* or draft, of his epic in 1559–60, he was already practising transposition and super-imposition.[72] The teenager had there the embassy of Alete and Argante, which he took over with only slight changes into the vulgate version of the *Liberata.* The Egyptians had actually sent two embassies to the Cru-saders, one at Antioch and one after Arqa, just before the Crusaders reached Egyptian territory.[73] The second concerned Jerusalem and the Egyptian demand that the Franks not invade Palestine.[74] Tasso duly re-produces this (*GL* 2.65), but the counteroffer made by Alete fits Antioch rather than Jerusalem.[75] He suggests an alliance against the Turks (of Anatolia and Antioch) and the "Persians" (the Turks of Mosul, or al-Mawsil).[76] Shiite Egypt had reason to fear the Sunni Turkish states, and Ibn al-Athir suggests they wanted a Syrian cushion between themselves and their Sunni rivals.[77] Such an offer makes no sense after Antioch, when the Crusaders had defeated the Turks from both regions and thought instead of Jerusalem, but Tasso already had Antioch in mind and was practising transposition. The technique underlay his whole approach to historical epic.

Even Tasso's heavy reliance on transposition could not furnish him with all the material he needed for his poem. The problem of history—that is, the paucity of material—still remained. Together, the Jerusalem siege and the technique of transposition gave Tasso slightly more than half of his poem: cantos 1–3, half of canto 5 (the quarrel), half of canto 8 (Sveno), canto 9, half of canto 10 (the political analysis or council in Jerusalem), canto 11, half of canto 13 (the drought), half of canto 17 (the muster of Egyptian troops), and cantos 18–20, which conclude the poem. This count gives a total of ten and a half cantos. The rest of the poem is fiction.

Though Tasso began by relying only on history in 1559–60, when he wrote his draft of what became cantos 1–3 of the vulgate text, he had already introduced fiction by 1566, when he told Ercole Tasso that he had reached the sixth canto of his "Gottifredo."[78] This fiction involved the introduction of Armida and Clorinda and thus prepared the ground for much of the love plots.[79] Tasso then justified this mixture of history and fiction in the *Discorsi dell' arte poetica,* where he argued that fiction keeps the poet from becoming a *mere* historian and that Italian as a language favors love.[80] Yet he still kept his fiction subordinate to the history, using Armida as a way to explain the defection and apostasy that plagued the Crusaders both at Antioch and at Jerusalem.

This restraint disappeared when Tasso composed the latter part of the

Liberata.[81] Fantasy, not merely fiction, dominates cantos 12–16 and takes up significant portions of cantos 17 and 18. Tasso had anticipated these wonders already in his *Discorsi dell'arte poetica,* when he argued that epic required marvels (1.354–55). This development linked him securely to the earlier romance tradition, to Pulci, Boiardo, and Ariosto, who all included magical operations, enchanted gardens, and exotic locales in their poems. Tasso's audience would have expected such scenes, and this material probably accounts in no small way for the popular success of the *Liberata.*

Even Tasso's Iberian counterparts, with their severer experiments in historical epic and romance, did not altogether escape the influence of the love god and his fantasies. Ercilla began by rejecting love from the *Araucana,* revising Ariosto's opening lines:[82]

> No las damas, amor, no gentilezas
> de caballeros, canto enamorados.
> (*Araucana,* 1.1.1, p. 1)

I sing neither women, love, nor the noble acts of knights in love.

He had to admit, however, that verse needs love to please an audience (*Araucana,* 1.15.1–5, pp. 239–40),[83] and he introduced amatory episodes into the second and third parts of the *Araucana.*[84] He begins the Dido episode by saying that he has followed such a narrow road that he needs breadth of subject matter and an open field. He tells his story of the Phoenician widow to divert the tired mind (*Araucana,* 3.32.50–51, p. 521).

Love also appears twice in *Os Lusiadas:* the vignette of Inês de Castro at the end of canto 3 and the Island of Love, which overlaps cantos 9 and 10. Inês's story qualifies the opposition between love and war, fiction and history, that we have seen in Tasso. Inês was a historical figure, and she reminds one that love can be as much a matter of history as war can be.

Ercilla too suggests a historical dimension to some of his love episodes. He tells the Dido story to correct Virgil and give an accurate history (*Araucana,* 3.32.43–46, 52–53, pp. 520, 522), and he claims to have met the war widow, Tegualda,[85] though the details of her story are clearly fictional.[86]

Tasso himself argues that his love fictions have at least some basis in history, citing remarks by the count of Rochese.[87] Given the nature of war, it is understandable that in military epic love episodes tend to be fictional, yet here especially the poet needs relief from scenes of fighting and killing. Ercilla, for example, tells the Dido story to the soldiers in his group, who are tired from the pursuit after Cañete (*Araucana,* 3.32.47,

PROBLEMS FOR THE POET

p. 521).[88] Like Tasso the Spanish poet requires diversion. Camões, in contrast, does not. He could mostly ignore love fictions or histories, since he chose a voyage and not a war for his topic.

Although both war poets, Tasso and Ercilla, included love stories, they differed radically in the proportions they allotted to love and fiction in their poems. Roughly three of thirty-seven cantos in the *Araucana* concern love, and another three and a half present Indian athletics and Fitón's marvels, so a total of six and a half, or about one-sixth of the whole.[89] As Ercilla explains in one place (*Araucana*, 1.15.4–5, p. 240), he simply has too much material to cover. Tasso, as we have seen, did not, and as a result he ended up balancing the two, making his epic an equal blend of the historical and the fictional, of war and love.

PART THREE

The Gun, or the New Technology

——SIX——

Negative Critiques
Ludovico Ariosto and John Milton

THE GUN POSED A PROBLEM FOR THE WRITERS OF ROMANCE and epic that had no parallels in tradition. Crossbows and the heavier armor they necessitated or the enceinte castles of the thirteenth century had not much altered the romancers' craft. But writers in the fifteenth and early sixteenth centuries were faced with the new technology of fire-power, developed between 1440 and 1530. The use of the gun in warfare challenged the basis of their fictions and provoked strong responses. Not surprisingly, most writers reacted negatively, like the majority of their contemporaries. They worked out a negative critique of the gun that is the focus of this chapter. Fortunately, J. R. Hale has already described public reaction to the introduction of guns in a long and careful article, and this frees me to concentrate on the poets, specifically Ariosto and Milton.[1] The Olimpia episode in Ariosto's *Orlando furioso* presented the negative critique of the gun in its classic form and set the model for writers outside of Italy. Milton, who comes after the period covered in this study, demonstrates the strength of the negative tradition. By the 1660s the gun had long been a standard weapon in warfare, yet the English poet in book 6 of *Paradise Lost* could still make the same complaint against firearms that Ariosto had uttered more than a century before.

A few poets opposed this negative line in varying degrees. Some attempted to assimilate guns somehow within their poems, while others espoused what I will call a modernist position. The latter group wrote not about the deep past but about contemporary naval warfare and colonial struggle. Most prominent among them were the Iberian poets Camões and Ercilla, whose work I analyze in chapter 7. To the present-day reader, it is both fascinating and confusing that the modernists shared the same value system as the other poets—a chivalric code inherited from the

Middle Ages. The works of both groups embodied this code. Thus, the poems of such writers as Camões and Ercilla present a mirror image of the romance world created by poets who espoused the negative critique. How could the chivalric code support both of the opposed positions? The concept of fraud, the vice traditionally opposed to the chivalric code in the older poetry, provides a key. Ariosto was the first to work out its problematic.

The epic poet was not obliged to reflect contemporary events, so Ariosto's inclusion of the gun in the *Furioso* is unusual. His ostensible topic, the wars of Charlemagne, long predated the age of the gun, and even his romance sources of the high and later Middle Ages came from a time before the use of cannon. Romance writers generally included present customs by a practice of discreet anachronism. Malory, for example, presupposes fifteenth-century-style tournaments in his translation of thirteenth-century texts. The gun, however, did not fit readily into this practice, because the changes it introduced in warfare were fundamental and far-reaching. Nonetheless, Ariosto began by presupposing the presence of cannonry, much as Malory had assumed tournaments. He made direct references to guns in the personal introductions he gave to his cantos. These remarks could have encouraged the positive or modernist position that Camões later argued. Afterward, however, Ariosto decided to introduce the gun directly to his plot, and when he did so he judged it negatively. This is his most important contribution to the literature of firearms, and it provides the focus of this chapter.

Ariosto had good reason to support the modernist position. His lord, the Ferrarese ruler Alfonso I d'Este, encouraged technological experiment. Ferrara was the first city to have angle bastions on its walls—that is, the first to use guns aggressively.[2] By his death Alfonso had collected 300 cannon, had personally supervised the casting of some, and had done his own shooting at Legnago, where his guns gave thirty to forty shots a day.[3] His cuirass bore the design of a flaming bombshell when he fought at Ravenna, and Titian portrayed him with his hand on a gun muzzle.[4] Ariosto himself knew of two battles where the Este artillery was decisive. At the second battle of Polesella (22 December 1509), the Este cannon destroyed a Venetian fleet on the Po.[5] The battle of Ravenna (1512) marked his poetry, even though he visited the battlefield only on the day after the event.

Alfonso and his cannon made victory possible for the French in their battle with the Spaniards at Ravenna. The duke contributed two-thirds of the cannon. After the initial barrage he turned them sideways to shoot across the field and forced the Spanish heavy cavalry to charge. This action in turn made the Spanish light cavalry opposite the cannon attack the Este artillery. In both cases the Spaniards left a strong defensive position and attacked a superior force. Ariosto twice compliments Alfonso for his tactics (*OF* 14.2, 33.40). They demonstrated what Cerignola (1503), Genoa (1507), and Agnadello (1509) had already intimated, that guns could turn around a battle. This time artillery broke up the then standard defensive-offensive strategy, whereby a smaller army took a fortified position and destroyed its larger enemy as the enemy attacked. The Spaniards at Ravenna were following this principle and had some of their guns placed defensively, as support for the infantry. By turning his guns, Alfonso forced them to leave a favorable position.[6] Ariosto assumes this technology in the Olimpia tale. Cimosco's gun is of the new versatile type, light enough so that Orlando can pick it up. Cimosco uses it for sieges, against field camps (*OF* 9.30–31),[7] and tactically against a horseman. Such uses, as much as Ariosto's comments, show the new style of warfare.

Ariosto wrote in a city that could have encouraged a positive attitude to innovation. Not only was Ferrara quick to adopt the gun, it also was where the modernists later defended Ariosto himself against the ancients.[8] Cinzio and others argued that the ancients had not anticipated romances because they had a different culture and language. The new society justified new literary forms, and Ariosto's romance served broader purposes than the epics of Homer and Virgil. Gunpowder and cannon suggested a similar argument, for the technology was unknown to antiquity.[9] The new warfare and the new poetry could have supported each other, and Ariosto might have anticipated Camões by forty years. He did not do so, however, and his comments on Ravenna reveal some of his reasons for adopting the negative critique of the gun.

Ravenna was perhaps the bloodiest battle of the century. Fourteen thousand people died, and at one point Alfonso's guns shot down men on both sides. Jacopo Guicciardini wrote to his brother the historian about these guns: "It was a horrible and terrible thing to see how every shot of the artillery made a lane through those men-at-arms [the Spanish heavy cavalry], and how helmets with the heads inside them, scattered limbs, halves of men, a vast quantity, were sent flying through the air." In *Elegy* 10 Ariosto described what he had seen the day after: the dead so crowded that no earth was visible for miles.[10] The major impact of Ravenna on

Ariosto's poetry is seen not in his stray comments but in his description of the carnage at Paris, the central military action of his epic. He makes the comparison explicit:

> Nei molti assalti e nei crudel conflitti,
> ch'avuti avea con Francia, Africa e Spagna
> morti erano infiniti, e derelitti
> al lupo, al covro, all'aquila griffagna;
> e ben che i Franchi fossero più afflitti,
> che tutta avean perduta la campagna,
> più si doleano i Saracin, per molti
> principi e gran baron ch'eran lor tolti.
>
> Ebbon vittorie così sanguinose,
> che lor poco avanzò di che allegrarsi.
> E se alle antique le moderne cose,
> invitto Alfonso, denno assimigliarsi;
> la gran vittoria, onde alle virtuose
> opere vostre può la gloria darsi,
> di ch'aver sempre lacrimose ciglia
> Ravenna debbe, a queste s'assimiglia.
>
>   (*OF* 14.1–2)

In the many assaults and cruel conflicts that Africa and Spain had with France, the dead were innumerable, left for the wolf, crow, and tearing eagle. And although the French suffered more, since they lost the whole field, the Saracens sorrowed more, for the many princes and great barons whom they lost.

There are victories so bloody that they bring little joy to the victors. And if I may compare modern things to ancient, unbeaten Alfonso, the great victory, the glory of which can be given to your acts of power, for which Ravenna must always have tearful eyelids, is like this one.

Ravenna both justifies the modernist position and explains Ariosto's reluctance to develop its implications.[11]

When Ariosto, now retired, revised his poem the last time for publication, he introduced to it the Olimpia story plus a direct meditation on guns, which he inserted at canto 11. In these passages he argues the standard negative theory of the gun: that it was a demonic invention made in the north.

Orlando says, when he throws Cimosco's gun into the North Sea:

> O maledetto, o abominoso ordigno,
> che fabricato nel tartareo fondo

> fosti per man di Belzebù maligno
> che ruinar per te disegnò il mondo,
> all'inferno, onde uscisti, ti rasigno.
>
> (*OF* 9.91)

O cursed, abominable engine, which malign Beelzebub put together in the Tartarean depth, who intended to ruin the world through you, I reassign you to the hell from which you came.

Ariosto continues the story in a monologue: recently a necromancer drew the gun back out of the ocean, and the devil helped the Germans learn how to use it (*OF* 11.22–28).[12] This theory was old already when Ariosto expressed it, as Hale indicates, and it represented the majority literary opinion in the period.[13]

The English later adopted the same position, composing variations on Ariosto's discourse. In his *Civile Wars* Samuel Daniel, speaking about York's entrenched camp near London, called artillery an instrument new brought from hell, framed to terrify men, to tear the earth, and to rend strong towers (6.26–27). A character named Nemesis later says that artillery enables people to scourge each other in a way a tyrant could never devise (*CW* 6.39–40). Two generations later Milton developed the story further; he had the devil both stimulate the invention of artillery among men (*PL* 6.501–6) and invent it himself, before human history and during the second day of the heavenly war (6.469–608).[14]

The story of the origins of gunpowder likewise assumed that northerners discovered the technology. For example, Ariosto sets his tale in Holland, and Cimosco rules Friesland. Practically everyone thought a German had invented gunpowder,[15] and elaborate accounts about its invention existed forty years before Ariosto wrote his *novella*. For Italians the belief could also form part of a larger theory, which credited all military innovation to the north. The poet here would be one with his contemporary Machiavelli.[16]

By coincidence this story exactly fits the biblical traditions behind the legend of Satan's revolt,[17] so that Milton had no difficulty assimilating it to *Paradise Lost*. The enemy god Baal built his palace on Mount Zephon or Casius in the extreme north of Syria,[18] and Isaiah parodied the story in his attack on the king of Babylon, who says he will ascend heaven, exalt his throne above the stars of God, and sit on the mountain of congregation in the north (Isaiah 14:12–15). Origen then applied the passage to Satan, and a northern location for Satan's revolt soon became commonplace for the biblical and literary tradition.[19] Near the beginning of

Paradise Lost Milton compares Satan's troops to the Germanic tribes that
swept away the western Roman Empire:

> A multitude, like which the populous North
> Pour'd never from her frozen loins, to pass
> *Rhene* or the *Danaw,* when her barbarous Sons
> Came like a Deluge on the South, and spread
> Beneath *Gibraltar* to the *Lybian* sands.
>
> (*PL* 1.351–55)

The poet closes the passage alluding to the Vandals, themselves bywords
for the destruction of art.[20]

The hint of barbarism suggests in classical form the main critique of
the gun, which again Ariosto originally expressed in very clear terms. The
destructive power of the gun, however, did not by itself bring about the
poet's denunciation, which he wrote long after Ravenna. Rather, the development of the harquebus, which immediately preceded the composition of the Olimpia episode, gave rise to his moral analysis that modern
technology was incompatible with chivalry (fig. 18).

Ariosto never describes Cimosco's gun except by periphrasis, and although these descriptions indicate a cannon (*OF* 9.75), the imprecision
allows him to have it function differently. It does not blow off hands and
scatter half-bodies, the way Alfonso's cannon did at Ravenna. Instead it
kills people the way a bullet would. Olimpia's father dies, shot between
the eyes. Her first brother, defending their field camp, receives a stroke
that breaks through his armor and goes into his heart. During another
battle her second brother is hit fleeing. A ball goes through his shoulder
and out his breast (*OF* 9.30–31). This sort of thing happened frequently
in the mid-1520s, when the harquebus replaced crossbows and all other
missile-throwing devices as a tactical weapon.

The harquebus had long been an important military weapon, but initially it was used more for harassment of the enemy than for precision
fire, and it was more important in sieges than in battle.[21] The matchlock,
introduced at the end of the fifteenth century, gave the weapon greater
accuracy. The gunner could now shoot from the shoulder and sight along
the barrel, and by the 1490s groups of mounted harquebusiers appeared.[22]
In the next decade they took important roles in major battles, beginning
with Cerignola (1504).[23] Further technological refinements gave the harquebus in the 1520s a new and decisive importance. The harquebus now
had a greater range (200 meters), and its bullets could pass through any
cuirass.[24] Harquebusiers formed their own companies and used alternat-

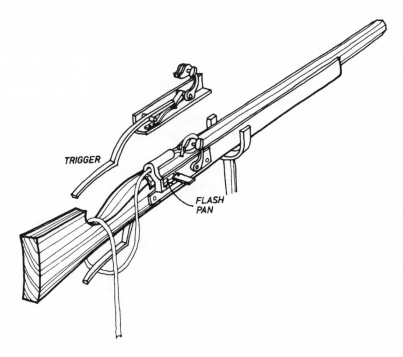

Figure 18. Harquebus, with its trigger mechanism. Reprinted from Pepper and Adams, *Firearms and Fortifications*. Copyright © 1986 by The University of Chicago.

ing fire.[25] Within a few years they had proved their worth against every other tactical arm: the pike (Bicocca, 1522, and Landriano, 1529), heavy cavalry (Pavia, 1525, and Gavinana, 1530), and light cavalry (Gavinana). For the romancer Pavia was the most serious event because it involved the heavily armed aristocrat on his horse. At that battle, the French were winning the battle of the knights, and Francis I had already told the seigneur de Lescun that he was now lord of Milan. Then the marquis of Pescara moved 1,500 Spanish harquebusiers and caught the French horse by flank fire. The first volley hit many French nobles, who were conspicuous by their dress. It caused confusion and panic, and allowed the Imperial cavalry to re-form and counterattack. In the end the Imperials annihilated the French knights: the king was a prisoner, and generals Bonnivet, La Trémouille, La Palice, and Lescun were dead, along with 6,000 other men. Paolo Giovio complained that cavalry, which had never fought so well, went down before ignoble infantry.[26] But Pavia was not the only alarming event for the romancers. Harquebus fire killed Bayard, the most famous of knights, on his horse at Romagnano Sesia, and an accurate volley from the trees killed the prince of Orange at Gavinana and put to flight his 400 men-at-arms.[27]

It is not surprising then that Ariosto finds the gun unchivalric and has Cimosco kill Orlando's horse. Orlando later says that it enables the bad to prevail over the good (*OF* 9.90). In his meditation on artillery Ariosto generalizes this observation. The gun destroys military glory. No mastery in arms, no courage or strength avails now, since the worse can win by the gun. A soldier, if he wants employment, should toss his weapons, even his sword, into the forge and shoulder a *scoppio,* or harquebus (*OF* 11.25–27). And this is what Ariosto's son did, when he became an artillery captain.[28]

This opinion of the poet, like his others, was a common one, and later writers like Cervantes returned to it.[29] Perhaps a more significant example, though not well known, is Juan Rufo. In his epic *Austriada* he celebrates the contemporary victory of Lepanto, a battle prominent for its cannonades. Yet Rufo introduces a denunciation of artillery into his discussion of the fighting on the Turkish royal galley (*Austriada,* 24.15–18), and he alludes to Ariosto. The horrendous artifice of Cimosco with its crude violence had no place there, Rufo says, for it was all sword work. Sword and lance are the crucible of valor and require a combination of mind, force, and dexterity to use them accurately. Artillery, on the other hand, is the epilepsy of fortitude.

The gunner, like the Germanic barbarian, operated outside civilized modes of warfare. For the romancers this meant outside their inherited chivalric code. The poets therefore assimilated firearms to a standard medieval category. Guns were held to exemplify fraud, the vice traditionally opposed to chivalry.

Ariosto associates Cimosco consistently with deceit. Olimpia correctly fears treachery (*OF* 9.51). When Orlando challenges Cimosco to a duel, the king instantly thinks of fraud. He sends a company of thirty horse and foot out another gate to ambush the hero (*OF* 9.63–65). Malory similarly connects cannon to fraud and treason: Mordred uses guns when he besieges Guinevere in the Tower of London (*Morte,* 21.1).[30] Those who cheat, those who do not follow the chivalric code, use guns.

Fraud, on the other hand, makes those who follow the chivalric code look innocent and inexperienced. Ariosto gives his characters a naïve view of technology. The poet twice describes Cimosco's gun, both times by periphrasis (*OF* 9.28–29, 73–75). He has to use circumlocution because he is describing the first gun, so that no one in his poem could experience it other than naïvely. Olimpia's father did not know what a gun could do and was shot down on the walls of a castle, walking in full view. There is a significant difference, however, between artistic and true naïveté. The Incas who first saw the Spaniards with their horses and guns thought they were gods. They called the harquebuses *yllapas*, or "thunder from heaven," and thunder was their second most important deity.[31] In contrast, Ariosto's characters see the same fraud that educated opinion of his day found in artillery.

Through this story Ariosto creates a sense of ethical outrage. He has Cimosco direct his weapon against innocent victims, people who know nothing about guns. The poet thus invents an unfair situation based on a false premise, since both sides used artillery in contemporary Europe. On the battlefield a tactical rather than an ethical question applied. One asked which side had the better guns, or which had more guns, or which side used them more effectively. Artificial naïveté, moreover, does not capture the Amerindian response to guns. In fact, the gun abroad reinforced rather than called into question the old ethical code, a topic I discuss in chapter 7.

Milton repeated Ariosto's scenario but in a more extreme form. Ariosto had posited the invention of artillery in the Middle Ages, but Milton had it happen before human history and outside our universe. He further modeled his story on what he believed to be the first tactical use of cannon in warfare. He read in Paolo Giovio's life of Bartolomeo Colleoni that for one battle the condottiere had *spingards,* an early type of gun, drawn up on small wagons behind his line.[32] At a trumpet signal the front opened on either side, leaving the wagons and guns facing the enemy, and the salvo shocked the enemy with a storm of projectiles. Milton assumes that Satan uses the same tactical maneuver, but he modernizes the technology. The devils have powder in grains (*PL* 6.575), and Milton imagines them using the new light field artillery introduced by Gustavus Adolphus, three rows deep and mounted on gun carriages.[33] Once the vanguard divides to the right and the left, the salvo has the same shock effect Colleoni produced in the mid-fifteenth century (*PL* 6.569–70, 589–90). Milton thus had Satan anticipate the historical invention of field artillery. The English poet replaced Ariosto's fictional version with an account derived from what he considered to be fact.

Milton also fit Ariosto's story into a different political and moral context. When Satan reveals his cannon on the second day of the heavenly war, the loyal angels maintain close formation (*PL* 6.581), and so the volley easily knocks them over. Not knowing what to expect, the good angels react like the members of Olimpia's family faced with Cimosco's gun. Naïveté invites deception, and Milton follows Ariosto in associating the gun with fraud (*PL* 6.555).[34] He could also have made a similar political application, if he had wished. James Freeman has shown that the Renaissance generally accepted fraud as a legitimate part of warfare, citing Ariosto's contemporaries, Machiavelli and More, and seventeenth-century treatises, including Milton's *De doctrina christiana*.[35] Yet the English poet provides a different political context, one that reveals the roots of this tradition in a way that Ariosto's work does not.

In the *Furioso* Cimosco resembles a condottiere lord or a Cesare Borgia. He tries to enforce debatable claims outside his inherited lands, and others see his actions as both tyrannical and aggressive. Satan in contrast is punished for sedition and rebellion against his legitimate overlord. God later calls the angelic revolt an act of fraud (*PL* 7.143–44). The technological fraud of artillery grows out of an original political fraud, fitly indicated by the night scene in which Satan initiates his action. No one ever mentions rebellion, yet Beelzebub understands Satan, and both generals talk ambiguously and play on angelic jealousy (*PL* 5.657–710). Milton thus understands the demonic revolt in terms of the fascination with fraud and sedition, which marked both Tudor and Stuart England.

Daniel gives the Tudor version, when he associates cannon with York's rebellion (*CW* 6.26–27), but it was the Gunpowder Plot that most deeply impressed the English and linked the new technology to sedition. As a student Milton had already worked out for his poems on that topic the very scenario he would later use for *Paradise Lost*. In *In quintum novembris* Satan again starts the plot by night, this time appearing to the pope in a dream (92–96) and telling him that he may use fraud against heretics (113–15), even as he himself deceives the pope under the false image of a Franciscan friar. In *Paradise Lost* Satan also manipulates Beelzebub, influencing his emotions (*PL* 5.694–95). In both scenes fraud breeds fraud, and ultimately politics and technology together outline a moral evil.

For epic and romance, however, the idea has ancient roots, far older than the period of the Tudors and Stuarts. Malory associates fraud with Gawain and his brothers, and Mordred comes from that family. In the *Chanson de Roland* it is Ganelon, and in the *Nibelungenlied*, Hagen. These men do not follow the chivalric code, and those who do— Lancelot, Roland, and Siegfried—can only see their activity as false and yet very dangerous. Mordred, and not the barons, Romans, or Saxons, brought down Arthur's kingdom.

The English writers followed Ariosto in another respect when they connected artillery to the construction of larger states. Cimosco is trying to unite some provinces of modern Holland into a single entity. For the English Daniel provides the most extensive discussion in his long excursus on Nemesis and Pandora. He begins with an idealized picture of medieval Europe, just before the development of firearms (*CW* 6.28–33). Europe had many states, none swollen out of form so as to disturb the rest. His note explains that Italy had more states then, as did the Germanies; France had free princes; and Iberia contained several kingdoms. Gunpowder, however, enabled larger states to expand, seizing smaller ones, so that a few great states appeared, like Spain and France, which could slaughter each other with greater power (*CW* 39–41). The gun certainly enabled the Spaniards to conquer Granada and permitted both Frenchman and Spaniard to range freely through Italy. Monster states led to what modern historians have called the gunpowder empires, and Ray Wolper cites both French and English opinion from the 1660s that connects the gun to empire building.[36] Milton turns the argument into a moral analysis. As we have seen, he links cannon to fraud and to its master, Satan, and then shows how Satan conquers our universe by fraud. The poet returns to this theme many times in *Paradise Lost* and *Paradise Regained*,[37] most especially in the passage where Satan relates to the fallen angels his successful temptation of Man:

> . . . Him by fraud I have seduc'd
> From his Creator, and the more to increase
> Your wonder, with an Apple; he thereat
> Offended, worth your laughter, hath giv'n up
> Both his beloved Man and all his world,
> To Sin and Death a prey, and so to us,
> Without our hazard, labor, or alarm,
> To range in, and to dwell, and over Man
> To rule, as over all he should have rul'd.
>
> (*PL* 10.485–93)

All three poets, Ariosto, Daniel, and Milton, react to periods of accelerated technological advance. Ariosto wrote the Olimpia story after the evolution of the gun was complete and after it had proved its worth in field engagements as well as in sieges and naval battles. By the time Daniel wrote the *Civile Wars* England had become a leading producer of iron cannon. The English founders had become the rage on the Continent by 1570 and made better guns than the Swedes.[38] In fact, mass production in Sweden and England began to alter the balance of power in favor of the Protestant north, and Milton saw its consequences. The Parliamentary armies, considered rebels by the Royalists, won the English Civil War and also initiated the most spectacular expansion of English power since the days of Henry V. Under Cromwell English soldiers occupied both Scotland and Ireland, and the navy seized Jamaica. Yet neither Daniel nor Milton adopted a modernist position, any more than Ariosto had done. All three denounced the gun and in so doing expressed their sense of a crisis that was literary as well as social and military.

Ariosto does not have Orlando simply defeat Cimosco, the agent of fraud, as Charlemagne punished Ganelon in the *Chanson de Roland*. Instead, he has Orlando take the gun and throw it into the sea, put it out of his world. By this action he signals the crisis. Ariosto is aiming at the whole new technology. It is not just Cimosco's gun but gunpowder as well. The poet puts a gunpowder explosion in a simile, which he applies, however, to Orlando:

> Chi vide mai dal ciel cadere il foco
> che con si orrendo suon Giove disserra,
> e penetrare ove un richiuso loco
> carbon con zolfo e con salnitro serra;
> ch'a pena arriva, a pena tocca un poco,
> che par ch'avampi il ciel, non che la terra;
> spezza le mura, e i gravi marmi svelle,
> e fai sassi volar sin alle stelle.
>
> (*OF* 9.78)

Whoever saw fire fall from heaven, which Jove unlocks with terrifying sound, and penetrate where an enclosed place shuts up carbon with sulphur and saltpeter saw that as soon as it arrives, as soon as it touches the powder even a little, it seems as if the sky as well as the earth blazes. It breaks walls, splinters heavy marble blocks, and makes the stones fly to the stars.[39]

Cimosco's gun has just struck Orlando's horse, so the simile carries over that sense of artificial lightning to the explosion of stored gunpowder, struck by natural lightning. Such an event occurred at the first battle of Polesella, when the Este cannon blew up a Venetian gunpowder ship (1509).[40] The simile also resembles another, which describes an explosive mine (*OF* 27.24).[41]

Ariosto suggested the various uses of gunpowder because he realized that it now affected every kind of warfare. The harquebus in the 1520s was the last in a series of developments. It began with sieges, when Jean Bureau's artillery blew the English out of France and Mehmed II's cannon pounded the walls of Constantinople. Then it was ships (Diu, 1509), field artillery (Ravenna, 1512), and finally the harquebus. In response to these developments, the new armies had to be versatile. They had to include more than one kind of infantry (pike and harquebus), plus light cavalry. Pavia, however, showed that heavy cavalry had a doubtful future, and this arm had been the traditional basis for romance epic.[42]

Romance began in the late twelfth and early thirteenth centuries as a celebration of a military aristocracy, the knight on horseback. In the ensuing 300 years this form survived major changes in the conduct of war, but could it survive the disappearance of the knight himself? The Olimpia episode indicates Ariosto's consciousness of the problem and answers the question in the negative.[43] The episode thus functions as an exorcism. Orlando's action indicates that the gap between the poet's fiction and contemporary warfare had become too great. To survive, romance had either to ignore the present or to undergo a change.

The poets did have more time to adjust than Ariosto may have thought. Matters that Ariosto could not anticipate softened the impact of firearms for another century. First of all, there was what Frances Yates in *Astraea* called the refeudalization of Europe, an escape into a medieval fantasy world, encouraged by aristocrats and government alike. The *Furioso* itself gave significant impetus to this movement, which had such success that later writers who talked about medieval manners or literature often tacitly assumed the sixteenth century, at least in northern Europe.[44] Eighteenth-century critics defended Spenser as a Gothic writer,[45] and in France, where neoclassicism made such a severe break with the past, later writers could assimilate the sixteenth century to their own medieval past.[46] France, in fact, experienced something of a medieval revival.[47] During the Wars of Religion the French manufacture of cannon dropped off, so cavalry could enjoy a partial recovery. Alessandro Farnese, duke of Parma, later dismissed Henri IV with the famous remark that he thought he was fighting a general, not a horse captain.[48] Finally, there was the slow pace of the military revolution itself. "Rifles" did not become generally practical until the next century, when they helped account for the successes of Gustavus Adolphus. Field artillery came to be distinguished from siege guns somewhat earlier but had to wait till the middle of the seventeenth century before it came into its own. The process of evolution did not reach completion until the bayonet replaced the sword in the late seventeenth century.[49] Ariosto had analyzed a revolution in slow motion, and later poets had sufficient time to experiment with a range of form and content perhaps more varied than at any earlier period in the history of romance and epic. Heroic poetry finally died at the end of the Renaissance, but its death resembled the supernova formed by a supergiant star, a brilliant burst going in all directions and widely observed.

Formal change involved the shift from romance to classical epic. Critics correctly explain this shift as a result of the revived Aristotelianism of the mid-century, but the new form also answered the military problem. Classical heroes fought on foot, and so do Tasso's. Rinaldo storms Jerusalem and rages through its streets on foot, and Tancredi is on foot when he kills Argante and Clorinda. The romance model for the latter fight was Boiardo's cavalry duel between Orlando and Agricane. Camões too uses a classical form, and his Portuguese, having no horses on their ships, use the infantry rush instead.

The change in content was more important. Poets responded to Ariosto's dilemma in three ways, though the categories are not mutually exclusive. Tasso maintained the old chivalry by going back to the time before the gun. He revived historical epic,[50] and his evocation of a heroic past aroused feelings of nostalgia in his audience. The Italians of his day lived under the "pax hispanica," and warfare was becoming a memory. Tasso thus responded to the gunpowder revolution in a highly original way, and his attempt anticipated the modern historical novel.

A second group of writers, mostly English, either limited the presentation of war as much as possible in their compositions or dropped it altogether. Those who limited their battle scenes still tried to maintain ties with the older tradition. Milton, although he confines war to a portion of a single book, nevertheless shows a very militarized heaven, as Hippolyte Taine complained in the nineteenth century:

> What a heaven! It is enough to disgust one with Paradise; one would rather enter Charles I's troop of lackeys, or Cromwell's Ironsides. We have orders of the day, a hierarchy, exact submission, extra-duties, disputes, regulated ceremonials, prostrations, etiquette, furbished arms, arsenals, depots of chariots and ammunition. Was it worthwhile leaving earth to find in heaven carriage-works, buildings, artillery, a manual of tactics?[51]

Satan arranges a military review in hell, which the poet describes in technical vocabulary; an angelic garrison guards Paradise; and the good angels regularly go in armed companies to visit Chaos. Robert Fallon correctly expresses the impression given by *Paradise Lost:* a stage crowded with military uniforms.[52]

More radical were those writers, like Spenser, who avoided war altogether, yet even he drew back from a decisive break with the past. At one point he promises something more like the old military poetry, when he addresses his Muse before the dragon fight:

> Faire Goddesse lay that furious fit aside,
> Till I of warres and bloudy *Mars* do sing,
> And Briton fields with Sarazin bloud bedyde,
> Twixt that great faery Queene and Paynim king,
> That with their horrour heauen and earth did ring,
> A worke of labour long, and endlesse prayse.
>
> (*FQ* 1.11.7)

Neither the extant fragments of *The Faerie Queene* nor the version projected in the letter to Raleigh, however, would allow for such a story. The poet postpones warfare to an indefinite future, perhaps to the epic of King Arthur, where he would celebrate the public virtues of his hero.[53] Meanwhile he compensates for the lack of war in *The Faerie Queene* by affirming throughout a code based on the old chivalry, which he illustrates constantly through the duels and adventures of his heroes.

No one else went as far as Marino, who both avoided war and did not maintain the old chivalric values in his *L'Adone*. In canto 16 he had the political issue decided not by combat but by a male beauty contest.

The Spanish and Portuguese worked out the third response to the new military technology and advocated the modernist position. Camões, where he depicts war, Alonso de Ercilla y Zuñiga in his *Araucana,* and also Gaspar de Villagrá in his *Historia de la Nueva Mexico* all accepted the gun and yet maintained the medieval military code. They found their subjects in the colonies, where a warfare closer to that of the old chivalry still persisted. A characteristic example is Ercilla's young man who lets down the drawbridge and challenges the Araucanian Indians to fight. When so many respond, he does not falter but goes forward alone to meet them (*Araucana*, 1.2.78–80, pp. 35–36). The conquistadors recalled the situation of the late eleventh century, when a few knights could conquer and hold Sicily and Palestine from the Muslims. This kind of epic resembled the first epics in one important respect: it too was chivalry at a distance, in space rather than time.

——SEVEN——

Positive Evaluations

Alonso de Ercilla y Zuñiga
and Luís Vaz de Camões

THE POETS WHO DEFENDED THE GUN OR AT LEAST TRIED TO
find room for it dealt with the same issues as those who adopted
the negative critique. They had to understand the use of guns within the
medieval military code, so they too raised the question of fraud. The
conclusion they reached, however, was very different. Where the majority
saw the ruin of heroism, these poets celebrated achievements they
claimed surpassed those of antiquity or any other period.

The poets who defended and even celebrated modern firepower fall
into two categories. The first is the Spanish poets who wrote of the battle
at Lepanto (7 October 1571) and who limit the gun's role in their work to
decoration. They assume—plausibly enough for a battle that marked the
climax and end of a long tradition of naval war—that firepower did not
essentially change the nature of battle. Therefore, they did not need to
raise the difficult moral questions that troubled Ariosto or Milton.[1] The
poets involved are three: Juan Latino, Hieronymo Corte Real, and Juan
Rufo. Latino, a high-school teacher of black African descent in Granada,
was the first to publish. He composed a brief epic in Latin that came out
in 1573 with the title *Austriadis libri duo.* Five years later the Portuguese
Corte Real published *Felicissima victoria,* a fifteen-book epic written in
Spanish and covering the Cypriot War through the battle of Lepanto.
Finally, Rufo of Cordoba released the *Austriada* in 1582, though he
claimed to have composed it a decade earlier.[2] His epic was a military
biography of Don Juan of Austria and covered both the Morisco Revolt
and Lepanto.

The second category concerns the poets of colonial enterprise, especially Ercilla in his *Araucana* and Camões in *Os Lusiadas.* Both men es-

poused the modernist position, facing the moral issue and its corollary: the fraud that subverts chivalry. Their resolution of this difficult question established some of the basic assumptions that determined later imperialist literature.

LEPANTO

All the poets who wrote of modern warfare used the gun decoratively, not just those who narrated Lepanto. A cannonade, especially, provided an occasion for sublimity or for elaborate pictorial effects. For example, Camões's most celebrated commentator, Manuel de Faria e Sousa, praised the poet's description of the bombardment of Mozambique:

> Eis nos batéis o fogo se levanta
> Na furiosa e dura artilharia;
> A plúmbea péla mata; o brado espanta;
> Ferido, o ar retumba e assovia.
> (*Lusiadas*, 1.89)

Behold, the fire raises itself in the boats in a furious and hard artillery. The leaden ball kills; the roar terrifies; the air, struck, echoes and hisses.

Faria e Sousa said that Camões described the salvo as if he had seen and heard it, and he especially praised the fourth line of the stanza for its use of onomatopoeia and gradation: the strike, the sound, then the echoing air.[3] The Portuguese poet in this brief passage certainly maintained the compression useful for the sublime.[4] Ercilla, in contrast, opted for an elaborate picture, modeling a description on the passage in the *Aeneid*, where Allecto, blowing a rustic horn, summons the Latins to battle (7.511–21). In the *Araucana* (2.16.36–38, p. 271) the Spaniards decide to test their artillery, while winter weather confines them to Quiriquina Island by Concepción. At the salvo the sea and ground tremble; the alpacas, vicuñas, tigers, and lions run about terrified; dolphins, Nereids, and Tritons hide in their deep sea caverns; rivers and fountains, confused, hold back their currents; and some Indians, awestruck, bow necks never bent before. Guns by their sound, fire, and smoke naturally fit an epic style and helped raise the narrative above the ordinary. What distinguished the Spanish Lepanto poets, however, was the central importance they gave to such aural and visual effects.

Most often the poets compared a cannonade to a storm. Latino uses this comparison three times in his *Austriadis libri duo*. One example will suffice: "Imbrem de coelo spissam cecidisse putares" (2.23r; "You would

Figure 19. Lepanto, battle of the flagships. Photograph: Roger-Viollet, Paris. Engraving in the Bibliothèque Nationale, Paris.

think a dense rainstorm to have fallen from heaven"). He reserves his most elaborate comparison for the initial barrage (*Austriadis libri duo,* 2.20v). Rufo likewise compares the barrage to a storm, both implicitly and then by simile (*Austriada,* 23.23, p. 126A), but a later passage in Rufo reveals the modernist point hidden in this group of metaphors and similes.[5] Rufo is describing the last salvo in the duel of the two royal galleys (fig. 19):

> ¿Quién hay entre los hombres que posea
> Animo tan feroz y escandaloso,
> Que al son terrible de un corrusco trueno
> Se halle de temor libre y ajeno,
>
> Con ser verdad que el rayo acelerado,
> Rompiendo por lo flaco de la nube,
> Las mas veces por alto levantado
> A buscar su elemento proprio sube;
> Y si alguno á bajar precipitado
> Hay que violentamente desennube,
> No puede á todo el mundo hacer guerra,
> Siendo tan ancho el globo de la tierra?

Pues: qué haria donde cada instante
Mil y mil rayos contra cada uno
Volaban con estruendo resonante
Sin podelles dejar reparo alguno?
Ya el sol se les quitaba de delante,
Ya arder se via el reino de Neptuno,
Y ya del ejercicio violento
Andaban todos casi sin aliento.
(*Austriada*, 24.8–10, p. 131A)

Who is there among men who has a mind so fierce and boisterous that at the terrible sound of a flashing thunderbolt feels free and detached from fear?

As a lightning bolt, breaking through the side of a cloud, most often climbs to seek its own element in the raised height, and if there is one, flung down, that violently unclouds itself, it cannot make war on the whole world, the globe of the earth being so broad, can it?

Then what will it be where each instant a thousand and a thousand rays against each one fly with resounding roar, without any defense being possible? Already the sun left them in front; already one sees the kingdom of Neptune burn; and already all went as if breathless from the violent exercise.

Earthly cannon outdoes heavenly thunder, and man by his own invention surpasses one of nature's most deadly weapons. Milton later attacked this modernist view, when he contrasted demonic artillery with the divine thunder, which chases the rebel angels to hell.[6] The modernist point stung the traditionalists, and it is most clearly seen in the battle of Lepanto. That event, which occasioned perhaps more poetry than any previous battle, also surpassed all earlier galley conflicts by the number of its guns and the intensity of its bombardment.

Guns were crucial at Lepanto and may have decided the outcome of the battle. Italian eyewitnesses support such an interpretation; they emphasize the initial barrage and the clash of the *reales*. In his letter to Sermoneta written just after the battle (9 October 1571), Onorato Caetani, a papal commander, says that the Turks shot from too far away and hit no one, while the Christians waited till the last minute and so inflicted the greatest damage on the enemy. The firepower of the galleasses at the center, moreover, sank three galleys immediately and forced the Turks out of formation.[7] Modern research indicates that the six galleasses may have actually sunk seventy enemy vessels.[8] The Venetian commander Sebastiano Veniero, argued that guns enabled Don Juan to win the battle of the *reales*.[9] The Christians, in fact, though outnumbered in ships, had an overwhelming superiority in firepower: 1,815 guns to 750 for the Turks. The Ottomans, moreover, did not have guns of the same quality. The Venetians captured 225 bronze cannon, which they later had melted down and remade because the metal was of such poor quality.[10] Venetians and scholars who study Venice tend to emphasize the technology of the battle, while the Spanish view emphasizes the quality of the soldiers who captured the enemy ships.[11]

The Iberian poets who celebrated Lepanto naturally tended to focus on the boarding of ships, but they by no means ignored the gun. Rufo more or less repeats Caetani's analysis of the initial barrage (*Austriada*, 23.29–31, p. 126A–B), adding further points. The Turks were intent on boarding and not on shooting, and the Christian galleys had lower prows, which made their gunnery more accurate (each galley carried a long gun in its prow). Rufo, indeed, never lets his audience forget the guns, and the repeated descriptions and references emphasize their importance. Other poets hint at the same point in a grander though less precise fashion, using apocalyptic rhetoric. For example, Ercilla twice compares the battle to the Last Day (*Araucana*, 2.24.52, 64, pp. 398, 400), and the initial volley seems to shake the world.[12] There is the smoke, fire, and noise, all the cries, and the smashing together of the prows as the galleys collide. It seems that the sea burns, the land collapses, and the heaven falls (*Araucana*, 2.24.40–42, pp. 395–96).

No other poet goes so far as Corte Real in pointing up the importance of guns. In his narrative missiles account for most of the casualties. Cannon fire sinks and cripples enemy ships as well as men.[13] Turkish harquebus balls kill or wound a whole series of prominent individuals, whom the poet names.[14] Although Corte Real mentions swordplay when he can, in his narrative it is missiles that decide the outcome at Lepanto. It is not surprising that Corte Real should give more attention to firepower than the other Iberian poets. Though he wrote in Spanish, Corte Real was Portuguese and published the *Felicissima victoria* in Lisbon. Portugal perhaps more than any other nation had pioneered the use of the gun at sea. Moreover, Corte Real composed his poem under the influence of Camões, whose *Lusiadas* had come out six years earlier.[15] Yet Corte Real draws no conclusions from his data and never states openly that firepower was decisive at Lepanto. He also does not develop the comparison to Actium the way the other poets do to emphasize the newness of Lepanto and its importance.[16]

The writers on Lepanto were almost forced to compare it to Actium, the greatest sea battle of antiquity, for the two conflicts took place in almost the same location.[17] Such a comparison invited a development of the modernist position, and writers in both prose and in poetry worked it out. The Venetian Tiziano Vecelli, for example, argued that cannon made Lepanto superior to Actium.[18] Among the poets Rufo comes closest to the full modernist position. He makes a triple argument (*Austriada*, 23.1–5, p. 125A) concerning why the past has no record of a similar conflict. First, the practice of the art of naval warfare in antiquity had not advanced so far.[19] Second, the defensive equipment with modern steel surpassed earlier technology. Third, and most important, the moderns had gunpowder, an argument that Rufo amplifies. He later correctly guesses that Lepanto will live in fame even without the poets (*Austriada*, 24.2–4, p. 130B), and in the argument to canto 24 he calls it the greatest naval action ever. Yet he ignores the implications of his argument and denounces cannon in another section of his epic (*Austriada*, 24.15–18, p. 131A–B), repeating the standard points made by the majority of writers and poets, who saw in firepower the ruin of the old military ethos (see discussion in chapter 6). Such ambivalence was common, though not universal (Corte Real, for example, nowhere denounces the gun). Ariosto also bemoaned guns and yet praised the Este cannon, and Blaise de Monluc could command harquebusiers and still condemn the weapon.[20] Such a position did not necessarily involve a contradiction. Rufo and Ariosto do not like guns but insist, nevertheless, that their states have the best and most advanced types. This ambivalence does, however, soften the poet's praise of Lepanto and blunt the modernist point.

The Lepanto poets did not need to consider the implications of the gun because the ramming and boarding among the galleys maintained continuity with traditional Mediterranean warfare.[21] Since boarding still involved swordplay, cannon and harquebuses made wonderful decoration without raising the ethical issues other poets had to consider. Alone among the Lepanto poets Ercilla analyzed the charge of fraud, which others like Ariosto commonly brought against the use of firearms. He did not use the case of Lepanto, however, but rather the example of a land battle, the Araucanian attack on Cañete, a fort in Chile. I reserve for chapter 10 my discussion of the actual battle with its shooting, since the slaughter there raised yet another moral question, that of the limits of violence in the conduct of war. Here I concentrate on Ercilla's presentation of fraud, which he detaches from the issue of technology.

CAÑETE

In cantos 30 and 31 of the *Araucana* Ercilla uses the opposed characters of Andresillo, a *yanacona* (Indian in the Spanish service), and Pran, an Araucanian spy, to present a drama of fraud that implicates both sides in the war. Ariosto anticipated this drama when he had Olimpia respond with deceit to the fraud she perceived in Cimosco's harquebus. She goes through a marriage ceremony with the son of her enemy, only to have him murdered in the bedroom. She stations a man behind a curtain, who strikes the youth over the head with a hatchet. Olimpia herself then jumps up and cuts his throat (*OF* 9.41–43). She thus fights fraud with fraud, just as Andresillo does when confronted by Pran.

Ercilla had Ariosto's story in mind when he composed his narrative of Cañete. On that occasion, he was in Cañete for only one full day. The battle took place on 5 February 1558. Ercilla arrived the day before, one of thirty cavalrymen rushed north, and left with his comrades the day after.[22] The story of intrigue he recounts is one he heard from members of the garrison (*Araucana,* 3.30.34, p. 492), yet his version differs from others'. For example, there is the question of the name of the *yanacona* who arranged the deception for the Spaniards. Gerónimo de Bibar, who wrote the earliest chronicle, leaves him unnamed; Ercilla calls him Andresillo (another chronicler, Captain Alonso de Góngora Marmolejo, gives the name Andrescio). But the later writers, Pedro Mariño de Lovera and Suarez de Figueroa, who follow the report of the garrison commander, Alonso de Reinoso, call the *yanacona* Baltazar.[23] Historically, a *yanacona* did help the garrison at Cañete, but which *yanacona* or what name he bore remains in doubt. This is not the only or the most important detail that distinguishes Ercilla's version.

All the others limit the fraud to the Spanish side, in particular to the *yanacona* who suggests the Indian plan of attack. Only the degree of his collusion with the local commander, Reinoso, is open to question. In Bibar's chronicle the *yanacona* alone sets the tactics. He had fled the fort and was captured by the enemy. Thinking quickly, he offered to betray Cañete to the Indian leader, here named Teopolican, and so escaped death. He received a reward instead and was allowed to return to the fort, where he informed Reinoso of what he had arranged.[24] Marmolejo credits Reinoso with the tactics instead. The commander draws the Indians into what he knows is a feigned peace, and then the *yanacona* sounds out one of the Indians and sets up a meeting for the following day. Reinoso tells the *yanacona* what to say and outlines the plan of attack the Indians should follow.[25] In between but closer to Marmolejo are Lovera and Figueroa.[26] None of these historians credits the Indians with the tactics of their attack or implicates them in fraud.

Their version would fit the model Ariosto established in his story of Olimpia. There the gun illustrates a pattern of fraud that characterizes Cimosco and his Frisians, who have invaded the province of Holland and offer the occasion for the poet's diatribe against firearms. Similarly here, the Spanish invader has the guns and sets up the elaborate deception that destroys the native opposition. Ercilla himself includes a severe denunciation of the *yanacona* at the beginning of canto 31, so he could have made his account follow much more closely that of Olimpia in the *Furioso*. Instead he develops a different narrative and denounces not the gun but fraud, which he finds and criticizes on both sides.

This insistence on mutual guilt produces a curious redundancy in Ercilla's narrative, as one character after another repeats and amplifies the same plan of attack. In the first place an unnamed spy gives the Indian leader Caupolicán the information that leads him initially to suggest the surprise attack during siesta.[27] He then coaches an intermediary, Pran, whom Ercilla describes as subtle, false, and malicious (*Araucana*, 3.30.43, p. 494). Pran repeats this tactical plan to the *yanacona* Andresillo (*Araucana*, 3.30.54–55, p. 496). Next Caupolicán himself outlines it to Andresillo (*Araucana*, 3.31.13, p. 502), who in this version merely urges its immediate implementation and sets the time for the following day (3.31.24, 26, p. 504). He cleverly advises what the enemy already intends.[28] Ercilla has the Spaniards deceive a deceptive enemy, find out his plans, and destroy him.[29]

Even with this significant difference, one could argue that Ercilla outlines the same circle of fraud that Ariosto had for his story. In Ariosto's version chronology is essential and shows that in a conflict where only one side has firearms, the guns give it such an advantage that the opposition has no recourse but fraud. This was Olimpia's answer, and it became that of the Araucanians. They fought their last open battle at Millarapue. After this, the fourth major defeat in three months, they resort to ambush at Purén, and Caupolicán advises a scorched-earth policy (*Araucana*, 2.29.5–7, pp. 470–71), arguing that they should burn their houses, clothing, and furniture. When honor no longer pertains to a place, he says, it is not good to have one. Soldiers should worry only about vengeance, while property would make them lukewarm. Soldiers must concentrate on taking honor, property, and life from the enemy: it is kill or be killed. He follows this speech with the sneak attack on Cañete and then has to hide in the woods, his army temporarily dispersed. Tactical inequality forces the Indians to guerrilla tactics, and their new methods in turn suggest fraud to the Spaniards, who use it at Cañete and later habitually.[30]

Ercilla, however, will have none of this. He condemns fraud on both sides. His Indian heroes do not take part in the assault on Cañete, since they consider fraud vile and cowardly and see such a victory as being without praise or glory (*Araucana*, 3.32.21–22, pp. 515–16).[31] We have already seen that the poet especially objects to the actions of the *yanacona*, Andresillo, for the Spaniards. Despite the gun Ercilla insists that neither Spaniard nor Indian use fraud. He does not allow that Spanish guns might justify fraud on the other side. He does not, in fact, see in firearms a subversion of the old military code but instead maintains that ethic in all its force.

Ercilla can do so because neither he nor his Indians connect the gun to fraud. Ercilla denounces fraud only here,[32] yet the Spaniards used guns in all their battles. General Mendoza filled a galleon with supplies, artillery, and ammunition, enough to supply the war needs of Chile for thirty years after Cañete.[33] Firepower was essential to many or all of his victories that Ercilla recounts: Penco (1557) in all versions and, as I show elsewhere, Purén (1558) and Cañete (1558).[34] Since there is no innate connection between firearms and fraud, Ercilla cannot allow fraud to the opposition. The poet has all the items of Ariosto's story, but he keeps them separate. Where Ariosto dramatized a threat to the chivalric code, Ercilla uses the same kind of story to reinforce the code. He insists that it applies both to those with and to those without guns. Ariosto's warning that firepower would subvert chivalry was not fulfilled. This is true both for Ercilla, who saw military action in Spanish America a generation later, and also for Camões, who served in the Portuguese colonies at the same time. Camões, in fact, revived the whole medieval set of oppositions between the chivalric hero and the practitioner of fraud, between Roland and Ganelon—only this time the hero carried a gun.

MOZAMBIQUE

Camões's episode takes place in southeast Africa (*Lusiadas*, 1.86–93). The sheik of the island city of Mozambique has arranged an ambush for the Portuguese (fig. 20). He knows that they need water, so he stations his men by the only springs in the area. The men are armed with shields, assegais, and poisoned arrows.[35] He keeps a small band visible to provoke the sailors and lure them into the ambush. For his part the Portuguese

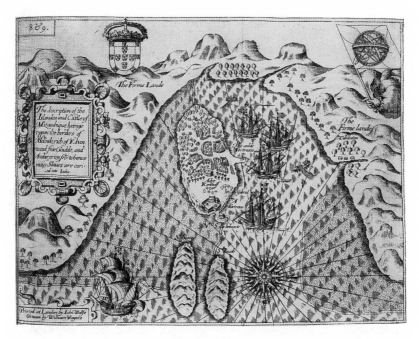

Figure 20. Rogers, map of Mozambique (the springs are by Calxiceira on the mainland at the right). Reprinted from Linschoten, *Discourse of Voyages*. Photograph courtesy the Newberry Library.

leader Vasco da Gama is suspicious and sends his men armed in three boats that carry bombards. The challenge works. The Portuguese rush onto land and simultaneously open fire.[36] At the great noise the "Moors" lose courage. Those in front die, those in ambush flee. The Portuguese now bombard the town, which lacks walls or any kind of defense. Some of the Moors curse amid the flames of the burning village, while others flee. In fury they shoot arrows and throw rocks and wood at their pursuers, but their terror makes this effort ineffectual. The Moors crowd into *almadias* (narrow boats like canoes that can carry sails) or try to swim across the narrow channel to the mainland, but the Portuguese bombardment blows up some of the boats, and some of the swimmers drown.[37] Rich with spoil, the victors can now draw water at leisure, and the defeated sheik must sue for peace.

In these few stanzas Camões presents the essentials of imperialist narrative and fiction. A few Europeans clash with men who speak a strange language and practice a different religion—in this case Islam—and whom the Portuguese, therefore, call Moors. The few Europeans easily

defeat a force much superior in numbers. Ariosto, talking of the Spaniards overseas, catches the scene with a biblical phrase: and ten shall chase
a thousand (*OF* 15.23). For the Spaniards it suffices to recall Cajamarca,
that first battle between the Incas and Pizarro's band of 150 men. At a
trumpet signal the Spaniards charged and fired point-blank at a crowd of
five or six thousand Indians. In the ensuing slaughter each Spaniard averaged fourteen or fifteen kills, and the main army of eighty thousand Indians fled as the Spanish soldiers approached.[38] Such victories are fantastic
and become comprehensible only after we remember the technological
superiority of the Europeans. Camões carefully indicates this technological advantage. For example, the people of Mozambique are said to wear
no armor, though they carry shields. Their cotton clothes (*Lusiadas*, 1.47)
would not stop a spear, much less a cannonball. On the other hand, the
sheik had asked to see Portuguese weaponry the day before (*Lusiadas*,
1.67–68), and they had shown him everything.[39] Da Gama, however, did
not demonstrate the firearms, so the Moor did not know what to expect
on the following day. The surprise was as complete as that which the
Incas experienced at Cajamarca, and the actual destruction was extensive:
many dead, the straw houses of the town on fire, and boats smashed.[40]

The incident, however, did not really happen that way. It was messier,
more protracted, and far less stunning. It is exemplary for the literature
of conquest because Camões made it so.

First of all, the poet reduced four military incidents to one, itself a
mixture of two of the four. Fernão Lopes de Castanheda and João de
Barros, his sources, narrate these two clashes as follows.[41] Having failed
to find water the previous night, late in the afternoon da Gama sends out
armed boats with a Moorish pilot. This time the pilot finds the springs,
but they are defended by twenty Moors armed with assegais. Da Gama
orders three bombards to shoot. The Moors, amazed and frightened by
the noise, flee into the bushes. The Portuguese now land and collect as
much water as they want. This incident provokes the second, for the
Moors now challenge the Portuguese, and da Gama and his captains decide to bombard the town.[42] They set off again in longboats with armed
companies, and bombards in the prows. The Moors have hastily erected
a palisade that conceals 2,000 men, and they leave 100 in front to guard
the beach.[43] There is a parley first, in which the Moors call the Portuguese
pirates. Talk fails, and the Moors start the fight. The 100 advance closer,
knowing little about guns. Bombard fire quickly drives them behind the
palisade and then flattens the palisade itself. The Portuguese continue the

barrage for three hours, while the Moors flee to town and leave two men dead on the field. The sailors now return to the ships for their noon meal, but they sail out afterward to take hostages. They find the Moors in boats, fleeing to the mainland, and overtake two. In one the Moors escape but leave some of the sheik's belongings. The other boat gives da Gama the hostages he wants, especially an old man who knows about the trading system. The sheik negotiates, however, only after the town suffers a second barrage.

Camões has reduced a military confrontation that extended over several days to one. He has also combined two places, for the island of Mozambique lacks water, and the springs are on the mainland. Castanheda is clear on this fact, and Camões probably knew Mozambique firsthand.[44] Condensation of this kind marks his treatment of the whole episode, not just of the military encounter. The many meetings between the Moors and the Portuguese become two, and Camões reduces the various pilots involved to one. Da Gama had hired two for the India voyage, but one had run away, and his attempt to get another helped provoke the armed clashes. Camões keeps the problem of the pilot but detaches it from the military encounter. Finally, he abbreviates the events that helped the Moors discover the religious identity of their visitors. They at first thought the well-armed strangers must be Turks and only gradually found out that they were Christians, their traditional enemy. Camões has da Gama explain his faith immediately, when he meets the sheik. Condensation marks every aspect of the epic version.

This abridgment serves to exalt the picture of Portuguese power. Since they were a few explorers in East Africa, da Gama and his sailors had tried to avoid clashes with the local powers. Camões eliminates all this. The Portuguese do not attempt first to get water during the night, as they did in fact, nor do they sail earlier to the islet of São Jorge, out of fear of the Muslims.[45] Moreover, the poet ignores the fact that the Portuguese were too few to risk a landing at the town.[46] There was no ruined town, no smashed boats. Victory depended on the psychological effect of the bombards rather than on gunfire accurate enough to sink canoes. It was the noise that scared the guards away from the springs, and the three-hour barrage, though it put the Moors to flight, killed only two of them.[47] Finally, the Portuguese of the epic show no fear, go directly into action, are good marksmen, and win a complete military victory.

Camões could justify these changes. *Os Lusiadas* celebrates not only da Gama but the whole Portuguese imperial adventure. The incident at

Mozambique, as the only military clash da Gama experienced on the way out, must stand for the typical kind of action that gave the Portuguese their power in the Indian Ocean.

The gun won many of their battles, and Camões shows how da Gama learns its importance. He had not demonstrated its capability to the sheik of Mozambique, but the military clash taught him better. Afterward, he regularly shows the gun to the natives. At Malindi, for example, the Portuguese close the first interview with music and a cannon salvo, and next day they greet the approach of the king with more cannon shot (*Lusiadas,* 2.92–100). Such scenes correspond to regular Portuguese practice.[48] Demonstrations of power forestall any hostile action. The incident at Mozambique justifies this bravado and shows its necessity.

Camões further restructures the military action to make it exemplary. Victory on land depends upon an infantry rush, a tactic the Portuguese continued to use as late as the eighteenth century. Naval fire wins and controls port cities. In the prophetic vision of book 10 Camões alludes to Alonso de Albuquerque's capture of Ormuz, Goa, and Malacca (*Lusiadas,* 10.40, 42, 44), three of the principal Portuguese bases in the East.[49] Finally, the smashed boats indicate the new naval warfare the Portuguese brought to the Indian Ocean and to the world. On his next voyage east da Gama defeated a large Muslim fleet off the Malabar coast (1502) by sailing "one astern of the other in a line" and keeping up a rapid artillery fire. King Manuel had already recommended these tactics to Pedro Alvares Cabral when he led the second Indies fleet out, saying that if the fleet met Muslim ships, "you are not to come to close quarters with them if you can avoid it, but you are to compel them with your artillery alone to strike sail, [so that] this war may be waged with greater safety, and . . . less loss may result to the people of your ships."[50] Camões himself refers to the more spectacular naval victory that Francisco de Almeida won in 1509 off Diu, over Emir Husein and a mixed Muslim fleet (*Lusiadas,* 2.50, 10.35–36). The Portuguese used cannon fire to sink the ships that came from Calicut. In that sector of the battle there was none of the traditional ramming and boarding.[51] More recently (1565) a single carrack with eighty sailors had defeated a Japanese flotilla, the guns causing 200 casualties.[52] All the unhistorical details in the original incident at Mozambique are there to indicate a later historical reality: the characteristic methods the Portuguese used in the East.

The apologist for the Portuguese Empire had to praise the gun, and he had also, therefore, to confront the charge of fraud. In this instance, fraud is the more striking because it is unnecessary. In this case Camões does not distort his sources to intimate truth, he changes them. The two incidents he used consisted in straightforward confrontations. The defenders at the springs openly defied the Portuguese, and the people of the town sent a challenge. They used the palisade as a defense against firearms. When he combines the two episodes, however, Camões introduces the notion of fraud. The soldiers behind the palisade become the ambush. This larger, concealed force makes the Portuguese infantry rush potentially dangerous, for they attack before they know the true situation. The poet himself raises the problem of fraud and blames not the gunner but his enemy.

One could, nevertheless, argue that fraud here represents the inevitable response of the weak to superior military force. The sheik has already seen the conventional armor and weapons the Portuguese brought with them to the East and that night plans the ambush. He never considers a straightforward confrontation.[53] He errs only in miscalculating the great advantage firepower gives the Portuguese, and after his defeat he resorts again to fraud. He sends da Gama a pilot whom he has instructed to lead the Portuguese to a more powerful Muslim city up the coast, where they can be captured or destroyed (*Lusiadas*, 1.8, 83, 93–94). Yet this argument works no better with Camões than it did with Ercilla.

Like the Spanish poet Camões carefully detaches fraud from the technology of war. The sheik of Mozambique has a hatred of Christians fixed in his soul, and once he finds out that the Portuguese are Christians, he wishes them evil, even before he forms any plans (*Lusiadas*, 1.69–71).[54] Muslim hatred indeed dogs the Portuguese everywhere on the littoral of the Indian Ocean, and it invariably expresses itself through fraud. The incident at Mozambique provokes another at Mombasa.[55] The Muslims there wish to avenge the defeat of their fellows at Mozambique. The pilot provided to da Gama by the sheik of Mozambique says falsely that the town contains a mixed population of Christians and Muslims. The Moors then welcome da Gama, intending to attack his ships in the harbor. They tie their boats to his, some climb on board, and all are proceeding toward the harbor entrance when Venus, the protectress of the Portuguese, stops da Gama's ship. The pilot and the Moors on board assume that da Gama has discovered the plot and jump off. The wary da Gama stays outside the harbor and leaves the area during the night, interrupting other Moors, who are sawing off his cables (*Lusiadas*, 2.64–66). Next, it is the Catual in Calicut who accepts bribes from the Muslim community and tries to delay the Portuguese there until the arrival of the Muslim fleet (*Lusiadas*, 8.76–77).

This enmity has global dimensions, partially through Islam itself. The Moor who first greets the Portuguese at Mozambique tacitly assumes that the Muslims rule the world, and after this meeting the Portuguese themselves wonder at the vast extent of the enemy religion, now found in another hemisphere.[56] Malice and fraud, however, mark more than Muslims. Whenever they visit a port, the Portuguese risk ambush or encounter fraud. It begins at Saint Helen's Bay, on the Atlantic coast of southern Africa, where the Africans of the area draw the Portuguese scout Veloso inland. They would have detained him beyond a peak, just out of sight, intending to force a rescue party and ambush it (*Lusiadas*, 5.31–36). He runs instead, and they pursue him with stones and arrows until the Portuguese come up. Camões expresses this malice mythologically through the figure of Bacchus.

The wine god sets up every Muslim act of fraud and does so by a means familiar in such stories: he deceives the deceivers. To the sheik of Mozambique he seems an old and trusted friend (*Lusiadas*, 1.77–81); to the Portuguese embassy at Mombasa, a Christian priest (2.10–13); and to a Muslim zealot at Calicut, Mohammed himself in a dream (8.47–50). In a rejected stanza the god himself expresses the logic behind such acts, addressing the sheik of Mozambique: "Que he bem olhado / Que quem quer enganar fique enganado" ("For I well believe that he who seeks to deceive should be deceived").[57] This, of course, is the pattern of Milton's Satan, who deceives his subordinates and both wins and tries to maintain his rule of the earth by fraud. It is not surprising, therefore, that Camões's commentator, Faria e Sousa, equates Bacchus with the devil.[58] Camões himself says that Christianity everywhere must face fraud (*Lusiadas*, 1.71), and so gives a theological solution to this ethical question.

The poets of classicizing epic normally allow the opposition a voice, even if demonic. Dido and Turnus in Virgil, Satan in Milton, all express their views, and so does Bacchus in Camões. He argues Ariosto's logic and charges that the gun-carrying Portuguese are deceivers. He tells the sheik of Mozambique that the Portuguese loot port cities under the pretence of trade and commit robbery on the high seas (*Lusiadas*, 1.78–79). They deceive others and do not live by civilized standards. They deserve fraudulent treatment. This argument has a basis in fact. Barros records this charge, and it was made at Mozambique.[59] The Samorin at Calicut gives the charge legal precision: the Portuguese are vagabonds and may be pirates (*Lusiadas*, 8.61, 63).[60]

The term *pirate* has a legal meaning common in all Western European languages. Camões has Bacchus give the modern dictionary definition in his speech to the sheik of Mozambique, when he uses four different forms of *roubar,* "to rob," within two stanzas (*Lusiadas,* 1.78–79).[61] A pirate is the naval equivalent of a highway robber, the kind whom Stevenson made famous for English-speaking readers when he created Captain Flint and Long John Silver for *Treasure Island.* Such a person preys on commercial shipping for private gain. In the sixteenth century Fernández Duro compared pirates to frigate birds, predators that lack the skill to fish for themselves and steal from the pelican.[62]

Even in antiquity, the term had Satanic overtones. The pirate is the enemy of the human race, or as Defoe says, "The pirate destroys all government and all order, by breaking all those ties and bonds that unite people in a civil society under any government."[63] English novelists like Stevenson and Conrad[64] have accordingly made pirates moral degenerates—a characterization, however, that would not fit da Gama, either in history or in Camões's epic. The contrast is striking. In the nineteenth-century novel the English judge their own as pirates and enemies of the human race, but within the *Lusiadas* it is the enemies of the Portuguese who make the charges: Bacchus and the Samorin. Their complaints indicate problems in the legal definition and usage of the term *pirate.*

Anne Pérotin-Duman sets out these problems succinctly. Piracy, though usually committed in international waters, was always tried locally, by national laws. The sea, however, lies *in between* nations, while judicial institutions belong to land communities.[65] Since land powers enforce the laws on piracy, the sense of their application in da Gama's case could well differ depending on whether one invoked the laws of Portugal or those in force at Mozambique or Calicut. Camões, of course, would understand the charge of piracy as a Portuguese. Da Gama, though he might fight against the merchants of other nations in the Indian Ocean, is not a pirate, since he does not attack his own nationals.

In such cases modern scholars often prefer to use the term *privateer.* These had a military function in the Renaissance roughly equivalent to that of the submarine in the two world wars of the twentieth century. Privateers wish to wreck enemy supply lines and have produced similar results in both eras. English and French privateers forced the Spaniards to adopt a convoy system between Seville and America, as the German U-boats did the English and Americans in the twentieth century.[66] Da Gama's destruction of a pilgrim ship during his second voyage gives a concrete instance. In Gaspar Correa's narrative da Gama first allows his men to pillage a large and rich ship, sailing from Mecca to Calicut, and then orders them to burn it. The ship's captain, instead, offers a boatload of pepper and drugs for ransom, an offer that has support from da Gama's own captains. He reminds them that they are in a state of war with Calicut and that the owner of the vessel had counseled the Samorin to kill and plunder the Portuguese there. The fleet eventually sinks the ship by gunfire.[67] As long as Calicut maintains hostilities, the Portuguese will destroy its shipping.

The distinction between privateer and pirate, though clear enough logically, unfortunately does not work very well practically. The English captain Richard Hawkins, captured by the Spaniards when out on a raid, puts the issue clearly. He complains that the Spaniards considered all English raiders corsairs (that is, pirates), despite the fact that a state of war existed between the two nations and that the English sailed with the implicit permission of their own government. The Spaniards did so because no one could arm a ship without a royal permit in their own system, and none had been given to the English. Basically, both the Spaniards and the Portuguese claimed monopolies on trade in their zones, monopolies that other powers never recognized. As a result, the Iberians considered anyone who violated their monopoly a pirate, whether the English, in the view of the Spaniards, or the people of Malabar, in the view of the Portuguese.[68]

Still more confusing is the gray area between the pirate and the privateer, especially when two powers maintain hostile stances toward each other over a long period. Peace treaties and truces never covered such activity. Philip's truce with the Ottomans (1578) did not stop the Barbary pirates, though they acknowledged the sultan as their overlord, and similar peace arrangements with England and Holland did not end piracy abroad in the early seventeenth century. Camões presumes such a situation between Christian and Muslim. Hostility always exists, and da Gama, immediately after sacking Mozambique, captures a Muslim ship and runs another aground, while sailing between Mombasa and Malindi (*Lusiadas*, 2.68–69). Camões makes no comment on these actions, and they fit Portuguese activity generally. The first notice of them in the chronicles of Hadramut in southern Arabia refers to seven vessels captured by the Portuguese and ends with a curse on the Westerners.[69] The hostility was mutual, as Camões assumed when he developed his theological explanation for these situations. By such logic the Portuguese would judge da Gama's violent acts heroic, and their enemies would consider them piratical.[70] Camões then allows Bacchus and the Samorin to say what they would have said *in any case,* and at the same time refutes the charge by representing da Gama as an epic hero.

The legal sense of the term *pirate* also misses the goal of such maritime violence. Da Gama does not commit these acts solely for private gain but as part of a state policy. Fernand Braudel formulated the principle behind such "piracy," in the context of the Mediterranean. It arises when two competing merchant states clash, the one forming and expanding, the other losing momentum and influence.[71] For example, when the English and the Dutch came to the Mediterranean (1575–80), being Protestants, they attacked Muslim and Catholic alike. Although they might trade with Venetians or Turks, they would also attack their shipping on the high seas.[72] Such ruthless methods helped them take over Mediterranean trade and supplant the Venetians in the East. We might say that this model applies best to da Gama and the Portuguese. They came seeking trade but acted like pirates against their competitors, the Arab Muslims of the Indian Ocean.

The Portuguese did even more. They came east to supplant an older trading system with their own. Instead of the Arabs, they themselves would become the universal middlemen of the Indian Ocean.[73] As a result, a state of war existed constantly between the rival traders, and Muslim attacks never stopped during the sixteenth century.[74] But the Portuguese also introduced a new kind of system to the Indian Ocean. Instead of merely trading in foreign ports, as the Arabs had done, the Portuguese established their own bases, factories, supply stations, and forts.[75] They created a maritime empire.

They had for models the systems constructed by the Venetians and Genoese in the Levant during the later Middle Ages, but they went far beyond anything envisaged by their Italian predecessors.[76] The Venetians and the Genoese maintained colonies in neighboring waters, never far away by oar or sail. The Portuguese, in contrast, set up an empire far away from their home both in space and in time. Da Gama had been out seven months before he reached Mozambique and had sailed into another ocean.[77] This system, the prototype for the later Dutch and British empires, had no precedent in previous history, and its very existence justified the modernist position.

Bacchus gives the negative version of this claim. Envy drives him on,[78] for he realizes that the Portuguese will eclipse his deeds and those of Alexander in India and Trajan in the Middle East (*Lusiadas,* 1.30–32, 1.74–76, 6.7, 6.27–34).[79] In this argument Camões merely elaborates on his source material, for Castanheda claimed in his prologue that the conquest of the Indies surpassed all previous acts. The historian too cited as an example Alexander, who had a weaker enemy and easier access to the land, not a sea journey of twenty months.[80] Of course, neither the poet nor the historian could claim that the Portuguese conquered more territory than Alexander. Instead they dwelled on the unique character of the Portuguese accomplishment and its difficulty, the effort to establish and maintain an empire that might as well have been on another planet. Camões hints at the grandeur of this new achievement in the cosmic vision that closes the epic. It begins with a compliment to the Spaniards, those other Iberians who had found a world in the West. The place is the Indian Ocean; the time is sunset, when Apollo drives his horses toward the lake that encircles Tenochtitlan (*Lusiadas,* 10.1). What follows includes both a sketch of the growth of the Portuguese Empire, a vision of its geographical area, and a vision of the cosmos itself. This is the appropriate context for da Gama's voyage.

Technology made the Portuguese achievement possible. Of the many inventions that humanists noted as unknown to the ancients, three stood out, two of which facilitated naval military action: the gun and the compass.[81] Without them the Portuguese could never have dreamed of the thalassacracy they established temporarily in the East.

Guns especially gave the Portuguese power, but in this respect the incident at Mozambique can be misleading. Guns were spreading rapidly around the Indian Ocean before the Portuguese came,[82] and India itself already had them.[83] The Portuguese did not normally fight unarmed merchants and natives, as happened at Mozambique, but rather enemies who used the same weapons they had. The Portuguese, however, had two advantages, which were decisive. First, the Indian vessels did not yet carry guns. Made with wooden nails, they could not bear heavy cannon or sustain a salvo.[84] Earlier in the century the Chinese had demonstrated the effectiveness of ships equipped with guns, when they anticipated the Portuguese achievement in reverse by sailing west to Africa and conquering Sri Lanka. To combat the Portuguese the Arab traders had to call in first the Mamluk and then the Ottoman navy. Second, the Portuguese had better guns. At the siege of Chaul (1571) their muskets carried a one-ounce shot with a range of 400 meters, while the Indians had but a half-ounce with a range of 200 meters.[85] Nor did the various native rulers of the subcontinent have cannon as good as the Portuguese. In 1525 the government of Portuguese India recommended that its people melt down captured enemy guns, so that they could cast better ones. As late as the eighteenth century they were still using some fifteenth-century-style cannon: large, clumsy guns made with iron strips.[86] The Portuguese won in the East because they had better guns, not because they faced opponents like those da Gama terrified at Mozambique or Cortez and Pizarro conquered in America.

Superior technology indicates superior knowledge, in ships as well as in firearms.[87] Camões conveys this point by abbreviation. All blundering and uncertainty are dropped. Ships do not run aground at the town, nor do they float backward on the Mozambique current, as happened in real life.[88] The Moors, not the Portuguese, suggest the need for pilots (*Lusiadas,* 1.55).[89] The sailors who, in Camões's expression, have run and navigated every part of the sea, in the north and under the Line, and rounded the whole African coast, do not ask directions (*Lusiadas,* 1.51). They have better ships and compasses than anything they will find in the Indian Ocean.

Technology likewise presupposes a superior material culture, and Camões accordingly alters his data. At their meeting he has da Gama give the sheik splendid gifts (*Lusiadas,* 1.61), though in fact the explorer had with him only trinkets for presents.[90] The real sheik despised the red hood and beads he received and asked instead for better cloth.[91]

As a logical corollary of this process, Camões lowers the material culture of the enemy, more by abbreviation and innuendo than by distortion. He describes, for example, the clothes of the common people (*Lusiadas,* 1.47) but not the splendid apparel of the sheik's party,[92] and in the battle the Portuguese are a noble race troubled by dogs (1.87).[93] Unlike later writers of imperialist narrative, Camões need not describe an alien magnificence. For wonder he has the gods and gives Neptune an underwater city more marvelous than those of India (*Lusiadas,* 6.8–25). In this respect, then, his approach differs fundamentally from that of nineteenth-century writers who romanticized the native. Camões takes two peoples, reasonably close to each other in some aspects of culture, and increases the distance between them. Technology and the military success it brings suggest that European culture must be superior in *all* things.[94]

This argument applies to time as well as to space and establishes the literary pretensions of the modernist poets. Rufo makes the more modest claim. For him, the truth of Lepanto equals the marvels of older fantasy (*Austriada,* 23.27–28, p. 126A): the wars of the gods and the giants, the enchanted lances and armor and diamond shields of the knights.[95] Camões puts the claim in a more extreme form. The Portuguese outdid the heroes of Italian epic, even if those fantasies had been historical (*Lusiadas,* 1.11–12). He reiterates the point with varying application throughout the epic.[96] Whatever their qualities as poets,[97] the moderns have the best topics, and they owe them to the new technology and mostly to the gun.

THE REVERSED MIRROR IMAGE

I have assumed throughout this discussion that those who attack the gun, like Ariosto and Milton, and those who defend it, like Ercilla and Camões, presuppose the same military code and, therefore, argue the same issue, that of fraud. They differ in their villains. For Ariosto and Milton the guilt of fraud applies to the gunner; for Camões, it fits the premodern soldier. The Portuguese poet similarly switches around the hero. Da Gama uses the gun, where Orlando fights against it. Camões thus reflects the other poets like a mirror, giving back a reversed image. This mirroring indicates the way an ethical code lags behind or resists technological change. Like other moral systems, chivalry posited a set of universal values, although based upon a certain stage of warfare. Changes in the military art at first provoked a reaffirmation of precepts held to be invariable. Camões can both praise the gun and support the same code as Ariosto. The Italian, however, has the advantage in this comparison because this shared system of values rested historically on the medieval world and not on the new technology. It remains to be seen how the modernists worked out their ethical position.

The naval poets, first of all, did not worry about fraud or guilt because both sides had guns, whether at Lepanto or in the clashes between the Spaniards and the English in the Atlantic and Pacific Oceans. At Lepanto the Christians had better guns, and the English used them more skillfully than the Spaniards, but the difference between the combatants was not sufficient to raise the issue of fraud. No technological gap existed of the sort that pitted Orlando with lance and sword against a harquebus or the inhabitants of Mozambique against Portuguese bombards. The issue Ariosto raised, therefore, had to be solved in the colonies, Portuguese or Spanish. How could the hero remain a hero and use a gun on those who lacked firearms altogether?

As we have seen, both Ercilla and Camões detach the charge of fraud from technology. Neither the Araucanians nor the sheik of Mozambique connects the gun to fraud or bases any complaints on the superior technology of the opponents, the way Olimpia and Orlando do in Ariosto. Yet by raising the issue of fraud the Iberian poets indicate their sense that fraud and technology somehow go together. They are uneasy in their ethical stances, and the best indication of this unease is how both poets double the charge of fraud. In the *Lusiadas* and the *Araucana* each side has reason to accuse the other of fraudulent activity. The Portuguese rightly suspect the Muslims of double dealing, while the Muslims claim the Portuguese are pirates masquerading as merchants. The Spaniards can say that the Araucanians, by switching to guerrilla tactics, have changed the rules of war, while the Araucanians rush into a trap set for them by Reinoso.

The two poets explain these repetitions differently, but they both incriminate the enemy in fraud, even though historical evidence indicates otherwise. The sheik did not use fraud at Mozambique, and no other source charges the Araucanians with fraud at Cañete. We must, therefore, infer that both poets *invent* fraud for the enemy, perhaps to spread around the guilt. This is a tactic they bequeathed to modern imperialist fiction, in which the natives regularly deceive their overlords.[98] Our poets, on the other hand, by their invention of enemy fraud tacitly admit that they cannot so easily work out a modernist position within the old medieval ethos. Only one factor, which I have not yet discussed, helped them: the odds in these battles.

Comparatively few Iberians went abroad. At the height of their power the Portuguese had only 10,000 men overseas. These had to control an empire that reached from the Brazilian coasts around Africa to India and Southeast Asia.[99] At Mozambique the Portuguese fought against odds, as did the Spaniards who campaigned in Chile and whose actions Ercilla narrates. Valdivia, who conquered Chile, died with a troop of 60 Spaniards and 2,000 allies fighting 20,000 Araucanians (*Araucana*, 1.3.17, 57–58, pp. 43, 51).[100] In the skirmish that followed 14 Spaniards defied 4,000 of the enemy (*Araucana*, 1.4 Arg., 51, pp. 59, 69). At Penco 130 faced 2,000 (*Araucana*, 2.17.19, 31, pp. 285, 287). The vast disproportion in numbers made the gunner heroic and blurred the technological gap. Like an Orlando, the colonial soldier fought against odds. He needed the gun to survive at all. Yet even here the old ethos had to undergo considerable reevaluation, in which the group replaced the individual hero.

——EIGHT——

The Heroic Few

Alonso de Ercilla y Zuñiga
and Gaspar Pérez de Villagrá

Halt sunt li pui e li val tenebrus,
Les roches bises, les destreiz merveíllus.

High are the mountains, and the valleys dark,
The rocks gray, and the narrows wondrous.
(*Chanson de Roland,* 66)

ONE SUMMER DAY IN 1558 A COMPANY OF SPANIARDS IN
Chile was bringing supplies north to the fort of Cañete from Imperial,
the modern Carahue in the province of Araucania. The poet Don Alonso
de Ercilla rode at the head of the column, and behind came a herd of
cattle plus packs and bags of food. As the party approached the coastal
range, they were joined by an eighty-man escort from Cañete. The Indians of the district ahead remained in rebellion, and the road passed
through the Cuesta de Purén, an oblique defile between the hills, two
leagues long (fig. 17). As they entered, two horsemen abreast filled the
road, which was made narrower by a stream.[1]

The Araucanian Indians had likewise made their preparations. They
had occupied a platform above the road, where they had rocks and missiles ready. When the whole column of Spaniards and cattle drivers was
inside the ravine and the vanguard neared the exit, the Indians attacked.
They shot arrows and stones from slings and hurled rocks, lances, and
darts. The missiles were so many and came so rapidly that Ercilla felt that
the hills themselves were breaking to pieces. The column stalled. The
Spaniards made a confused swirl as they took cover, some crawling on all
fours or dragging crippled limbs, behind a rock or into a hollow. Aiming
their harquebuses, they quickly shot many of the Indians, but the bodies,

rolling down with rocks, caused further confusion. In the rear the Indians were already sacking the baggage, attacking the guard and servants, and running off with the supplies.

The poet, seeing certain defeat for his party, took a chance. He rode his horse through the Indian blockade and came on ten soldiers hidden in a hollow beyond. He explained his plan, and the eleven rode their horses straight up a knifelike ridge to the top, covered with thick brambles and trees.[2] The ridge overlooked the platform where the Indians had their missiles and had been ignored by them, since it was too far for throwing rocks into the defile below. The climb had exhausted the horses, which stood panting, unable to move. The Spaniards dismounted, and Ercilla led them back above the tumult at the baggage train. They now shot their harquebuses and threw rocks at the Indians just below. Soon other Spaniards joined the eleven. The harquebusiers killed many of the enemy, but the sudden fear did more. Attacked from above and below, the Indians in their turn swirled, broke, and fled in all directions. A few who stayed to get more booty lost their lives.

Ercilla thought the results of this action were mixed. The Araucanians had captured much food, but they fell into disorder, taking plunder before they had won the battle, and their general punished some of them afterward. The Spaniards, though battered, had won a tactical victory.[3]

This account mixes old and new elements, both determined by Ercilla's stance as an eyewitness narrator and participant. Among the traditional elements are the odds: 100 or 150 Spaniards defeat a huge army of Indians, 6,000 of them according to the chronicler Bibar.[4] Another is the weapons of the enemy, for spears, darts, arrows, and rocks have been present in epic since Homer. A nontraditional element is the disparity in technology that Purén illustrates. The Spaniards use horse and gun against an infantry army equipped with stone-age weapons. New also is the anonymity of the participants. In his version Ercilla names no one on either side—not the commanders, not even the ten who rode up the hill with him and turned the tide of battle.[5] Purén is a heroic clash without heroes. Finally, another new element is the guerilla style of the war. Although Ercilla describes conventional battles, such as Mareguano, the Bío-Bío, and Millarapue, he includes an equal number of ambushes, traps, and surprise assaults on isolated forts: Tucapel, the Rio Claro, Mataquito, Cañete. Such skirmishes are characteristic of colonial epic, and Captain Gaspar de Villagrá likewise has them in his *Historia de la Nueva Mexico* (1610), that companion piece to the *Araucana,* set on the northern frontier. The novelty of guerilla warfare relates directly to the traditional unequal odds, for it is regularly the few who fight such battles along the frontier. For this reason I treat both topics together in this discussion. Throughout I emphasize the skirmishes and assaults the poets themselves witnessed. Ercilla saw most of the battles by which Mendoza reconquered Araucania in 1557–58: Penco, the Bío-Bío, Millarapue, Purén, and Cañete.[6] Of these battles Purén and Cañete fit the guerilla pattern (*Araucana*, 2.28.53–71, pp. 464–67; 3.30.38–32.25, pp. 493–516). Villagrá includes three battles in his epic, two of which he witnessed in 1598–99: the ambush of the Alarabes, or Apaches, in the desert (*NM* 12.94–281) and the capture of Ácoma (cantos 28–34 but especially 28.195–31.338).[7] Purén and the attack on the Alarabes are the principal focus of my analysis.

THE FEW

On a diminutive scale the Purén ambush recapitulates the origins of vernacular epic in the *Chanson de Roland*. Although Ercilla's acocunt does not resemble its artistic representation with the famous paladins and the eclectic army of Saracens, his story does recall the historical ambush that occurred in 778 and inspired the *Chanson*. Basques ambushed the Frankish rearguard and baggage train as they passed through the deep cleft of Roncesvalles on their return to France. Like the Araucanians, the natives occupied the cliffs and hurled missiles and rolled rocks down upon their enemies.[8] It was an incident in the long border war that eventually became the Reconquista and marked the whole Spanish Middle Ages. It is appropriate that eyewitness epic should return not to the first poem but to the probable facts behind that poem.

The *Chanson de Roland* itself founded the cult of the heroic few and provided its most famous example: Roland and his friends successfully repelling the attack of a Saracen horde and dying on the field.[9] For Ercilla and Villagrá, however, the classical model had an equal importance, and that model was historical, not poetic. The Greeks had the larger army in the *Iliad*, but the Lacedaemonians at Thermopylae acted much like the imaginary paladins of France and fought to the death against a huge Persian army. We shall see that this historical model determines some unique aspects of the Spanish poets' representation of colonial war.

It is always the few in Ercilla and Villagrá. At Tucapel Valdivia has 60 Spaniards and 2,000 allied Indians (*Araucana*, 1.3.57–58, p. 51), but an Indian friend estimates the enemy at 20,000.[10] The 14 heroes who arrive late fight against a large Indian force, only to have 4,000 more appear late in the afternoon (*Araucana*, 1.4.51, p. 69). At Mareguano the Indians outnumber the Spaniards fifty to one in the fight at the guns (*Araucana*, 1.5.31, p. 87). Villagrá recounts the three-hour defense eighteen Spaniards make against the Indians of Ácoma, where seven escape. Finally, the Keres Indian leader Zutacapan cannot believe that the Spaniards would send a mere seventy to assault his sky fortress (*NM* 27.125–32, p. 141v), but the odds become even worse as the battle develops. Twelve men scale the rock and establish a foothold there, despite Indian counterattacks, and the next day 13 struggle against 500 (*NM* 30.21–34, p. 155r; 120–40, p. 156r–v).

Epic statistics correspond to what the chroniclers relate, and the battles the poets narrate are typical.[11] Cortés and Pizarro provide the famous examples, but there are others from the zones presupposed in the *Araucana* and the *Historia de la Nueva Mexico*. At Santiago 32 cavalry and 18 infantry fought against 8,000–10,000 Indians (1541). Valdivia and 60 horse defeated 300 near the Itata (1546), and at Andalien he had 300 Spaniards plus Indian allies versus a large force that the chronicler Pedro Mariño de Lovera overestimates at 150,000. Finally, Coronado's vanguard of sixty horse plus some infantry and Mexican allies sufficed to capture Arenal pueblo.[12]

Analysis qualifies the heroic status of these statistics. First, the Spaniards had a technological advantage, as did the Spartans at Thermopylae, who had better armor and longer spears than the Persians.[13] Second, Spanish chroniclers and poets alike seldom mention their Indian allies. Tucapel is a rare case, where Ercilla's figures indicate a ratio of thirty-three allies to one Spaniard. At Mataquito the poet mentions 400 allies (*Araucana*, 1.14.16, p. 230), and we know from Lovera that the Spaniards numbered 120, a ratio of more than three to one. The proportion was three to one for Coronado's expedition to New Mexico.[14] Alonso Gonzalez de Najera, writing at the low point of the Araucanian War (1614), argued that the Spaniards could never have maintained the war without their Indian allies. They were the cheapest soldiers in the royal service, made up the majority in the army, and provided many services besides fighting. They cared for the horses, built forts, fortified camps, and carried messages through dangerous territory.[15] The modern historian H. E. Bolton compares the Spaniards to an officer class or elite corps and argues: "It might well be said that the Spaniards did not conquer America—the natives, led by the Spaniards, conquered each other."[16]

Both explanations, the technological and the numerical, help make the Spanish achievement comprehensible, but they do not completely explain it.[17] For example, Pérez de Luxán, who narrated the Espejo expedition to New Mexico and Arizona, remarked that at Anatobi pueblo 12,000 Hopis trembled before 10 Spaniards. He exaggerated the number of Hopis and ignored the 150–80 Zuñi allies and the Concho and Indian servants, but the contrast is still remarkable.[18] And there were cases where the Spaniards fought alone. Villagrá was part of a tiny scouting group that routed 200 Apache (*NM* 12.94–281, pp. 61r–63v), and 12 or 13 Spaniards probably fought alone on the rock of Acoma.

It is not fortuitous that the Purén skirmish should recall, however faintly, the *Chanson de Roland,* for colonial warfare revived the tactical and strategic situation of the eleventh century, which itself gave rise to the chansons de geste and the romances. The Normans had only 130 heavy cavalry in 1062, while they were conquering Sicily, and the Crusaders had 1,000 knights in Palestine after the conquest, a mere 675 under Baldwin IV (1174–85).[19] But they established effective control over limited areas—Sicily and the Levantine coast—while Spanish arms in thirty years spread from the Caribbean north to New Mexico and south to the Rio Itata in Chile, a distance of roughly 4,000 miles by land. The Portuguese, whom I have discussed in chapter 7, likewise made spectacular achievements. Such feats depended not only on equipment and alliances but also on the capabilities of the colonial army and the men who constituted it.

These armies fought in winter, an uncommon practice in the Renaissance. A winter storm nearly wrecked Mendoza's fleet sailing to the war zone, and Ercilla remembers their wait on the sterile island of Quiriquina, while the land army was blocked by swollen rivers to the north. For two months they ate moldy biscuits and drank rainwater (*Araucana*, 2.20.23, p. 328). Francisco Vásquez de Coronado's campaign against the Tiwa pueblos[20] and Juan de Oñate's war with Ácoma took place in winter. Villagrá wakes during the night to a snowstorm (*NM* 19.142–46, p. 105r), just before the Indians start the war. Soon after, on their way back to San Juan the Spaniards collect snow from the rocks and melt it over the fire, using their helmets as containers (*NM* 24.208–16, p. 129v). They capture Ácoma in January.

In canto 20 Villagrá describes the soldier who made such exploits possible. He celebrates not the universal man made famous by the humanists but a jack-of-all-trades. The soldier sews, cooks, and washes; knows how to find salt, wood, and water; farms; cuts hair; and cures dangerous wounds. He sees to all his military needs. He can shorten arms to fit a horse, and he tames, shoes, bleeds, and cures horses. He stitches saddles. He knows how to remail corselets, paint helmets, make lovely drums, and straighten a harquebus. Meanwhile he endures an animal existence. Covered in iron, he must be ready to act at any hour of the day or night.

He is subject to the rigor of a burning sun, drenched in water, and whipped by the wind. He suffers nakedness, hunger, thirst, and exhaustion. He sleeps on the ground and sometimes wakes buried in snow. Without shelter he endures cloudbursts, and his clothes dry while he wears them. His drinking water at times freezes, and to save his life amid deep snow he hangs onto horsetails and lets himself be dragged through drifts. He eats anything: roots, plants, seeds no one wants, even dogs (*NM* 20.69–168, pp. 109r–10r). A thirty-year veteran, Villagrá speaks with authority, and his poem is his record. Much of what he describes he suffered personally.[21]

Difficulty tests the worth of a soldier. However good he may be, he cannot demonstrate his prowess in an easy victory. The place and the person of the enemy, either singly or in combination, provide the necessary opposition. The guerilla war of the frontier had both for the colonial warrior.

Soldiers naturally gravitated to the frontier. The Spanish Indies lacked a standing army, so soldiers found employment in guard duty and raiding on the north or south frontiers.[22] These areas challenged a Spaniard even without the presence of an enemy. The landscape of the *Araucana* is one of forests, ravines, and low mountains.[23] The Spaniards finally capture Caupolicán, the Indian leader, when he winters at a rancho set in the midst of the bush, surrounded by swamps. To find him the Spaniards must follow a narrow winding path over great hills and up a streambed (*Araucana*, 3.33.55–66, pp. 542–44). Najera later argued that the land was the Indians' principal fortress. He considered it the ruggedest country in the New World, an area easier to defend than to conquer. He noted that it has many large rivers as well as the swamps, where a soldier must use his hands as well as his feet to get through. The hills have difficult passes where one man can stop a hundred. The Indians have no homes but the forest, yet the land is so fertile that the Spaniards cannot starve them out. It is impossible to cut down all the trees, much less flatten the hills or dry up the streams and bogs.[24] Nuñez de Pineda y Bascuñan, who traveled across Araucania during the winter, verified Najera's analysis and vividly described the rainstorms and cold of winter.[25]

The northern frontier offered a different landscape and climate but an analogous problem. New Mexico was far beyond the zone of Spanish settlement. After Oñate had established the colony, supplies went back and forth to Mexico only at intervals of five to six years.[26] The straight road led across nearly 350 miles of desert, broken only by the Rio Grande at El Paso. Villagrá had to explore much of this area and narrates his sufferings. The scouts went three days without food or water amid rocky hills and sand dunes (*NM* 12.85–97, p. 61r) and later experienced a week of continuous rain. Their metal shirts tore on thorn bushes, and the horses became exhausted by the rough climbing, so the Spaniards had to go shakily on bare and swollen feet across burning sand dunes that wounded their eyes and gave them headaches (*NM* 14.35–70, pp. 72v–73r). Finally, they went another four days without water, and the horses, blind with thirst, bumped into trees (*NM* 14.90–99, p. 73r–v). Besides the inhospitable land between Old and New Mexico, the Spaniards complained generally of the climate of New Mexico itself, particularly of the cold. Villagrá conveys this feeling through his résumé of the Coronado expedition. The scout Juan de Zaldívar returns broken down by the rough road, by hunger, and by the cold of the high plateau (*NM* 3.327–33, p. 13v). Coronado's men upon their return complain of hunger, nudity, exhaustion, and tell of terrible ice, snow, and winds, a punishing sun, rain, and hail (*NM* 4.84–89, p. 16v). Coronado himself spoke of the cold winter plus the lack of suitable wood, clothing, and blankets.[27] Whether a freezing desert or a rainy, impenetrable forest, either frontier tested the Spanish soldiers.

More important than the land was the enemy, and Ercilla is only the first of many to praise the Araucanian warrior. He is a member of a warrior class, always ready for battle. Training begins in childhood, and each soldier practices only one type of weapon (*Araucana*, 1.1.15–18, pp. 5–6). In the prologue to part 2 the poet emphasizes the Indians' overall achievement and indicates their guerrilla style of warfare. They have defended for thirty years not great cities and accumulated wealth but rocky and uncultivated fields, for they have burned their own homes and belongings to frustrate the enemy (*Araucana*, "Al Lector," pp. 261–62). It is difficult to overcome a people who destroy all they have and still continue to fight. Villagrá describes a variant of this situation at Ácoma, where the Indian warriors prefer suicide to surrender. Like the Araucanians they also fought to the death for something that had little attraction for the Spaniards. The colonists speculated that Araucania had mineral and agricultural resources, but they all agreed that New Mexico was poor.[28] A warlike poverty resists conquest and does not attract colonists. It defines a frontier.

The requirements of honor led the Spanish poets to write as much about the limits of empire as about the great conquests. Chile attracted as much poetry as Cortés. In effect the colonial epic revived the older frontier tradition that had marked the Spanish Middle Ages and had produced the *Cid* and many *romanceros*. Najera suggests the link when he argues that the mountains of Chile both make the Indians bellicose and keep them independent. He cites three outside examples, two of them drawn from the Iberian peninsula. The Arabs and Berbers conquered the plains but could never subdue the mountain people, who later recovered the whole land. Conversely, the Moors of Granada had the Sierra Nevada and the Alpujarras as an effective defense.[29] Spaniards had fought on all these frontiers—only the enemy had changed, the Indian replacing the Moor. Both Indians and Moors offered an exotic and alien culture, and —in epic at least—they had the same kind of soldiers, the *furioso* whose rages won battles.

THE INDIANS

Indians used old forms of weapons, and as a result the poets portrayed them as holding older values as well. The Apache hunters whom the Spaniards ambushed in the deserts of Chihuahua carried only bows and arrows (*NM* 12.160, p. 62r).[30] At Purén the Araucanians used a greater variety of missiles: arrows, stones, lances, darts, and slingshots (*Araucana*, 2.28.55, p. 464). For close fighting they depended more on pikes and clubs,[31] as did the Keres tribe in Acoma (*NM* 27.158–61, p. 142r).[32] The Indians had no metal weapons of their own.

Such equipment suggests the warriors of an earlier age. The heroes of the *Iliad*, the members of the Greek phalanx, and the Roman legionnaire all fought on foot with spears. This parallel may have led Ercilla to project upon his Araucanians Homeric qualities, as critics have noted.[33] Lautaro's scene with Guacolda (*Araucana*, 2.13.43–57, pp. 222–25) imitates Hector's farewell to Andromache (*Il.* 6.390–502), and the Araucanians engage in classical athletic competition (*Araucana*, 1.10–11, pp. 159–90).[34] For example, Colocolo resolves a wrestling match by the award of double prizes (*Araucana*, 1.11.29–30, p. 179), as Achilles had once calmed Odysseus and Ajax (*Il.* 23.725–39). By extension Ercilla uses Homeric techniques to describe battles with Indians. He piles up nature similes,[35] and warriors are wounded and die with the surgical precision of the *Iliad*.[36] Villagrá in contrast tends to assimilate his Indians to the Saracens and Arabs of medieval and Renaissance epic. On their rock the Ácomas, clothed only in war paint, shout abuse at the Spaniards below (*NM* 27.113–19, p. 141r; 155–83, p. 142r–v), as the Saracens had blasphemed a Christian procession at Jerusalem (*GL* 11.12). The poet calls the Apaches in the Chihuahua desert *Alarabes* and applies the same term to other Indians on occasion.[37]

The word—an Arabic word with the usual inclusion of the article—can mean any uncouth or brutal person, but it originally signified *Arab*. In earlier epic, whether classical or medieval, warriors had frequently been described as *furiosi*, rushing across the battlefield and gaining glory (see chapter 10). The Indians do the same.

In older heroic poetry a *furioso* might appear on either side of a battle. Hector rages as well as Achilles, and Boiardo contrasts proper and improper *furor* in the persons of Orlando and Rodamonte. Parity of character reflects parity of equipment, since both sides used the same arms. With the development of the gun, however, parity disappears, and the *furioso* survives best among the warriors who still carry the old weapons.[38] The Indian reminded European writers of their own very recent past and embodied values many of them still shared or had given up with reluctance.[39]

Ercilla and Villagrá both project *furioso* characteristics on Indians generally and on their heroes. Ercilla claims that the Araucanians are impatient and ferocious from birth (*Araucana*, 1.1.45, p. 11) and shows them raging in the first skirmish (1.2.83, p. 36). Chroniclers and colonial writers generally agreed with the poet. Najera quotes the *Araucana* approvingly, where the poet says that the planet Mars accounts for their warlike character. Najera argues that land determines character, so that the rough topography of Araucania accounts for the ferocity of its inhabitants.[40] The evaluation may be correct, but Villagrá shows how it involves an older European model. He admits that the Pueblo Indians are a gentle and peaceful people (*NM* 15.321, p. 86r) but nevertheless assimilates the Ácomas to the *furioso* type. In assemblies Zutacapan can easily stir up a war spirit (*NM* 18.54–64, pp. 97v–98r); 21.42, p. 114r), and in battle the Keres furiously resist a peace offer (31.185–95, p. 161v), finally choosing suicide over surrender.[41]

People who use old-style weapons must behave like old-style heroes. Tucapel and Rengo in the *Araucana*, Zutacapan and Gicombo in the *Historia de la Nueva Mexico* are typical examples. Tucapel is particularly interesting because he illustrates the link between the hero and the group. He may have begun as a personification. Ercilla considered the Indians of the district of Tucapel the most warlike in Chile and Peru, and most Spaniards agreed.[42] The name *Tucapel* is taken from the district and merely signifies its chief, yet Ercilla indicates that Caupolicán was the war leader there, who commands in the battles around Tucapel and is eventually captured nearby.[43] A chief named Tucapel no doubt existed, but the poet gave him his character. Through Tucapel Ercilla personifies the qualities of the Indians who live in the war zone, and he models his figure on the traditional *furioso*. Angered, Tucapel shoots living fire from his eyes (*Araucana*, 2.16.55, p. 275), and he does not distinguish friend from foe in his battle rage, any more than did Ranaldo at Montealbano (*Araucana*, 1.8.51, p. 129, referring to *OI* 2.24.30). His fury grows as does his peril (*Araucana*, 2.25.32–33, p. 416). Forced out of Penco fort, he leaps down a great cliff, followed by a cloud of missiles. He receives ten wounds and becomes so angry that despite the continuing rain of missiles, he circles the cliff and tries five or six times to climb back up (*Araucana*, 2.20.7–13, pp. 325–26). Ercilla turned this personification into a powerful fictional character by drawing upon the same *furioso* tradition. He modeled Tucapel on the Rodamonte of Italian epics, who likewise inspired Tasso's Argante and Marlowe's Tamburlaine. In battle Tucapel acts like Rodamonte, twice leaping into the enemy fort,[44] and in council he gives Rodamonte's speech (*Araucana*, 1.8.27–30, p. 125). Whether the Spaniards are divine or human, he will destroy them, he says. Chile is not enough; he will follow them to Spain and then make war on the sky. Next he rages against the old sorcerer Puchecalco, as Rodamonte had against the king of Garamanta, and starts a fight (*Araucana*, 1.8.44–52, pp. 128–30). He is the anarchic warrior, as dangerous to his allies as to the enemy.[45]

Unlike their Saracen predecessors the Indians normally rage in defeat. Boiardo had associated Rodamonte with Saracen victories (Monaco, Montealbano), but Tucapel and Rengo, Gicombo and Bempol do not participate in Indian triumphs.[46] More characteristic are Rengo at the Bío-Bío and Gicombo on Ácoma. The Araucanian, as he flounders about in a swamp with mud up to his waist, baits his enemies and clubs a few, including the poet.[47] He goes insane with rage as the harquebusiers decimate his men, but still has to lead a retreat out by a mountain path (*Araucana*, 2.22.33–44, pp. 362–64). At Ácoma a furious Gicombo is rousing his men when the sergeant major shoots him in the arm. The poet then compares the Indian to a bull, tired out and encircled, bellowing, foaming at the mouth, and shaking its head (*NM* 29.133–55, p. 151v). Gicombo rages on, but his men do not succeed in expelling the twelve Spaniards who have scaled the rock.

The old heroism no longer worked, and both poets present a powerful image of its futility: the *furioso* voluntarily hanging himself. In the *Araucana* it is Galbarino. Ercilla would have spared his life, but Galbarino eloquently pleads for death, arguing that the Indians can be killed but not conquered and that suicide would deny the Spaniards the glory of sparing him. He then persuades a young chief, who had asked for mercy, to die with him and the other leaders, and the convert follows Galbarino to the hanging, choosing a tall branch for himself.[48] Villagrá closes his epic with an equally strong image of heroic but frustrated defiance. The Spaniards have shut Cotumbo and Tempal in a kiva. The Indians tear up the ladder and hold out for three days, but hunger and thirst force them to ask for a knife to kill themselves. They are given two ropes instead and come out with them tied around their necks. They quickly clamber up two tall poplars and give a last speech. They promise vengeance if they can return from death. Villagrá then describes their death graphically: the whites of the eyes, the bitten tongue, the foaming mouth, and the corpse suspended and motionless (*NM* 34.238–381, pp. 179r–80v). Such scenes indicate not only the depth of Indian resistance on the frontier but a continuing European sensibility to an ethic, recently their own and only half surrendered.

THE HORSE AND THE GUN

A combination of horse and gun reduced the heroism of the *furioso* to futility. The Purén ambush is one of many examples in colonial epic that illustrates the new warfare; another is the ambush of the Alarabes in the Chihuahua desert (*NM* 12.94–281, pp. 61r–63v).

A scouting party of eight Spaniards, lost in the desert, had not eaten or drunk for three days. Their horses were in even worse shape, and three died during the night that followed. Suddenly, as it grew dark, they saw a great number of lights. Two men—the sergeant major, Vicente de Zaldívar, and the poet Villagrá—went out to reconnoiter. They saw huts, 200 Apache warriors armed with bows and arrows, and a larger crowd. All at once seven Indians threw hides on them from behind, gave them some quick, hard blows, and ran. The two men returned to camp, trembling, and the little party made its plans. At dawn harquebus shots stampeded some of the horses through the Indian huts. The scouts rode along, and the Indians quickly fled, like hares from wolves. Three Spaniards jumped off their horses and took two captives apiece, since they were looking for guides. The poet led the rest, destroying all the bows and arrows they could find,[49] so that if the Indians should return, they would lack arms. The results, however, were less decisive than the ambush. The Spaniards found food and water, saving their lives, but the captive guides soon escaped.

In this skirmish both sides act in ignorance. The scouts are trying to find the Rio Grande, though they have never crossed this desert before.

Villagrá compares them to blind men, feeling their way by touch (*NM* 12.75–79, p. 61r), and later talks of Theseus in the Cretan labyrinth (12.118–20, p. 61v). This ignorance determines Spanish tactics. The Alarabes attacked two scouts the night before, so the Spaniards, on the point of death and outnumbered twenty-five to one, have to assume the Indians are hostile and act quickly. The Indians, on the other hand, are unaware of the Spaniards. Those who jumped Villagrá and Zaldívar the night before thought the two were Indians and played a practical joke. The Spaniards do not know this, of course, so they attack the next day.

The whole action bears some resemblance to Purén and has an analogous tactical pattern. This time it is the Spaniards rather than the Indians who ambush the "enemy," trying to take his supplies. In this case surprise and shock are sufficient to win the action, and the Spaniards do almost no fighting. In both ambushes a combination of horse and gun accounts for the victory. In the *Araucana*, horses quickly carried Ercilla and ten Spaniards up a steep hill, and guns scattered the enemy below. Here harquebus shots stampede the horses and simultaneously create the illusion of a larger attacking force, while the horses rushing through town confuse an enemy caught sleeping and carry the Spaniards to their objectives. Horse and gun express the advantage the European had over his stone-age opponents.

During the sixteenth century the Indians *never* learned how to use guns.[50] Guns alone could permit one group to win a battle,[51] as could cavalry. Whether together or separately, the two tactical arms gave the few the confidence necessary to overcome a more numerous enemy.

The exploits of the fourteen under Juan Gomez de Almagro indicate the power of cavalry (*Araucana*, 1.4.6–74, pp. 60–74).[52] Valdivia had summoned them to Tucapel, and passing through the Purén ravine, they rode within sight of the ruined fort, though they saw Indians assembling and knew that they were blocking the return route. The Indians told them that Valdivia was dead, but the Spaniards wanted proof and twice scattered the natives who closed the road with their spears. They retreated only when they were convinced by seeing some of the Indians wearing Spanish clothes. Choosing a level place, encircled by a low rise, they fought off two large squadrons led by Lincoya. The Spaniards charged in pairs, first with lance, then with sword, and soon Indian and Spaniard were mixed up with the usual confusion of individual combats that marked a cavalry battle. Toward sunset Lautaro and 4,000 more came to the attack and forced the Spaniards to retreat. On the way they had to follow a narrow road in the hills, edged by a lake. Soon the fourteen were reduced to seven, but a violent electric storm scattered the Indians, and the remaining Spaniards escaped. Juan Gomez had to make his way back through the woods on foot. When they returned to Purén, the Spaniards had been fighting for three hours and riding for twenty-four.

The tactical advantage given the Spaniards by the horse, unlike that given by firearms, was not absolute, and it narrowed as time passed. The initial effect was overwhelming. As a Spanish force rides south toward Chiloe, Ercilla has an Indian relate that the strangers fight on running, ferocious animals, governed only by thought (*Araucana*, 3.34.57, p. 563).[53] Even though the Indians north of the Mexican frontier had seen Spaniards before, they still responded fearfully to Oñate's cavalry. At Ácoma the Indians wonder whether the neighs of a horse are speech and watch motionless and silent as the Spaniards go through maneuvers (*NM* 18.225–36, p. 100r). Later, when the poet rides up alone, they stay at a distance of six arm lengths, thinking that his horse would tear them to pieces (*NM* 19.55–58, pp. 103v–4r).[54] After the Indians became more familiar with horses, they still could use only defensive measures against them. They set horse traps and favored rough ground for battles.[55] Even on rough ground the Spaniards would use horses if they could, as at Purén, where Ercilla rode up a steep hill to turn the tide of battle. More significant for the future is the interchange between Lautaro and Marcos Veas that Ercilla relates (*Araucana*, 1.12.19–22, pp. 195–96). Lautaro had been Valdivia's stable boy and was trying to teach the Indians to ride horses. He had six of them, armed with painted shields and large lances, ride before Marcos. The Spaniard was not impressed and challenged all of them. By the seventeenth century the Araucanians had more horses than the colonials, but the Spaniards still considered them inferior cavalrymen.[56]

The mounted harquebusier blurred the distinction between gunner and horseman. He normally rode to battle and then dismounted to shoot, as did Ercilla and the other Spaniards at Purén. Ercilla was a lancer, but at Purén he functioned like a mounted harquebusier. Villagrá sponsored six for the New Mexico expedition.[57] By the 1590s the mounted harquebusier was gradually replacing the regular or light cavalryman.[58]

Besides horse and gun the Spaniards had the advantage of metal over stone. The light cavalryman, for example, had a metal-tipped lance and a double-edged cutting sword, later a thruster. He could wear armor weighing up to sixty pounds, though by the end of the century he preferred a half suit with a metal shirt and might content himself with padded cloth armor against Indians.[59] The Ácomas were impressed by the seeming invulnerability of men covered in steel and iron (*NM* 18.221–24, p. 100r), and at Purén the shower of arrows and rocks only dented Spanish armor (*Araucana*, 2.28.55, p. 464). Ercilla best conveys the contrast of the two technologies, for he makes us hear the sound of steel and flesh (*Araucana*, 1.14.34–35, p. 234). The Indians hit tempered harnesses, like the blacksmith using iron to beat iron plates on his anvil. The Spaniards break flesh and bones and sound like birds tearing flesh with their talons.[60] The few needed the enemy hordes, for without the numerical disadvantage their victories would have lacked honor.

The few differed from their enemies in another particular, at least insofar as they both appear in the *Araucana*. Fame belongs to the few as a group, not to individuals. Ercilla's Spaniards lack named heroes. Where the Indians normally have a Tucapel or Rengo in battle, Spanish soldiers at best achieve brief cameo roles, never to reappear. Juan Gomez and the survivors of the fourteen illustrate this point: they drop out of the poem afterward. Juan Gomez kills two men at Mataquito, but a single stanza is not enough to maintain his status in the epic (*Araucana*, 1.15.15, p. 246). More characteristic is Ercilla's earlier remark (*Araucana*, 1.4.72, p. 74) that although with a few men Juan Gomez defended Purén fort against superior enemy forces, the poet does not present this incident since it does not pertain to his history. Valor in battle does not grant a person status in the epic and, therefore, does not provide fame. Spanish heroism is anonymous. We remember the fourteen, not Juan Gomez.

NAMELESSNESS

In some battles the poets name hardly anyone at all. Purén is an example. Ercilla is its only hero, of necessity, since he reports what he saw and his action changed the result of this particular skirmish.[61] Villagrá does name people for the desert ambush, but there were only eight involved. For the siege at Ácoma he celebrates few men by name: the poet saves a bridge, Zaldívar revenges his brother, and Diego Robledo has two encounters (*NM* 31.94–147, pp. 160v–61r; 32.250–63, p. 167v). The contrast between these battles and those of previous epic could not be more pronounced. The poets who sang about the fighting at Troy, Latium, Albraca, and Paris regularly narrated exploits by heroes on both sides. Not so these Spanish poets, who leave one side without heroes. Their technique has a double rationale, tactical and methodological.

The tactical analysis provides a partial explanation for anonymity. The struggle in the Purén ravine depended on missiles, not on close combat.

Similarly, at Ácoma the Keres Indians prefer fighting at a distance. They shower arrows and stones onto the twelve who scale their rock (*NM* 29.75–77, p. 150v), and the next day they bury the thirteen under rocks (30.184–89, p. 157r). Their generals encourage arrow shooting when the main Spanish force crosses over to their side of the mesa (*NM* 30.243–48, p. 158r). The predominant comparison is to a rainstorm.[62] Missile exchanges are inherently anonymous. No one knows, for example, who killed Lautaro at Mataquito. He rushed out of his hut, without armor, and an arrow hit him in the heart, killing him instantly (*Araucana*, 1.14.14–17, pp. 230–31). Probably an allied Indian shot the youth. Again the contrast with previous epic is great. Heroes are normally killed by heroes: Hector has Achilles; Turnus, Aeneas; Agricane, Orlando; and Rodamonte, Ruggiero. Lautaro has no hero, not even a Spaniard.[63]

The colonial troops likewise used missiles. The harquebus replaced the bow and arrow. Harquebuses lacked the precision of modern guns and were more effective when fired simultaneously. The harquebus thus requires coordination to be an effective weapon, and tactical success requires more than one volley.[64] The eighteen Spaniards who were attacked by surprise on Ácoma, when the Indians began the war, never got a chance to shoot twice (*NM* 22.165–70, p. 119r–v), nor did the thirteen ambushed on the mesa during the siege (30.140–47, p. 156v). The day before the ambush, on the other hand, twelve men had done great damage with two salvos (*NM* 29.80–88, p. 150v) and had gained a foothold on the rock. This kind of fighting encourages heroism of the group rather than of the individual, since effective shooting depends on joint effort.

The technological explanation, though helpful, is insufficient by itself. It does not account for the anonymity of cavalry actions, nor does it apply in cases where the Indians sought close combat, as they did the first time, when they fought the eighteen on Ácoma. Moreover, the Indians sometimes are nameless as well. The ambushes discussed here, as well as Cañete, lack *furioso* heroes, and the Indians fade into a nameless attacking horde.[65] Both sides are anonymous, and there are few or no heroes.

The fundamental rationale for this namelessness comes from the poets' historical method. In one place Ercilla claims that there was no one wounded whom he did not name (*Araucana*, 1.12.71, p. 205). Fact, however, constrains him as well as Villagrá. The latter poet recounts the quartermaster's duel with the Apache in the desert but merely lists his name for Ácoma among those shouting at Indians on a wall (*NM* 29.186, p. 152r). The Indians at Purén probably have no names because Ercilla as an eyewitness could not find out who they were. Villagrá calls the desert Indians Alarabes most likely for the same reason. I infer from the location that they were Suma Apaches, but the poet did not know. For a writer pursuing the historical method, lack of information requires anonymity.

Even when the poet names names, he often gives them as they would be given in a chronicle: bare lists. Six stanzas suffice for the Spanish heroes at Millarapue (*Araucana*, 2.25.26–27, pp. 414–15; 57–60, p. 421), and Villagrá gives two lists for Ácoma.[66] Lists themselves imply groups, however, and it was classical writers who gave Ercilla and Villagrá the model for writing about collectives.

Ancient historians and the poets of historical epic emphasize the group as well as the individual, particularly in scenes of fear. Lucan, for example, provided Ercilla with models for group panic. His dramatic account of the hasty evacuation of Rome by everyone, terrified by rumors of Caesar's approaching army (*De bello civili*, 1.466–522), helped Ercilla construct one of his most effective episodes, the civilian panic that emptied Concepción and left it open to the enemy. Fear of the Araucanians, victorious at Mareguano, makes the people think they must leave the city, since it cannot sustain an attack. Such thinking makes a defensible place defenseless (*Araucana*, 1.7.9–14, pp. 107–8). Ercilla's picture of the panicked evacuation is one of his most memorable passages (*Araucana*, 1.7.14–21, pp. 108–9; 31, p. 111). People trudge out of town, taking their pets and their chickens, and women go without shoes, dragging their dresses in the mud (*Araucana*, 7.21.31, p. 111). Lucan also suggested the way one might represent battle panic (*De bello civili*, 7.528–35, 543–44), but he has nothing like the extended sequence Ercilla develops for Mareguano. The Spanish cavalry begin to ride off, deserting the infantry, deaf to friendly pleas. A few men try to make a last stand, but once they falter the soldiers lose control. Those in front ride off like the wind. Some try to catch horses, throwing off and killing the riders. Some hang onto horses' tails, pleading friendship, but it is no time for friends (*Araucana*, 1.6.20–33, pp. 97–100). The poet closes with a vision of terror (*Araucana*, 1.6.50–55, pp. 103–4): horses running wild or stopped, trembling; people abandoning shield and lance or even their own bodies to slaughter.[67]

Like classical histories, the epics of the colonial poets have two kinds of rhetorical scene. One resembles that of classical epic, when the writer has specific persons address an assembly or each other. Villagrá has a series of such scenes, as the Ácomas argue themselves into war. The second type is unique to the historians and their colonial imitators, when the writer has whole groups speak. In Thucydides, for example, Corinthians describe Athenians.[68] Villagrá has a peculiar variation on this presentation of group speakers. Several times he assigns a single speech to two people, always people whom he links together by friendship or politics. General Gicombo and his Navajo friend Bempol twice speak jointly to the Ácomas: to reject surrender (*NM* 31.282–308, p. 163r) and to denounce the pueblo itself (32.287–302, pp. 167v–68r). At the close of the epic Cotumbo and Tempal together plead for death (*NM* 34.278–90, p. 179v) and together promise vengeance before they die (347–66, p. 180v). Such speeches turn individuals into tiny groups and at the same time maintain the elevated status of the group.

Epic poets and historians of the classical period and their Renaissance imitators had several stylistic formulas to describe group action. One of the most common was the "alii . . . alii" construction, which English clumsily expresses as "the one . . . the other," or "some . . . others." Epic poets usually alternated such formulaic passages with others about individual heroics. Historians on the other hand might give *only* group action, adding at most orders given by opposing generals.[69] Lucan takes over this historical version of the formula in at least one place, when he describes the battle of Pharsalus. In his comparatively brief narration Lucan draws attention to only two individuals other than the commanders.[70] Ercilla, however, uses this technique throughout his epic.

He breaks the action at Purén into three parts: the Indian attack, the near defeat of the Spaniards, and the outflanking movement that won the battle. Each sequence culminates in one of these syntactic units, followed by similes in the first two cases and by a moral and summary in the last. The first unit expresses the Spanish reaction to the attack, as the soldiers rush for cover:

> Unos al suelo van descalabrados
> sin poder en las sillas sostenerse;
> otros, cual rana o sapo, aporreados
> no pueden, aunque quieren, removerse;
> otros a gatas, otros derrengados,
> arrastrando procuran acogerse
> a algún reparo o hueco de la senda,
> que de aquel torbellino los defienda.
> (*Araucana,* 2.28.56, p. 464)

Some went to the ground, unhorsed, unable to sustain themselves in their saddles. Others, beaten like a frog or toad, could not move, though they wished to. Others on all fours, others crippled, managed to take refuge by dragging themselves to some shelter or hollow in the path that might defend them from that whirlwind.

Next it is the Indians, sacking the baggage train:

> Quién con carne, con pan, fruta o pescado
> sube ligeramente a la alta cumbre;
> quién de petaca o de fradel cargado
> corre sin embarazo y pesadumbre.
>
> (*Araucana*, 2.28.62, p. 466)

One climbed lightly to the high hilltop with meat, bread, fruit, or fish; another ran easily and effortlessly, carrying pack and bag.

Last, this syntax expresses the Indian flight:

> Cuál por aquella parte, cuál por esta,
> (cargado de fardel o saco) guía;
> cuál por lo más espeso de la cuesta
> arrastrando el ganado se metía:
> cuál con hambre y codicia deshonesta,
> por solo llevar más se detenía,
> costando a más de diez allí la vida
> la carga y la codicia desmedida.
>
> (*Araucana*, 2.28.69, p. 467)

One was going this way, one that, laden with a bag or sack. One was plunging into the thickest bush of the hill, dragging livestock. One, out of hunger and irrational greed, was staying merely to carry more, the load and the uncontrolled greed there costing more than ten of their lives.

Ercilla uses both formulas ("unos . . . otros," "quién . . . quién") with the same application, for the second gives a single person as typical of a group. The first and the third contrast Spanish and Indian reactions to a surprise attack from above. Both swirl ("un confuso remolino," "remolinando torpemente") and then scatter, the Spaniards to continue the fight, the Indians to escape. The swirling of the latter is, therefore, shameful. A *remolino* is also a whirlwind, which Ercilla develops as a simile immediately after the first unit. The Spaniards scatter for shelter like men and animals under the menace of a great electric storm, and he continues this frame of reference throughout, since it fits a battle fought primarily with missiles. In place of the simile he ends the last unit with the moral reflection dear to colonial writers: greed and its consequences. In contrast to these two units, the second expresses an action, one crucial to the outcome of the battle. The Indians begin to plunder the baggage before they have won, like doves descending on grain in summer. Hence the conclusion on greed is apt.

Ercilla favors a rhythm of action, generalized description (often by the "one . . . one" formula), simile, and moral reflection. This pattern characterizes his presentation of Lepanto and Cañete, as well as a conventional battle, such as Millarapue.[71] The "one . . . one" formula marks his style as much as his similes drawn from nature. He does not confine the formula to warfare. He applies it to men building a fort (*Araucana*, 2.17.24, p. 286), to hunting (2.17.48, p. 291), to sailors in a storm (1.15.80–81, p. 255); in fact, he uses it much too often.[72] The later poets of colonial warfare were less insistent, though they still used the formula.[73]

The formula itself is not necessary, but it serves to indicate the generalizing style. Villagrá employs this generalized mode even to describe an individual event, such as the death of the *maestre de campo,* Juan de Zaldívar. Similes disguise the degree to which the whole sequence conveys generalized action. Juan makes a broad field among his attackers, knocks down and cripples people, and they all run (*NM* 23.36–41, p. 123v). A long simile follows to convey the movements of the Indians, who flee like doves (*NM* 23.42–49, p. 123v). Later a list of attackers (*NM* 23.62–65, p. 124r) becomes a generalized reflection on mob courage (23.66–80). Villagrá uses the technique to characterize the crowd that finally kills the commander. He shows that there are many ways to convey group response or action, the "one . . . one" formula being the type that shows the origins of the style.[74]

Neither the colonial poet nor the classical historian tried to avoid heroes. A strict historical method, however, does not allow for traditional epic heroes like Orlando, who can perform glorious deeds regularly, in battle after battle. The hero of one action may do nothing memorable in the next, and the group counts for as much or more in a modern tactical encounter. The Iberian poets created a factual heroic poetry without heroes, the cult of the glorious few. Later it would be the British square in India and Africa, the Foreign Legion in the Sahara, and the U.S. cavalry out west—part of the same tradition but without the epic poetry.

———NINE———

The Officers Take Over

Juan Rufo and Pedro de Oña

THE POETS OF NAVAL BATTLES, ESPECIALLY THOSE WHO wrote about Lepanto, introduced a new hero to epic narrative: the commanding officer. Two rather different but overlapping factors account for this hero. First and most important, the nature of naval battles —whether encounters between hostile fleets or small clashes with privateers and pirates—led to such a choice. Second, in the late sixteenth century the rapprochement of epic and history experienced a trend opposite to that which Ercilla developed (see chapter 8), one that favored heroes over groups. Patronage partially explains this trend, but the written news accounts, the historical sources, and perhaps also oral reports encouraged this preference among poets.

Naval warfare had two sharply divergent forms in the sixteenth century, depending on whether it occurred in an enclosed sea like the Mediterranean or on the ocean, whether by galley or by sailing ships. The galley, though near the end of its long history, still dominated Mediterranean warfare and reached its final development at the battle of Lepanto, where the ships were larger and heavier, carried more guns, and had much larger numbers of men on board than ever before. The gun, of course, was changing the nature of naval as well as land warfare and would eventually make the galley obsolete. At Lepanto in 1571, however, boarding and capturing an enemy galley rather than sinking by cannon fire remained the essential tactic. Governments partly covered their expenses and paid their troops from booty and prizes. For this reason, they did not wish to sink an enemy, as had been done in classical times. The beak of a Renaissance galley did not extend underwater to puncture the hull but stretched upward to pierce the dead work, or that part of the enemy galley that is above water, so as to hold it fast for capture and yet not damage the hull. This operation required many men to row and to fight. It indicates another factor that distinguished galley warfare from engagements between sailing ships.[1]

A late sixteenth-century galley could have anywhere from 200 to 300 men, two-thirds of them rowers.[2] Traditionally rowers had doubled as fighters, and they still did in the Levant.[3] Moreover, they often took part in land operations. At Nicosia (1570) 100 rowers from each Turkish ship participated in the final assault.[4] Warfare was amphibious rather than strictly naval, and the line between army and navy was blurred.[5] Rulers did not worry about whether the commanders of their fleets had much naval experience. Many commanders at Lepanto lacked extensive practice at sea, and Don Juan in particular had almost none.[6] In the *Austriada* he explains to the allied council that, while a pilot knows how to govern a ship, war is the general's business (20.18–21, p. 106B).[7]

A Western trend to separate soldier from rower and sailor did not eliminate this blur, for the nature of the fighting remained the same. Spain, Genoa, and Malta in the late sixteenth century used slave or convict rowers, who could not be trusted to fight,[8] and the Spaniards after Jerba (1560) had to substitute regular infantrymen for their marines.[9] At Lepanto they persuaded the Venetians to use both mercenary and Spanish troops on board their ships,[10] and after this battle the Turks had lost, probably forever, their own trained marines.[11] Yet this tendency to use soldiers and generals without naval experience merely heightened the resemblance between land and galley battles, and this similarity was crucial for poets.

The epic artist inherited a rich variety of techniques to represent land warfare. For galley battles he had only to stress the man-to-man combat that boarding required. Such dueling and spoiling were as old as Homer. Cannon he could include as decoration and hint at their importance. He had, moreover, recent models for their use in the poetry of Camões and Ercilla. As long as he still had close combat, the poet was not at a loss when he wished to represent mimetically a battle like Lepanto.

No subject could have been more appropriate for such poets. Lepanto was both the greatest naval battle since Actium and the bloodiest slaughter of any kind in the sixteenth century. Corte Real, one of the Lepanto poets, estimated the Turkish losses at 240 galleys and 20,000 dead.[12] It involved a great reversal, for the Turks, who had won a succession of victories at sea, suddenly lost almost their entire fleet. Accordingly, it attracted much attention among Western writers. There were many eyewitness descriptions and formal histories to aid a poet who wished to recreate the battle.

Many Italian and Iberian writers celebrated the victory.[13] Here I focus on those who wrote in Spanish, partly to balance the current impression of the battle created for English-language readers by recent scholars who have used Italian sources, but mostly because only Spain fought both kinds of naval war and produced poetry about both. Lepanto inspired three epics—Latino's *Austriadis libri duo,* Corte Real's *Felicissima victoria,*[14] and Rufo's *Austriada*—and drew considerable reference to itself in two others.[15] Ercilla devoted a canto of part 2 of his *Araucana* (1578) to Lepanto, and Cristóbal de Virues, an eyewitness, included it in a catalogue of naval battles that took up much of canto 4 of his *Historia de Monserrate* (1588).[16] In my analysis I refer to all these poets, but I concentrate on the *Austriada.* Of the three who devoted much of their epics to Lepanto, Cervantes praised only Rufo (*Don Quijote de la Mancha,* 1.6.75). Don Juan had Rufo accompany him on his campaigns, and the poet composed the epic at the command of Don Juan's sister (*Austriada,* Dedication, p. 1). His picture of the battle thus has a quasi-official status, and he pioneered the kind of narrative oriented to officers.

Ocean warfare required very different tactics from galley battles and thus presented a different problem for the poet. In such conflicts the sailing ship became a floating gun platform,[17] and the tactical objective was to sink or disable the enemy by a cannonade. For such clashes, where boarding did not occur as often, captains needed only small crews.[18] On the other hand, such encounters took longer. Lepanto was over in a few hours, but it took the Spaniards three days to capture a single ocean vessel, the *Daintie* of Richard Hawkins, in the fight I discuss below. The effective range of cannon was short and fire discontinuous, so the sinking of another ship took time as the cannon slowly hammered away.[19]

By the end of the sixteenth century these broadside duels had become the principal naval encounter on the oceans and remained so for centuries. Pioneered by the Portuguese, developed further by the English, this manner of warfare characterized the English fights with the Spanish Armada in 1588, as ramming and boarding had characterized Lepanto sixteen years previously.

Poets did not inherit literary techniques to present this kind of warfare. It lacked the traditional hand-to-hand fighting and featured only cannon. As a result, the poets tended to avoid taking such clashes as their subject matter. Camões, the great poet of sail, chose a subject that did not involve naval battles of this kind, though he referred to victories won this way.[20] Lope de Vega wrote a brief epic on Drake's last campaign, *Dragontea* (1598), but he too avoided having to describe a sailing battle. Aside from a brief description of Drake's attack on San Juan, Puerto Rico (*Dragontea,* 4.260–83), he concentrated on the land operations at Panama. The Armada, the great victory for the new military methods, stimulated none of the poetry inspired by a traditional battle like Lepanto. Spenser alludes to it allegorically, but he does not represent it. The only poet of any ability who tried to portray such battles was Pedro de Oña, a member of the faculty at the university in Lima.[21] He began a narration of the conflict between Don Beltram de Castro's tiny Spanish fleet and the *Daintie* of Richard Hawkins, which occurred at Esmeraldas off the coast of Ecuador (30 June–2 July 1594). The poet wanted the battle both to conclude part 1 of his *Arauco domado* (1596) and to begin a second part, which he never wrote. Consequently, he did not get beyond the first day of a three-day battle. His narrative, despite its fragmentary nature and the tactical differences between sail and oar, nevertheless fits the story pattern set by the poets of Lepanto. Oña produced a narrative concerned with officers.

LEPANTO

The Iberian poets who narrated Lepanto were reasonably clear about the tactics that decided the battle at the Christian center and right, and they gave two reasons for the success there. The first was the more effective firepower of Western artillery and small arms. This missile exchange continues throughout canto 23 of the *Austriada,* and contemporary accounts supported the poets' emphasis.[22] The second was the decisive role of the engagement between the commanders' galleys. The poets credit the commanders with the victory or blame them for the defeat. This conception of the tactics determines their preliminaries, for they introduce the battle with opposed portraits of the two generals, Don Juan and Ali Paşa. For this purpose they use a classical historical convention in which the generals give speeches just before a fight. The poets found an epic precedent in Lucan, who had Pompey and Caesar address their armies before Pharsalus.[23]

Don Juan did in fact give a brief speech, going in a small boat past as many of the galleys as he could. The form of this speech varies in the eyewitness accounts and from poet to poet, but the basic point remains the same. He claimed that God was with the Christians.[24] Poets and historians likewise agree that he inspired his men with the confidence that won the battle.²⁵ Rufo contrasts Don Juan with Pompey, who guessed the result of Pharsalus and showed his misgivings (*Austriada,* 23.19, p. 125B). The attitude of the commander, positive or negative, affects everyone.²⁶

The same logic requires that the enemy commander act like Pompey. In most of the poetic versions Ali Paşa so enters the fight, though like Aeneas he may conceal his fears when he addresses his men.²⁷ The poets, however, adduce slightly different versions of these misgivings. In Ercilla Ali simply senses the hour of fate and his coming death.²⁸ Latino has him perceive the change of wind, which had previously favored the Turks, and the unusual boldness of an enemy they had often defeated as bad omens, and his fears affect his own council (*Austriadis libri duo,* 1.6r–v, 2.17v–18v). In particular Don Juan's audacity upsets him. The Christian general stands fearless and seems like Neptune riding the waves (*Austriadis libri duo,* 1.4v). Ali later compares him to the eagle, which has taken little birds, setting out after the rest or to the lion, shaking its mane and stalking its prey (*Austriadis libri duo,* 1.14v–15r). Latino summarizes this view mythologically (*Austriadis libri duo,* 2.17r–v). The oceanic gods favor Don Juan, and Triton sings that the Fates are cutting the threads of Ali's life. The poet thus views Ali in the same way as Ercilla but gives specific causes for the general's feelings.

Corte Real develops a variant of this version. The battle has just begun, and Ali Paşa reacts not to the devastating galleass fire but to the Spanish and Western contingent he faces and to Don Juan's *real,* or flagship, in particular (*FV* 13.149–84, f. 174r–v). He fears losing, and some of his advisers say he should not attack. He recovers confidence, however, and goes to the attack, saying he should go only where the peril is greatest (*FV* 13.185–218, ff. 174v–75r). Rufo picks up this last detail and paints the most elaborate picture. Xilues the necromancer warns Ali the night before that he has seen the ghost of Süleyman and that the stars oppose the Turks (*Austriada,* 22.72–84, pp. 120B–21B). The general, cheered by the favorable wind, rejects these prognostics, and in this Rufo is correct historically. After the battle the captives Mehmet Bey and Caur Ali said that their commander had desired battle and had overridden the cautious opinions of some of his council.²⁹ Rufo, therefore, has Ali enter battle confidently, but he soon learns fear. The poet contrasts a serene Don Juan and a terrified Ali Paşa (*Austriada,* 23.73–74, p. 128B). Don Juan stands in the poop, subject to the perils of a miserable soldier, but his heart despises the risk, and his calm expression assures others of victory. A fearful Ali, meanwhile, promises Mohammed a temple and a reliquary. Then the death of the ağa of the Janissaries nearby dismays the Turks around him (*Austriada,* 99–101, pp. 129B–30A). A fortuneteller had said their fate this day depended on this man. Finally, Ali dies cursing (*Austriada,* 24.24, 26, p. 131B). Rufo, though he honors historical fact, nevertheless keeps the established pattern. The spirit of the commander and of his circle indicates the impending success or failure of the navy.

The duel of the *reales* of the two fleets continues this emphasis, despite the complexity of the action, which the poets carefully present. Most of the best ships and the highest ranking officers on both sides clustered around their commanders, and dead soldiers were replaced by a relay system in which reserves moved from other ships to the *real.* It is not surprising, therefore, that the capture of the flagship and the death of Ali Paşa should dismay the Turks generally. The poets all agree that Ottoman resistance collapsed at this point, and many of the historians held the same view.[30]

Throughout their descriptions of this duel the poets keep the commanders in view. Latino shows us Ali Paşa, fighting with bow and sword, calling on his men by name, reminding them of Sultan Selim's order (*Austriadis libri duo,* 2.21r). He closes with a picture of the leader's head impaled on a long spear, with terrible eyes and a swollen face, oozing black pus (*Austriadis libri duo,* 2.23v). Corte Real presents essentially the same scenario with a more elegant closure (*FV* 14.217–356, ff. 191v–94r). The god Mars hurls a dart that penetrates the general's entrails, and he falls dead among the confused crowd of corpses.[31] Corte Real portrays Don Juan as well, fighting with his sword, which sends out rays and blinds the Turks.[32] The other poets emphasize Don Juan only. Ercilla shows the commander and his officers in action (*Araucana,* 24.61–63, pp. 399–400), Don Juan himself covered in blood (68, p. 401),[33] and his fury enabling his men to take Ali's galley (87–88, p. 405). Rufo, who constantly returns to the duel of the *reales* during his description of the battle,[34] has Don Juan pray first and then the Christians successfully sweep the Turkish galley (*Austriada,* 24.6–7, 11–31, pp. 130B–32A). The poet then invents a dialogue between two Turkish deserters, who watch the battle from land and praise Don Juan. He closes with hyperbole: an eagle among falcons, Don Juan conquers by his very shadow (*Austriada,* 24.80–81, p. 134B). The commander both animates his men and takes part in the action that determines victory or failure for all.

The logic of these presentations presupposes the validity of commands—that is, that command has consequences. Philip in his congratulatory letter to his half-brother said as much. He was pleased that Don Juan had ordered all in his own person, telling the others what to do. The king thought this was the principal cause of the victory.[35] Don Juan did not personally kill Ali Paşa; that feat was accomplished by men acting under his orders. A general or admiral with a well-drilled military force could expect his battle plans to be executed. Don Juan in fact reviewed and exercised his fleet and made them row toward Lepanto in battle order.[36] He could hope that his plans would have effect, and his contemporaries agreed with this approach. Right after the event pictures and diagrams appeared, showing the positions of the two fleets and sometimes the stages of the battle.[37] The historians and poets who emphasized the encounter of the *reales* argued the same point by different means. Ercilla is the strongest evidence because he normally focused upon groups rather than individual officers in his presentation of warfare; where possible, he does so here as well. The "alii . . . alii" formula he favored for group action (see chapter 8) appears regularly in canto 24 of the *Araucana*. His use of the device is sometimes brilliant, as in his picture of boarding an enemy galley (*Araucana*, 24.50–51, p. 397) and of the dead (24.56, p. 398).[38] Each characteristic stage of a sea fight receives its own generalized description. Yet even Ercilla credits Don Juan with the victory. This suggests that the nature of naval battles may have required an analysis geared to commanders. At least this naval battle for these Renaissance writers depended on its officers.

This view has precedents. By one analysis Cleopatra lost her nerve at Actium and fled, drawing Mark Antony after her and causing ruin for their fleet. A similar argument could be made for Alexander's double victories over Darius III at Issus and Guagamela. In both the Macedonian charged directly at his adversary's chariot, Darius fled, and the Persians lost heart.[39] Taking a different view, many modern historians have claimed that Lepanto was a free-for-all. The most recent military historian of the battle, Francis Guilmartin, however, has argued the reverse. He bases his thesis on Don Juan's orders of 9 September 1571. The commander wanted to crush the enemy center with the greater weight of his own before the Turks with their larger number of ships could outflank the Christian fleet. Both sides executed their plans, but Don Juan was able to carry his through shortly before Uluj Ali moved to outflank the Christian center on its right. Don Juan could then turn the ships of his center first to meet this threat and next to the left, where the Venetians had stopped a similar flanking maneuver along the coast.[40] Crucial to the allied success was Don Juan's presence of mind to forego the prizes won by his ships at the center and help the wings instead.[41] Thus the old poetic view of the battle still has its defenders.

Among the poets of Lepanto, Corte Real and Rufo turned this analysis into a general method. For them the whole sea fight was an affair of those princes, aristocrats, and officers who served Philip II directly or indirectly.[42] Their discussions of the Christian battle dispositions are really catalogues of officers, and their narratives tend toward lists of names.[43] At times the officer functions as synecdoche for his ship and men. So in Rufo, Juan de Cardona, though wounded, stops Uluj Ali, as if they were engaged in a personal combat.[44] Later Diego de Mendoza, who supervised four galleys, accomplished deeds befitting his rank, and his kills made the sea red (*Austriada*, 93–94, p. 129B). The poet names not the ship but the officer and credits him with the heroism of his men.

By this technique Corte Real and Rufo introduced to the epic a mode of military narrative that dominated military discourse up to World War II. It had its roots in Roman historiography, which glorified generals,[45] but it was the great naval battle of Lepanto that occasioned this transformation of the old epic heroes into officers. Other poets who narrated Lepanto made the same assumption, though they did not turn their view into a general method.

We might expect a different sort of presentation when sailing ships clash on the ocean, since the tactics are so different from those used in galley warfare. The engagement at Esmeraldas, which Oña included in his *Arauco domado*, illustrates this difference. The Spaniards won it not by boarding but by bombardment.[46] Yet even here the pattern set by the poets of Lepanto persists, for like them Oña glorifies the commanding officer.

ESMERALDAS

After many days of searching northward from Lima, Don Beltram de Castro y de la Cueva and his pursuit fleet of two ships rounded the point of Galera and came upon the enemy.[47] The great ship of Richard Hawkins, which the English called the *Daintie* and the Spaniards the *Linda*, was just weighing anchor. It was 4 p.m. on 17 June 1594. Of the ensuing three-day battle Pedro de Oña relates only the events of that first day, but he is unusually precise in his terms and presentation of tactics, perhaps because the engagement happened only two years before the poem was published. Oña functions as a kind of reporter,[48] and the few hours' struggle he narrates well illustrates the new style of ocean warfare.

Don Beltram had as his *capitana*, or what the English called an admiral, the one ship of his previous fleet that had survived a storm off Chincha on the Peruvian coast, a galleon with thirty guns.[49] With it he had a *galizabra* (a small fast ship with lateen rigging) built on this coast.[50] Together the two ships carried 280 men.[51] Opposed to them, Richard Hawkins had what Oña terms a rich and lovely ship, well armed (*AD* 18.42, pp. 623–24; 19.75, p. 671). Lope de Vega in his parallel account compared it to a mountain or island (*Dragontea*, 3.148) and said that nothing similar had ever appeared in the South Sea.[52] But the ship, however impressive, lacked a crew large enough to board an enemy vessel of war. Both Hawkins and Don Beltram had pinnaces that they used to check out ports, and Hawkins immediately sent his out to reconnoiter the newcomers.[53] This action started the battle.

The pinnace was a fishing boat Hawkins had captured. It used both oar and sail, and Hawkins put his captain and ten men aboard. Don Beltram sent against it the *galizabra*, which fired three guns through its portholes, missing its target. The launch quickly turned back toward the *Daintie*, but the Spanish ship chased it toward the coast until the *galizabra* had to drop the pursuit or risk running aground. Meanwhile the main fight had begun, and the *galizabra* tacked back quickly to join it.

The duel between the *capitana* and the *Daintie* goes through three stages.[54] In the first stage Hawkins comes directly at Don Beltram, who tries to block the escape route of the *Daintie*. The Spaniard is to windward, no small advantage. The English shoot first, from the *amura* (the place where the ship narrows toward the prow). They hit, and the Spaniards answer with two culverins from the prow. As the prows almost touch, Hawkins doubles around his enemy and shoots from port. Don Beltram has to turn downwind to continue the fight and loses his advantageous position. He wants to board the *Daintie*, but Hawkins with his small crew keeps his distance and gives a cannonade at the right side of the Spanish ship. These maneuvers are standard, and Hawkins maintains broadsides, hoping to disable or sink the *capitana*. The third, crucial stage occurs as the ships pass so close that they almost scrape. A battle between sterncastles follows, and the exchange of shots hurts both sides. Hawkins tries to lasso the Spanish standard, but a harquebus wounds him in the neck, and a shot from a *pedreñal* takes flesh from his arm.[55] At the same time an English ball pierces the covering of the sterncastle and cuts across both sides of the deck, breaking lances but not hurting anyone. Another, however, kills a gunner loading a culverin and disembowels Ercinal, an old man who is rolling it forward.[56] He presses his entrails in with a towel and moves the gun into firing position. The English ship pulls away, while Hawkins stands all bloody over the poop covering. The poet closes his narrative as the *Daintie* goes to meet the *galizabra,* now approaching, its men with swords out, ready for boarding.

Hawkins, a very good sailor, sets the tactics of the battle.[57] He forces the enemy into an artillery duel, which he can do because he outmaneuvers the Spaniards.[58] Though he has a slower ship, he soon gets to windward of his enemy, an action that forces the *galizabra* to give up its pursuit of the pinnace since the *capitana* was now in danger. A ship to leeward exposed part of its hull below the water line, the standard target for English gunners.[59] Oña represents this style of fighting accurately, even if he does not offer an explanation of its tactics.

As befits such tactics, Oña emphasizes guns in his narrative. He prefers a lyrical style and conveys the effects of the initial cannonade (*AD* 19.89–90, pp. 675–76). A cloud of saltpeter takes away the sky. The sea, fine silver before, seems enveloped in a dark veil. Fire and water are at war. A huge mountain crumbles and disappears at the sound that touches it. Rock shakes, when the ball buzzes by, and resounds in caverns. The echo rebounds from valleys and canyons. So far the poet stresses in standard fashion the cloud of smoke and the great noise characteristic of cannon, but he achieves a baroque freedom in describing the effects of an English barrage (*AD* 93–94, pp. 676–77). The crystalline field of Neptune colors with crimson. Bodies turned to ash fly through the diaphanous of Juno (air). The burning ball splinters wood and takes one side of the ship away. It grinds and breaks leather, flesh, and bones, and sows white bones on the red sea. One man is left crippled, another twisted. Here the ball does not kill on impact but afterward, on the rebound. Here you see a man's chest open, there one with a split head. Here lies an armless body; there another in a thousand pieces.

Oña rightly emphasizes artillery, especially that of the English, but he cannot go further than this, partly for lack of information, partly for lack of understanding. He probably did not know that the Spaniards had twice as many guns,[60] or that Hawkins considered their brass pieces, though they shot smaller balls, to be larger and heavier than the English iron cannon. Spanish shot pierced better but was designed to injure and kill people rather than to destroy ships. It was therefore less effective in an artillery duel than the weightier shot of the English. Hawkins explains that the English shot shakes and shivers what it strikes and often does as much damage by its splinters. In fact, the shorter iron gun, or cannon, that fired the weightier shot soon gave its name to all large guns.[61]

Oña probably would not have understood Hawkins's other point about long guns. Don Beltram lost his windward position because his men could not use such guns there, when the ship lay shaking in the wind (*AD* 56.277–78). To shoot he had to lose the initiative.[62] Oña successfully represents a battle he only partly comprehends, and this split helps to explain why he can continue the narrative pattern of Lepanto, even though this battle is conducted differently.

The poet makes Esmeraldas another affair of officers. There is some justification for this choice. Oña lists the officers who defended the Spaniards against Hawkins and the gunners (*AD* 19.97–98, pp. 677–78; 105–6, pp. 680–81). He memorializes them in the graphic picture of the disemboweled old man, pushing a gun into place while holding his wound. The poet also rightly emphasizes the role of the English commander, since Hawkins took an active part on the first day. His seamanship kept the odds even, and he did much of the shooting himself. The chief gunner on the *Daintie* lost heart, and Hawkins and the ship's master took over his duties (*Observations*, 53.271–72). His personality likewise impressed the Spanish poets. Oña calls him gallant, valiant, affable, noble, and generous (*AD* 18.41, p. 623), and Lope de Vega portrays him sympathetically in the *Dragontea*. Don Beltram de Castro is another matter.

The poet begins his narrative saying that the Spanish commander deserves an alabaster statue and in death altars consecrated to his fame (*AD* 18.75, pp. 634–35). During the battle itself he contrasts the bloody, wounded Hawkins with the grave Spanish leader, who animates his men (*AD* 19.107–10, pp. 681–82). But these compliments do not disguise the fact that Don Beltram does nothing during the sea fight as far as Oña tells it. He lacks even the commands and speeches of the admirals at Lepanto. The poet gives him such a prominent role for two reasons. He is still thinking of galley rather than ocean warfare, despite his accurate representation of the battle, and he is affected by the new orientation to officers that marked much historical poetry in the late sixteenth century.

Oña was not alone in confusing galley and ocean warfare; the Spanish high command in Peru had the same attitude. The viceroy gave Don Beltram a small army, and each soldier wore armor. Don Beltram had his men arranged as a commander would distribute his troops on land: van and rear (fore and aft), wings, and the main "battle," stationed at the *plaza de armas*, or aft of the mainmast.[63] The Spanish thought this way because they still had as their goal the capture of the enemy ship. As in galley battles, they tried three times that first day to board the *Daintie* and went over to an artillery duel only with reluctance. In this respect the poet reflects the military theory still current in the colonies, one that Villagrá in the north might have shared as well, since his marine similes tend to involve galleys in those cases where he specifies the kind of vessel.[64] Oña thinks of Esmeraldas as if it were a Mediterranean clash because it never occurred to him to see it otherwise.

Hawkins had a complementary but slightly different explanation for the Spanish tactics at Esmeraldas. He blamed what he considered their poor seamanship on the use of land generals as commanders, an explanation still current in some historical circles, and in support of it is the fact that Don Beltram had previously held an army post. In this respect the Peruvian high command merely reflected traditional Castilian attitudes, which valued soldiers over sailors and normally put two soldiers to every sailor on board.[65] Against this argument are the facts of the Armada. The English commander, Lord Howard, had no more naval experience than the Spanish Medina Sidonia, but both had very able naval advisers: Drake and Hawkins's father for Howard; Recalde, Oquendo, and Bertendona, all of whom had extensive naval experience, for Medina Sidonia.[66] The use of land generals does not explain why the two sides fought differently in either battle.

The changeover from galley-style combat to artillery duels, like the whole military revolution, took time and spread over more than a century. The Portuguese, who invented the tactics of the artillery duel, used them around Africa and in the East, while many of those who fought in the north Atlantic and in European waters continued to favor grapple-and-board tactics. Philip's great admiral, Santa Cruz, defeated the French with such tactics in the Azores as late as 1582, and Philip, well aware that the English favored artillery duels, still ordered Medina Sidonia to grapple and board. Elizabeth's ministers thought similarly and kept telling Howard to board enemy ships.[67] Even the failure of the Armada did not convince the Spanish high command to change tactics. In the disaster of the Downs (1639) the experienced naval commander Oquendo tried to grapple with the Dutch enemy. The Spaniards won often enough to give support to the old theory. The year before the Downs, Hoces defeated both the French and the Dutch in European waters and took thirty-eight prizes on the way home. Even the great defeats did not necessarily refute this viewpoint. At Matanzas (1628) and the Downs the Dutch had overwhelming numerical superiority.[68]

This viewpoint may have made Oña's poetry possible. We have seen that the similarity of galley to land warfare made it easy for the poets to describe sea battles in their poems. Oña thinks the same way and composes a narrative in that tradition despite the fact that the tactics he visualizes are alien. Camões and later poets, who probably knew better, never attempted the same feat.

The focus on officers follows the same pattern, because galley warfare highlights the commander. At the same time this emphasis reflects a historiographical trend. In his parallel version of this battle, Lope de Vega likewise stresses officers (*Dragontea,* 3.166–72). This trend reverses the emphasis of fifteenth-century romance. Orlando commands because he is a hero, Don Beltram is a hero because he commands.

THE OFFICER HERO

When epic poets turned to contemporary history, they could choose among several alternatives. An eyewitness narrator, for example, might emphasize group action, as did Ercilla, or he might write from the viewpoint of the common soldier or sailor, as did Aurelio Scetti, who served as a convict rower at Lepanto, or he might concentrate on the commanders, as did Rufo.[69] But officers wrote most of the eyewitness accounts, and their narratives naturally reflect the commander's view of an action. The majority of historical epics tended to reflect this outlook, particularly when the poet depended on written sources.

Lepanto exemplifies this tendency. The commanders at Lepanto receive considerable attention even in Ercilla's version, partly because of the kind of naval battle it was and partly because the Spanish poet in this case probably used both oral and written sources. Ercilla, Latino, Corte Real: none was an eyewitness to the battle. Precisely what accounts these poets used has not yet been established, but the standard eyewitness versions of Lepanto are officers' narratives. This fact surely helps explain the tactical bias in the poetic versions. These accounts take the form of semiofficial letters, or relations. For example, Romegas, a French officer who served with the Knights of Malta, and Onorato Caetani, the commander of the papal infantry, wrote letters to Rome; Sebastiano Veniero, the Venetian captain general, composed a relation; and Don Juan himself probably sent the one Cayetano Rosell printed in his *Historia del combate naval de Lepanto* (Madrid, 1853). These officers all served in the center, which helps explain the poets' comparative ignorance of the fighting elsewhere. Moreover, they probably used purely Spanish sources, which would naturally concentrate on the center, where Don Juan commanded, and to a lesser extent on the right and reserve, where Gian Andrea Doria, Philip's admiral, and the Marqués de Santa Cruz commanded.[70]

This tendency to versify officers' narratives also applies to the oceanic strife with privateers in the New World. Oña used the relation of Balaguer de Salcedo, but the standard English account would have supported the same viewpoint. Hawkins's *Observations* (1622) apologize for his disaster and blame his men.[71] For his *Dragontea* Lope de Vega used the relation sent to Spain by the Real Audiencia of Panama. His poem frequently reads like a chronicle in verse, and the officers attract most of his attention.[72]

Although poets could in some cases achieve a certain independence from their sources, they could not overcome the cumulative bias of those sources. Lepanto, for example, gave rise to many narratives. Corte Real, trying to get the most truthful information, followed standard historiographical practice. Drawing on various sources, he followed common opinion (*FV* Prologue to Philip II, *3r–v). Rufo similarly recognized the existence of different opinions, as in all cases where many relations exist. He tells readers he has tried to be certain and in doubtful cases has followed the likeliest version (*Austriada,* To the Reader, 2). His caution and the multiplicity of his sources, however, do not alter the concentration on officers in his narrative.

There is another reason for this bias. Most poets wrote for patrons or wished to attract patrons who were either themselves the officers or relatives or friends of the commanders involved. For example, Latino directs his poem to Deza, the governor of Granada who had received Don Juan during the Morisco Revolt (*Austriadis libri duo,* 1.2r–v). The poet himself had met Don Juan in the same city, when the general visited Granada in 1569.[73] Corte Real emphasizes his relative, Santa Cruz, as well as dedicating his poem to Philip II.[74] Rufo served Don Juan directly, and his sister requested the poem.[75] Oña wrote for the viceroy, Don Garcia Hurtado de Mendoza, whose deeds and the successes of whose administration he celebrates in the *Arauco domado.* Don Beltram de Castro was the viceroy's brother-in-law. Patronage reinforces the viewpoint of the poet's sources and requires that the commander function as the hero of the epic.

Rufo and Oña, poets of both kinds of naval warfare, best illustrate this double bias, for they extend this viewpoint to land as well as sea battles. For Mendoza, Oña rewrote Ercilla, putting Don Garcia and his half-brother Don Felipe into the battles and having them personally defeat Ercilla's Indian heroes. Rufo, however, anticipated Oña by a decade, and I draw my example from him.

At the beginning of the Morisco Revolt Mondejar wins a skirmish that illustrates the evaluative tendencies in an officer's narrative (*Austriada*, 3.71–87, p. 19A–B). Mondejar attacked the Moriscos in Dulcar, where they had retired. The fighting began during the night and was a blind confusion, where a man struck friend as well as foe. Four hundred Spaniards and five hundred Moriscos died, and the Morisco survivors fled toward the sierra, while the Spanish cavalry tried to block the passes. At dawn Mondejar nevertheless sounded a retreat. His troops were raw and needed reordering. His men instead lost courage, and the army began to disintegrate. Enraged, Mondejar upbraided them for fleeing from a fleeing enemy. They reacted with shame and turned back to fight, but by then the Moriscos had presumably made their escape, since Rufo mentions only an advance to the bridge of Tablate, where the Spaniards made camp.

In this account and others like it, the officer receives credit for a success, while any confusions or defeats require a different explanation. Mondejar's men were inexperienced, and it took all his efforts to get the limited victory he won. Similarly, Hawkins blames his men for his defeat in the Pacific, and Oña attributes Don Beltram's initial failure at Chincha to the weather. Only a storm saved Hawkins from capture (*AD* 19.24–25, p. 654). These explanations are based, of course, on truth.[76] Logically, however, an officer deserves blame for defeats, if he insists on credit for victories. Weather might have troubled the Spaniards at Chincha, but it helped them at Lepanto.

Success more than defeat shows the characteristics of the new form of epic. A brief comparison to Malory clarifies this change. At Bedgrayne the leaders similarly monopolize the narrator's attention.[77] When King Ban enters the battle, Lot, the northern commander, despairs. Ban and the King of the Hundred Knights unhorse each other, but Ban knocks him cold and fells his seneschal Morganor. He then stands amid the corpses of men and horses and clears an area as far as his sword can reach. Leaders like Ban win by their own fighting, the reason why a medieval hero may or may not be a general. It is the fighting that counts, not the plans and commands. In Ariosto Orlando defeats two squadrons by himself (*OF* 12.69–85). In contrast, Don Juan, though he fought at Lepanto, did not win the battle by his prowess. A bullet and not his sword killed the enemy general.[78] Not for him the climax at Salisbury Field, when Arthur and Mordred concluded the battle with a duel (*Morte*, 21.4). History does not allow such idealizing fantasies. Rufo and Oña needed some explanation other than prowess to account for an officer's success and hence for his status as a hero.

Writers such as Rufo and Oña could not use Tasso's method, either, which depended on allegory. Tasso turns Goffredo, who had been a great warrior, into the modern commander hero. Although he fights, his authority depends mainly on his moral and spiritual status. God moved his election as captain (*GL* 1.32), and his mere presence quells a mutiny (8.77–85). Tasso assigns the important fighting to the romance hero Rinaldo, who alone in the epic has a superhuman strength that recalls Orlando. He carries through all the actions essential to victory. He is first on the walls of Jerusalem (*GL* 18.72–79), and his approach makes Solimano leave the passage free to Goffredo and his warriors in their movable tower (18.99). Against the Egyptians Rinaldo scatters Armida's knights at the center and draws Altamoro away from the Egyptian left wing, which collapses (*GL* 20.59–71). He then kills the leaders on the other wing— Adrasto, Tisaferno, and Solimano—and the rout becomes complete (*GL* 20.101–8, 112–16). Tasso unites the two heroes by his psychological allegory. Goffredo is the head and Rinaldo his right hand.[79] Rufo, though he drops romance heroes, uses the same idea to account for his commander, Don Juan.

Rufo develops for Lepanto what amounts to a theory of moral causation. He introduces the final canto and the turning point of the battle this way:

> . . . tú, claro don Juan, ejemplo has sido,
> Mostrándonos cómo eres invencible,
> Del derecho que lleva en las porfías
> Quien defiende la causa que seguías.
> (*Austriada*, 24.4)

Famous Don Juan, you have been an example, showing us how you are invincible, by the right that helps in combats whoever defends the cause that you follow.

It is not Don Juan's prowess but his confidence in his just cause that encourages his men and leads to victory. As befits a moral theory, its mechanics are psychological. Latino and Corte Real make the same point without the theory. Latino's hero talks continually before the conflict (*Austriadis libri duo,* 1.10r–11v). All eyes are on the eager general, who sees in vision the world waiting on news of the battle (*Austriadis libri duo,* 1.7r). He wears a look of victory and so strengthens others (*Austriadis libri duo,* 1.13r). In Corte Real's work, Don Juan gives a proper example, as the balls fly past and battle rages on the *real* (*FV* 14.221–60, 191v–92r). He animates his men with a speech, pointing to the banner of the crucified

Jesus, and then starts fighting himself. For all three poets a moral cause, visibly present in the commander, accounts for victory.

Virgil provided the technical means for the presentation of this kind of hero. Lepanto was inevitably compared to Actium, a battle to which all the poets specifically refer.[80] Virgil put Actium on the shield of Aeneas and emphasized the visible presence of Augustus during the battle: "stans celsa in puppi, geminas cui tempora flammas / laeta vomunt patriumque aperitur vertice sidus" (*Ae.* 8.680–81; "He stands on the high poop. His temples emit twin flames, and above his head appears his paternal star"). Servius explained that the eyes of Augustus blazed, citing an anecdote from Suetonius, and that he had himself depicted with a star on his helmet to recall the funeral games of his father, when a star appeared during the day.[81] In the poetic version Augustus radiated the presence of the gods and showed to all the coming victory. Latino did the same for Don Juan, stressing his look of victory. Oña used the scene in another context, modeling on Augustus his Mendoza, who stands on the deck, unmoved during a fierce storm (*AD* 4.5–8, pp. 133–34). The picture in the *Aeneid*, moreover, helps to clarify the differences between the Spanish poets and Tasso, when they use the analogy of the body politic.

For Tasso Goffredo is the mind, but Rufo equates Don Juan with the heart:

> Averiguada cosa es y sabida
> Que en tantos ministerios diferentes
> Como en los que consiste nuestra vida,
> Preside el corazon, y de sus fuentes
> Procede la virtud esclarecida
> Que hace osados brazos y valientes
> Y que sin él, la fuerza y la destreza
> No merece llamarse fortaleza.
>
> Así de aquel mancebo generoso
> Ardiente corazon de aquella liga,
> Un vigor redundaba poderoso,
> Que se extendia por la gente amiga.
>   (*Austriada*, 23.109–10, p. 130A–B)

It is a thing discovered and known that in so many different ministries, as in those in which our life consists, the heart presides, and from its fountains shining strength proceeds, which makes arms bold and valiant, and that without it force and dexterity do not merit the name fortitude.

So from this generous young man, the burning heat of that League, a powerful vigor overflowed that extended itself through the allied people.

Accordingly, it is fitting that Don Juan turn the tide of battle by his prayer (*Austriada*, 24.6–7, pp. 130B–31A). Immediately afterward his men board the enemy flagship and kill Ali Paşa. Similarly, Oña has Mendoza save his men through prayer during the storm at sea. Just after, the broken foresail, swinging wildly and dragging an anchor, sticks in the horizontal pole at the front of the ship, which steadies itself, and they come to harbor (*AD* 4.9–18, pp. 134–37). The prayer of the leader carries his men safely through both natural and human tempests, and for this action the heart serves better than the mind as an analogy.

Rufo is not consistent, however. Later in the same canto he compares the opposing commander Ali Paşa to the brain. When the brain is sick, the members suffer (*Austriada*, 24.31, p. 132A). He uses the analogy again to explain the turn of the battle. The Christians have just killed Ali Paşa, and his followers lose their nerve. Rufo employs the same idea as Tasso, but he varies the application. In all cases, nevertheless, he insists, as had Latino, on visibility. The men see Don Juan, they see the death of Ali Paşa, and what they see changes the battle.

Tasso need not insist on physical presence, for he uses the idea of the body politic allegorically. Goffredo is the brain or mind by interpretation. For this end the poet preferred consistency of application but could dispense with epiphanies of the sort that Virgil imagined for Augustus and that the Spanish poets imitated.[82] Rufo does not require consistency but must have some kind of sensible manifestation because he is writing purely historical poetry. He allows no allegory in the *Austriada* and alludes instead to the example Don Juan affords for his readers. His deeds, the visible acts of his life, provide models for imitation. History traditionally instructs by example,[83] and Rufo claims no more for himself. At the same time the Spanish poet created a curious doubling or mirroring. Historical poetry moves by example, but historical causation also depends on example. The looks and deeds of Don Juan influence his men and bring about a victory, just as Ali Paşa's misgivings affect his. The interaction of men in history, where the officer molds his soldiers, resembles the interaction of epic and society, where the poet strives to form morals in his audience. In such cases history and poetry are one.

PART FOUR

Violence

TEN

Are There Limits to Violence?

Matteo Maria Boiardo, Torquato Tasso, and Alonso de Ercilla y Zuñiga

ALL POETS OF ROMANCE AND EPIC HAD TO WORRY OVER THE conduct of the war they presented. They had to decide whether restraints applied *during* a battle or not. In the Renaissance they recognized and debated two answers to this question, which correspond roughly to the modern distinction between limited and total war. It was the latter that aroused the controversy—what the Spaniards, who did most of the arguing over the question, called "guerra a fuego y sangre" ("war by fire and blood").[1]

The poets never resolved the issue, but the manner of debate changed noticeably in the late sixteenth century. A century earlier Boiardo had contrasted the two positions within his poem, working out a dialectic between his heroes, but by the 1570s poets had polarized over the issue. Tasso and Ercilla in particular developed elaborate cases for the opposing sides. Even literary imitation became ideological, for the use of Virgil in this context came to signal a supporter of total war.

Following Boiardo came Ariosto, who registered the increasing seriousness of the issue. Next Tasso spoke for a generation of poets accustomed to "guerra a fuego y sangre." Finally Ercilla attacked that concept and practice, anticipating the mood with which the century closed.

BOIARDO AND ARIOSTO

At Boiardo's Montealbano, Emperor Carlo, unhorsed and surrounded by the Saracens of Spain, summons Orlando and Ranaldo. Orlando responds to the message first with quiet sorrow, then with fury. His face becomes fiery, and he grinds his teeth. As he rides toward Carlo, all those who can do so give way to him. Orlando uses his sword on the rest and kills many of them. In his emotional turmoil he *barely* distinguishes friend from foe (*OI* 2.24.24–25). However, Ranaldo is the first to reach and assist the emperor. Unlike Orlando, he makes no distinction between friend and foe, knocking over Saracen and Christian alike till he reaches Carlo and helps him to remount (*OI* 2.24.30–39).

Ranaldo's success raises the ethical question that is the focus of this chapter: was the success owing to his swift horse Baiardo or to his indiscriminate tactics, or both? Are there moral criteria for such tactics? In larger terms, does victory justify indiscriminate killing? Ranaldo is not an isolated case in the *Innamorato*. Agricane, angry and trying to stop the rout of his Tatars, likewise kills friend and foe (*OI* 1.10.52–11.1). The Saracen Marfisa provides a variant example, for she switches sides (*OI* 1.20.37–38, 41). Enraged that King Galafrone interrupted her duel with Ranaldo, she attacks her erstwhile ally, making a rout along the River Drada, which runs bloody and fills with horses and men, fleeing her. Later, as the cavalry and King Galafrone escape to Albraca, Marfisa kills those without horses at the ditch. Though the enemy is fleeing, she does not stop. Her fury is great because she knows her enemy has reached safety. Yet she and Ranaldo have turned the tide of battle and won a great victory. Boiardo makes no comment on this scene, and he mutes the moral circumstances of Ranaldo's rampage at Montealbano.

The poet lists only Saracens among the killed and wounded, while he substitutes a comic scene for the Christians, in which Ranaldo overthrows Carlo's chaplain, who is fatter than his fat mule. Such scenes pass in the *Innamorato* either without commentary or with humor. Yet it would be inaccurate to say that Boiardo evades the moral issue.

Boiardo could be reticent because his readers understood the problem, that of *furor*. Orlando barely succeeds in controlling it, while Ranaldo and Marfisa do not even try. Classical models indicate the difficulty. It is not just Achilles or the younger Aeneas, carried away by passion during the fall of Troy.[2] It is Virgil's now mature Aeneas, who struggles in book 12 to master his rage but ends up killing indiscriminately. At first, concentrating on Turnus, Aeneas does not pursue the other Latins (*Ae.* 12.464–67). Then, frustrated in this pursuit, he falls into wrath and kills everyone (*Ae.* 12.494–99). When he finally duels with the Latin hero and wins, pity only stops his anger for a moment before he stabs him, ending the epic (*Ae.* 12.946–47).[3]

Judgments of such actions vary. The Virgilian critic Ralph Johnson sees in Aeneas's rage the dark power of Juno, which finally takes over.[4] Yet the fury of a hero also brings glory and wins battles. Achilles gives no

other evidence for his worth as a fighter than the rampage that leads to
the Trojan defeat and Hector's death. By killing Turnus Aeneas wins the
war. These heroes, like Orlando, struggle with their anger, yet those who
do not achieve similar glory. It is not just Ranaldo or Marfisa, it is the
Viking berserk, who turned fury into a profitable vocation.[5] Their careers
imply that glory and carnage must go together and that fury has no limits
other than the training and character of the hero.

Boiardo allows for such a reading. He has another sequence involving
Orlando and Ranaldo, where the two warriors feel no rage yet react similarly. The sequence concerns Falerina's mob, which escorts prisoners to a
monstrous execution. Orlando merely scatters this crowd and does not
pursue the fugitives (*OI* 2.3.53–59). Ranaldo, enjoying their fear, chases
them for two miles, killing as he goes (*OI* 1.17.23–32). Humor again mod-
ifies one's reactions. Ranaldo first cuts the leader in half—a 600 pound
ruffian, who never rose fasting.[6] Difference of character does not invite a
negative moral evaluation of the lesser hero, for Boiardo has a wider
pattern in mind.

The poet contrasts Orlando not just with Ranaldo but also with the
other heroes.[7] In the scene just mentioned Orlando contents himself with
tactical victory. When he has defeated or dispersed the enemy, he ceases
fighting. The others pursue total victory and kill everyone. In the poem
this second policy sometimes has more success. At Montealbano Ranaldo
rescues the emperor, and in the incident of Falerina's mob, Ranaldo's terror tactics help Orlando. The captain of the mob flees, thinking that Orlando is Ranaldo. These achievements qualify the temptation to make
Orlando the ideal, for Boiardo refuses to condemn the others, an attitude
comprehensible in his historical context.

The Italian scene allowed Boiardo a detachment impossible for later
poets. Standard practice in the *Innamorato* corresponded to nothing in
Italy, for the condottieri imitated Orlando. Modern scholarship supports
Machiavelli's claim that they fought a war without deaths.[8] In such scenes
Boiardo rather criticizes the exaggerated figures and slaughters of romance. The deaths exist only in fiction, or rather the proportions fit the
larger European and Mediterranean context, where Italy, like Orlando
among the heroes, was an exception to the general rule.

Italians who ventured abroad had some experience with this other
kind of war, for they knew about Turkish terror tactics. Mehmed II regularly had Italian soldiers killed, beginning with the Venetian leaders who
helped defend Constantinople in 1453, and later at a Venetian colony the
Turks sawed in half all Westerners who surrendered.[9] Their example

seems to have affected the Venetians, who sacked and burned Smyrna (1472), bringing 215 heads as trophies to their ships.[10] This pattern corresponds to that in the *Innamorato*. From the viewpoint of Westerners, Saracens slaughter everyone. Like the Venetians, Ranaldo reacts in kind.

Mass killing also characterized northern warfare. The infantry fought a war to the death in the Hundred Years War, and the land suffered as well. Toward the end the war zone in northern France was empty, reverting where possible to forest. Afterward, during the Wars of the Roses, the victors regularly slaughtered all knights on the defeated side.[11] Meanwhile the Burgundian dukes fought a *guerre mortelle* first with their subjects in Ghent (1451–53), then with those of Liège (1466–68). Three thousand people from Ghent died to atone for Cornelius, the bastard of Burgundy, killed by a pike thrust at Rupelmonde. The enemy responded in kind, taking no prisoners.[12] Farther south, the Swiss took no prisoners, would pillage towns that had capitulated, and would violate the terms of surrender given a hostile garrison.[13] Although they did not torture and execute people in Levantine fashion, northerners fought a war quite as ruthless as the Turks.

The north brought these tactics to Italy. In their campaigns of 1494 and 1495 the French made mass killing an Italian reality. At Fivizzano on the Tuscan frontier (1494) and at Monte di San Giovanni (1495), they massacred the populace and burned the towns. At Fornovo the Venetian commander, Gonzaga, learned afterward that the French had killed all fallen horsemen. The uncle and three cousins he wanted to ransom were all dead.[14] The terror of massacre helped the French strategically. The sack of little Monte di San Giovanni terrified Capua into surrender. Alessandria, the fortress town that controlled access to Milan, is another example. The French first captured two outlying castles and slaughtered everyone. The terror such actions aroused drove all the surrounding towns to surrender. Alessandria itself quickly fell by assault, as the commander deserted and the garrison was divided.[15] Other nations soon emulated the French example: first the Spaniards (1503), then the Germans (1509).[16] Ruthlessness now could characterize tactics anywhere, and the change can be seen in Ariosto, who continued Boiardo's poem.

Ariosto condemned the French sack of Ravenna, though his duke acted as a French ally. The outburst vividly evokes an army out of control:[17]

> . . . le man rapaci e ladre,
> che suore, e frati e bianchi e neri e bigi

> violato hanno, e sposa e figlia e madre;
> gittato in terra Cristo in sacramento,
> per torgli un tabernaculo d'argento.
>
> (*OF* 14.8)

Hands, rapacious and stealing, which violated nuns and friars, white, black, and gray, and wife, daughter, and mother. Christ in the sacrament was thrown to the ground to take a silver tabernacle.

The deaths involved probably did not surpass those caused by Boiardo's Marfisa, but Boiardo wrote fantasy. Reality obliterates the possibility of detachment for Ariosto. These new tactics of terror marked the wars that continued throughout Ariosto's life and climaxed with the sack of Rome in 1527. Yet such terror had its own ethical suppositions.

In Orcagna Orlando assumes that Falerina's people can be friends. He has come to liberate the land from her tyranny, and his success depends partially on information given by a lady who serves the queen. Ranaldo in contrast presupposes an intractable enemy—a not unreasonable assumption, since he is traveling in Saracen territory.[18] If not intractable, the enemy is at least foreign, not someone with whom a warrior could normally have close bonds. This presumably would be the point of view of the foreign soldiers in Italy. Although they did not demonize their enemies, they were fighting in a land strange to them against people who spoke a different language. Ariosto, of course, could never share this attitude. For him the people of Ravenna were neighbors and could be allies at a future time. Alliances shifted among the city states, and a foe could easily become a friend, so the sack of Ravenna made no sense. The immediate strategic advantage of terror, the submission of the neighboring towns of Faenza and Rimini (*OF* 14.9), would not outweigh the hatred caused; in fact, the French soon lost the occupied territories and had to invade Italy all over again.

Where religious or profound cultural differences existed, Ranaldo's ethic ruled. It reached a climax in the 1570s with the Dutch War in the north, the clash of Saracen and Christian in the Mediterranean, and the interminable border wars Spain fought with American Indians on its northern and southern frontiers. Ercilla and Tasso produced their epics precisely in this decade, and they polarized over the issue. Ercilla condemned such practices, while Tasso at least tacitly supported the tactics of total victory. Neither could emulate Boiardo and present both alternatives more or less impartially.

Tasso presented the kind of war that aroused the controversy. He dramatized a victory that others have condemned as a massacre, and he worked out the literary method for such presentations that became basic to other poets of the period.

TASSO

In studying the First Crusade, Tasso encountered a ruthlessness equal to any in the Renaissance. The poet was spared the grisly details recorded by Fulcher of Chartres: blood up to the ankles in the Temple of Solomon or Aqṣā Mosque, the bodies of the dead or burning cut open to get swallowed money, the corpses still rotting a half year later and making a stench around Jerusalem.[19] Yet his principal source, the *Historia rerum in partibus transmarinis gestarum* of William of Tyre, gave him the essential information.[20] William said that the Crusaders were terrifying to see after the slaughter, covered in blood from head to foot, and he does not conceal the killing inside the Aqṣā Mosque. The historical record did not allow for any apologies based on emotions. The massacre was not the result of a riot; rather, it fit previous procedure. The Crusaders had already killed all the Muslims in Antioch, and their mass killings may have shocked the Near East quite as much as French actions had Italy in 1494–95.[21]

The poet's literary theory forced him to confront this record directly. Tasso believed that a poet had to base his epic on documented history. Although he could alter that history in many ways, he had to work within the general contours of a major event and could not change significantly the end of an action.[22] Jerusalem fit both requirements, since the Crusaders had left Europe intending to capture the city and its fall climaxed their campaign. Theory also dictated the form he used to face the problem, a different form than Boiardo chose. For verisimilitude Tasso limited a hero's prowess in epic, with the exception of his dynastic hero, Rinaldo (and even his actions had precedent in those of the historical Tancredi).[23] This new realism turned the problem of the *furioso* hero into that of the commanding officer.[24] For Tasso this meant that his previous characterization of Goffredo affected his presentation of the mass killing, since he wrote canto 18 after he had already established that character.[25]

Two choices concerning Goffredo determined Tasso's version of the killings. First, Tasso had projected backward Goffredo's election as leader, so he became general commander of the Crusader army for the whole invasion of Palestine.[26] He thus became responsible for the actions of the Crusaders at Jerusalem. Scholastic theory held the leader, not the individual soldier, responsible for the conduct of a war.[27] Second, the poet had chosen to make Goffredo into a positive moral example for his audience.[28] Both choices created the same problem: an idealized Goffredo could not simply preside over a massacre. Tasso has Goffredo criticize his soldiers afterward:

> Ite, e curate quei c'han fatto acquisto
> di questa patria a noi co'l sangue loro.
> Ciò più conviensi a i cavalier di Cristo,
> che desio di vendetta o di tesoro.
> Troppo, ahi! troppo di strage oggi s'è visto,
> troppa in alcuni avidità de l'oro;
> rapir più oltra, e incrudelir i' vieto.
>
> (GL 19.52)

Go and heal those who have acquired with their blood this home for us. This more befits the knights of Christ than desire for revenge or treasure. Today, alas, much too much slaughter has been seen, too much gold lust in some. It is forbidden to take more and to commit cruelties.

Such an apology by itself greatly understated the mass killing that occurred at Jerusalem, and although it preserved the idealized image of Goffredo, it would not have absolved him from responsibility as a commander. Tasso needed something more than this speech, and he found what he needed in Virgil.[29]

The Roman poet concluded his epic with Aeneas killing an opponent who had appealed for leniency. This harsh ending seemed to justify the tactics of total war, for by this kill Aeneas won a secure position for the Trojans in Italy and guaranteed the Roman future. Villagrá later remembered it for his *Historia de la Nueva Mexico*. Tasso accepted the logic and, when he defended Virgil's ending, appealed to reason of state. For his own epic, however, he preferred to imitate book 2 of the *Aeneid*.[30]

Virgil's presentation of the fall of Troy has become the paradigm in the West for the atrocities of war and civilian massacre. Of many scenes the most famous is the rampage of Pyrrhus, who breaks into Priam's palace, kills a prince before the king's eyes, and then drags the monarch, slipping in his child's blood, to an altar, around which his wife and daughters cluster. There Pyrrhus kills him and leaves behind a headless corpse without a name (*Ae.* 2.526–58). Such scenes equaled those of the First Crusade and would have fit Tasso's poetic practice, since he regularly used classical descriptions to present historical fact. Yet he found more than pictures in Virgil.

Less well known but no less influential was the logic with which Virgil presents such scenes. Virgil assumes the fall of Troy to be inevitable. Two

episodes make this point, that of Laocoon and Aeneas's interview with
Venus. Laocoon suspects the Trojan horse and would pray to Neptune
that he sink the Greek fleet. Athena instead sends serpents that kill him
and his two sons, and this marvel invalidates his advice about the horse.[31]
The Trojans, therefore, draw the horse up to the citadel, where the snakes
vanish under Athena's image (*Ae.* 2.225–27) and where the deceiver Sinon
will go that night, guarded by the Fates and the will of the gods (257–59).
In the second episode Venus shows her son the gods destroying Troy (*Ae.*
2.602–3, 608–23), among them that same Athena, standing on the citadel. The mode is tragic, and Virgil regularly drew on the Attic tragedians
whenever he was not imitating Homer.[32] The Roman poet, however,
never used such a mode to justify the slaughter at Troy, as Villagrá later
did for Ácoma and as Tasso comes close to doing for Jerusalem.

Critics have long known that Tasso imposes a Virgilian pattern on the
fall of Jerusalem. The Saracen Argante quotes Aeneas:

> Penso . . . a la città del regno
> di Giudea antichissima regina,
> che vinta or cade, e indarno esser sostegno
> io procurai de la fatal ruina.
> (*GL* 19.10 [= *Ae.* 2.363])

I think about the city, the most ancient queen of the kingdom of Judea,
which now falls conquered, and in vain I tried to be her support from
inevitable ruin.

Next the Judean king becomes Priam. He sets forth to fight, an old man,
trembling under the weight of armor, long unused (*GL* 18.67; *Ae.* 2.509–
11). He next talks like the priest Panthus, lamenting that they *were* and
that the last day has come (*GL* 19.40; *Ae.* 2.324–26). Finally, and most
important, Rinaldo at the Aqṣā Mosque imitates Pyrrhus breaking into
Priam's palace (*GL* 19.33–37; *Ae.* 2.469–500). In effect, the Crusaders act
like Greeks and the Saracens like Trojans, acquiring a pathos they had
not had before.

The pattern assumes a tragic logic. Jerusalem like Troy falls by divine
decree. Tasso transfers Aeneas's vision to Goffredo, substituting dead
Crusaders for the old gods destroying the city (*GL* 18.92–96; *Ae.* 2.602–
23). Ugone like Neptune shakes down the walls. Dudone replaces Juno
at the main gate, and the cleric Ademaro recalls Jupiter presiding over the
attack from a distance. Here, however, Tasso crosses his set of equations.
Aeneas, a Trojan, sees the gods he worships obliterating his own city and
culture, while Goffredo sees the angels and saints capturing an enemy

city for him, and the experience radiates triumph not tragedy.[33] Tasso's Virgilian imitation clearly has problems, which in turn illustrate his ethical difficulties.

The tragic pattern does not really fit the rest of the poem. Critics have noted how it wrenches the characters of the leading Saracens and makes them inconsistent. The furious Argante suddenly becomes reflective and pensive,[34] and the Herodian Aladino awkwardly assumes the role of Priam. One could defend Tasso's attempt by arguing that he uses the Virgilian parallels to criticize Crusader violence, turning the Christians momentarily into the brutal Greeks of book 2 of the *Aeneid.* Such an interpretation, however, does not explain Goffredo's vision and cannot account for the rupture that this imitation makes with the rest of the poem and with how Tasso otherwise tries to minimize the massacre.

Where Virgil emphasizes the carnage, Tasso reduces it to a few stanzas (*GL* 18.105, 19.29–30, 38). Rinaldo shows the difference. Tasso limits to him William of Tyre's description of *all* the Crusaders, bloody from head to foot.[35] The poet had assigned to Rinaldo the role of the historical Tancredi, who broke into the Aqṣā Mosque and plundered the Dome of the Rock. Yet Rinaldo abstains from plunder and imitates Boiardo's Orlando. He attacks only armed leaders and merely scares the unarmed by his look and cry (*GL* 19.31–32). Nor does he kill anyone inside the Temple of Solomon, for Tasso drops Virgil's scene between Priam and Pyrrhus.[36] It was evidently not the Virgilian critique of violence that attracted Tasso but more likely the pattern of fate that could rationalize it.

Tragedy justifies the tactics of total war. If the fall of the city is predetermined, the manner of its fall may also be inevitable. A Saracen enemy at least is intractable, so the killing follows of necessity. Tasso in fact kills all his Saracen warriors and commanders, though some actually outlived the First Crusade.[37] For the slaughter in the Aqṣā Mosque Tasso quotes William of Tyre, a bishop, who saw in the event heavenly justice. The impious pagan washed with his blood the temple he had profaned (*GL* 19.38).[38] Crusader violence merely enacts divine vengeance. Such a perspective could justify even the killing of the unarmed, and Renaissance proponents of "guerra a fuego y sangre" could defend the bloodshed in the Aqṣā Mosque.

Military codes protected civilians at home but not always in enemy territory. The theologian Fray Francisco de Vitoria, asked about the status of noncombatants, said the victors could kill everyone. And the distinction was difficult to draw in the first place. At Siena, the last great siege in Italy, women made up the pick-and-shovel brigade.[39] In practice, a fallen town depended on the mood of the army and of its commanders, and no distinctions existed between a town taken by storm and one that surrendered to terms.[40] All this, of course, fits the logic of Boiardo's Ranaldo and could apply to Tasso and even to Virgil. It is the logic that Villagrá, another reader of Virgil, develops for Ácoma.

In such a view ethics governs the beginning rather than the conduct of war. The Spanish poets use identical logic, though they draw radically different conclusions about conduct. If the war is just, all can follow as part of the nature of war. Villagrá devotes an entire canto of the *Historia de la Nueva Mexico,* filled with documents quoted or paraphrased, to justify the attack on Ácoma. Among them he includes the Franciscan opinion that the conquered and their goods are at the mercy of the victor in a just war (*NM* 25, p. 132r–v). Ercilla is more explicit. In a just war the victorious may strike, take, enslave, or kill (*Araucana,* 3.37.7, p. 591). Tasso similarly justifies the First Crusade and so need not pass moral judgment on all the killings in the city. God commands the Crusaders to move against Jerusalem, and Tasso inserts the novella of Sofronia and Olindo to explain why. The persecution of Christians in Palestine justifies the war and makes poetic justice of the killings at the end. Before the siege the Muslims had expelled the Christians from Jerusalem, so the Crusaders killed only enemies.[41] Although they did not distinguish between unarmed and armed enemies, they did avoid the extremes of Boiardo's raging heroes. They did not confound friend with foe.

Tasso rationalizes a situation that all the poets of war in the later sixteenth century confronted. Since he treats real events, he must solve an ethical question different from that which concerned Boiardo and Ariosto. In actual war no person could perform the deeds of Orlando, either of the *Innamorato* or of the *Furioso.* Only a group could achieve such feats, and the ethical responsibility for the actions of a military group rests with the commander. As a result, the poet worries about policy and moments of decision. Those who support or accept the tactics of total war locate that choice solely at the beginning. Once the military action starts, it operates by its own logic until the opponent has been exterminated. The poet conveys his sense of this automatic sequence through imitation of the *Aeneid,* and Virgilian tragedy justifies mass killing.

Two factors mitigate this ferocity. First, Tasso wrote as a civilian who had never witnessed war. His is an academic fierceness learned from books and conversation. He was writing for a court that did not participate even in the Lepanto campaign. Second, the poet simply expresses the mood of his times.

While Tasso was finishing his poem, conflict outside Italy flared up and generally followed the pattern of "guerra a fuego y sangre." Christian and Muslim clashed both in Spain and the Levant, and all Italians knew both about Bragadino, the Venetian commander skinned alive at Famagusta in Cyprus (1571), and about Lepanto (1571), the bloodiest battle of the century. The Massacre of St. Bartholomew came in the following year (24 August 1572), and the duke of Alba conducted an especially ferocious campaign in the Low Countries through 1572–73.[42] Previously, the Levant had added a cruelty to its ruthlessness that was not found in the north, but that difference now vanished. Alba regarded the inhabitants of the Low Countries not only as rebels—as had the dukes of Burgundy in the previous century—but also as heretics. The Calvinist poet Agrippa d'Aubigné, speaking of France, notes the cruelties that religious hostility added to normal fighting. In villages the victors hung people by the fingers and crying children by the feet. They roasted some over wood fires and tortured others with pincers dipped in burning fat (*Les tragiques*, 1.345–52). At the same time the poet shared in the ferocity, at least mentally. He imagined a compatriot in heaven who, while singing a hymn, bathed his feet in the blood of Catholics and threw the blood up into the air (*Les tragiques*, 3.1049–50). Fighting both in the Levant and in the north now involved a clash of religions or sects and sometimes of cultures, and the participants were pitiless.

The other poets of the decade register these same practices. Camões (1572) tacitly assumes them when he narrates the victory at Mozambique (*Lusiadas*, 1.86–93). The Portuguese pursue the fugitives with gunboats, though they have already bombarded the town (see chapter 7). Juan Rufo has the longest list of atrocities, for in his *Austriada* (1582) he presented mostly the revolt of the Moriscos, during which both sides adopted tactics of terror and extermination. Muslims violated Spanish women in the sight of their families, cut off the hands and feet of some, burned others slowly over fires, and skinned still others with flints. Women inflicted a thousand wounds on some Christians, using their brooches. Finally, the rebels crucified two young brothers who refused to apostasize (*Austriada*, 4.10, 14–16, p. 21A–B).[43] Christians reacted with a corresponding harshness. The Moriscos who surrendered at Guájaras were killed (*Austriada*, 4.89–95, p. 25A–B), and at Galera the Spaniards took no prisoners and were slowed at their entry only by corpses (16.83–84, p. 86B). Most telling was Guéjar (*Austriada,* 15.57, p. 80B). The Spaniards found only old people there but killed them nevertheless. Harshness appears even in part 1 of the *Araucana* (1569), and the poet Villagrá could cite it later to support "guerra a fuego y sangre" (see appendix 3).

Despite the harshness of part 1, in parts 2 (1578) and 3 (1589) of the *Araucana* Ercilla explicitly rejected total war. For him violence was not a learned dream but a reality, since he himself fought in the Araucanian war and saw the casualties. He voiced his critique most clearly in his story of Cañete, in part 3 (fig. 17). Since the *Araucana* is not well known to English and American audiences, I summarize the episode before analyzing it.

ERCILLA

The action at Cañete began around noon on 5 February 1558, when a spy came to the fort disguised as an Indian on forced labor. His contact in the fort showed him the gates open, the men asleep with their armor off, and the horses unsaddled. The spy immediately ran back to his army by a shortcut (*Araucana,* 3.31.36–41, pp. 506–7).[44] The Spaniards, who had been warned, barely had time to arm themselves before the Araucanians approached the fort from two sides. Both armies waited in silence, then 2,000 Indians charged the gates, against which the commander Reinoso had directed his large guns.[45] The poet emphasizes the slaughter that followed. No gun or missile missed, since the Spaniards were shooting into a crowd (*Araucana,* 3.32.6, 10, pp. 512–13). Meanwhile the cavalry, in which the poet served, broke up the crowd outside the gates, and the sudden onslaught left the Indians stunned. Again no lancer could miss his mark, and the horsemen killed more than the gunners (*Araucana,* 3.32.11–12, pp. 513–14). The Indians behind tried to retreat in a quick but organized fashion, scattering and rejoining, some turning to slow the pursuit. The cavalry followed closely, cutting down the last ones (*Araucana,* 3.32.16–19, pp. 514–15).[46] The Indians left many of their men behind, dead or captive, and could no longer maintain an army in the field.

The Spanish victory was so great and the casualties so numerous as to raise questions related to those posed by the Crusader sack of Jerusalem. This time, however, the poet provided a critique rather than an apology.

Ercilla thought Cañete involved too much slaughter, and he made it a study in visual horror. A dawn with clouded light signals the coming kills, the sun rising slowly and the moon turning its white face away rather than look on Araucania (*Araucana*, 3.31.34–35, p. 506). Next the poet itemizes the deaths, first those caused by the guns:

> Unos vieran de claro atravesados
> otros llevados la cabeza y brazos,
> otros sin forma alguna machucados,
> y muchos barrenados de picazos;
> miembros sin cuerpos, cuerpos desmembrados,
> lloviendo lejos trozos y pedazos,
> higados, intestinos, rotos huesos,
> entrañas vivas y bullentes sesos.
>
> (*Araucana*, 3.32.8, p. 513)

Some they see clearly cut across, others with heads and arms cut off, others pounded out of any form, and many drilled with hits: members without bodies and dismembered bodies raining far off chunks and pieces, livers, intestines, broken bones, living entrails, and boiling brains.

Next he describes the cavalry kills:

> Unos atropellados de caballos,
> otros los pechos y cabeza abiertos;
> otros, que era gran lastima mirallos,
> las entrañas y sesos descubiertos,
> vieran otros deshechos y hechos piezas,
> otros cuerpos enteros sin cabezas.
>
> Los voces, los lamentos, los gemidos,
> el miserable y lastimoso duelo,
> el rumor de las armas y alaridos
> hinchen el aire y cóncavo del cielo:
> luchando con la muerte los caídos
> se tuercen y revuelcan por el suelo,
> saliendo à un mismo tiempo tantas vidas
> por diversos lugares y heridas.
>
> (*Araucana*, 3.32.13–14, p. 514)

Some trampled by horses, others with chests and head opened, others, who were a great pity to see, with entrails and brains uncovered. They see others unmade and made pieces, and others, whole bodies without heads.

The voices, laments, groans, the miserable and pitiful lamentation, the noise of arms and cries swelled the air and the dome of the sky. The fallen, wrestling with death, twisted and rolled on the ground, so many lives going out at one time in different places and with different wounds.

Ercilla also dramatizes his own narration of the horror. Twice he breaks off his story, unable to continue. The first time, he shows a mind divided

by contraries, between pity and hate, a desire to condemn and his promise to narrate the war, a wish to distance himself and the fact of his partici-
pation in the battle (*Araucana*, 3.31.49–50, p. 509).⁴⁷ The initial shooting
provokes the second:

> Nunca se vió morir tantos á una,
> y así, aunque yo apresure más la mano,
> no puedo proseguir, que me divierte
> tanto golpe, herida, tanta muerte.
> (*Araucana*, 3.32.10, p. 513)

Never was seen so many die together; and, though I hasten the pen, I
cannot go on because so great a blow, wound, and so much death dis-
tract me.

The poet becomes a speaker, so upset over the slaughter that he can barely
talk. In fact, though the war continued through the assault on Quipeo,
Ercilla narrates no more battles. Cañete with its mangled corpses closes
that portion of his story.⁴⁸

No one shared the poet's complaint; the other chroniclers and witnesses merely note the many dead.⁴⁹ Certainly the commander Reinoso
carried out a conscious policy of terror. After the battle he shot thirteen
caciques, or chiefs, out of a cannon.⁵⁰ He followed up his victory with the
capture and impaling of Caupolicán, the Indian leader.⁵¹ Reinoso in turn
merely implemented the policies of his general, Don Garcia Hurtado de
Mendoza.⁵² The poet had already complained, for example, that the pursuit after Millarapue tarnished the victory because the Spaniards spared
no one (*Araucana*, 2.26.5–8, pp. 428–29), and there are other such incidents. The poet's commanders systematically killed or terrorized as many
Indians as possible, anticipating by a decade the "guerra a fuego y sangre"
that dominated Europe and America in the 1570s.

Ercilla's critique of such warfare is essentially political. He thinks not
only of the violence during battle but also of what occurs afterward. The
poet had witnessed the mutilation of Galbarino after the battle at the
lagunillas by the Bío-Bío River. Don Garcia had both hands of the Indian
lopped off. The victim fell in despair to the ground, biting his bloodless
stumps, and then tried to beat and eat an allied Indian carrying plunder.⁵³
It is against such practices that the poet directs the moralizing discourse
with which he introduces the battle of Cañete (*Araucana*, 3.32.1–5,
pp. 511–12).

Killing in cold blood is vengeance, cruelty, and tyranny, Ercilla says.
Even killing in a rage, though it can be forgiven, provokes resistance. The

double statement covers all the kills at Cañete. Deaths by gunfire would be morally evil, since Reinoso consciously set up the guns to kill as many as possible and then used them to execute captives. The horsemen, rushing about, acted in fury, but their kills, while morally neutral, merely stiffened Indian resistance for the war generally. Ercilla allows the common opinion that the victor may do what he wishes, but he still thinks the slaughter at Cañete was excessive and counterproductive, and he implies that terrorism lost the hope for peace. His criticism had special weight by 1589, the year he published his account of Cañete, for by then the war in Chile had lasted for more than thirty years.

To terror the poet opposes clemency, and here he refers to classical precedent. Rome conquered more nations by mercy than by the sword, and men praise the captain who is less bloody. The Chilean war unfortunately affords Ercilla no examples of clemency, so he must argue negatively. Both before and after Cañete he shows that terror encourages rather than deters resistance.

The story of Galbarino's mutilation offers an example. Ercilla published it in 1578, at the height of the period when commanders favored "guerra a fuego y sangre." Galbarino's exemplary punishment drew from him a vow of perpetual enmity (*Araucana*, 2.22.52–53, p. 366). He attended an Indian war council where he argued successfully against peace and so provoked the battle of Millarapue (*Araucana*, 2.23.3–17, pp. 368–71). Terror in this case helped prolong the war.[54]

Ercilla follows the account of Cañete with a critique of the Spanish march south. Men destroyed livestock and food, sacked towns, killed *caciques,* and raped women without regard to place or age. This terror worked to the disadvantage of the Spanish army and caused great suffering when they left on an exploratory journey farther south. The local Indians hid their supplies (*Araucana*, 3.34.59, 65, pp. 563–64) and gave the Spaniards a false guide who led them through the worst country and then vanished (3.35.24–29, pp. 570–71). Seven days of wandering followed, leading to fallen horses and to shoeless men in rags, bathed in blood, mud, and sweat, with broken feet and arms (*Araucana*, 3.35.30–40, pp. 571–73). In this case terror nearly destroyed its own agents.

Ercilla's critique presupposes the thinking we have already seen in Boiardo. Not for him—any more than for Orlando—the pursuit and extermination of the enemy after a victory. The soldier should limit bloodshed and look to the end of the war. Orlando first fought against the people of Orcagna and then found help from one of them, who gave him the information necessary for him to overthrow the unlawful ruler of the

land. Ercilla thought the Spaniards should have followed a similar pattern
in Chile.

Ercilla gives some of the pragmatic reasons behind the scholastic theory of a just war.[55] Such a war has as its end the reestablishment of peace,
and the commander should not always do what is allowed, if that action
would obstruct peace.[56] In fact, a war that is initially just can become
unjust by the way it is conducted or if it inflicts more evil than the evil
cause.

By this presentation Ercilla returns us to Boiardo, and yet a real shift
has taken place. What was new was not the basic analysis but the moral
passion with which poets debated the issue. The new hero helps to explain this change. The officer hero served an essentially ethical role and
so focused attention on the problem in a way that the old *furioso* did not.
Ercilla shows Reinoso planning the battle of Cañete, not fighting it. He
is therefore responsible for its casualties, where the *furioso* hero had to
answer only for his personal kills. Yet even the new hero only partly explains the moral anguish in these poems. The crucial difference lies elsewhere. Boiardo could have diminished the commander's responsibility by
an alteration of the story, but Ercilla could not change what happened at
Cañete. Ercilla was not inventing a story but narrating a historical event.
Ercilla, Tasso, Camões, Rufo—none could alter significantly the history
in their narratives. Ercilla saw all the dead at Cañete, some of whom he
probably killed, and he could not afford the detachment of Boiardo. Instead of the Italian's humor—the 600-pounder Ranaldo kills or Carlo's
fat chaplain—Ercilla gives us a narrator so upset he can barely tell his
story.

Seriousness forced the poets to be much more explicit. They may have
argued the same positions as their predecessors, but they worked out
those positions in such detail that they clarify the whole debate for us.
Ethically, it had two parts, one that produced a consensus, one that
caused disagreement.

Both sides agreed that a war had to be just, and they took elaborate
means to demonstrate this. Tasso made God part of his plot and had him
order and support the First Crusade. Ercilla devoted the long introduction of his last canto to the subject (*Araucana*, 3.37.1–25, pp. 589–94) and
justified Philip's takeover of Portugal as a legitimate inheritance. Earlier,
Boiardo provided examples, though he left the matter implicit rather
than explicit. Gradasso invades western Europe to get some military
equipment for himself, and Agricane begins the gigantic siege of Albraca
for a woman. Such wars are illegitimate, and Boiardo ends them appro-

priately with a comic duel and the besiegers in possession of an empty tower.[57]

The poets polarized over the conduct of war, in particular over "guerra a fuego y sangre." Could they accept mass killing and terror as part of war, a more or less automatic process that they could present tragically, as Tasso did through his Virgilian imitation? Or did it require the moral condemnation Ercilla insisted upon? This debate was practical as well as moral: Ercilla thought that terror prolonged the war in Chile.

This profound disagreement also affected the poets' literary presentations of fighting. Boiardo uses humor to mute the effect of the indiscriminate slaughtering done by his heroes. Tasso tries a different means but has the same end in mind. He limits the horrors of the Crusader sack of Jerusalem, mostly by abbreviation but also by softening details in his picture, particularly through Rinaldo, who looks terrifying but acts like Boiardo's Orlando. The poet thus tacitly admits to discomfort with his assumptions. In contrast, Ercilla, who rejects total war, emphasizes the violence by making his audience see the dying, mutilated, and wounded. For him such visualization achieves more than any moralizing discourse.

Polarization allows for no middle ground, no compromise. Instead an alternation between the two positions marked the later sixteenth century, now one side, now the other, receiving wide assent. The debate itself never came to a resolution.

——ELEVEN——

Ácoma

Gaspar Pérez de Villagrá

IN 1599, AT ÁCOMA PUEBLO IN NEW MEXICO, THE SPANIARDS
achieved a tactical success so great that it raised questions about a possible
massacre. They won with slender resources. The sergeant major, Vicente
de Zaldívar, brought only seventy-some Spaniards (*NM* 25.137–38, p.
134v),[1] such a small number that the enemy leader, Zutacapan, could not
believe they would risk fighting (27.125–32, p. 141v). The Spaniards had
provisions for just two weeks, and the well was five miles away from camp
(*NM* 28.28–29, p. 145r). The Indians, on the other hand, had all the advantages. First, they had what seemed an impregnable location, one the
Spaniards failed to carry a century later.[2] The village was built on a mesa
consisting of two great rocks, with cliffs that Villagrá compared to mountains, one point rising in his estimation to above 400 feet (*NM* 27.118–24,
28.304–9, 32.220–24, pp. 141v, 148v, 167r) (see fig. 21).[3] A chasm 300 paces
wide separated the North and South Mesas.[4] The settlement, situated on
the North Mesa, suggested to the poet a great labyrinth because of its size
and its caves, entrances, and exits (*NM* 31.260–67, 32.284, pp. 162v,
168r).[5] The Indians, moreover, had a good supply of water and, Villagrá
guessed, enough provisions for six years (*NM* 28.36–39, p. 145r).[6] He
probably erred here, as he did on the numbers, but he was correct in
assuming that the Ácomas had considerably more men than the Spaniards had. Finally, the Spaniards attacked in January and had already
suffered from winter snows.[7] In the Indian debate some said it would be
cowardly to fear the Spaniards and to think they could harm the Indians
in their lofty fort (*NM* 26.158–63, p. 137r). Yet the Spaniards captured
Ácoma in three days.

The sergeant major feinted at the North Mesa, where the Indians concentrated their forces, while he himself and eleven others climbed the

Figure 21. Two views of Ácoma. Reprinted form Lt. Col. W. H. Emory, *Notes of a Military Reconnaissance, from Fort Leavenworth . . . to San Diego.* (Washington, D.C., 1848). Courtesy Michael Murrin.

South Mesa by ladder (*NM* 28.42–44, 88–91, 250–54, 273–334, pp. 145r–v, 148r–49r).[8] Among the eleven was the poet Villagrá (*NM* 29.32, p. 150r). The Spaniards then held that position until nightfall, repelling with their harquebuses two attacks at the passage that joined the two mesa tops (*NM* 29.55–57, p. 150r).[9] Most of the fighting occurred on the second day, beginning with an ambush. Lured by what seemed an empty pueblo, thirteen Spaniards on their own initiative crossed over to the North Mesa and were instantly attacked (*NM* 30.120–89, pp. 156r–57r). The other Spaniards could not help them. Two ditches cut the passage between the two mesas, and the thirteen had taken the gangplank with them. The poet himself saved the situation, leaping the first ditch and bringing back the gangplank. The Spaniards now attacked the North Mesa in force (*NM* 30.190–209, p. 157r–v). A furious missile battle followed, the Indians charging directly at the harquebuses (*NM* 30.217–31.50, pp. 157v–59v), until Zaldívar had two cannon brought up (31.51–93, pp. 159v–60v), and other Spaniards set fire to the houses (31.150–57, p. 161r). The day ended in peace offers and renewed fighting (*NM* 31.173–209, pp. 161v–62r). The third day brought ruin. The exhausted Indians returned to fight (*NM* 31.231–38, p. 162r), but the fire also recovered strength (31.239–51, p. 162r–v). Roofs exploded, and the entrances[10] breathed out a thick, black, slow-moving smoke cloud, as sparks and cinders flew.[11] The high roofs, walls, and lofts broke apart and crumbled, suddenly burying their neighbors in fire and earth. Nothing remained unburned (*NM* 34.15–26, p. 176r). Finally, 600 Indians surrendered (*NM* 34.97–104, p. 177r).[12]

Few Indians remained because so many had committed suicide that day. Warriors killed themselves and each other (*NM* 31.252–59, p. 162v). Women also stabbed themselves, threw themselves into the flames, or leaped from the cliff, and they killed their children (*NM* 31.315–32, p. 163v). Villagrá describes the plazas and walls of Ácoma wrapped in streams, puddles, and lakes of fresh blood, and a great number of corpses (*NM* 32.45–55, p. 164v). As the pueblo burned down, the suicides continued, people leaping from the summits to shatter their bodies below (*NM* 34.27–31, p. 176r).[13] Villagrá dramatizes this tragedy especially through two warriors, the fictional Gicombo and his Navajo companion, Bempol.[14]

Gicombo had opposed war with the Spaniards and was not present at the massacre of Juan de Zaldívar (brother of Vicente) and other Spaniards the previous December, the action that started the conflict (*NM* 26.9–16, p. 135r). To prove his courage, nevertheless, he agreed to defend his village (*NM* 26.321–28, p. 139v) and later was elected war captain, after the Spaniards had already captured the South Mesa (29.303–8, p. 153v). In return he exacted from the Ácomas a vow, confirmed by oath: they would fight to the death and commit suicide if necessary (*NM* 29.330–33, 30.7–20, p. 154r–v). After much carnage and a Spanish peace offer, he later reminded them of this oath (*NM* 31.268–308, p. 163r).[15] This reply started the mass suicide, as Gicombo himself went home to die. He found his house burning and broke through to his wife, whom he clubbed to death. At this point the sergeant major and the Spaniards arrived. Zaldívar made him an offer beyond his instructions: Gicombo could govern the Ácomas as king. The Indian replied with a challenge, and Zaldívar had him shot (*NM* 32.304–82, pp. 168r–69r). The other women in his house then ran to his friend Bempol, asking that he take them wherever he thought best. They set Gicombo's little daughter before him (*NM* 33.85–121, pp. 170v–71r). Taking her, he answered that if they wanted freedom, they should follow him, and he leaped from the cliff. Fearless, the women all followed (*NM* 33.128–49, p. 171r–v). Villagrá compares the two warriors to Brutus and Cassius, who could not live subject to another (*NM* 32.275–77, p. 167v). They fill the roles of tragic heroes, Gicombo especially. Caught by his military ethic, he defends his guilty city, and that same code determines the mass suicide that ends the war.

Self-destruction by a group has many historical parallels, both before and after Ácoma.[16] Villagrá himself alludes to Numantia (*NM* 28.118–20, p. 146r), a story that concerned early Iberian history. Reduced by famine and faced with a demand for unconditional surrender, the Numantines received from the Roman commander, Scipio Aemilianus, a day for suicide. They then killed their captains, burned their town, and killed themselves.[17] A closer parallel, however—so close that Ácoma almost seems a repetition of it—was an incident from the Araucanian War, the battle of Reinaco (10 June 1554). This was an Indian fort on a mesa-shaped hill, steep on the east side, rocky on the others, protected on the south by a stream and thick stand of trees. Another Villagrá, Pedro, led the assault with a feint on the east side. Meanwhile he sent ten harquebusiers around by the other side, who fought their way in easily while the Araucanians were devoting all their attention to Pedro. The Indians, faced with a battle on two fronts, were cut to pieces. Some, preferring death to captivity, jumped over the cliff, while others were captured.[18] All these cases present the same tragic pattern, which the poet Villagrá developed through a set of invented characters, who rationalized the historical actions of the enemy.

The character Gicombo illustrates the poet's procedure. He reflects the historical Caoma, whom the Spaniards identified as a captain of one of the wards of Ácoma and who gave evidence at the trial of the surviving Indians, which the Spaniards held later. Like Gicombo he was in the country the day of the December massacre and learned about it only afterward.[19] The absence of a commander at a crucial military action could suggest a divided pueblo, something that other Indian witnesses indicate.[20] Taxio stated that when Vicente de Zaldívar made his peace offer before the assault, the old people and the leaders did not want peace and so attacked with arrows and stones. Xunusta draws the inference: because they were split, they did not submit.[21] Both these witnesses were in their early twenties, and their evidence indicates a generational division at Ácoma. The old favor war; the young, who must fight it, oppose. Villagrá develops this opposition within a fictional Indian family, opposing the lowborn adventurer Zutacapan who instigates the December massacre[22] to his teen-age son, Zutancalpo, who appeals to good sense (*NM* 18.93–100, p. 98r–v). A series of debates dramatizes this clash and conforms to Xunusta's testimony.[23] Paralyzed by internal discord, Ácoma could not respond positively to Zaldívar's overtures, and the three-day battle followed of necessity. The pattern is tragic, and the literary model Virgilian.

Villagrá gave his epic a Virgilian structure. In the first or Odyssean half, the colonists journey to New Mexico, and in the second or Iliadic part they fight to stay in the land after the natives have initially accepted them. In this second half Villagrá makes specific comparisons to the *Aeneid,* especially to book 2, as had Tasso before him.[24] Chumpo recalls Priam. An aged Indian, he surrenders amid his fallen city, reminiscing over all the dead he has had the misfortune to see, the bloody kills, and the corpses eaten by their own dogs (*NM* 33.211–71, pp. 172v–73r).[25] The Trojan horse appears in a simile (*NM* 32.240–44, p. 167r–v),[26] and Zaldívar holds an Indian audience with his speech as Aeneas had held Dido (*NM* 34.221–25, p. 178v). More important than these specific references, however, is the tragic pattern they imply, which Villagrá develops. His ending makes this parallel explicit.

Villagrá closes the *Historia* with a violence equal to that of Virgil's *Aeneid.* Cotumbo and Tempal, two leaders of the war party and close associates of Zutacapan, commit suicide by hanging.[27] They give two speeches that show a hatred of the Spaniards that no diplomacy could ever alleviate.[28] Theirs is the kind of enmity that paralyzed the pueblo before the battle and inflamed the Indians even during defeat. Spanish guns merely increased it:

> . . . qual vemos,
> Crecer y lebantar las bravas llamas,
> De poderosos vientos combatidas,
> Que mientras mas las soplan y combaten,
> Mas es su brava fuerça y gran pujança,

Assi feroces todos rebramando,
A boca de cañon arremetian.

(*NM* 31.29–35, p. 159v)

As we see brave flames grow and rise, beaten by powerful winds that, while
they blow and buffet them the more, the more is their brave force and
great strength, so all ferocious, bellowing loudly, they charged into the
mouth of the cannon.

Next they respond to Zaldívar's peace offer with arrows and the cry for
mass suicide (*NM* 31.185–94, p. 161v). Hatred caused the war, and the
fighting in turn deepens that hatred.[29] Extermination alone ends the
cycle, and Villagrá expresses this tragic logic through a thematic of fate.[30]

The theme has two aspects, both of which the Navajo Bempol illustrates. He hopes death will end his cruel fate (*NM* 33.32–40, p. 170r),[31]
yet he sees that fate as providential, wondering what gods the city had
offended (70–80, p. 170v). The Indians, in fact, see Our Lady and Santiago helping the Spaniards (*NM* 34.189–99, 228–32, p. 178r-v). Villagrá
thus reproduces the Virgilian pattern already imitated by Tasso. Fate ful-
fills a divine decree, and a miraculous vision justifies the capture of
Ácoma.

All this fits the thinking behind total war discussed earlier in relation
to Tasso (see chapter 10). A conflict, once begun, follows an automatic,
if tragic, process. Ethics, therefore, applies only to its commencement,
and Villagrá accordingly focuses on Zutacapan, who initiated the December massacre. Other Indians blame him for their misfortune,[32] and
afterward women beat his corpse for the same reason (*NM* 34.115–58,
p. 177r-v). Villagrá himself discusses the matter in a long passage (*NM*
32.1–45, p. 164r-v). Zutacapan provides an example of pride. By it he
moved an unjust war and caused the end of so many lives, including that
of his own son, and the burning of so many houses. Since the Indians
began the war, the ethical question concerns them alone and among them
the man whose orders initiated it. The poet thus presents the same logic
with which Tasso justified the Crusader sack of Jerusalem, and like the
older poet, he too was arguing over a morally complicated situation.

Villagrá published his epic the year after the viceregal court in Mexico
had completed its investigation of Spanish conduct in New Mexico and
formulated charges against Governor Juan de Oñate, Zaldívar, and the
poet himself.[33] One major charge concerned Ácoma and was directed
against Villagrá's commanders. The poet, now in Spain, tried to present
the defendants' case before the trial, which took place in 1614. Two docu-

ments present his argument. The first was the *Historia de la Nueva Mexico*
itself, which, following epic requirements, gave a purified version of the
assault on Ácoma. There Villagrá gave a simplified account of disputed
matters like the peace negotiations and their breakdown at the end of
the second and beginning of the third day, and he dropped the judicial
mutilation and enslavement of the captives, which happened sometime
after the battle. Instead he devoted a pamphlet to these and similar
charges. He published his pamphlet in the year the trial was announced
(1612) and titled it *Justificación de las muertes, justicias, y castigos.* . . . Modern historians have judged his epic account, however idealized, to be accurate; even those who regard Zaldívar and the Spaniards harshly accept
Villagrá's story, simply changing the interpretation.[34] The poet and his
commanders, however, had many and powerful enemies, and neither epic
nor pamphlet was enough to save them.

Villagrá directed his pamphlet at some "outlaws," who repeated in
Spain the charges current in Mexico. These "outlaws" had deserted
Oñate's expedition in the famine year of 1601, while the governor led an
exploratory party to the plains. In fact, a majority of the colonists left
New Mexico then, making fifty-seven charges against Oñate.[35] Captain
Luis de Velasco best expresses their views. He was the viceroy's agent, and
his letter on Ácoma set up the charges of massacre (*OD* 2.609, 614–15).
Still more serious enemies, perhaps, were the Franciscans and in particular the commissary general, Friar Juan de Escalona. He encouraged the
desertion of 1601 and criticized the Ácoma war generally.[36] His complaints and those of Velasco reached the Council of the Indies and started
the investigations (*OD* 2.972).

The trial of 1614 found the Spaniards at Ácoma guilty on two counts.
First, it faulted Governor Oñate because he chose for the command of
the army a man too emotionally involved after his brother's death at the
hands of the Acomas the previous December. Villagrá carefully allows for
this charge in his account. Vicente kills the man he sees wearing his
brother's clothes, and the poet describes the action by one of his effective similes:

> Qual suele un bravo sacre arrebatado,
> Que de muy alta cumbre se abalança,
> Sobre la blanca garza, y de encuentro,
> La priva de sentido, y luego à pique,
> Hecha un ovillo toda à tierra viene.
>   (*NM* 29.120–24, p. 151r)

As a brave hawk, in fury, is accustomed to do, which swoops upon the
white heron from the tallest height and stuns it by the encounter, and it
comes quickly to the ground, curled up.

After the battle he throws himself tearfully on the bloodstained spot
where his brother died and makes a decorative lament.[37] Second, the
court decided that the Spaniards had acted too severely at Ácoma, a judgment that concerns both Oñate's instructions and Zaldívar's actions (OD
2.IIII, 1114). The court came to this decision despite the fact that the
policy had been determined in a public meeting.[38]

The logic of this double judgment presupposes the new military situation alluded to in chapter 10. Ethical questions concern the officers, who
have replaced the old furioso heroes, so the court sentences Oñate and
Zaldívar, not the men generally. (Oñate was sentenced to perpetual exile
from New Mexico and four years' exile from Mexico City and had to pay
a fine of 6,000 ducats; Zaldívar was exiled from New Mexico for eight
years and from Mexico City for two years and was fined 2,000 ducats
[OD 2.1113–15].) The substance of the charge then rests on the second
conviction, for severity proves Zaldívar's unsuitability as a commander.
Yet not even severity would suffice by itself. Captain Velasco had also
charged that Zaldívar later burned one of the Saline pueblos, killing 900
people and leveling the village. Yet the court judged him not guilty in
this case (OD 2.615, 1115), where he had no emotional involvement. Presumably, the court considered Zaldívar's actions at Ácoma too severe because the Indians had made a peace offer. They had shown that they were
not intractable. Their slaughter, therefore, suggested a massacre.

Villagrá presents the evidence one way in the epic and another in the
testimony he delivered at the Indian trial after the battle. In the epic
the sergeant major twice offers the Indians a chance to surrender, before
the assault and toward the end of the second day. The second is the crucial gesture, to which the Indians respond with a shower of arrows; with
redoubled efforts, using arms, teeth, and fists; and with the cry that their
women and children would die too. Villagrá compares them to rabid
dogs (NM 31.186, p. 161v), and they attack with such force that they
amaze and upset the Spaniards. Zutacapan provides the single exception.
He asks for peace but slinks away when he learns the conditions, for the
sergeant major excludes from his offer those who started the war. By this
scene the poet rationalizes the situation and explains why the Indians
could never surrender (NM 31.173–208, pp. 161v–62r). In accordance with

their public meeting Oñate had instructed Zaldívar to demand the surrender of the leaders who had instigated the massacre and had further required that the Indians move to the plain below and that the Spaniards burn the pueblo, lest it be used again as a fortress.[39] Given such instructions, Zaldívar could offer peace, but he could not seriously expect the Indians to accept it.

Villagrá omits from his epic the Indian counteroffer made at 5 P.M. on the second day. In his prose testimony he says that the Ácomas brought turkeys and blankets, but Zaldívar had him return them. Other witnesses give his reason, which again concerns his orders. Zaldívar came not for blankets but to find out why the Indians had killed Spaniards in December. The Ácomas, nevertheless, left the goods as a pledge.[40] Next morning the sergeant major entered the village and began to arrest men and women and jail them in an *estufa* (kiva). At this they broke away through concealed tunnels, which opened into the adjoining houses, or barricaded themselves. The Spaniards decided to smoke them out, and Zaldívar ordered battle without quarter and commanded that the houses be burned.[41] Villagrá notes this resistance[42] but dramatizes it rather for Cotumbo and Tempal, the two Indians whose deaths close the epic. It was this sequence of events that Captain Velasco presented in such a manner as to suggest a premeditated massacre (*OD* 2.614–15).

In Velasco's account Zaldívar, after placing the Indians in the *estufa*, stationed a black with some other soldiers at the entrance and had the Indians come out, one by one. They were immediately executed and hurled over the cliff. Frightened by these murders, the other Indians made a last stand in their *estufas* and houses. Men killed one another rather than fall into enemy hands. The Spaniards in turn burned the village, trying to smoke them out. The viceregal court accepted this version against the others and so found Oñate and Zaldívar guilty.[43] This judgment, however, depends on faulty evidence.

In his appeal of 1617 Oñate states that the six witnesses at the trial gave conflicting reports on Ácoma. Two provided a version that agrees with that of Villagrá and the eyewitness testimony collected after the assault. Four, who had deserted during the famine year, supported Velasco's version (*OD* 2.1127–28). This one, unfortunately, seems based on indirect evidence. Velasco was treasurer of the expedition and probably did not go to Ácoma (*OD* 1.249–50, the Salazar Inspection). The documents do not mention his presence there, and his version of the war clashes too often with the eyewitness accounts and contains too many small errors of the sort typical of someone reporting a matter secondhand. For example, he has the Indians offer maize on the second day, something not mentioned in any other account,[44] and he gets his figures wrong throughout. He claims that Juan de Zaldívar demanded blankets as well as provisions before the December massacre, a detail corroborated only by one other person, an Indian who was not present.[45] The Franciscan evidence has even less support. Escalona, who wrote the accusatory letter, only arrived in New Mexico a year later.[46] Friar Alonso Martínez, the previous commissary, did accompany the army to Ácoma, but he stayed below and did not witness any of the fighting on the mesa.[47] It seems that the viceregal court, when it condemned Oñate and Zaldívar, followed not eyewitness but secondhand testimony.[48] The court probably did so because sentiment in Mexico had already turned against the kind of methods used by Oñate and favored instead the approach to the frontier that gave the Franciscans a privileged position. Hence the importance of Escalona's letter, whatever its basis in evidence. This viewpoint as well as Oñate's methods came out of the long Chichimeca War, which lasted from ca. 1550 to ca. 1610, although the main fighting ended by 1590.

The Chichimeca War revolved around the silver mines discovered first at Zacatecas and then at other places, far to the north of Mexico City. Harsh tactics characterized the war up to 1585. The Spaniards looked to Indians for mine workers and at the same time feared them. The prospecting families lived in isolated communities, and communication with the capital was difficult. At the same time the nomadic Chichimecas, attracted by the supply trains and enraged over slaving, started a guerilla war. They used terrorist tactics, scalping living victims by pulling the skin off the head and face, cutting off the genitals and stuffing them in the victim's mouth, impaling or dismembering Spaniards slowly till they died.[49] The colonists replied in kind, anything from execution by decapitation, hanging, or burning to amputation of feet, hands, or fingers. Enslavement reached a peak in the decade 1575–85.[50]

The Oñate and Zaldívar families were deeply involved with the silver mines and with this war. Two Zaldívars played leading roles. Another Vicente had been lieutenant captain general for the Chichimeca War and still held that office when Oñate left for New Mexico. Another Juan helped pacify the Chichimecas at Colotlán (1597–1600).[51] Oñate had himself fought the Chichimecas for twenty years (*OD* 1.42–43), and his family had been among the pioneers who originally developed the silver mines at Zacatecas.[52] In fact, the venture to New Mexico followed the same pattern, a search for mineral wealth far beyond the frontier, another leap in the dark.

Oñate and Zaldívar carried over to New Mexico the stern methods of war developed for the Chichimecas.[53] Villagrá gives the theory in his *Justificación,* the pamphlet in which he defended their procedures in the Ácoma war. He claims that cruelty is the mother of fear, which is the most important thing in war. The practice of Christian commanders in the sixteenth century sanctions the methods of total war, and Villagrá has no difficulty citing for Ácoma numerous sacks and civilian slaughters: Tunis, Dura, Antwerp, and Paris.[54] Because the Ácomas began the war, killing the *maese de campo,* or army commander, and ten to twelve others, they became liable to these severe methods of war and bore the responsibility for the ruin of their own pueblo.[55]

The war council or public debate before the Ácoma campaign worked out the pragmatics. The situation of the colonists—a few people occupying a salient that protruded far beyond the regular frontier[56]—required a prompt crushing of what they considered a rebellion. One of the survivors of the December massacre, Captain Tabora, outlines the Spanish reaction. Ácoma is an impregnable rock, now fortified, and can serve as a rallying point for Indian resistance. If it is not destroyed, New Mexico will become too dangerous for the colonists. Its punishment, on the other hand, will make the other Indians obedient.[57] Juan de León claims in support of this analysis that Ácoma is a place where Indians will take refuge in time of war.[58] The Spaniards, therefore, must destroy the pueblo and make the mesa uninhabitable. Such attitudes help explain why the Indians probably never could have accepted Spanish terms or surrendered. They could not have saved their pueblo in any case.[59]

The same theory of war explains Oñate's harsh treatment of the captives. They were judged as a group, most being enslaved and men over twenty-five mutilated.[60] Villagrá defends the justice of this action, answering the legal objection that such punishments confounded the innocent with the guilty. In a marginal note to his pamphlet the poet cites authorities who allow the offended to chastise one person for another's crime. In fact, judicial mutilation was an acceptable punishment in Europe and had been used in the Chichimeca War.[61] In practical terms, such justice functions as a chastisement, and success justifies all the killings and mutilations, as Villagrá argues in his pamphlet. New Mexico has had peace since then, and fewer than fifty Spanish soldiers control the vast province.[62] In fact, the Spaniards enjoyed relative security until the Apache raid of 1640 and had no serious difficulty with the Pueblo Indians till 1650.[63] If the Spaniards had not chastised Ácoma, Villagrá argues, they would have had to kill all the Indians, little by little, or else they would have had to endure a great war lasting many years, as they did in Chile and in the Gran Chichimeca.[64] Initial violence, however bloody, ultimately saved lives and avoided a serious war.[65] But however successful, "guerra a fuego y sangre" did not fit current viceregal policy, which itself reflected a different phase of the old Chichimeca War.

Harsh tactics had not won that war, and by the 1580s the clergy became convinced that they actually prolonged it. The army itself was the root cause. Soldiers did not receive enough pay and needed the slave trade to supplement their income.[66] The clergy charged that they provoked war even with peaceful Indians so that they might continue that trade. Each conquest caused war with the next Indian tribe, fearful that they too would suffer enslavement.[67] So argued the archbishop of Guadalajara in 1584, and Escalona later made the same critique of Oñate.[68] Though one of the silver millionaires, Oñate did not command sufficient resources for the conquest and had to impose tributes on the Pueblo Indians, which in turn provoked the wars of 1599–1600 and the enslavement of captives. Escalona merely expressed the standard critique of total war that had governed viceregal policy since 1585. Not soldiers but missionaries had ended the Chichimeca war.

Philip Wayne Powell in his *Soldiers, Indians, and Silver* describes the new system. It had four parts: (1) diplomatic efforts to make peace with the Chichimeca tribes; (2) an intensified missionary effort; (3) the transplantation of sedentary Indians to the frontier; (4) the use of military money to finance the operation.[69] Peace became possible once most of the soldiers left and systematic slave raids ceased.[70] With the military money thus saved, the viceroy bribed the Chichimecas to settle down and learn farming, encouraged by the new presence of Tlaxcalans and other sedentary tribes. The friars provided the education and commanded the few soldiers stationed at their missions. The archbishop of Guadalajara, whose speech inaugurated this policy, argued that defensive colonization despite its bribes cost much less than a militarized frontier.[71] With the new methods the war quickly died down, and by 1600 the nomadic Chichimecas were already disappearing.[72] Villagrá himself learned to work more or less under this system, when he returned to Mexico in 1599 and served as *alcalde mayor* (sheriff) at Guanaceví (1601–3).[73] He had to operate with Jesuits and try soft means to draw the Tepeguanes from war. During his term the land was quiet.[74]

The trial of 1614 repeated the old critique of "guerra a fuego y sangre" already made in the 1580s and thus supported the new mission system that governed Spanish frontier policy for the next 200 years. It also fit the mood of the times: the truce with the Dutch and the end of religious strife generally in Europe, whether in the Low Countries, France, or Ireland. Ercilla best expressed the new attitude for poets, when he revived the old condottieri notions of military conduct for the later parts of his *Araucana*. A soldier must treat every enemy as a potential friend.

This new attitude did not last. The Mexican model, though it worked in the Gran Chichimeca, failed in other places. Its proponents imposed their standards on New Mexico only to leave a colony polarized between governor and Franciscan, a split that lasted up to the Pueblo Revolt of 1680. Nor did it work in Chile. Governor Loyola tried to bring about a lasting peace with the Araucanians, but they killed him instead and won their independence.[75] Villagrá used Loyola's failure to justify the Spanish treatment of Ácoma and faulted even the pacification of the Chichimecas. He could point to still existing war zones, complain about taxes to bribe the enemy, and claim that he won peace in Nueva Vizcaya without such payments.[76] He further stated that success and not morality determined the choice between the two modes of war. Cortés flattened New Spain with fire and blood, but the king said nothing despite Las Casas's attack. If Oñate had found a rich land—even if he had done all the same chastisements—they would have raised him above the moon.[77] Villagrá, of course, speaks with bitterness and sarcasm, anticipating his trial, yet his analysis requires attention. The attitude Ercilla and the Mexican court expressed did perhaps dominate thinking by the end of the century, but many still disagreed. Neither approach had regular success, and four years after the trial, the Thirty Years' War began.[78]

PART FIVE

The Epic without War

TWELVE

The English

Sir Philip Sidney, Michael Drayton, and Samuel Daniel

SO FAR I HAVE SAID LITTLE ABOUT THE ENGLISH CONTRIBU-
tion to romance and epic during the sixteenth century. After Malory, in
fact, English writers concentrated primarily on translation. In the reign
of Henry VIII, Sir John Bourchier, Lord Berners, Englished most of the
Huon cycle of romances. Many worked on Virgil: Gavin Douglas in
Scotland; Henry Howard, earl of Surrey, and Thomas Phaer in England.
At century's end John Harington translated Ariosto, and Edward Fairfax
translated Tasso. At the same time, in the 1580s and 1590s, other English
writers composed a cluster of original heroic narratives: Sidney, Spenser,
Michael Drayton, and Samuel Daniel. Together these works mark a new
stage in the development of epic and romance that affected the major
such works of the following century.

One might have expected very different representations of war from
Sidney, on the one hand, and Drayton and Daniel on the other. Aside
from considerable stylistic variations, these late sixteenth-century poets
had sharp theoretical differences over the nature of literature itself. Sidney
identified poetry with fiction. In his celebrated formulation poets cannot
lie, since they affirm nothing. Narration is instead "an imaginative
groundplot of a profitable invention" (*Defence*, 185). Scholars have understood this claim variously, relating it to Italian Aristotelianism of the mid-
century or to still earlier traditions of northern skepticism.[1] Whatever its
antecedents, this position could not contrast more strongly with Daniel's
remarks on historical epic, which he made part of his *Civile Wars* (1595–
1609).[2] He invokes Memory and claims a story: "Unintermixt with fiction's fantasies, / I versifie the troth, not Poetize" (*CW* 1.6).[3] He later introduces the ghost of Henry V, who develops the point (*CW* 5.4–5). The
ghost wonders why poets seek feigned paladins and do not give glory to

the true designs of men like Talbot. Daniel thus argues for a conception of epic that fits the most recent trends set by Mediterranean authors— Tasso, Camões, and Spanish poets, such as Ercilla and Villagrá. Nothing could be further from Sidney, who stressed rather the fictional side of history.[4]

Despite these fundamental differences, both Sidney and Daniel as well as Drayton[5] share a basic approach to representations of warfare. They also share certain mimetic techniques and shy away generally from war in their narratives. All three men reduce war to a small part of their stories and so set the pattern of the following century, that of the epic without war.

Three narratives are the focus of my discussion: Sidney's *Arcadia,* Drayton's *Barons Warres,* and Daniel's *Civile Wars.* All three present complicated textual histories. Like the Italians, the three Englishmen kept revising their texts, so one must clarify which version of a particular battle is under discussion. For Sidney the situation is clear, since he included battles only in his revision of the *Arcadia,* which Fulke Greville first published in 1590 but which most people read in the version edited by Mary Sidney, countess of Pembroke (1593).[6] The case of Drayton is more difficult, for he never stopped tinkering with his text. He began with the *Mortimeriados* in rhyme royal (1596), reworked it as the *Barons Warres* in ottava rima (1603), and still had changes for the 1619 edition. I have used this last version, which presents his final intention, but with an eye to the original version done in the 1590s.[7] Daniel poses another kind of problem. Besides revising his *Civile Wars,* he gradually expanded it, publishing books 1–4 in 1594 and book 5 in 1599, rearranging them as seven books in 1601, and adding an eighth in 1609.[8] By then Daniel had ceased changing his text, so the 1609 edition represents his final intent.

BATTLES

From all the various types of fighting that make up a war—naval battles, sieges and assaults, guerilla ambushes—these English poets chose to represent primarily one form. Their choice was the classic mode with which we began this book: the open field engagement. Sidney dramatizes the skirmish that begins the siege of Cecropia's castle.[9] Drayton portrays two battles, those of Burton and Borough Bridges, both in book 2, but he emphasizes the former. Daniel has three: Shrewsbury (1403) in book 4, Castillon (1453) in book 6, and Towton (1461) in book 8. In my discussion I emphasize Castillon, since the field camp fortified by cannon that Jean

Bureau set up before the battle illustrates a characteristic of early modern warfare that made narrative difficult for romancers and poets. I do not focus upon the events of these battles but rather on the manner of their presentation—or, really, nonpresentation—for the English made their contribution not by their choice among possible military encounters but by the literary techniques they employed.

All three poets prefer cavalry battles. Although Sidney mentions foot soldiers at the beginning of his skirmish (*NA* 7.467), they never appear in his narrative. Cavalry, in fact, dominates all actions in the *New Arcadia*. Anaxius brings only horse to relieve the castle (*NA* 15.521).[10] Daniel also features cavalry where possible, especially at Shrewsbury, where Douglas keeps unhorsing dummy kings, trying to kill Henry IV (*CW* 4.49–52).[11] Drayton likewise assumes that Burton Bridge was a cavalry struggle.[12]

The three thus revert to the methods of medieval and Italian romance but with various degrees of justification. Sidney, since he has no commitment to history, may do as he pleases. In his view the author ranges freely within the zodiac of wit and has a "high flying liberty of conceit."[13] Therefore, he can make his battles classical, medieval, early modern, or some combination thereof, as long as he keeps them internally consistent. Drayton dramatizes English warfare just before its transformation under Edward III, the last time such cavalry clashes regularly occurred. His assumptions accordingly fit his subject. Daniel, on the other hand, has more difficulty. Although he prefers cavalry, he must refer as well to infantry, since even the knights of the fifteenth century fought on foot.

Although a view of war as consisting of cavalry engagements did not fit current trends in Spain and the Low Countries, it did have some justification in the late sixteenth century. During the French religious wars most battles turned on cavalry, and the Huguenots had the best cavalry troops.[14] Cavalry had also experienced a revival in England. At Pinkie (1547) the duke of Somerset held off the Scottish pike with cavalry charges until he could use missiles against their flanks.[15] In Ireland English cavalry routinely routed horse or foot at odds of one to ten.[16] Leicester took a thousand horse to Holland in 1585.[17] Sidney participated in that expedition and had previously praised cavalry more than once. He studied horsemanship at the court of Emperor Maximilian II and talked about it in his *Defence* (150). In the *Arcadia* he also emphasized Musidorus's proficiency as a horseman (*NA* 2.5.247–49). At the same time this revival did not introduce anything like the old horse battles of the high Middle Ages, which had set the pattern for romance narrative. Leicester's force consisted mainly of infantry at a proportion of eight to one, and it

fought against Spanish *tercios,* which likewise had mostly foot soldiers.
Even the Huguenots faced Catholic or royal armies that had excellent
infantry contingents and won most of the battles.[18] The limited revival
of cavalry did not mean a return to medieval methods of war, so a considerable distance separated the poets' narratives from current practice.[19]

The poets convey this sense of remoteness stylistically in two ways, by
generalized and by impressionistic description. Daniel specializes in the
first mode, Drayton in the second, but both men make use of both
modes. Sidney has generalizing passages but avoids impressionism, instead devoting careful attention to the duels of his heroes.

Castillon best illustrates the generalized style (*CW* 6.88–98). Consider
the following passage:

> Frank of their owne, greedy of others blood,
> No strokes they give, but wounds, no wound, but kills:
> Neere to their hate, close to their work they stood,
> Hit where they would, their hand obeyes their wills;
> Scorning the blow from far, that doth no good,
> Loathing the cracke, unlesse some blood it spils:
> No wounds could let-out life that wrath held in,
> Till others wounds, reveng'd, did first begin.
>
> (*CW* 6.90)

This passage could describe any close-in fighting between infantrymen,
from the Greek phalanxes to U.S. marines with bayonets. All poets need
such descriptions, of course, but most either locate them topographically
or alternate them with other kinds of passages that lend specificity to the
battle. Drayton, for example, makes his casualties proper to Burton
Bridge in an otherwise conventional use of the formula of "the one . . .
the other": "One his assayling enemie beguiles, / As from the bridge he
fearfully doth fall, / Crush'd with his weight upon the stakes and pyles"
(*BW* 2.41). Sidney prefers the other method, that of alternation. He has
generalized passages, but he also supplies a different description for each
of Amphialus's kills (*NA* 3.7.469–71). Daniel, however, keeps his battle
generalized, even when he uses different techniques. Personifications like
Wrath, Fury, and Fortune, or similes of opposed winds and a falling oak
tree do not lend specificity to his presentation. Daniel describes not Castillon but a typical battle. Drayton does not go so far, but he shows this
tendency. Over the years he tended to eliminate specifics from his narrative of Burton Bridge. In the *Mortimeriados* he stated that Burton Bridge,
where the fighting that he narrates occurred, was very long, having forty

arches (280), and that the barons charged it initially with 300 horse (372). The final version dropped both points.

Others in the late sixteenth century used such a style but with different effects. I have noted earlier its presence in Villagrá and Ercilla (see chapter 8), but they also gave topographical specifics and used other literary techniques. Unlike Daniel, they did not give *only* generalized descriptions. Their readers, moreover, could supply specifics based on their own experiences in the same battles or in similar encounters. The English poets, in contrast, described action that had occurred long ago or in an imaginary Arcadian world. Their readers could supply no specifics other than those given them. For Castillon Daniel provided only an outline, a fading image at the margins of memory.

Lyric impressionism, which seems the opposite of the generalized style, nevertheless serves a similar function in these narratives. The poets provide specific images or details but no coherent picture or view of a military encounter. Drayton, for example, evokes the start of battle, with its noise and music: "What with the showt, and with the dreadfull show, / The heards of beasts ran bellowing to the wood; / When drums and trumpets to the charge did sound, / As they would shake the grosse clouds to the ground" (*BW* 2.32). Later he gives a precise visual picture of the fighting on the bridge, as the pennons fly whirling from the helmets like snowflakes (*BW* 2.38). He added in his revised version a whole sequence of stanzas giving the heraldic ensigns of some of the nobles involved (*BW* 22–27). Daniel likewise opted for scattered pictures when he wrote his last battle, that of Towton. The Yorkists send an arrow shower like clouds of steel that "new-night" the sky (*CW* 8.16), and at battle's end the wounded and weary crawl helpless in the river (20–21). Such passages give the illusion of immediacy to a battle narrative: particular sense impressions instead of generalized description. They do not, however, help the reader understand how the battle developed or why one side won.[20] Neither the generalized nor the impressionistic mode clarifies the tactics of a battle.

Both Sidney and Drayton, nevertheless, set up the initial tactics and give a sense of a battle's end. For his skirmish Sidney tells us that Amphialus takes 200 horse to meet the advancing army and conceals 500 foot soldiers in a wood on the slope of a hill. At the end Amphialus must break off his duel with Musidorus because the enemy army is getting between him and his castle.[21] Drayton similarly explains where Edward and the rebel barons camp and states that the king splits his army, sending half of it across a ford to outflank the enemy (*BW* 2.29). A reader unfamiliar with Drayton's first version of the battle might think that Kent's charge at the bridge won the day.[22] In this respect both poets are true to the original romance tradition, which reflected the cavalry battles of the high medieval period. Commanders could position their men before battle but had little control once it started.

A crucial difference separates Sidney and Drayton from the Vulgate author of the *Mort le roi Artu* or from Pulci and Boiardo. No medieval or Italian romancer would have an ambush set up and never mention it again. Bradamante's sudden attack, late in the day at Montealbano, and the appearance of Ban and Bors on the barons' flank, as they struggle with Arthur at Bedgrayne, affect each battle decisively.[23] Not so with Sidney and Drayton. Sidney never again mentions the band of 500 foot soldiers, and Drayton in his final version says nothing about the half of the king's army that forded the Trent before the battle.[24] The poets are content to give the impression of tactics but do not work them out. Daniel goes further. Fortune signals the crisis point at Castillon (*CW* 6.91), and the poet thus substitutes a personification for an analysis.[25]

The English could dispense with tactics because their audience and perhaps they themselves lacked a sense for or interest in the necessary details. No one had fought that way in England since the days of Edward II, 250 years before. They were thus content to suggest and wise enough not to develop the tactics for cavalry clashes outside the range of their experience.

The English poets did have an interest in such warfare, but an interest of a very different kind. They substituted for realism a romantic view of medieval warfare. Sidney orchestrates his battle in the manner of a tournament. He gives careful accounts of the jousts and duels of Amphialus, Philanax, and Musidorus. The older romancers, even Tasso, would have done the same, but the context gave a different sense of war. They would not have blurred the tactics, and they would have developed differently the intervals of fighting during the siege. Sidney's handling of Phalantus illustrates the difference. After the skirmish he challenges Amphialus to a joust but leaves afterward, seeking adventures (*NA* 3.11.499), and thus vanishes from the story. The older romancers would have followed him on those adventures, as Boiardo did Brandimarte and Orlando at Albraca or as Tasso did with Rinaldo and Tancredi at Jerusalem. Sidney instead stays with Amphialus at the castle and gives us a series of jousts. Again, the romancers would have had some such duels, like that between Rinaldo and Orlando at Albraca or the one between Tancredi and Argante in Tasso, but they would have devoted most of their attention to adventures elsewhere: Orlando in Falerina's garden or Rinaldo away with Armida in the Fortunate Islands. Sidney gives us *only* duels, whether in battle or in the intervals between. He thus harmonizes warfare and tournaments, or rather makes war seem like a series of jousts, the kind that occurred in Elizabethan tournaments, since he devotes so much attention to such encounters.[26]

At the time when romance began, in the late twelfth and early thirteenth centuries, there was little to separate the open mêlée of a tournament from an actual cavalry clash, but this was not the situation in the late sixteenth century. Much has been said about the Elizabethan neomedieval revival and its Burgundian antecedents, but these elaborate pageants—with their outfits, so expensive only aristocrats could afford them[27]—had little in common with the warfare that killed Sidney in Holland. Instead of muskets, mines, and mud, the poet imagines a brilliant world of color and personal symbolism for his fiction. One remembers Phalantus in his blue armor, riding a white horse, its mane and tail dyed strawberry red to match its freckles, its reins vine branches, which become grapes in the horse's mouth, the shield with a greyhound catching but not hurting a hare, and the motto: "The glory, not the prey" (*NA* 3.11.496–97). The poet thus evokes a view of the Middle Ages that endures to this day: colorful armor, elaborate tournaments, duels, and symbolic ceremonial.

Drayton achieves the same effect by his impressionism. The nobles ride to Burton Bridge in similar garb, and Drayton describes some of the outfits. Vernon, for example, wears a white coronet with a red fret, the pennon on his lance being of the same color (*BW* 2.24), and the royal leopards appear on both sides, carried by the king and by Lancaster. In the fighting on the bridge these pennons float and whirl slowly in the air (*BW* 2.38). Colors and vivid, sometimes bloody, images mark Burton Bridge. Daniel opts rather for nostalgia, commemorating at Castillon the figure of Talbot, the last great English general in a foreign war. Despite his misgivings Talbot encourages his troops, fights, and dies heroically. Through him Daniel recalls the medieval period he idealizes elsewhere (*CW* 6.28–33) and the greater England that once controlled large tracts of land on the Continent.

This romanticism involves a temporal blur. Drayton provides the simplest example by doing what romancers had regularly done: modernizing the battles. Mining areas send pickax men to dig trenches (*BW* 1.43), though field camps became common only in the mid-fifteenth century. The soldiers similarly use a variety of fifteenth- and sixteenth-century

weapons, such as the poleax (*BW* 1.41) and the pike (2.37), and Edward
II has a modern coastal defense with beacons and watches (4.21). Anachronism brings the past closer, makes it more accessible to an audience,
but the technique must be used with caution. Drayton avoids anything
that presupposes guns, anything that would spoil his medieval picture.
Sidney is not so successful, since some of his modern touches make no
tactical sense.[28] For example, he has Basilius surround Cecropia's castle
town with trenches and gradually move them closer. When the trenches
are close enough, the king sets up forts to answer to each other (*NA*
3.11.493).[29] Such a contemporary procedure presupposes gun platforms
and cannon, which would normally keep an attacker at a distance, but
which Sidney ordinarily banishes to similes.[30] A medieval siege did not
require such a cautious approach. Sidney similarly betrays an uncertain
sense for Mediterranean galley warfare, since he has Pyrocles and Musidorus go to war in sailing ships (*NA* 2.7.260–61).[31] Daniel, however, is
the most confusing. In current Renaissance fashion he sees all his battles
as affairs of officers, so at Castillon he follows the fortunes of Talbot and
his son, Lord Lisle.[32] At the same time he never mentions Jean Bureau's
fortified camp or its guns, which destroyed so much of the English
force—six per shot, once Talbot had them attack at point-blank range.[33]
As we have seen in chapter 9, the gun was one of the main reasons the
medieval knight became the modern officer. Daniel thus uses the wrong
technique to present his subject. Where Sidney confuses details, Daniel
gives a misleading view of the whole. Castillon was not a typical medieval
battle but one of the first in a new kind of encounter: the assault on a
fortified camp.[34]

   All three English writers prefer imaginative projection to truth. Sidney
does so by theory, inventing a faroff Arcadian world where characters bear
classical names and may have classical gods[35] but where they fight medieval cavalry battles modeled for their details on Elizabethan tournaments.
Drayton and Daniel take a foreshortened view of their medieval subjects.
The battles happened so long ago that various stages of warfare blend
together. Tasso here provides the contrast. He too narrated a war that
occurred nearly half a millennium previously, but he read the chronicles
and wove a story full of truthful details, one that conveyed a real sense of
war later to Chateaubriand.[36] Any details Daniel gives for Castillon could
very well be wrong. Although Talbot did rout a small enemy force initially, the thousand archers at St. Laurent's Priory, he did not then meet
a new arriving force (*CW* 6.79). Jean Bureau had had pioneers working
on his fortified camp for three days before 16 July, and Talbot had to

attack it.[37] It was the English and not the French who moved. Similarly, Talbot did not cut his way through the closest ranks before he died (*CW* 6.93–94); he did not even wear armor. Cannon got his horse, and Michel Peronin brained the fallen leader. Most especially, his son, Lord Lisle, did not charge into a battalion near the French monarch and die of many wounds there (*CW* 96). Charles VII was leading another army and was not even present at the battle. Daniel imagines a typical battle that corresponds hardly at all to the real fight at Castillon.

The English as a group, therefore, differ sharply from current Mediterranean trends. They prefer imagination to history, at least when they narrate wars. Such a choice fits Sidney's theory well enough but would seem to undercut Daniel's claim to serve truth and versify history, except that he devotes so little of his poem to war. Daniel relates essentially political history, and it is there that a scholar must assess his truth claims. Sidney and Drayton may emphasize different topics, but they likewise deemphasize war.

ROMANCE AND EPIC WITHOUT WAR

Sidney limits his representations of war to four sequences that cover five chapters, a tiny fraction of the *New Arcadia*, which has seventy-seven chapters in all.[38] He does so despite the link between epic and war that he emphasizes in the *Defence of Poesie*. In that work he notes that Alexander the Great had his copy of Homer and that Ennius was buried in the tomb of the Scipios, and argues that the *Orlando furioso* or an Arthurian romance provides appropriate reading for the modern soldier.[39] In practice Sidney carefully sets up a fiction where war seems omnipresent. The retrospectives in book 2 summarize eight separate wars, and the siege of Cecropia's castle town stretches across most of the fragmentary book 3, which breaks off as yet another besieging army arrives.[40] The constant references, the protracted siege, make the *Arcadia* seem more warlike than it is.

The other two poets follow a similar pattern. Drayton limits his military representations even though he narrates the civil wars between Edward II and his barons. Out of the many battles that marked this period, he presents only two, in all just 47 stanzas out of 457, or 10 percent of his poem. As for Daniel, Ben Jonson complained that he "wrote *Civil Wars*, and yet hath not one battle in all his book."[41] In fact, Daniel narrates three, which by a generous count amount to 61 stanzas out of 871 in *The Civile Wars*, or about 7 percent.[42] The two poets thus contrast strikingly with Marlowe and Shakespeare, the dramatists who covered the same material. They did not shy away from battles even though the dramatic medium is *less* well suited to such representations.

Spenser took this tendency to its logical conclusion. *The Faerie Queene* occasionally allegorizes but hardly represents war. At most the poet shows us one or two knights or a "robot" like Talus dispersing a multitude.[43] While Sidney tended to reduce war to jousts and duels, Spenser has almost nothing else.[44] He thus looks back past the Renaissance to the late medieval tradition of Arthurian prose romance, to the *Roman de Tristan en prose,* and the *Palamedes.* Within the Renaissance the move is unprecedented—that such a lengthy poem should never really bring its knights to a battlefield—but not without influence. Drayton likewise banished war from his long geographical romance, the *Polyolbion.* The English writers as a group, therefore, developed the peaceful epic, whether like Sidney they limited war to a fraction of their compositions or, more radically, eliminated it altogether.[45]

In doing so the English poets both reflected and responded to a profound social change. Late medieval England had been involved in war continuously for more than 150 years (1330s–1485), but fighting became more and more sporadic under the Tudors. It is a truism to say that Elizabeth ruled over one of the first civilian populations in modern times. Civilians, of course, did not read stories the way the members of the old military aristocracy had. They lacked the military experience and perhaps also the interest. This transformation is revealed in several ways. Here, I will consider two: foreign evaluations of the English and the careers of the poets.

The Berry Herald, writing his *Livre de la description des pays* in the early fifteenth century, said of the English that they are all good archers and soldiers but also a cruel and bloodthirsty people, who war on all nations and among themselves.[46] At the end of the sixteenth century Lope de Vega characterizes them very differently in his *Dragontea.* A band of Drake's men, out looting in the countryside of modern Panama, comes upon a straw hut inhabited by a woman, her two small boys, sick husband, and old father. Trying to find treasure, the English tie up the men and threaten the woman, putting a sword to her breast and throwing her babies to the ground. Frustrated in this attempt, they turn to revel and dancing, and five of them fall asleep inside the hut. The woman then goes out with her children, unties the men, and they burn down the hut on the sleeping English. Lope uses the incident to illustrate the barbarity

of the English and their lack of discipline (*Dragontea*, 5.357–85). The facts
bear him out. The English soldiers in the 1580s received almost no training, and impressment brought men of poor discipline and doubtful
morale into the army.[47] The English military historian, Sir Charles
Oman, felt shame over their military conduct on land and cites the journey of Portugal (1589) as an example. The soldiers plundered the land
their leaders hoped would support the pretender, Don Antonio, and the
men basically drank themselves to death.[48]

The poets themselves had no military expertise, and in this respect
they contrasted sharply with their Iberian contemporaries. Camões, Ercilla, Villagrá, and de Vega all did military service.[49] None of the English
had any military experience except Sidney, but even he wrote the *Arcadia*
before he went to Holland. Scholars are undecided whether Spenser
had any military experience. He lived in a zone of intermittent war
and initially served Lord Grey, but his occasional unrealistic descriptions suggest that he never had any real experience of battle.[50] Milton
provides the most striking instance. Living through the English civil
wars, he never joined the army or saw a battle. The English poets
lacked direct experience of war and also lacked an audience for the
literature of war.

The English led in the development of the epic without war, but they
were not alone. The successful epics of the seventeenth century generally
followed this pattern. Poets either limited war to small portions of their
narratives, as Milton did for *Paradise Lost*, or they dropped it altogether,
as did Marino in *L'Adone* and Milton in *Paradise Regained*.[51] A social or
rhetorical explanation would not account for this pan-European development, for it involved countries like Portugal, which still had a living military tradition in the 1570s, as well as those like Italy and England, which
had become increasingly civilian.[52]

For this wider movement one must paradoxically appeal to a more
restricted or literary hypothesis, one that Drayton and Daniel suggest.
They both claim that no glory follows fighting in a civil war, so they
refuse to celebrate any military heroes.[53] Drayton further makes his narrative of Burton Bridge subserve a lament for civil strife. He begins it with
a pathetic fallacy of the rain as tears, delays his action with apostrophes,
and provides vivid pictures of the dead and wounded (*BW* 2.16, 27, 30–31,
40–41). Daniel puts the matter bluntly in a stanza he later removed from
The Civile Wars. The best in such battles are the worst, since they are
killing many of their own citizens.[54] He later wrote a soliloquy for Henry

VI, which makes the same point (*CW* 8.22–24). The king watches the battle of Towton from a hill and thinks that the Lancastrian and Yorkist rivalry does not merit all this slaughter.

Such an attitude calls into question the poets' choice of topic, since they both allow for heroism abroad. Drayton says that if the barons at Burton Bridge had done such deeds in Palestine, he would have commended them (*BW* 2.45). Daniel similarly celebrates Henry V and Talbot, the heroes of the war in France. A critic may ask why either poet chose a topic unsuitable for epic by their own standards, and they partially respond to this potential charge by looking instead to tragedy. Drayton calls his narrative a tragic story (*BW* 1.4), and Daniel has Pandora order Nemesis to make of England a black stage for bloody tragedies, from which other European states can draw examples (*CW* 6.43). These appeals carry added weight because Marlowe and Shakespeare made tragedies of the same stories.[55]

The two poets highlight the generic dilemma of epic at the end of the sixteenth century. Daniel comes closest to verbalizing it, when he interrupts his narrative of Shrewsbury with an apostrophe to war (*CW* 4.46). He calls war a child of malice and hate, begot in pride and luxury, the foul refiner of the state, the unjust-just scourge of human iniquity. Such a view fits the specific situation in the poet's narrative, but it makes one wonder how Daniel could write epic at all, at least epic as it was then understood.

Daniel and Drayton evaluate morally a dilemma I analyzed earlier technologically. With the Gunpowder Revolution the general practice of war in Europe changed so radically that the traditional methods of romance and epic could no longer represent it. Poets succeeded only with colonial and perhaps naval warfare, and this is one reason why Spanish authors, who effectively narrated battles in North and South America, had no influence on Europe generally. It was not that others ignored Spain; Cervantes and even St. Teresa had a broad readership outside the peninsula. Rather, the other European nations, which lacked colonies, did not provide poets with the special circumstances necessary for them to celebrate heroism. The Italians had lost most of theirs; the English, French, and Dutch had yet to gain colonies in 1600. Hence no one could follow the Iberian experiment. It is not surprising, therefore, that Europe as a whole developed the epic without war.

This transformation of the genre had both positive and negative consequences. On the positive side, the avoidance of war gave epic and romance another century of life, from Camões (1572) to Milton (1667).

The Roman epic tradition provides an illustrative contrast. Ovid's two brilliant exercises in the nonmilitary epic, the *Metamorphoses* and the unfinished *Fasti,* did not substantially alter a tradition so strong that Valerius Flaccus put wars into his *Argonautica,* where Apollonius of Rhodes had not had them. Tasso could later rightly refer to the common idea that the Romans specialized in the military epic.[56] Camões in contrast started a trend that changed the genre.

This transformation may have had effects well beyond the limits of epic. It may have affected first its own dialectical opposite, those prose narratives that scholars loosely classify as picaresque. Where heroic narrative normally views military life from the top[57]—focusing upon leaders and officers, their conferences, plans, and actions—the picaresque views the same from the bottom. Thomas Nashe, for example, who composed *The Unfortunate Traveller* at about the same time the English poets invented their romances and historical epics, concentrates on victualers, accountants, and the like and later describes the artisans who made up the Anabaptist army at Münster.[58] Grimmelshausen, whose *Abenteuerliche Simplicissimus* (1669) is perhaps the most famous picaresque tale of warfare, has as his hero an uneducated farm boy who serves mostly as a dragoon and musketeer.[59] Yet these writers register the same changes as do Drayton, Daniel, and Sidney.

Nashe, like the English poets, lacked military experience and avoided descriptions of battles and sieges as much as possible.[60] He says nothing about the actual siege of Tournai (1513) with which he begins his tale and limits himself to the aftermath of Marignano (1515).[61] The closest he comes to an actual depiction of warfare is the brief but effective evocation of the guns at Münster (*UT* 285–86). Moreover, he shares with the English poets the temporal blur, though his history is not so distant, covering events early in the reign of Henry VIII. His hero leaves England in 1513 (*UT* 254) and at the end goes to the Field of the Cloth of Gold (1520).[62] Yet in between he travels from Marignano to Münster, a temporal leap of nineteen years, and meets people in an impossible chronology.[63] The mirror image of epic thus has the same peculiarities as its heroic counterpart: a hazy sense of history and a tendency to reduce the description of military encounters as much as possible or preferably to avoid them altogether.

One might expect more of Grimmelshausen, who drew on his own military experience when he invented the story of Simplicius Simplicissimus. Like Ercilla he shows scenes of guerilla activity, of soldiers foraging and plundering, but he specializes in these and gives them a satiric thrust.[64] The hero begins, for example, by seeing soldiers sack his own farmhouse, raping the women in one room and torturing each man individually in another. A soldier shoves one man into a bread oven and lights the fire. Later, when Simplicius visits Hanau, the Protestant troops there raise supplies by plundering the village of Orb, sacking Braunfels, and burning Staden to the ground. Grimmelshausen later says that *foraging* is military language for theft and plunder.[65] Yet he too avoids battles, though he carefully dates his hero's career by famous battles and sieges in the Thirty Years' War.[66] He does provide one lively description, that of the battle of Wittstock (4 October 1636), and, like Nashe, effectively suggests the sounds of war. Unfortunately, he borrows the passage from the German edition of Sidney's *Arcadia,* which had come out in 1629, so his description remains strictly literary. The only other battle he describes is an old-style cavalry clash between Russians and Tatars, part of the exotic coda of the story, and he limits it to a few paragraphs.[67]

The parameters set by late Renaissance heroic narrative and by the picaresque held true for the new genre that followed: the novel. Of course, a critic can easily find in the long history of the novel ones that do present warfare or have some kind of military scenes, from Uncle Toby's play battles in *Tristram Shandy* to the Napoleonic conflicts Tolstoy has in *War and Peace* and, in the twentieth century, Hemingway's *Farewell to Arms* and Solzhenitsyn's *1914.* By a statistical count many have been the novels written about World War II, though few if any of them have high merit. The genre in general, as represented by the works that have canonical status, has tended to avoid war. The reader of Austen's *Pride and Prejudice,* for example, has little sense that the story occurs in wartime. Thomas Mann, who lived through two world wars, ends his most famous work, *Der Zauberberg,* with Hans Castorp on the western front in 1914, but the novel has little else on the subject. Most novelists have limited war to an episode or eliminated it altogether. This is exactly the pattern I have just outlined for late epic: either no war or very little.

Such a transformation also had its negative consequences, at least outside England. The fact that narrative artists no longer treated war did not mean that Europe had become more peaceful. The incidence of war did not decline appreciably in the seventeenth and eighteenth centuries[68] and had a revival in the first half of the twentieth. Even that interval of peace, the nineteenth century (1815–1912), had more war than one generally allows. Local conflicts marked the 1820s and 1830s and again the years 1848–71, and the Balkans struggled toward independence and among themselves. War was a major industry in Europe for a very long time

(1330s–1815),[69] one reflected and evaluated by the writers of romance and epic and by Grimmelshausen as late as the mid-seventeenth century. As we have seen, Renaissance writers engaged in intense debate over the technology of war and the limits of violence. Later, however, the writers fall silent.

Perhaps if later writers had been able to devise an appropriate genre and had continued to portray war, they might have diminished or at least criticized both its general practice and its most terrible manifestations, the way Grimmelshausen reacted to the Thirty Years' War.[70] This did not happen, and the development illustrates the old principle that when one thing, in this case a genre, replaces another, much is lost as well as gained.

Readers and critics take for granted the great gains won by the novelists of the modern period, so many things the older genres lacked. One thinks of the precise social milieu Stendhal presents in *Le rouge et le noir* and which Auerbach celebrated in *Mimesis*.[71] Julien Sorel, the petit-bourgeois upstart, lives out his short life in an upper-class setting carefully placed at the end of the Restoration (1830), and Stendhal gives a rich psychological portrait of his hero, the awkward seducer of Madame de Renal.[72]

Yet by other standards the novel had a narrower, not a wider, scope than the older romance and epic. Julien Sorel never goes to war, he only reads about it.[73] Stendhal's other hero, Fabrice del Dongo, starts at Waterloo in a typical picaresque sequence but spends the rest of *La chartreuse de Parme* away from battlefields and war.[74] Yet the period covered in both novels was not really peaceful. Spanish troops fought a major colonial war in the New World, while the French went to Algiers. In Europe itself the French intervened in Spain and the Austrians in Naples. The period seems peaceful in comparison to the convulsions that preceded it and because its novelists preferred peaceful scenes. In France most of the time, and in England before the twentieth century, they could indulge in this illusion of peace, since their governments regularly managed to fight their wars somewhere else. Many in Stendhal's audience, however, could have recognized this preference as a generic limitation, since so many had served in the army or lost family members in the protracted wars of the Revolution and Napoleon. With wars all around them, novelists looked in another direction.

—APPENDIX 1—

Malory and the *Suite du Merlin*

THE *SUITE* WAS ANOTHER CONTINUATION OF THE VULGATE *Merlin*.[1] It survives mainly in two manuscripts, London, British Library, Additional MS 38117, called the Huth manuscript, and Cambridge University Library, Additional MS 7071. Malory used the latter,[2] which differs from other versions of the *Suite* in that it includes the Vulgate war between Arthur and the kings.[3] It also presupposes the enlarged version of the Vulgate, which it in turn expands.[4] Use of the Cambridge manuscript affected Malory's version by art and by error or omission. The latter types of effect are the more important.

Errors in numbers in the Cambridge *Suite* created exaggerations in Malory. The writer of the *Suite* assumed with the Vulgate that the enemy kings brought a force of 40,000 to Bedigran.[5] But it is easy to confuse *xl* and *lx*, so the scribe of the Cambridge version gives the kings 60,000 men for the battle (Cambridge *Suite*, 217r). Malory reproduces the larger figure, and a similar escalation of 40,000 to 60,000 marks his version of the *Morte*.[6]

An omission explains a more important change. The Cambridge scribe did not specify the enemy in Uther's last battle. He may have omitted to state that they were Saxons because he considered that obvious. They were the grand enemy previously, and in this instance the Saxon captives go over to the enemy army (*Suite*, 197r). Yet the omission gave Malory the freedom to reinterpret, particularly since he dropped the career of Uther before Arthur's conception. This starting point reduced the presence of the Saxons to a single episode, the attack against the enemy kings. As a result, the political emphasis changed. The Vulgate author had imagined a Britain threatened by a persistent invader and now falling into civil war. For Malory, however, the internal problem became almost the sole problem.

Boiardo's Translation
of Herodotus

SINCE BOIARDO TRANSLATED HERODOTUS'S *HISTORIES* BE-
fore he wrote the *Orlando innamorato*, the scholar must consider that
translation to see what the poet did to Herodotus, with a particular concern for the sections that might have influenced the *Innamorato*. These
sections concern the Persians and their attacks on the Greeks (books 1
and 7) and Herodotus's description of North Africa in the latter part of
book 4 (sections 145–205).

In his discussion of Boiardo's translation of Herodotus, Giulio Reichenbach notes two characteristics. First, the translation is rather free and
contains additions not found in Valla's Latin version or in the Greek original. Second, the translation contains errors, which come partially from
the printer who set up the first edition of the Valla translation (1474) and
partially from Boiardo himself in interpreting the Latin. To these I add a
third characteristic: Boiardo's abbreviation of the original in his translation. This is the principal change he made.

I compared the Italian directly with the Greek for *Hist.* 1, 4.145–205,
and 7, and checked all divergencies against Valla's Latin. For the translation I used the microfilm of the text of the first printed edition (Venice,
1533) taken from the copy in Vatican City, Biblioteca apostolica Vaticana,
Ferraioli V.4623. The printer mispaginates the 200s as 100s for much of
book 7. I have corrected this mistake. For Valla I have used my own copy
(Paris, 1510). I have noted when Boiardo's variation depends on Valla.
Otherwise the data presented here include Boiardo's variations both from
Valla and from the Greek.

Boiardo abbreviates slightly in books 4 and 7, much in book 1 (up to
a quarter of the whole). In book 1 some of these abbreviations are due to
Valla. For example, there is 92 (Herodotus, *Historiae,* trans. Valla, xvi

recto; trans. Boiardo, 22r), the list of offerings sent to various temples by Croesus, which would be a footnote in a modern history. Since Valla drops the list, it does not appear in Boiardo. Valla also eliminates Deioces's rise to power (96–100; Valla, xvi recto–verso; Boiardo, 22v); the description of Esagila (181–83; Valla, xxi verso; Boiardo, 29r); and the prostitution of women in Babylonian temples (199; Valla, xxiv recto; Boiardo, 32v). Most noticeable is his elimination of the Persian conquest of Ionia, Caria, and Lycia. Boiardo on his own drops repetitions, as at 9–10 (Boiardo, 3r), where Gyges receives his instructions and then follows them. He omits Sandanis's important description of the Persians at 71 (Boiardo, 16r). He also skips Herodotus's statement that the sailors wanted to hear Arion's song (24; Boiardo, 6r). In book 4, however, the poet abridges very little. An example would be 165 (Boiardo, 149v). Boiardo maintains the same pattern in book 7. He drops matter at 41 (Boiardo, 224r; the detail about the apples), 96 (Boiardo, 232v; a methodological statement), 117 (Boiardo, 236v; the references to *sumphoré*), 120 (Boiardo, 237r; part of the joke), and 192 (Boiardo, 254r; the reference to the second day and the libation). In one case abbreviation creates error (86; Boiardo, 213r), where he excludes the Indians from those who used horses and chariots. Minor omissions occur at 9 (Boiardo, 215v–16r), 17 (Boiardo, 219r–v), 19 (Boiardo, 219v–20r), 85 (Boiardo, 231r), 95 (Boiardo, 232r), 102 (Boiardo, 233v), and 174 (Boiardo, 250v).

Some of the additions to book 1 are explanatory. Boiardo says of the Lydian boar hunters that they threw spears from horses (43; Boiardo, 9v) and amplifies the description of the plain and forces before Sardis, where the Persians defeated the Lydians (80; Boiardo, 18v). Occasionally the explanation is anachronistic. The children who play with Cyrus come to the country with their mothers for the summer season (114; Boiardo, 24v), and Cyrus personally invests Cambyses as his heir (208; Boiardo, 34r). Otherwise the additions are details, as at 62 (Boiardo, 13v; the oracle is made explicit), 79 (Boiardo, 18r–v; praise of the Lydian cavalry), 180 (Boiardo, 29r; Babylon gets streets of polished stone); and 189 (Boiardo, 30r; the white horse that drowns in the Gyndes is identified and gets a boy rider). In book 4 he follows the same pattern. Valla contributed one of the interpretations when he rationalized the Psylli, whose wells simply dry up so that the tribe goes south, looking for another country (173; Valla, ci verso; Boiardo, 150v–51r). Valla may also unintentionally have helped Boiardo to ascribe motives to the Samians who followed Arcesilas (163; Vallo, c recto; Boiardo, 149r). The other interpretations are the poet's. He approves Demonax's constitution limiting the monarchy (161;

Boiardo, 148v), and he corrects Herodotus in one place, perhaps drawing on *Ae.* 1.184–93, 4.153–59. The Greek historian said that there were no deer or boar in Libya, but Boiardo claims they can be found by the coast (192; Boiardo, 154v). Finally, he expands the epitaphs for the fallen at Thermopylae (228; Boiardo, 261r–v). Additions that concern minor details are at 146 (Boiardo, 144v–45r) and 177 (Boiardo, 151r). In book 7 Boiardo's expansions are mostly brief explanations. Valla is behind those at 61 (Valla, cli recto; Boiardo, 228r), 64 (Valla, cli verso; Boiardo, 228v), 115 (Valla, clvi recto; Boiardo, 236r), 125 (Valla, clvii recto; Boiardo, 237v), and 216 (Valla, clxviii recto; Boiardo, 259r). A special case is 6 (Valla, cxlii recto; Boiardo, 214v), where Valla omits the examples for Onomacritus's oracles before Xerxes and Boiardo supplies his own examples. Boiardo himself accounts for the expansions at 26 (Boiardo, 221v), 27 (Boiardo, 221v), 35 (Boiardo, 222v), 106 (Boiardo, 234v), 159 (Boiardo, 246r–v), 207 (Boiardo, 257r), 223 (Boiardo, 260r–v), 226 (Boiardo, 261r), and 228 (Boiardo, 261v).

Errors in book 1 are few, partially because the translation is free. A manuscript tradition gives Arion a *large* statue at Taenarum (24; Valla, iv verso; Boiardo, 5v). Boiardo errs when he has the royal canal go to Nineveh (193; Boiardo, 31r), and Babylonian lovers fumigate *before* intercourse (198; Boiardo, 32v). More errors can be detected in book 4 because Boiardo follows the original more closely. Generally, however, the translation is quite accurate. Valla is behind four mistakes. At 172.1 (Valla, ci recto; Boiardo, 150v) the Nasamones grind dates rather than locusts for food; at 152.1 (Valla, xcviii verso; Boiardo, 146r) the Samians are returning from instead of going to Egypt; at 148 (Valla, xcviii recto; Boiardo, 145r–v) Boiardo compounds Valla's error by a misreading and puts cities conquered by the Minyae in Thera, not Elis; and at 152.3 (Valla, xcviii verso; Boiardo, 146r) the griffons on the crater face each other. Boiardo is responsible for the error at 198.2 (Boiardo, 155v), where he thinks *no* rain falls at the River Cinyps. Not surprisingly, he has trouble with numbers and directions. At 183 (Boiardo, 152v) he has the troglodytes live thirty days away from an oasis, when the oasis itself is thirty days from the coast; at 185 (Boiardo, 153r–v) he thinks the salt mines lie toward the coast. A pardonable error is 169.2 (Boiardo, 150r), repeated at 192.3 (Boiardo, 154v), where he follows other geographers and decides that *silphium* is a district.

Errors in book 7 concern geography, peoples, and poetry. Valla is behind not a few. At 153 (Valla, clxi verso; Boiardo, 244v) *oikétor* becomes a proper name, and Boiardo or the printer confuse the Lindians with the

Indians. Valla puts Anthela right at Thermopylae rather than between the Phoenix and Thermopylae (200; Valla, clxvi recto; Boiardo, 255v). The Syrians of Palestine become the Syrians and Palestinians, so Valla and Boiardo give the Egyptian equipment to the Palestinians (89; Valla, cliii recto; Boiardo, 231v), and they both put 34,000 for 24,000 on the Thracian ships at 185 (Valla, clxiv recto; Boiardo, 252v). In the poetry Valla accounts for the numerical error at 228 (Valla, clxix recto; Boiardo, 261r–v), where he gives the Peloponnesians 2,000 men, not 4,000. Among miscellaneous errors Valla passed on to the poet are those at 188 (Valla, clxiv verso; Boiardo, 253r), where the great wind that comes after a serene dawn becomes a wind blowing in a clear sky; and at 190 (Valla, clxv recto; Boiardo, 253v), where Ameinocles instead of killing a child lacks one. More important is the error at 99 (Valla, cliv recto; Boiardo, 232v), where Artemisia comes to the war because her son is so young. Boiardo makes several mistakes on his own in book 7. Three are geographical. He puts Sale and Zone in Samothrace (59; Boiardo, 227v), confuses two towns with mountains (112; Boiardo, 235v), and at one point makes the ground swampy, not rutted (176; Boiardo, 251r). The printer may be responsible for the error at 204 (Boiardo, 256r), where Leonidas becomes king of Macedonia. In the catalogues Boiardo adds the Magi to the Assyrians (63; Boiardo, 228r), and Lycian goatskins become shields (92; Boiardo, 232r). There are other errors as well. Boiardo has Xerxes wait at Sardis for the return of his envoys (33; Boiardo, 222r–v), makes all three spies sent to Sardis Athenian (146; Boiardo, 242v), and turns deserters into spies (219; Boiardo, 259v). Finally, Onetes, who could have known the area, becomes a man who did not know the area well (214; Boiardo, 258v).

Marks of the romancer appear here and there. The Lydian cavalry wear white for their final battle (1.80; Boiardo, 18v). Both Valla and Boiardo drop references to tyranny at 1.96–100 (Valla, xvi recto–verso; Boiardo, 22v) and at 7.10 g.2 (Valla, cxliii verso; Boiardo, 217r).

——APPENDIX 3——

Araucana I (1569)

THE POET GASPAR PÉREZ DE VILLAGRÁ TWICE USES PART I OF
Ercilla's *Araucana* to support "guerra a fuego y sangre." He sets up the
first by literary imitation, modeling the dialogue of his Gicombo and
Luzcoija just before the fatal battle at Ácoma (*NM* 29.275–83, p. 153r–v)
on that between Lautaro and Gualcolda before Mataquito (*Araucana*,
1.13.43–57, pp. 222–25).[1] The Spanish victory at Mataquito itself resembles both Cañete and Ácoma in its completeness and in the casualties
inflicted (*Araucana*, 1.14.6–15.55, pp. 228–50). By a forced march Francisco de Villagrá comes upon Lautaro's fort at dawn (*Araucana*, 1.12.61–
68, 13.41, 14.4–5, pp. 203–5, 221, 228). He finds the walls unguarded because the sentinels are just retiring to rest. The Spaniards instantly attack,
and the local Indians who had joined Lautaro run away. He himself dies
instantly, and the remaining Araucanians are surrounded. They fight, so
densely crowded together that the dead have no room to fall (*Araucana*,
1.14.33–35, p. 234). Villagrá offers clemency to the one-eighth who still
live, and the Spaniards withdraw, but the Indians only shout, "Death,
death!" Some, on their knees, whirl swords, and some, lying on the
ground, strike at people's feet. The Spaniards have to kill them all, climbing over the arms and bodies (*Araucana*, 1.15.42–48, pp. 248–49). One
survivor, Mallén, commits suicide (*Araucana*, 1.15.55, p. 250).[2]

This action parallels that of Ácoma in two respects. Both battles have
a high number of casualties, and in both the Spanish commander tries to
arrange a surrender, which the Indians refuse. Ercilla shows this intracta-
bility through his fictional hero Rengo, who survives the battle to fight
again. The resemblance, however, may also reflect the officers' manner of
reporting a battle. The poet Gaspar Pérez de Villagrá, himself a captain,
presented Ácoma in a way sympathetic to his commander, Vicente de

Zaldívar. Ercilla did not fight at Mataquito but probably drew his information from the commander, whom he likely met in Lima after his own service in Chile.[3]

The battles may seem to resemble each other more than they actually do, for some evidence indicates a major difference between them. At Mataquito the Cauqenes (local Indians; Lautaro is fighting north of Araucania) are opportunistic. Some join him (*Araucana*, 1.12.57, p. 203) but bolt as soon as the Spaniards attack. Four hundred others help Francisco de Villagrá and provide crucial aid. One first informs and then guides him to Lautaro's fort. Another kills Lautaro with an arrow as he runs out of his hut. Only some of the Indians at Mataquito were intractable.

In his second use of part 1 of the *Araucana*, the poet Villagrá twice refers to Ercilla's moralizing discourse, which initiates canto 4 of the *Araucana*. Villagrá uses it both for his epic and for his pamphlet, the *Justificación*. In the *Historia* Villagrá talks about the need to punish rebellion instantly, as Governor Oñate did to Ácoma and as Valdivia did not do to the Araucanians in Tucapel:

> Desto dechado grande nos han dado,
> Aquellos bravos barvaros de Arauco,
> Pues por no mas de averles dilatado,
> El deuido castigo à tales culpas,
> Sincuenta largos años son passados,
> Que en efusion de sangre Castellana,
> Sus omicidas armas no se han visto,
> Enjutas, ni cansadas, de verterla.
> (*NM* 27.10–17, p. 140r)

Those brave barbarians of Arauco have given us a great model of this because, for no more than having delayed the required punishment for such sins, fifty long years have passed that their murderous arms have not been dry from pouring out Castilian blood nor have they tired in pouring it out.

He cites the same passage again in the *Justificación* (5v), yet this parallel too could allow for a contrary reading.

Ercilla attributes both the revolt and the initial success of the Araucanians to Spanish greed. Avarice led the Spaniards south and forced the Indians to hard labor. Valdivia began poor but ended with 50,000 vassals, who gave him twelve marks of gold *daily* (*Araucana*, 1.3.1–4, pp. 39–40). At Tucapel the Indians refer to this lust for gold as they attack, shouting that the robbers must pay their debts (*Araucana*, 1.3.21, p. 43). Greed also explains Valdivia's fatal delay. He took a difficult route to Tucapel so that he might collect tribute at a gold mine (*Araucana*, 2.92–93, p. 38). Ercilla closes the moral discourse, which Villagrá paraphrases, by saying that avarice gave the evil time to take root (*Araucana,* 1.4.3, p. 60).[4]

The poet stops short of justifying the Araucanian revolt.[5] Concerning the battle that follows, which brings death to Valdivia, he says that fortune decided the unjust cause was just (*Araucana,* 1.3.57, p. 51). Like the later proponents of the mission system, Ercilla does not question the Spanish right to rule Indian lands—a fundamental assumption shared by advocates both of limited and of total war. They disagree about the means, not about the end.

At best part 1 of the *Araucana* provides ambiguous evidence for Ercilla's view on total and limited war. It provided Villagrá with precedents to justify Spanish methods at Ácoma. It could also fit the arguments for limited war that make up parts 2 and 3 of the *Araucana.* For example, the poet carries the theme of avarice through his whole epic. In part 2 Galbarino reminds the Araucanian leaders that desire for gold led the Spaniards there (*Araucana,* 2.23.12–13, p. 370), and in part 3 Tuncanabal advises the Indians who live farther south to appear poor so as not to draw a permanent Spanish presence (*Araucana,* 3.34.59–60, p. 563). Both speak as enemies of the Spaniards and keep the reader aware of the problem that caused the rebellion in the first place.[6] The modern critic, then, may argue that Ercilla maintained a consistent attitude throughout the *Araucana.* Or, accepting Villagrá's reading of part 1, the critic could say that the poet initially flirted with the then fashionable notion of total war but later rejected it.

NOTES

All translations are my own unless otherwise indicated.

INTRODUCTION

1. Rossignol, *Pierre d'Aubusson*, 275. The bastion was a platform projecting in front of the Tower of Aragon, on the west side of Rhodes.

2. Boulanger, *Greece*, 817; Bradford, *Shield and Sword*, 118–20.

3. The Ottomans had begun to arrive in late June and early July of 1522 (Bradford, *Shield and Sword*, 113), but the actual bombardment and attacks began only in August (Rossignol, *Pierre d'Aubusson*, 258). The large balls are mentioned by Bradford (114).

4. Rossignol, *Pierre d'Aubusson*, 261–64. The gunfire came from the Auvergne sector just to the north.

5. Ibid., 265–271, 275.

6. Kollias, *City of Rhodes*, 63.

7. Rossignol, *Pierre d'Aubusson*, 93.

8. The Italian Tower and curtain still have embedded cannonballs (Boulanger, *Greece*, 818), probably from the siege of 1522. Pierre d'Aubusson, the grand master in 1480, calculated that the Ottomans shot a thousand balls a day into the town (Bradford, *Shield and Sword*, 94), but a modern estimate suggests that the town received only 3,500 balls during the whole siege (Contamine, *War in the Middle Ages*, 200–201).

9. Brockman, *Two Sieges of Rhodes*, 44–45. The Turks still could not elevate or depress their larger cannon.

10. Kollias, *City of Rhodes*, 72; Bradford, *Shield and Sword*, 112. The Knights began this work and ended it with Italian engineers (Brockman, *Two Sieges of Rhodes*, 34; Bradford, *Shield and Sword*, 110; Kollias, *City of Rhodes*, 65). Kollias indicates (64–65) that the role of the Greeks was unclear. Were they only master masons or engineers? He also believes that Italian thinking had little to do with the final form of the walls, which resembles constructions in Provence and Spain (68). For the hard labor as opposed to the engineering, the Knights used captured Muslims when possible (Rossignol, *Pierre d'Aubusson*, 125). The modern tourist sees the walls almost exactly as they were in 1522 (Kollias, *City of Rhodes*, 65).

11. Boulanger, *Greece*, 817. The last built tower, that of Caretto, had a huge, circular terreplein some fifteen meters across and again loopholes for cannon fire into the moat

(818). The Gate of Saint John the Baptist or Koskinou provides the clearest illustration of this modernization. Huge horseshoe-shaped bastions, with ravelins and embrasures for artillery, now enclose the old medieval square tower with its small openings and battlements. For the galleries see Rossignol, *Pierre d'Aubusson*, 258.

12. Brockman, *Two Sieges of Rhodes*, 38. Kollias likewise stresses the Western thinking behind this new defense, pointing to parallels in southern France: Avignon and Villeneuve-les-Avignon (*City of Rhodes*, 68). He further notes (77) that the buildings put up between 1481 and 1522 resemble those of southern France.

13. Contamine, *War in the Middle Ages*, 204; Brockman, *Two Sieges of Rhodes*, 52; Rossignol, *Pierre d'Aubusson*, 266, 269.

14. Pepper and Adams argue that the star-shaped forts came in more slowly than previously believed and had to compete with gun towers, more like those used at Rhodes and popular in northern Europe. This contention is a major part of their argumentation in *Firearms and Fortifications*, but see especially 22–24, 159–60, 172.

15. This is the analysis of Hale, "Early Development of the Bastion," 466–94, and now reprinted in his *Renaissance War Studies*, 1–29.

16. Martorell and Galba, *Tirant lo blanc*, trans. Rosenthal, vii, x.

17. The colophon to the whole work dates it to the ninth year of the reign of Edward IV.

18. Parker, *Military Revolution*, 1. The fourteenth and fifteenth centuries show a similar pattern. See Contamine, *War in the Middle Ages*, 123–25.

19. Spanish epics are cited by canto, stanza, and page number, since the editions do not number stanzas.

20. The Spaniards began to standardize shot sizes after the Armada (Martin and Parker, *Spanish Armada*, 209). On imprecision see ibid., 215.

21. He had a place or fellowship in the Real Collegio Mayor de San Felipe and San Marcos in Lima (*AD*, title page and note; note at 19.53, p. 663).

22. Francisco de Figueroa in his dedicatory *Canción* says the poet comes from barbarian Chile (p. 8). The title page indicates that he came from the infantry stationed at Angol, an origin confirmed by Gaspar de Villarroel y Coruña in his dedicatory sonnet (p. 22). The poet himself tells us that he learned the language of the Araucanians (the warlike Indians of southern Chile) and uses technical terms from it (*AD* 2.57, p. 85). He uses correct Indian names at 6.7, p. 199.

23. At *AD* 19.30, p. 656, the editor Medina notes that Oña borrowed from Salcedo the phrase "de romania" for the falling masts of the *San Juan*. Moreover, Oña was versifying recent and local history. The poem came out in 1596, only two years after the incident. The imprimatur and license to publish are dated to 10–11 January of that year (*AD*, pp. 4–5). The poet published it in Lima. His readers would have expected accuracy.

24. *AD* 18.70–71, pp. 632–33. The *Relación* assigns twenty-eight large bronze guns to the *capitana*, which it calls a *naos*, and thirty to the *almiranta* (Vega, *Dragontea*, 2:121 [doc. 97]). Medina, the editor of *Arauco domado*, could find no information on Tejeda. Hawkins observes that the Spaniards had only recently begun to make cannon on the Pacific coast (*Observations*, 42.234).

25. The *Relación* also gives it fourteen (Vega, *Dragontea*, 2:121), as does Figueroa in his biography of Mendoza (*Hechos*, 135).

26. Martin and Parker, *Spanish Armada*, 216; *AD* 19.101–4, pp. 679–80. The *almiranta* or second ship had become the *capitana* or first ship by the time the Spaniards cornered Hawkins in Esmeraldas.

27. The *Relación* puts them in the prows of the *patajes*, along with the *versos* (Vega, *Dragontea*, 2:121).

28. *AD* 18.97, p. 642. The *Relación* mentions balls of bronze, razor, chain, and diamond point (Vega, *Dragontea*, 2:121).

29. Martin and Parker, *Spanish Armada*, 216. Their list indicates that the Armada still had some.

30. The first two were Drake (1579) and Cavendish (1587).

31. Martin and Parker so classify them (*Spanish Armada*, 216).

32. Ibid., 35, 50–51, especially 158. Such tactics won the Battle of the Azores in 1582 (95).

33. Against Trump in the English Channel, Oquendo tried to grapple and board, in the battle preliminary to the disaster of the Downs (1639). See Phillips, *Six Galleons*, 216.

34. Martin and Parker (*Spanish Armada*, 261) list only odes in Holland and ballads in England inspired by the defeat of the Armada.

35. Perrault's poem "Le siècle de Louis le Grand," given to the Académie Française in 1687, started the quarrel of the ancients and moderns.

36. Quint has already begun to remedy this defect. In *Epic and Empire* he devotes considerable attention to both Ercilla and Villagrá. See especially 99–106, 157–85.

37. In *Epic and Empire* Quint similarly stresses history, but he concentrates on politics and propaganda rather than on war.

38. The *Iliad* has scenes of chariot fighting but emphasizes encounters between dismounted warriors. One remembers the many duels or the race of Hector and Achilles around Troy. In the *Odyssey* the hero plays the role of a bowman, standing on a raised platform in his own hall and shooting his enemies.

39. Weinberg criticizes some humanists for classifying poetry as a kind of history and dates their efforts largely before 1560, though most of his examples have a later date (*History of Literary Criticism*, 1:13–16). Hathaway, in contrast, thought the debate over the relation between poetry and history grew out of Aristotle (*Age of Criticism*, 188, also 131, 133–34).

40. Nelson assumes the dichotomy but understands the difficulties it causes, since no clear line separates history and fiction (*Fact or Fiction*, 38–39). Levao has Sidney as his critical focus, a poet-critic who assumes the Aristotelian ladder for his *Defence of Poesie* and so emphasizes the differences between history and poetry. Levao sketches a tradition of northern skepticism behind Sidney, involving Nicholas of Cusa, Erasmus, and Cornelius Agrippa. He contends that for these writers the "only access to reality is through fiction and conjecture" ("Sidney's Feigned Apology," 229). Levao elaborates these arguments in *Renaissance Minds*, where he also stresses the Platonic equation between poetry and lying.

41. Nelson outlines a complicated development, which begins at the end of the sixteenth century and runs through the seventeenth. As historians became more concerned with the authenticity of their sources, they drew further away from poetry (*Fact or Fiction,* 41). Samuel Daniel illustrates the trend, since he was both historian and poet. He began with historical fiction in *The Complaint of Rosamond* (1592); moved to the *Civile Wars* (1595), in which he says he "will not poetize"; and ended with the *Collections of the Historie of England* (1612), a prose work in which he restricts himself to the ascertainable past (Nelson, *Fact or Fiction,* 106). Other creative writers responded to this trend differently and claimed truth for their narratives (94–98). Many romances were read as disguised accounts of contemporary events (101–3), and French writers after 1640 emphasized historical matter, yet with a significant shift in emphasis. In Camões's *Lusiadas* and Michael Drayton's *Mortimeriados* fiction enhances history, but in the later French romances history enhances fiction (99–100). Nelson thus admits that the real move toward history occurred among poets of the late sixteenth century, the ones I discuss in this book.

42. *Discorsi dell'arte poetica,* in *Prose,* ed. Mazzali, 1:351–52. See also his letter of 12 March 1576, *Prose,* 772.

43. Kennedy, for example, uses the work of Clifford Geertz (*Knighthood,* vii, 1–2), as did Greenblatt in *Renaissance Self-Fashioning* (3–4, 255).

44. Rossignol (*Pierre d'Aubusson,* 17) assumes the Ottomans had 200,000 on Rhodes and lost half of this army. Jacques de Bourbon, an eyewitness narrator of the siege, is the source for this figure. He cites a remark of the Ottoman general, Ahmed Paşa, to one of the Knights' ambassadors, Antoine de Grollée. Hammer-Purgstall, the great nineteenth-century historian of the Ottoman Empire, accepted this figure. On the other hand, Ramadan, himself an Ottoman, limits casualties to 18,000–20,000, but Rossignol does not consider his account reliable (274–75).

45. Bradford, *Shield and Sword,* 119.

CHAPTER 1: THE TACTICS OF RONCESVALLES

1. Pio Rajna, as usual, did the basic research on Pulci's sources, and Ageno carefully records all the borrowings in her edition. Jordan (*Pulci's "Morgante,"* 46n.4) provides bibliographical information, including the more recent studies by Ruggieri, *L'umanesimo cavalleresco italiano,* and Gianni, *Pulci uno e due.* Ruggieri argues that the *Entrée* was authoritative in Italy (271) and says that Pulci preserves Roncesvalles largely unchanged, having probably memorized the *Spagna* and *Rotta* (223–24). He also notes that the *Spagna* was a recent text (251–52). Orvieto (*Pulci medievale,* 271–72 and notes) supplies additional bibliographical references. By a careful stylistic analysis, Orvieto argues that Pulci composed a poetry that was not anchored in reality. Instead, his reality is literary and produces a literature of literature. See especially his chapter 8 and the conclusion on p. 321. My argument, based on other criteria, should act as a corrective to Orvieto's discussion.

2. *Chanson de Roland,* ed. Bédier, p. iii. The battle happened on 15 August 778, though Pulci dates it to 8 May 806 (*M,* 27.111–12). At Roncesvalles itself the Chapel of the Holy Spirit was said to have been built over the ditch where the knights were buried. It is kept open during May, when masses are said for Roland and the peers. See Monmarché, *Pyré-*

nées, 120. Pulci also gets his May date from the old feast that commemorated an appearance of the archangel Michael on Monte Gargano. In traditional fashion Pulci assumes that the archangel presided over the battle and wonders whether he intervened in it (*M,* 27.77–78, 113, 115).

3. He used the *Suite de Merlin* (thirteenth century) and the Alliterative *Morte Arthure* and Stanzaic *Morte Arthur* (fourteenth century). The last-named goes back to the Vulgate *Mort* (thirteenth century).

4. Pulci entered the service of Roberto da San Severino in 1474, serving as an intermediary between him and the Medici (Jordan, *Pulci's "Morgante,"* 34). He had already begun acting as a go-between the previous summer (Pulci, *Morgante,* ed. Ageno, x). Jordan speculates that he may have continued to do so during the Pazzi War (35–36), a conjecture that requires that Pulci's Letter 46 be dated to 1479. For San Severino in that war, see Pieri, *Il rinascimento,* 297. Allegretti notes his activity at Serazzano and his intervention in Milan (*Diarj,* entries for 19 June, p. 789; 31 August, p. 792; 12 September, p. 793). For his activity in the Ferrara War, see Mallett, *Mercenaries,* 171–72.

5. It was the coup in Milan that drew Ercole out of the Pazzi War. See Allegretti, *Diarj,* entry for 31 August 1479, p. 792. For the publication of the expanded *Morgante,* see Pulci, *Morgante,* ed. Weston, 2:484; and especially Wilkins, "Dates of Composition," 250. Wilkins indicates that Pulci began cantare 24 in or after 1476 and wrote cantare 28 between 25 March and the end of 1482. The publication date was 7 February 1483.

6. Zorzi, "Un vicentino," 422, 425–26. Chiericati was seeking employment under the new pope, Sixtus IV, but got none.

7. Ibid., 369, 373, 419.

8. Visconti, ed., "Ordine," 448–52 and n. 2. Filippo was castellan of Pavia, and the twenty documents in his collection run from 28 November 1472 to 12 March 1475.

9. Pieri, "Il 'Governo,'" 101–3.

10. Ibid., 101, 119–20. Carafa may have known Joanot Martorell, who visited Naples in 1454–55 and perhaps in 1442. See Martorell and Galba, *Tirant lo blanc,* trans. Rosenthal, x. For the north, Contamine (*War in the Middle Ages,* 120–21, 125, 214) lists Jean de Bueil, *Le jouvencel avancé pour guerra* (1460–70); Honoré Bovet, *Arbre des batailles* (1386–87); and the *Correspondence de Charles VIII et de ses conseillers avec Louis II de la Trémoille pendant la guerre de Bretagne,* ed. L. de la Trémoille (Paris, 1875).

11. Chiericati was born early in the century and died in 1477 (Zorzi, "Un vicentino," 369, 371), so he was probably in his sixties when he wrote his "Trattatello." San Severino was seventy when he drowned in the Adige in 1487, fighting the Austrians at Calliano (see Pieri, *Il rinascimento,* 315–19; Mallett, *Mercenaries,* 234). He was, therefore, fifty-five or fifty-six when he helped compose the "Ordine." Orsini was nearly seventy when he wrote the "Governo," and he died on campaign during the Pazzi War (5 July 1479). Carafa was already over seventy when he composed the two *Memoriali.* See Pieri, "Il 'Governo,'" 103.

12. San Severino served both Galeazzo Maria and Ludovico Sforza. Orsini was a disciple of Francesco Sforza, whom he first fought and then served in the 1440s. See Pieri, "Il 'Governo,'" 101–2. Musio Attendolo Sforza (1369–1424) founded the school; see Mallett, *Mercenaries,* 67–69.

13. The condottieri treatises ignore Charles the Bold's sophisticated use of traditional methods and the triumphs of the Swiss pike. See Pieri, "Il 'Governo,'" 116–18; Contamine, *War in the Middle Ages*, 134–37, 233–35.

14. For the battle with Baligant in the *Chanson de Roland*, Charlemagne arranges his army by a similar logic. He increases the numbers of his back files so as to keep hitting the Saracens with stronger and stronger attacks (216–25).

15. Contamine, *War in the Middle Ages*, 229–30.

16. Pulci uses *sguardo* and *schiera* to translate the terms for first battle and second battle (*M* 25.102). In strict as opposed to poetic usage, *schiera* corresponds to French *échelle* (see *Chanson de Roland*, 217–18). Contamine says *échelle* designated a section of a battle, but he allows that Jean de Bueil uses *bataille* and *échelle* as synonyms (*War in the Middle Ages*, 230n.73). Boiardo uses *schiera* for battle (*OI* 1.4.27–28).

17. Pieri, "Il 'Governo,'" 115, 118.

18. Braccio da Montone (1368–1424) broke his army into small groups and based his tactics on such small groups.

19. Mallett, *Mercenaries*, 68; Carafa, second "Memoriale," 4.204–5, in Pieri, "Il 'Governo'"; Pieri, "Il 'Governo,'" 122–24.

20. Pieri, *Il rinascimento*, 283–84n.1. Guicciardini gives a complementary and more detailed description of the same tactics at Fornovo.

21. The crucial units on each side are the French cavalry under Ranaldo, which Marsilio places second, and the troops from Gradasso's own kingdom of Sericana, which he places last and makes the royal battle. His front divisions are all outlanders, the subjects of his newly made tropical empire: Ceylonese, Arabians, Persians, Macrobians, and Ethiopians.

22. None, however, is as elaborate as the battle of Salisbury in the *Mort le roi Artu* (ed. Frappier, 180–81), where Mordred pits twenty battles against Arthur's ten.

23. Lieutenants lead the first battle; Bors, the second; and Ban, the third. A cavalry army normally rides to a fight in three battles and sometimes delivers its attack in the same way, as here. Lancelot has the same arrangement at Joyous Garde. Out of three gates issue the van under Lionell, the main battle under Lancelot, and the rear under Bors (*Morte*, 20.12). In actual battles, however, the distinction of van and rear is often technical, since they can become the right and left flanks on the battlefield and do not necessarily attack seriatim. Malory's readers would have had no more difficulty with these imagined tactics than Pulci's readers. For Tewkesbury (4 May 1471), Edward IV, anticipating a conflict, divided his army into three battles. For the battle see Goodman, *Wars of the Roses*, 82, 168, 172–73.

24. Pieri, "Il 'Governo,'" 121; Pieri, *Il rinascimento*, 283n.1; Mallett, *Mercenaries*, 71–72.

25. The two battles are Barcelona and Paris. At Barcelona the French fight as allies of King Marsilio.

26. With the crucial difference that Lot wants to rotate huge masses of men.

27. And at Barcelona Marsilio leads the reserves on the other side. A medieval example is the *Mort le roi Artu* (ed. Frappier, 180–81), in which Arthur and Mordred command their respective reserves at Salisbury.

28. Carafa, second "Memoriale," 6.207, in Pieri, "Il 'Governo.'"

29. Contamine, *War in the Middle Ages,* 236 and n. 91.

30. Mallet, *Mercenaries,* 108–9; Contamine, *War in the Middle Ages,* 168–71.

31. Orsini, "Il Governo," 30.167–68.

32. Pieri, *Il rinascimento,* 208–10.

33. Pieri, "Il 'Governo,'" 205–6 (note 3 to Carafa, second "Memoriale," 5).

34. Oman, *Middle Ages,* 1:483–90.

35. *Merlin,* ed. Paris and Ulrich, 1:259–62. Similarly, in the *Chanson de Roland* the Saracens flee after Charlemagne kills their leader Baligant (261–64).

36. Contamine, *War in the Middle Ages,* 259.

37. The initial skirmish of the Roman War provides another example, where Gawain, Bors, and Idres have the heroics (*Morte,* 5.6).

38. *Istorie fiorentine,* 8.16, cited by Pieri, "Il 'Governo,'" 205–6 (note 3 to Carafa, second "Memoriale," 5).

39. The unexpected appearance of Rinaldo, who attacks the second battle under Bianciardino, upsets Marsilio's plan (*M* 26.81–82, 92–93). Fearing treason, when he sees the disorder in an uncommitted battle, Marsilio comes down from his mountain (*M* 26.95–97) and soon sends both the second and third battles prematurely into the fight (*M* 26.125–31).

40. The other two are the battles of the prisoner escort and the forest (*Morte,* 5.6–7, 10–11).

41. Pieri, *Il rinascimento,* 208–10; Van Overstraeten, *Des principes de la guerre à travers les âges* (Brussels, 1926), 1:30, quoted by Contamine, *War in the Middle Ages,* 209; Contamine, *War in the Middle Ages,* 229.

42. Birds in flight were stunned, and one thought it was an earthquake. This scene provides the model for Astolfo's horn in the *Orlando furioso.*

43. Oman, *Middle Ages,* 2:197–200, 381–86. Orsini points to these battles and remarks that Edward III conquered France by caution and military strength but lost it when he lost prudence ("Il Governo," 35.174). Discussing the use of infantry just after the Hundred Years War, Jean de Bueil recommends that infantry not attack: "Everywhere and on all occasions that footsoldiers march against their enemy face to face, those who march lose and those who remain standing still and holding firm win" (quoted in Contamine, *War in the Middle Ages,* 231). For a romance analogue see *Tirant,* 286.804–288.808. The Greek army drove off a party of sappers, who fled to a marshy pass. The Saracen cavalry, however, rode on to a deserted village, where they had cavalry in a wood, ready for ambush. The Christians debated whether to attack, and finally the duke of Pera forced an attack. The Christians had to dismount at the ditch and broken wall of the village, at which point the Saracens attacked from two sides. All the dismounted knights were killed or captured, five hundred of them in all (289.811–12).

44. Carafa, second "Memoriale," 7.207–8, in Pieri, "Il 'Governo'"; Pieri, *Il rinascimento,* 283.

45. Tirant has also arranged an ambush of foot soldiers, who are to attack late and complete the destruction of the enemy. Their commander, Diaphebus, loses patience

and moves too soon, so the main Saracen army manages to escape, though with heavy losses.

46. Oman, *Middle Ages,* 2:381–86.

47. Even the cautious Carafa thinks a commander can win a field encounter, if the enemy outnumbers him by only 10 percent (first "Memoriale," 20.198–200, in Pieri, "Il 'Governo'").

48. Pieri, *Il rinascimento,* 304; Visconti, ed., "Ordine," 11.498. Monferrato advises Galeazzo Maria not to leave anything behind an army that can harm it (13.502). Chiericati begins his treatise by stating that leaders need prudence and discretion. He praises Antonello da Correto, who was never captured and always returned safely, having taken prisoners or driven the enemy back (Zorzi, "Un vicentino," 426).

49. Carafa, second "Memoriale," 7.208, in Pieri, "Il 'Governo.'"

50. Machiavelli's statement has been generally accepted by scholars. Mallett agrees, though he points out that Machiavelli falsified numbers to make his point (*Mercenaries,* 197–200). Del Treppo ("Gli aspetti organizzativi," 273–75) bears out both authors by his statistics. In more than twenty-five years Micheletto's company of 512 had only 25 deaths, 15 of these in battle. See also Oman, *Middle Ages,* 2:307–8.

51. Pieri, *Il rinascimento,* 307 and n. 2; Mallett, *Mercenaries,* 233–34.

52. Mallett, *Mercenaries,* 198; Pieri, *Il rinascimento,* 304. Carafa advises the duke of Calabria that he can maintain better cohesion in his army if he takes no prisoners. A captured man-at-arms requires a guard, so both sides lose a man (second "Memoriale," 3.203, in Pieri, "Il 'Governo'").

53. *M* 26.1, 13, 41, 138, 142; 27.57–58, 180.

54. In the catalogue of Lucius's troops Palestine is Saracen, and Tatary and Turkey send troops. Lucius puts a Saracen garrison in Cullayne (*Morte,* 5.2). Saracens appear in the battle with the prisoner escort (5.7), and the Rhodian knight, Feraunte, is a rebel against God (5.11).

55. For the siege see Babinger, *Mehmed der Eroberer,* 300–303; and Lane, *Venice,* 358–59.

56. Contamine, *War in the Middle Ages,* 257–59. He speaks of the eleventh through fifteenth centuries but draws all his examples from the fourteenth and fifteenth centuries.

57. Oman, *Middle Ages,* 2:381–86, 408.

58. Orsini, "Il Governo," 2.127. The experience of the twentieth century certainly fits his assumption, since the defeated state either underwent a change of political systems or disappeared. Russia (1917), Germany (1918, 1945), Italy (1944), and Japan (1945) exemplify the former; the Ottoman Empire (1918), Austria-Hungary (1918), Poland (1939), and South Vietnam (1975), the latter.

59. Carafa, first "Memoriale," 7.185 and n. 4, in Pieri, "Il 'Governo.'"

60. The campaign of Jena and Auerstädt provides an instructive parallel. On 14 October 1807 the French vanguard of 26,000 under Davout collided with and defeated the main Prussian force of 70,000 at Auerstädt. At the same time Napoleon with 56,000 destroyed the Prussian rear guard of 50,000 under Hohenlohe. The Prussians sustained 27,000 casualties plus 18,000 prisoners and lost their field guns. An energetic pursuit

captured another 20,000 and soon most of Prussia itself. As Chateaubriand expressed it in his *Mémoires d'outre-tombe* (vol. 1, part 3, bk. 20, chap. 6, p. 753): "A Auerstaedt et à Iéna, le 14 octobre, la Prusse disparaît dans une double bataille; je ne la retrouvai plus à mon retour de Jérusalem." Lefebvre provides the figures in *Napoleon*, 259–60.

61. Belloc, *Eye-Witness*, 82. He assumes that the battle began at dusk and was over long before dawn. The *Chanson de Roland* has its second battle, like the first, last all day, concluding at dusk (*Chanson de Roland*, 252, 258).

62. Pieri, *Il rinascimento*, 210–11.

63. Orsini, "Il Governo," 4.129, 22.159. In fact, the number exceeds any data we have. See Mallett, *Mercenaries*, 116–20. Pulci's exact figure is 20,600.

64. For the Milanese army, see Mallett, *Mercenaries*, 118–19. Pulci's figures are those of the *Chanson de Roland* (215–16), which also has 100,000 watch the duel for Ganelon's life at Aix (280–81). For the battle with Baligant, Charlemagne has 350,000 (*Chanson de Roland*, 217–25). In 1494 Charles VIII brought to Italy an army of 30,000. See Mallett, *Mercenaries*, 238.

65. See note 60 above.

66. A knight could dismount, of course, to make a kill.

67. The Italian use of infantry declined from 1400 to 1450, but foot soldiers never disappeared and were experiencing a steady growth during Pulci's lifetime. See Contamine, *War in the Middle Ages*, 132–37. Chiericati assumes a 5:1 ratio of horse to foot, recommending that no captain general have more than 1,500 horse and 300 infantry (Zorzi, "Un vicentino," 432).

68. Cavalry, in fact, made Carolingian expansion possible, but the real enemy at Roncesvalles, at least, was the Basques, who fought on foot. See Belloc, *Eye-Witness*, 82.

69. Mallett, *Mercenaries*, 148–49. In Malory's tale, Lancelot cannot walk to Mellyagaunce's castle, though it is only two miles away (*Morte*, 19.4). His dilemma is that of the fifteenth-century knight, a prisoner of his heavy armor. The stout and middle-aged Edward of York died of a heart attack at Agincourt, and at Dendermonde (1452) a man fell and was unable to rise. See Oman, *Middle Ages*, 2:377–78.

70. Orsini, "Il Governo," 11.139.

71. Pieri, "Il 'Governo,'" 111–12.

72. Contamine, *War in the Middle Ages*, 127–28. He cites a condotta between Ercole Bentivoglio and Florence for 1483. This was the year of publication of the expanded *Morgante*. Mallett (*Mercenaries*, 149) dates the change to the 1470s. Chiericati remarks that a man-at-arms in the recent wars had from three to five horses, but he then recommends from six to ten for the men-at-arms in the "lanze spezzate" (Zorzi, "Un vicentino," 427, 430).

73. The "Ordine" (1.453–55) assumes six or seven horses per man-at-arms. The French "lance fornie" or "lance garnie" had six by 1445. See Pieri, "Il 'Governo,'" 108–10; Contamine, *War in the Middle Ages*, 129. Brittany and Burgundy soon adopted the same ratio (1450–75). Here, however, the *fighting* unit was three (Contamine, *War in the Middle Ages*, 127). Charles the Bold had the largest units after 1472, when a lance involved nine people. See also Vale, *War and Chivalry*, 121–25.

74. By the regulation of Charles the Bold (1473), a *coutilier* or squire wore a brigandine, or jack, in the German style, a *sallet* (helmet), and a *gorgerin* (neckpiece), and had his legs and arms protected. He carried a sword, a two-edged dagger, and a javelin, which could function as a short lance. See Contamine, *War in the Middle Ages,* 128. Condottieri theory influenced Charles, who wanted Bartolomeo Colleoni at his court. See Pieri, "Il 'Governo,'" 115; Mallett, *Mercenaries,* 236.

75. Foot soldiers served as individual assistants to knights. They took prisoners, collected the fallen, and carried lances.

76. Vico, *Principj,* par. 559. This explanation would not apply to twelfth-century narratives, when the lance as a unit did not yet exist.

77. One normally argues that the romancer speaks to the concerns of an aristocratic audience. Boiardo begins the *Innamorato* by addressing "signori e cavallier," and Pulci talks to Lucrezia Tornabuoni. On the other hand, such a rhetorical explanation has its limits. It overlooks the popular nature of many romance stories, especially those sung in the public squares, and the fact that Florence did not have an aristocratic society.

78. Orsini, "Il Governo," 17.150.

79. Carafa, first "Memoriale," 1.180, in Pieri, "Il 'Governo.'" Berry Herald in *Le livre de la description des pays* thought that Naples had the best cavalry in Italy. See Contamine, *War in the Middle Ages,* 124.

80. Orsini, "Il Governo," 36.174, cites examples. His earliest is Aquila (1424), where Braccio lost the battle because he did not fortify his camp. For the north we know that Jack Cade fortified his encampment at Blackheath in 1450. There are several examples later in that decade, including Dartford (1452) and Ludford Bridge (1459). See Goodman, *Wars of the Roses,* 20–22, 30, 167, 170–71, 214. Using Jean de Bueil, Vale describes French practice for the same period (*War and Chivalry,* 142). Chiericati stresses the importance of infantry in building, attacking, and defending fortified camps (Zorzi, "Un vicentino," 433).

81. Visconti, ed., "Ordine," 5.482–83; 16.509. See also Pieri, "Il 'Governo,'" note 2 to Orsini, "Il Governo," 18.151.

82. Carafa, first "Memoriale," 3.182, and second "Memoriale," 7.208, in Pieri, "Il 'Governo.'"

83. He mentions Caesar's camp at Alesia ("Il Governo," 33.171). Vitruvius, Vegetius, and Hyginus provided the information on such camps (Oman, *Middle Ages,* 2:217).

84. Orsini, "Il Governo," 18.150–54; Pieri, "Il 'Governo,'" 120–21, 124. I follow Pieri on the word *bastion.* It must not be construed in its later sense; here it means simply a reinforcement of wood, sticks, or earth.

85. For Castillon see Burne, *Agincourt War,* 332–45; Seward, *The 100 Years War,* 259–62; Jacob, *Fifteenth Century,* 505–6; Goodman, *Wars of the Roses,* 164–65; Oman, *Middle Ages,* 2:403–4.

86. Allegretti, *Diarj,* entry for 7–8 September 1479, p. 793; Pieri, "Il 'Governo,'" 118n.1; Carafa, first "Memoriale," 10.187, n. 1, in Pieri, "Il 'Governo.'"

87. Orsini, "Il Governo," 36.174.

88. Oman, *Middle Ages,* 1:204–5.

89. Mallett, *Mercenaries*, 108–9; Contamine, *War in the Middle Ages*, 168–71, 254–55.

90. Carafa defers to Federigo of Urbino (second "Memoriale," 1.201), and he praises him as a cautious and prudent commander (first "Memoriale," 8.185–86), qualities he learned from Francesco Sforza (second "Memoriale," 7.209, in Pieri, "Il 'Governo'").

91. Impatient with the long cavalry battle and anxious to share the glory, Diaphebus sprang his ambush prematurely, so the bulk of the Saracen army was able to escape.

92. Oman, *Middle Ages*, 2:304.

93. Mallett, *Mercenaries*, 108. Chiericati assumes the same numbers, saying that the "lanze spezzate" should be organized in squadrons of twenty-five men-at-arms each (Zorzi, "Un vicentino," 430). He assigns twenty-five to thirty-four infantrymen per squadron (ibid., 430, 434). For other examples in Pulci, see *M* 26.64–65.

94. Visconti, ed., "Ordine," 1.453–55, 9.490, 14.505. Orsini has twenty men-at-arms per squadron ("Il Governo," 17.149 and n. 3).

95. Contamine, *War in the Middle Ages*, 233–35. Despite his elaborate blueprint for Morat, Charles the Bold altered his plan there to fit the terrain. For the condottieri and Charles the Bold, see note 73 above. Mallett criticizes Ridolfo Gonzaga's battle plan at Fornovo as too complicated. Gonzaga was a veteran of the Burgundian wars. See Mallett, *Mercenaries*, 241–47; Pieri, *Il rinascimento*, 343–53.

96. Contamine, *War in the Middle Ages*, 157–58, 160–61; Mallett, *Mercenaries*, 26–27.

97. Lord Agramunt wounds the king of Egypt, as he dismounts to kill the fallen Tirant, and Hippolytus gives the commander his own horse.

98. This is Mallett's description (*Mercenaries*, 202–3). Vegetius was, of course, the most popular of the classical manuals.

99. For the battle of Pelis Tirant rustles mares (*Tirant*, 132.362) and drives them into the enemy camp so the stallions run wild (133.373). In Africa he follows the advice of the Genoese Almedixer and times an attack to follow a cattle stampede through the enemy camp (*Tirant*, 339.939, 340.941).

100. Martorell and Galba, *Tirant lo blanc*, trans. Rosenthal, viii–x. Martorell exchanged thirteen challenge letters with Joan de Montpalau in the 1430s and then challenged don Gonçalbo de Hijar, lord of Montalbán (1446–50). See ibid., 630n.5. In the dedication, Martorell claims that the book will give light for a moral chivalry (*Tirant lo blanc*, ed. Riquer, 6), and he says in the prologue that the romance instructs by example (8).

101. He must fight the Muntalbà brothers, for example, because he killed a then unknown knight in a joust (*Tirant*, 74.177, 77.181–82, 81.190).

102. The glimpses he gives fit the traditional pattern: duels between heroes, and the fight between the two generals, Orlando and Sicumoro, which decides the battle.

103. Camylarde is the exception (*Morte*, 1.18).

104. Malory knew the Vulgate version through the Stanzaic *Morte Arthur*. For the Vulgate version, see *Mort le roi Artu*, ed. Frappier, 180–90.

105. Galba's narrative of Caramèn comes closest (*Tirant*, 384.1026–387.1034). He gives a list of battles and the initial clashes. Galba uses *esquadres* and *batalla* here interchangeably (387.1031–32).

106. The Vulgate *Mort* flanks Salisbury with Arthur's battle against the Romans (161–62) and Lancelot's against Mordred's two sons (197–98), both of which it abbreviates.

107. Our four romances appeared in print between 1483 and 1495. Ariosto composed the Olimpia episode, where he discusses the new manner of war, for the third edition of *Orlando furioso* (1532). See chapter 7.

CHAPTER 2: ARTHUR'S RISE TO POWER

1. Delbrück observed that medieval warfare lacked a theory, since clerics and not soldiers were the writers (*Medieval Warfare*, 5.8.636). Frontinus defines strategy as whatever a commander does (*Stratagems*, 1.Proem.6). His editor, Mary McElwain, says in a note that this paragraph is probably an interpolation (Frontinus, *Stratagems*, ed. McElwain, 10).

2. Vegetius wrote his *Epitoma rei militaris* or *De re militari* in the late fourth century. In it he described an ideal, the old legions of the past (Oman, *Middle Ages*, 1:17). Delbrück lists some of his adapters (*Medieval Warfare*, 5.8.636–40). Contamine lists both translations and adaptations (*War in the Middle Ages*, 210–11). For English versions see Mahoney, "Malory's Great Guns," 293n.20; and especially Bornstein, "Military Strategy in Malory," 124; and Bornstein, "Military Manuals," 470–75. Four English versions were made in the fifteenth century, of which Malory could have seen two, possibly three. Vegetius lists Frontinus among his sources (Bornstein, "Military Manuals," 469).

3. Mallett, *Mercenaries*, 202–5. For Martorell and Galba see chapter 1. Contamine mentions a French translation early in the reign of Charles VII, and Antoine de la Sale included copious extracts in *La salade* (1444), which he wrote for John of Calabria (*War in the Middle Ages*, 212). Frontinus probably wrote the *Stratagems* shortly after he returned from Britain, where he had campaigned against the Silures in Wales (Frontinus, *Stratagems*, ed. McElwain, xii), an area that regularly troubled the Arthur of the romancers.

4. The Cambridge or expanded *Suite* includes the Vulgate wars, which do not exist in the shorter version of the *Suite,* the so-called Huth *Merlin*. For the relation of the Cambridge version to Malory, see appendix 1.

5. The difference between "Renaissance" and "Autumn" or "Indian Summer" arises from the kind of books imitated, but it is well not to draw the line too sharply between Italy and the North. Courtiers in north Italy read widely in vernacular romances.

6. Malory, *Works*, ed. Vinaver, 3:1499; Goodman, "Malory and Caxton's Chivalric Series," 261. Benson parallels the fictional Alexander's exploit with that of the Bastard of Saint Pol, who defended the "belle pèlerin" for a month on a road between Saint Omer and Calais (1449). See Benson, *Malory's "Morte Darthur,"* 180.

7. Whitaker, *Arthur's Kingdom,* 10. She cites Sir Thomas Gray, *Scalacronica* (fourteenth century), and Caxton's preface to Malory.

8. Pochoda, *Arthurian Propaganda,* 29–30. She cites Laura Keeler, "Geoffrey of Monmouth and the Late Latin Chroniclers," *University of California Publications in English* 17, no. 1 (1946).

9. Pochoda, *Arthurian Propaganda,* 12, 69, 71–72. She cites D. S. Brewer, "'The Hoole Book'," in *Essays on Malory,* ed. J. A. W. Bennett (Oxford: Clarendon Press, 1963), 41–63.

10. Benson points out that romancers normally set up a scribal tradition that established an authority (*Malory's "Morte Darthur,"* 8–9), but the thirteenth-century romancers whom I have read do not cite multiple authorities or allow for disagreement. Elizabeth Kirk reads this procedure differently. She thinks Malory makes contradictory claims about the validity of his historical witness. The story demands assent to truth for itself, but Malory calls attention to the fragmentary basis for this narrative and to his own limited authority (Kirk, "'Clerkes, Poetes and Historiographs'," 290–91).

11. Delbrück, *Medieval Warfare,* 5.8.640. Although Jean de Bueil contributed part of *Le jouvencel,* three of his retainers actually wrote most of it. Contamine lists it among other texts that the soldier Bertrand de Béarn owned in 1497 (*War in the Middle Ages,* 215).

12. Riquer, *Cavalleria,* 8. For *Jehan de Saintré* see ibid., 5, 69–70, 73, 75. Benson remarks, "To a surprising degree fifteenth-century romance is a realistic genre, elevated in style but often mimetically true to the aristocratic life of the time" (*Malory's "Morte Darthur,"* 138–39). C. S. Lewis in his *Discarded Image* ([Cambridge: Cambridge University Press, 1964], 179–82) makes this closeness a basic principle. He argues that one ought not to distinguish history and fiction when thinking of medieval literature and its reception. Both genres have fancy as well as reality and comment on actual problems, tendencies, and events. Göller cites this approvingly ("Arthurian Chivalry," 53), but I prefer the time-based definition and would limit the rapprochement to the medieval revival of the late fourteenth and fifteenth centuries.

13. Malory has bequeathed to the English tradition the spelling errors of the Cambridge *Suite du Merlin:* Bedgrayne for Bedigran, Camylarde for Carmelide, Lodegraunce for Leodegan. So as not to confuse matters further, I will follow the spellings of the Cambridge *Suite* and of Malory, which are by now conventional in English.

14. The romancers here imitate the Trojan model as transmitted to them by Dares and Dictys. The Achaeans must defeat not only the Trojans but also a series of relief armies: the Thracians under Rhesus (Dictys, 2.45–46), the Amazons under Penthesilea (4.2–3), and the Ethiopians and Indians under Memnon (4.4–8).

15. Albraca provides the one possible exception.

16. This truism would apply to any of the three Malorys whom current scholars have identified with the writer.

17. Keen, *Chivalry,* 221–22.

18. In the Vulgate, Merlin conjures a firestorm, which destroys the enemy camp and occurs simultaneously with the charge of Arthur's knights. Malory drops the magic and so must make the odds more realistic. For both battles the romancers give lists of the contingents plus overall totals. The numbers do not always correspond, and the lists are sometimes partial. For Caerleon the Vulgate has 2,800 for a partial catalogue of enemy knights but at the battle 4,000 plus many squires, sergeants, and crossbowmen. Arthur has 350 knights (Vulgate *Merlin,* 88). The Cambridge *Suite* has 2,700 for the catalogue and 3,000 enemy knights for the battle, plus 3,000 infantry, squires, and crossbowmen (*Suite,* 203r, 204v). Arthur has 450 knights. Malory has 2,800 versus 500 knights but assumes that 300 go over to Arthur before the battle, convinced of Arthur's legitimacy. The total then is 2,500 to 800 (*Morte,* 1.8.17–9.19). At Bedgrayne the Vulgate manuscripts

have two figures, 44,000 plus infantry for the barons or 60,000, while in both Arthur has 25,000–26,000 (Vulgate *Merlin,* 109–12). Sommer lists the higher figure for the enemy kings (Malory, *Morte,* ed. Sommer, 53). The Cambridge *Suite* has the lower figure for the catalogue and the higher figure for the battle (*Suite,* 216r, 217r). Arthur again has 25,000. Malory narrows the gap slightly: 60,000 to 30,000 (*Morte,* 1.11.25–12.26). In the catalogues minor variations and changed attributions are frequent. The variation between 40,000 and 60,000 is a simple manuscript variant: *xl* or *lx.*

19. The Vulgate author has "li menus pueples" support Arthur after Merlin proves his legitimate birth (Vulgate *Merlin,* 91). The phrase signifies those who have no importance. In Malory they have clubs and staves (*Morte,* 1.9.19).

20. The kings lose half their army. The Cambridge *Suite* specifies 20,000 dead, a number that assumes the lower total of 40,000 for the enemy army, since 20,000 are still alive to rally next morning (*Suite,* 219r–v). Sommer (Malory, *Morte,* ed. Sommer, 46) notes that Merlin predicts that Arthur's own losses will be 4,000.

21. The kings fall back, try to rally, but fail, and the retreat becomes a flight. In the expanded Vulgate, Merlin predicts that the enemy will lose hundreds and hundreds but Arthur only eighty (Vulgate *Merlin,* 111).

22. Malory preserves this action with two changes. First, he puts the emphasis on the day battle. The enemy losses at night total only half the Vulgate number, so Merlin's second ambush now wins a battle against a superior army. Second, the enemy never loses formation or flees, though the enemy forces do retreat (*Morte,* 1.13.26–17.37). The Cambridge *Suite* suggested this interpretation. The enemy makes a better rally and maintains formation in retreat. The pursuers kill only those who fall under the horses' feet (*Suite,* 223v).

23. Tirant catches the Saracen army besieging Pelidas by a night march and by stampeding mares into the enemy camp, which drive the stallions wild (*Tirant,* 133.373–75). He next separates the two halves of the enemy army when he burns the bridge over the Trasimene by night (*Tirant,* 141.407–8), and at Malveí he places his lieutenant, Diaphebus, in ambush (155.481–82). Galba has Tirant arrange a variant on this plan in Africa (*Tirant,* 334.928) and then another version of the attack conjoined with a stampede, this time of cattle. He follows this ambush next day with a surprise attack at dawn (*Tirant,* 339.939–340.943). The Saracens had used ambush from swampy ground against the Greeks before Tirant's arrival, luring the Christians to attack across a deep river (*Tirant,* 131.358–59). Later they catch the Greeks and Franks dismounted at a deserted village (*Tirant,* 286.804–288.808). In Africa they ambush a party of Christians during a truce (*Tirant,* 340.945).

24. Martorell drew probably on a French prose version of an Anglo-Norman romance of the thirteenth century. See Martorell and Galba, *Tirant lo blanc,* trans. Rosenthal, xi. The strategy in the Vulgate and that in *Tirant* thus originate in the same period.

25. Fulvius Nobilior with an enemy army close behind came to a river, the swift current of which would delay him. He left a legion in ambush on the enemy side. The enemy, despising the smallness of his army, followed the Romans into the stream. Fulvius then sprang the ambush and destroyed the army.

26. See note 20 above.

27. All travelers were to be sent to the king and could lose a limb or their lives (Vulgate *Merlin,* 109). The expanded version has Arthur's camp itself guarded, so that none could leave and inform the enemy (Vulgate *Merlin,* 111).

28. Vulgate *Merlin,* 110; *Morte,* 1.13.26. The Cambridge *Suite* elaborates further. All Arthur's troops travel to Bedgrayne by night (*Suite,* 215r–v).

29. He is Cipres of Paternò (*Tirant,* 149.450–53). A renegade Christian of Famagusta, he wishes to reconvert and becomes Tirant's spy. In *Jouvencel* King Amydas learns the enemy plan of campaign when informers betray it to one of his messengers (3.1.196–97).

30. Delbrück, *Medieval Warfare,* 5.8.640.

31. Robert de Balsac is still emphasizing the need for espionage around 1500. See Contamine, *War in the Middle Ages,* 226.

32. At Bedgrayne Arthur brings 10,000–11,000 and the Bretons, 15,000 (Vulgate *Merlin,* 109, 112). The Vulgate author models the situation on Geoffrey of Monmouth. There Hoel of Brittany brings the same number of troops to help Arthur against the Saxons, who have similarly increased the size of their army (*Historia,* 144). The *Brute* preserves this episode (*Brute,* 73).

33. At Caerleon those who rejected Arthur were Kings Lot, Uriens, Carados, and Agustans (Vulgate *Merlin,* 88). At Bedgrayne Agustans does not appear, but the kings have added Escant de Cambenic, Clarions of Northumberland, the king of Chent, and Tradelmans of Norgales (Vulgate *Merlin,* 110). The Cambridge *Suite* adds the King of the Hundred Knights (*Suite,* 203r).

34. The Cambridge *Suite,* Malory's immediate source, had given different lists for Caerleon and Bedgrayne. Malory puts them together and comes up with eleven rulers. The Cambridge list for Bedgrayne is Escans de Cambenic, Brengoires, Clariant, the King of the Hundred Knights, Lot, Uriens, and Ydres (*Suite,* 216r), and it assumes Tradelmans for the actual battle. Malory adds Angwysshauns, Nentres, and Carados from the Cambridge list for Caerleon.

35. The Cambridge *Suite* adds that the giants who live in Ryons's land will not stay a day's journey from the frontier, once Arthur marries Guinevere (*Suite,* 214v).

36. In the Vulgate, Merlin invented the Round Table for King Uther (Vulgate *Merlin,* 55–58). After his death the knights left the realm because of the great disloyalty they saw and served Lodegreaunce instead (Vulgate *Merlin,* 92).

37. Ban and Bors had presumably served Uther, and Ulfius and Bretel had often been to Brittany. Arthur summons them to an obligatory court. All who hold lands from him must come (Vulgate *Merlin,* 98). When asked to do homage, Ban and Bors ask only that the king and Merlin demonstrate the legitimacy of his title. They assume throughout that the English monarch is their liege lord.

38. The Vulgate author could have found a model in the Arthur of Geoffrey of Monmouth, who spends all his money on his followers and then begins the Saxon war for plunder (*Historia,* 143).

39. Kennedy, *Knighthood,* 36–37.

40. Orsini says much the same: men, arms, money. G. J. Trivulzio was more extreme: money, money, money (Orsini, "Il Governo," 26.162 and Pieri's note).

41. Martorell also gives Saracen pay (*Tirant,* 140.400) and states that the Grand Kara-man raises 300,000 ducats for the war (163.529).

42. Orsini would also have the heirs provided for ("Il Governo," 3.127–28).

43. Zorzi, "Un vicentino," 427–29; see also 433 (infantry) and 413.

44. Kennedy has some brief remarks on "bastard feudalism," a phrase coined in 1945 by K. B. McFarlane to describe a system that resembled the old feudal arrangements but replaced fief and homage with cash fees (*Knighthood,* 52).

45. Mallett, *Mercenaries,* 227–28.

46. For this campaign see Burne, *Agincourt War,* 332–45; Seward, *The 100 Years War,* 259–62; Jacob, *Fifteenth Century,* 505–6; Goodman, *Wars of the Roses,* 165. Martorell may have used Talbot's copy of the romance of William of Warwick for the first section of *Tirant,* a copy Talbot gave to Henry VI as a wedding present in 1444 or 1445 (Martorell and Galba, *Tirant lo blanc,* trans. Rosenthal, xi–xii).

47. I use the translation of Rosenthal (Martorell and Galba, *Tirant lo blanc,* trans. Rosenthal, xxix).

48. See Gaston Paris's introduction to the Huth *Merlin* (*Merlin,* ed. Paris and Ulrich, x–xii). Robert is similarly confused about Northumberland. Twice it is a region, mostly uninhabited (*Lestoire de Merlin,* 46, 65), but a messenger talks as if it were a town (65).

49. The kings reach the city by a night's ride (Vulgate *Merlin,* 124). Sommer notes that they meet in the marshes of Gore (Wales) and Scotland (Malory, *Morte,* ed. Sommer, 53).

50. Merlin stops the pursuit at a makeshift bridge (Vulgate *Merlin,* 121).

51. Kennedy, speaking of Malory, argues that Merlin here also stops the killing be-cause it is immoral to kill those in flight (*Knighthood,* 27).

52. For Galescins see Vulgate *Merlin,* 127–28.

53. Gaston Paris originally noted that the *Suite* derived its English geography from Robert de Boron and the Prose *Lancelot* (*Merlin,* ed. Paris and Ulrich, lxviii). It has Rob-ert's confusion over Northumberland. Niviene's father is a king in Brittany who rules Northumberland (Huth *Merlin,* 136, 140–41). The romancer presupposes two Northumb-erlands, one bordering on Brittany and the other separating Logres and Gore (Huth *Mer-lin,* 43, 140–41, 143). As in the Prose *Lancelot,* Sorelois instead of the Irish Sea is beyond Norgales (Huth *Merlin,* 159–60). There are indications in the whole Vulgate of a real geography for England. The expanded *Merlin* puts a castle of Arthur at Arundel (Vulgate *Merlin,* 133), and the *Mort le roi Artu* has Winchester and Salisbury (*Mort Artu,* 5–6, 8–9, 129, 178). It is unclear whether these references are any more specific than those in Robert de Boron. After the battle of Salisbury the wounded Arthur goes to the Noire Chapele, by the *sea* (*Mort Artu,* 191, 194).

54. Riquer, *Cavalleria,* 27, 35–36. He cites from the *Viatge al Purgatori* of Ramon de Perellós.

55. Benson, ed., *King Arthur's Death,* xviii.

56. Ibid. For Winchester, Stanzaic *Morte Arthur,* 41–42; for Rochester and Carlisle, 2254–57; for Glastonbury, 3960–61.

57. After Bedgrayne the kings provide for the defense of Cornwall, Wales, and the north (*Morte,* 1.18.40–41). Malory precisely identifies many more places. From the north

come the king of the Scots, Lot, Clarions of Northumberland, and Carados, whom Malory later puts in Scotland (*Morte,* 19.11.1147). From the west come Uriens and Cradelmans (Wales), Idres (Cornwall), and Angwysshauns (Ireland). For the lists see *Morte,* 1.8.17 (Caerleon), and 1.12.25–26 (Bedgrayne). At Caerleon it is mostly Wales and Scotland. At Bedgrayne, Cornwall, Ireland, and Northumberland are added.

58. Malory puts the battles in the same place, Castle Terrable, ten miles from Tintagel (*Morte,* 1.1.8, 2.10.75).

59. Arthur makes Brastias warden of the north: "Fro Trent forwardes, for it was that tyme the most party the kynges enemyes" (*Morte,* 1.7.16). Merlin requires passports from all soldiers *this* side of Trent (*Morte,* 1.11.25). For Sherwood Forest, see *Morte,* 1.17.38. Sommer first noted that this location was Malory's invention (*Morte,* ed. Sommer, 44, 57). Vinaver remarks that Malory treats the area north of the Trent as enemy territory throughout the Tale of King Arthur, that is, until the Roman War (Malory, *Works,* ed. Vinaver, 3:1287). Knight observes that Malory's war zone was realistic by contemporary standards. Rebellion in the west and north had marked the Middle Ages generally but especially the fifteenth century. Edward IV had constant trouble in the north in the early 1460s. Knight wrongly attributes to the *Suite,* however, the emphasis on the northern barons (*Arthurian Literature,* 108–9).

60. Oman, *Middle Ages,* 2:302, citing Machiavelli, *Principe,* 12. Contamine notes that sieges could drag through a winter and says that the troops of Liège fought in January nine times during the fifteenth century (*War in the Middle Ages,* 227–28).

61. For details on the Yorkist engagement, see Jacob, *Fifteenth Century,* 528–30, 532; Goodman, *Wars of the Roses,* 57, 59–64, 157. Arthur makes arrangements with Ban and Bors during an All Saints' Day tournament (*Morte,* 1.10.22, 24), and after the battle of Bedgrayne Merlin visits Blaise and returns to Arthur the day after Candlemas, or February 3 (*Morte,* 1.17.38).

62. Bornstein, "Military Strategy in Malory," 127; Christine de Pisan, *Fayttes,* 1.18.64–65.

63. Benson (*Malory's "Morte Darthur,"* 166, 182–84) discusses tournaments, noting the lists of names, like those kept by heralds, the jousting armor, and the barriers set up to prevent head-on collisions between horses. All these were marks of fifteenth-century tournaments.

64. *Tirant* brings in "Moors" from the Canary Islands (*Tirant,* 5.18)!

65. Here, the "old story" includes the intermediate version preserved in the *Suite,* Malory's direct source. There the kings repent and ask peace of Arthur when he returns from Camylarde. Both then raise armies against the Saxons who, frightened by the united action, flee to their ships. The army of the petty kings catches up with them and wins a great victory. The battle restores stature to the kings and makes worthwhile their movement to Arthur's side (*Suite,* 227v–29v). For a discussion see Bogdanow, *Romance of the Grail,* 31–33.

66. Uther besieges the duke of Cornwall in Castle Terrable, ten miles from Tintagel (*Morte,* 1.2.9). For the second battle the Cambridge scribe did not specify the enemy but assumes Saxons, since he mentions that the Saxon captives went over to the enemy army (*Suite,* 197r).

67. Pieri, *Il rinascimento,* 207–11. In a countryside covered with castles battles were rarely decisive.

68. Knights fought on foot, and their heavy armor made flight unlikely. Moreover, a captive could not expect mercy or ransom in a civil war (Oman, *Middle Ages,* 2:410–11). Here are some examples from the Continuation of the *Brute.* The Lancastrians lost at St. Albans I and left the duke of Somerset, the earl of Northumberland, and Lord Clifford dead on the field (*Brute,* 256, app. X). They lost again at Northampton, where the duke of Buckingham, the earl of Shrewsbury, Viscount Beaumont, and Lord Egremond died (*Brute,* 261, app. X). It was the Yorkists' turn at Wakefield. York, Rutland, and Thomas Nevile died in the battle, and Salisbury was executed later at Pomfret Castle (*Brute,* 262, app. X). At Mortimer's Cross or Wygmore, Edward of York had Owen Tedder, the father of the earl of Pembroke, beheaded after the battle (ibid.). After St. Albans II the Lancastrians executed two lords and many others (ibid.). At Towton the Lancastrians lost another Northumberland, and Clifford and Sir John Nevile, the brother of the earl of Northumberland (*Brute,* 263, app. XI). Finally, at Barnet, Warwick and his brother, Marquess Montague, died on the field, and Edward IV slew Prince Edward of Lancaster after the battle (ibid.).

69. An exception is the presence of Lot.

70. Both these episodes derive from the *Suite du Merlin.*

71. On Assumption it is Arthur and the king of the Scots versus the king of Norgales, King Angwysshauns of Ireland, the King of the Hundred Knights, Galahaute the Haute Prince, and King Clarivaus of Northumberland. All but one of these fought against Arthur at Bedgrayne. At Allhallows it is Arthur and the rulers of Ireland, Northumberland, and Scotland against the king of Norgales, the King of the Hundred Knights, and Galahaute. The latter two are not named initially but are at the tournament and would balance the odds. At Candlemas, which is Malory's invention, Arthur, Norgales, Ireland, Northumberland, and Galahaute combat Scotland, Gore, Brittany, and the duke of Clarence.

72. The kings of Scotland and Norgales, King Angwysshauns of Ireland, the King of the Hundred Knights, and the king of Northumberland (*Morte,* 19.11.1147).

73. Pochoda (*Arthurian Propaganda,* xi) argues that political theory proved just as troublesome. This is the thesis of her book.

74. Jacob, *Fifteenth Century,* 528–30, 532; Goodman, *Wars of the Roses,* 57, 59–64, 157; Mahoney, "Malory's Great Guns," 292, 300.

75. Goodman observes that the old static siege warfare was not used (*Wars of the Roses,* 181, 183).

76. Pochoda goes so far as to say that "the cumulative effect of Malory's tragedy is that of separation from the past and from the notion of recreating the past" (*Arthurian Propaganda,* 34).

77. Malory did some alteration but no radical experimentation with Arthur's Roman War. Vinaver dated it early (Malory, *Works,* ed. Vinaver, introd., 1:lii–lv). McCarthy also considers it an early composition. See his two essays: "Order of Composition in the *Morte Darthur,*" and "The Sequence of Malory's Tales." See also Spisak's remarks ("Recent Trends," 8).

CHAPTER 3: AGRAMANTE'S WAR

1. Martorell and Galba, *Tirant lo blanc,* trans. Rosenthal, xii–xv. Martorell also used John Hunyadi as a model for his hero.

2. Benvenuti cites the Sienese Bernardo Illicino, who in his commentary on Petrarch's *Trionfi* says that the romances had a core of fact. He grants that Charlemagne had warriors reside in his palace, who were accordingly called paladins (*I libri,* 26).

3. Boiardo treats his main historical source, the pseudo-Turpin, comically. See, for example, the interchange between Turpin and Rugiero (*OI* 3.4.40–45).

4. He does variations on "bella istoria" at 1.13.58, 1.19.65, 2.1.3, 2.4.86, 2.11.1, 2.13.2, 2.16.1, 2.19.3, 2.31.50, 3.1.2, 3.8.2, 3.8.66. Otherwise it is simply the "istoria": 1.24.1, 1.26.3, 1.29.55, 2.4.1, 2.12.62, 2.18.3, 2.22.61, 2.23.2, 2.25.52, 2.27.2, 2.28.55, 2.31.2, 3.8.1. Neither list is exhaustive. In personal communications, Charles Ross of Purdue University pointed to one example where *istoria* means only "story" (*OI* 2.11.13), and David Quint of Yale University suggested that Petrarch 187 might be behind *OI* 2.22.1–3.

5. Bertoni, *Biblioteca Estense,* 18.

6. Boiardo made the point about his "low" style in the proem to *OI* 2.19. In spite of his claim about following the historian, Marinelli argues that book 2 is closer to epic, pointing to the dynastic material (*Ariosto and Boiardo,* 53).

7. This trend was perhaps encouraged also by the *poemetti bellici,* or short narratives of contemporary battles and sieges. Marina Beer has recently edited these poems.

8. Martorell provides an instructive contrast. He likes to cite Livy but does not imitate his formal devices and technique. See, for example, *Tirant,* 137.230, 357.984, and perhaps 143.417–18.

9. The private focus concerns the love interests of the characters and those adventures that do not relate directly to the war.

10. Ponte, *La personalità del Boiardo,* 81, 85, and note. Ponte also points to the use of *Hist.* 3 for passages that concern Egypt and India. He also cites Livy and the invasion of Hannibal as a source, one which Boiardo himself indicates at *OI* 2.29.2.

11. Ponte, *La personalità del Boiardo,* 11. Boiardo would have finished his translation *before* Ercole became duke.

12. Boiardo may have originally picked up the term from Lorenzo Valla's translation: "quos Cambyses in expeditione contra Macrobios aethiopes sumpta subegit" (Valla, lxx verso). For 7.18, however, Valla simply gives *Aethiopes* (Valla, clxv verso). The term may also be due to modernization, since Macrobia appears in some fifteenth-century maps where modern Ethiopia is located. It is a case of an epithet, "long-lived," taking on an existence of its own, so that Herodotus's "Aithíopas toùs makrobíous" (*Hist.* 3.21.3) became two separate peoples, located in the same area. The name may involve a pun, since the Ethiopian king gives the Persian spies a bow they cannot string. This is the second meaning in Liddell-Scott, citing a gloss in the *Etymologicum Magnum* (3.23).

13. Ponte, "L'*Orlando innamorato* nella civiltà letteraria," 413. He contrasts Boiardo with Pulci, who used only two sources.

14. Two details directly link *Orlando innamorato* to Herodotus. First, the Greek histo-

rian stated that the Caspian was fifteen days' rowing in length (*Hist.* 1.203.1), a detail Boiardo reproduces at *OI* 2.10.50–51, 2.13.30. Second, Cyrus finds Babylon supplied with food for a siege of many years (*Hist.* 1.190.2), as does Agricane at Albraca (*OI* 1.10.24). Beyond these details Boiardo would have found hints for certain plot situations. Cyrus offers marriage to a queen in Turkestan, goes to war when refused (*Hist.* 1.205), and dies there. This is the pattern of Agricane and Angelica, and the area is the same. Also, Boiardo's notion of a two-part invasion of France transforms the double Persian assault on Athens. Marathon becomes Rodamonte's attempted naval landing in Monaco, with similar results: the invader suffers complete defeat. This force is followed by the main army, which goes overland and wins an initial victory that nevertheless indicates the tactical superiority of the defenders (Thermopylae, Montealbano). In neither case, however, does Boiardo derive any details of plot from Herodotus, and the parallels are too general to rule out other sources. The same can be said for two sets of scenes. In one set Gradasso must rely on his personal troops to win a battle (Barcelona, Paris), just as Xerxes and Mardonius normally turn to Persians, Medes, and Elamites (Thermopylae, Plataea). Second, the dramatized barbarism of the Rocca Crudele may owe something to Pheretima's revenge at Barca, when she impales her enemies and sets them around the walls of the town (*Hist.* 4.202).

15. He begins his first speech by saying that he will listen to the elders' advice (*Hist.* 7.8.a.1) and immediately cites what he has learned from them: the accomplishments of his predecessors. On the second day he explains that he has not yet matured in wisdom and apologizes for his words to his uncle Artabanus. However, as How and Wells indicate, he had a married son, a fact to which Herodotus alludes at 9.108. See How and Wells, *Commentary,* note to *Hist.* 7.13. Wells wrote the commentary for *Hist.* 1–4, while How was responsible for commenting on *Hist.* 5–9.

16. Perhaps as a result of their youthfulness the two kings do not truly lead. Mardonius talks Xerxes into the Greek war (*Hist.* 7.5), and then Artabanus changes his mind. In the *Innamorato* Agramante cannot control the hawks in his army. Rodamonte organizes his own expedition. At Montealbano the other hawks simply attack the French, without royal command, and Agramante can only follow with the rest of his army (*OI* 2.29.48).

17. Boiardo also summarizes Alexander's career at *OI* 2.1.5–13.

18. The capture of Barca did not balance the disaster in Russia, and the acquisition of Macedonia and some Aegean islands did not compensate for Marathon.

19. Hubris is, of course, a major concern in Herodotus. Frequently, its signal is the unnecessary war. Croesus loses his kingdom in a war he begins with a have-not, as his adviser Sandanis warned him would happen (*Hist.* 1.71), and Cyrus goes to his death in a needless war.

20. He thus would fit the astrological type of Mars, as described in the *Sphaera,* a work preserved in a manuscript in the Este library (Bertoni, *Biblioteca Estense,* 194–95). These verses accompany the miniature of Mars: "Il bellicoso *Marte* sempre infiama / Li animi alteri al guerreggiare et sforza / Hor questo hor quello ne satia sua brama / In l'acquistar: ma più sempre rinforza." Boiardo keeps his type pure because he suppresses the revenge motif. Xerxes discusses it, especially in his second speech (*Hist.* 7.11), but Agra-

mante, who has more justification since he lost family members in Europe, does not refer to the previous war.

21. Mardonius has argued privately that a war of revenge is necessary to deter others from attacking Persians and that Europe is worth winning, a lovely land with every kind of the best trees (*Hist.* 7.5–6).

22. Artabanus repeats this argument at Abydus (*Hist.* 7.46.4). For the comparison to Greek tyrants, see the anecdotes of Thrasybulus at 5.92.

23. Herodotus remarks that the nomads of North Africa worship only the sun and the moon (*Hist.* 4.188). Pizigani in his portulan (1367) says that the Garamantes are named after Garat, a son of Apollo, who founded the town Garama. See Kamal, *Monumenta,* 4:iv.1482.

24. The use of the catalogues is common to epic and romance as well as to history. Reichenbach (*L'"Orlando innamorato" di M. M. Boiardo,* 110) cites, for example, the *Spagna in rima.* Paratore discusses parallels in the *Aeneid,* but his evidence indicates that Herodotus and not the Roman poet would fit Boiardo. Virgil insists on numbers and on known familiar surroundings, not on the names of kings and exotic places ("L' *Orlando innamorato* e l' *Eneide,*" 357).

25. Most of the cities in Agramante's kingdom appear, for example, in the Catalan Atlas (1375?; reproduced in Kamal, *Monumenta,* 4:iii.1304v–5v) or in the Atlas of Nicolaus de Combitis (end of the fourteenth century; ibid., 4:iii.1333). Ross notes a source in the Hebrew Bible for the enemy army. Agramante, like Ben Hadad of Damascus, leads thirty-two kings to battle (1 Kings 20). See Boiardo, *Orlando innamorato,* trans. Ross, 26.

26. For the elect troops, see *OI* 2.29.17–20. The others come from the old Cyrenaica: Tolometta, Bernica (Bernice), and Rassa, a narrow point with white beaches located in contemporary maps eastward toward Egypt. See the *Sfera* of Dati (before 1424; Kamal, *Monumenta,* 4:iv.1493v) and Maestro de Portii (ibid., 4:iv.1444). Garbato guessed rightly that the name Rassa is the Arabic word for a headland (*ras*) turned into a proper name; see his note to the same passage (Boiardo, *Orlando innamorato,* ed. Garbato). Boiardo also alludes to the good military equipment of these soldiers (*OI* 2.22.30). Alzerbe is the spelling of the portulans, which, as is often the case, includes the Arabic article in the name. See, for example, Maestro de Portii (Kamal, *Monumenta,* 4:iv.1444r).

27. Boiardo puts it next to Oran going east (*OI* 2.22.23). This is the Belmarye of Chaucer's General Prologue, 57. It does not appear on the maps and may be a romance inheritance, as is perhaps Normandia.

28. Larache, the medieval Ana, is Banī Arūs (the vine arbors of the Bani Arus). Boiardo equates it with the Isole Felici because Pliny the Elder made that identification for Punic and Roman Lixus, the predecessor of Larache. The marshes of the River Loukos were the Gardens of the Hesperides. See *Morocco,* 72. The windings of the river suggested the serpent that guarded the golden apples. I am indebted to Charles Daniels of the Department of Archaeology of the University of Newcastle upon Tyne for this suggestion. Marmonda probably belongs here as well, south of Arzila. It is a fishing kingdom on the ocean (*OI* 2.22.16), whose leader is an admiral (2.17.24).

29. This is the argument made by Admiral Achaemenes (*Hist.* 7.236) and had been

the procedure when the Persians went to Europe: in Thrace (4.85–89) and in Macedonia (6.43–45). For an analysis see How and Wells, *Commentary,* app. 20.

30. In fact, only the Mamluks among Islamic powers used ensigns. See Atil, *Art of the Mamluks,* 20–21.

31. For examples from Herodotus, see the Nubians or West Ethiopians (*Hist.* 7.69), the East Ethiopians (7.65, 70), or the Sagartii with their lassoes (7.85).

32. See the portulan of Maestro de Portii (toward 1424; Kamal, *Monumenta,* 4:iv.1444r). The Portuguese had captured the place in 1458.

33. The portulans put Getulia in the Tell of Algeria and Tunisia. See, for example, the Anonymous (Kamal, *Monumenta,* 5:i.1493r); Pierre d'Ailly, *Ymago Mundi* (1410; ibid., 4:iii.1357v); or Fra Mauro's *Mappa-mondo* (1457–59), which Beazley reproduces in *Prince Henry the Navigator,* 302. Classical maps, however, put Getulia in the North Sahara, a location that accords with Boiardo's description: far from the sea and hot (*OI* 2.22.17). See, for example, Pirrus de Noha, Preface to Pomponius Mela (ca. 1414; Kamal, *Monumenta,* 4:iii.1376v); or the Ptolemaic map of 1478, published at Rome (ibid., 5:i.1502r).

34. The first time the Garamantes are an unwarlike, shy race, living in the wilds above the desert (*Hist.* 4.174; Valla, ci verso). Modern editors of Herodotus substitute the Gamphasantes of Pliny the Elder (5.44–45), and Pomponius Mela (1.47). See the note in How and Wells, *Commentary.* Valla has "Garabantes" for the second mention of the Garamantes (*Hist.* 4.183; Valla, cii verso).

35. Boiardo slyly remarks that Turpin has them eat locusts, a statement Herodotus applies to the Nasamones (*Hist.* 4.172).

36. Salmasius later emended the first to "Atarantes." See the note in How and Wells, *Commentary.* In Valla's translation, it is cii verso.

37. The Trivulziana manuscript of *Orlando innamorato* has misled editors, who read "Fersa" here and at 2.3.39. The Venice edition of 1486 reads "Fiessa," which is the spelling of the maps. See the Anomymous Portulan of 1457 and the *Sfera* of Dati from before 1424 (Kamal, *Monumenta,* 5:i, 4:iv.1437v). Anonymous lists it as the Regnum Fesse (the Marinid kingdom), but its location varies on the maps, and it sometimes wanders south of the Atlas. Ross states that the Trivulziana manuscript and the early printed texts generally do not fit Boiardo's spelling (Boiardo, *Orlando innamorato,* trans. Ross, 29).

38. Valla has the spelling of the portulans, "Trimison." It regularly appears on the nautical maps. Dati's *Sfera* locates it a journey of three days inland (Kamal, *Monumenta,* 4:iv.1439r). Boiardo puts it on "our sea," the Mediterranean, and follows it with Oran (*OI* 2.22.21–22).

39. The portulans always mark Mount Carena or the Atlas range and have a standard description. It is fertile land, producing bread, wine, oil, and fruit, and it supports a dense population. This description probably suggested to Boiardo the location for Atlante's garden. For a whole list of examples see Kamal, *Monumenta,* 4:iv.1473v. It is also on Dati's *Sfera* (ibid., 1437v) and the portulan of Baptista Becharius (1426; ibid., 1454v). Guilelmus Soleri (toward 1385) adds that the area has many ferocious animals: leopards, lions, wolves, and boar. The boy Rugiero feeds on lions (*OI* 2.1.74) and hunts wild animals (3.3.35–37). Almasilla is the modern M'Sila, on a line south of Bejaïa (Bugia) and the Atlas. Ibn Khal-

dun locates it near the Zab and has the original for the Italian spelling. See the *Kitab al-'lbar* (Book of Admonitions), cited in Kamal, *Monumenta*, 4:iii.134v.

40. Herodotus may have influenced Boiardo in his conception of these black cultures. Three, possibly six, realms contribute black soldiers to Agramante's army. The poet so identifies the troops from Libicana (*OI* 2.22.5), the coastal land of Maurina (2.22.21), and Esperia, at the far edge of the world (2.22.6). He may likewise classify Cosca and Mulga, zones beyond the horizon (*OI* 2.22.27–28). The king of Mulga at least is black. One might tentatively put Norizia here, a land a thousand miles beyond Ceuta (*OI* 2.22.9). Finally, though just appointed ruler of Tingitana (North Morocco), the pygmy Brunello leads a group of black pygmies to the war. His origins seem to be West African, since he knows the king of Fiessa (Fez), and Boiardo makes the blacks of Maurina people of small stature. The poet may have been thinking of Herodotus's story (*Hist.* 2.32–33), in which Nasamones cross the desert going west and find pygmies on the Niger. If so, he again interprets nautical information through a classical source.

41. The Almoravids ruled from Senegal to Spain; the Almohads, from Spain and Morocco to Tunisia.

42. Only the Lydians are equipped like the Greeks (*Hist.* 7.74.1). Two contingents, the Assyrian and an unnamed one, contribute medium troops, who have regular helmets, shields, and spears but lack metal breastplates (*Hist.* 7.63, 76).

43. Persians, Medes, and Elamites all wear armor and carry large bows. Their shields are wooden and their spears short (*Hist.* 7.61–62). Like them are the Median exiles (*Hist.* 7.80) and the Hyrcanians (62.2). Other contingents equipped for double duty include the Bactrians, Sacae, and Scythians (*Hist.* 64); the Arians, Parthians, Chorasmians, Sogdians, Gandarans, and Dodicae (66); and Caspians and Sarangae (67)—that is, the tribes of the eastern plateau of Iran and of Turkestan, plus the Nubians (69).

44. The unarmed archers are Pactuans, Indians, East Ethiopians, and Arabians (*Hist.* 7.65, 67–70). Many of the Anatolian javelin throwers are well equipped with offensive arms but still lack armor: the Paphlagonians, Ligues, Matieni, Marianchuni, Cappadocians, and Phrygians (*Hist.* 7.72–73), and the Colchians, Alarodians, and Saspeires (79).

45. The Persians, Medes, and Elamites have the same armor as the infantry (*Hist.* 7.84–86). Besides other mobile units (*Hist.* 7.86–88), Xerxes picks up cavalry in Thessaly.

46. These are the elite troops that have both infantry and cavalry (Tripoli, Bernica/ Rassa, Tolometta) and the elite that are not so specified (Biserta, Tunis) at *OI* 2.22.30, 29.17–19. Otherwise those of Bugia have armor, shield, and lance (*OI* 2.22.25), those from Bellamarina (2.22.23) and perhaps Septa (2.22.15) are acceptable, and Tremison contributes heavy archers who wear regular armor and carry lance and shield besides (2.22.21–22).

47. There is no information for four groups, not even inference: those from Marmonda, Constantine, Garbo, and Alzerbe.

48. These are Almasilla, of whom none are worthy (*OI* 2.22.7); Bulga or the troglodytes (2.22.10); the unarmed Nasamones (2.22.12); Amonia, whose men Boiardo compares to lice (2.22.14, 2.29.11); those of Getulia, who are naked and worthless (2.22.17); and the ignorant nomads of Nurizia (2.22.9). The other nomads and oasis dwellers would

presumably also lack worth: the Garamantes, those of Fizano, and the dumb folk of Fiessa (*OI* 2.22.11).

49. Those of Alghezera lack armor and carry Stone Age weapons (*OI* 2.22.18), as do those from Canara (2.22.30). The troops from Alvaracchie wear skins and carry clubs (*OI* 2.22.13). Those from Arzila and Azumara would presumably fit the same pattern.

50. Boiardo evaluates only two of the black troops: the unarmed rout from Libicana (*OI* 2.22.5) and the more sophisticated blacks from Maurina, of whom, however, hardly one in a thousand had arms (2.22.21).

51. At Plataea the Persians grab the Spartan spears and try to break them (*Hist.* 9.62). How and Wells also suggest that the larger shields of the Greeks made a difference (*Commentary*, note to 7.211, citing *Hist.* 9.62 and Diodorus Siculus, 11.7).

52. See his arguments with Demaratus at Doriscus (*Hist.* 7.102–3) and Thermopylae (7.209.5). He estimates 2 million infantry and 100,000 cavalry, chariots, and camels.

53. See *OI* 2.29.48, 50; 2.30.8, 39, 44; 3.4.11, 37. The poet uses the same term for the Spaniards: 2.23.24, 52, 67; 2.24.22.

54. At the end fewer than 1,100 Greeks face the Persian army (*Hist.* 7.202, 222). At Montealbano the *canaglia* comes like a river in flood and wins the battle (*OI* 3.4.31).

55. Three thousand survive Plataea (*Hist.* 9.70.5).

56. Hess, *Forgotten Frontier*, 17–18, 60–61. Kemal Reis began the new piracy when he went west in 1487 and raided out of Bejaïa, Annaba (Bone), and Jerba for eight years. In contrast, Portugal had taken over several coastal cities in North Africa (26–30). Galba in his continuation of *Tirant lo blanc* mirrors the true situation, since he portrays a Christian offensive in the area. The piracy of Kemal Reis then was a defensive response to Western aggression.

57. The ducal library had a copy of Andrea's version. See Bertoni, *Biblioteca Estense*, app. 3, no. 20.

58. Hess, *Forgotten Frontier*, 21–24, 34, 52.

59. For example, an Italian translation of Strabo is listed as 447 in the 1495 inventory. The 1467 list included two copies of Pomponius Mela, plus Paulus Orosius, *De plagis mundi* (nos. 2, 17, 25, 133), not to mention many other geographical texts in both lists. Bertoni, *Biblioteca Estense*, reprints the lists in his appendices.

60. Ruggieri points out that the Turkish threat also affected Pulci (*L'umanesimo cavalleresco italiano*, 217–18). In his letters written to Lorenzo during 1471, Pulci discusses Neapolitan naval preparations against the Turks (Letter 19 of 27 February, Letter 21 of 19 March, Letter 22 of 21 March). See Pulci, *Lettere*, ed. Bongi, 88, 94, 99.

61. Babinger, *Mehmed der Eroberer*, 277–78.

62. Pieri, *Il rinascimento*, 38 and note. The raids took place in 1471–72 and 1477. For the view from Venice, see Lane, *Venice*, 236.

63. *Hist.* 8.72; Lopez, "Il principio della guerra veneto-turca," 81.

64. *Hist.* 7.139; for the building of the wall, 8.71.

65. Lopez, "Il principio della guerra veneto-turca," 80–81.

66. The figures are Lane's (*Venice*, 358–59). Babinger gives him even less: thirty-six galleys and six cargo ships (*Mehmed der Eroberer*, 299–300).

67. Babinger, *Mehmed der Eroberer,* 300–302; Lane, *Venice,* 358–59.

68. The Franks are less homogeneous than the Greeks. Ranaldo has Hungarians at Monaco.

69. Machiavelli, *Arte della guerra,* 2.392–94, 399, also 6.481.

70. By 1483 Venice had six squadrons of Stradiots. See Mallett, *Mercenaries,* 119.

71. Ibid., 152–53; Miller, *Latins in the Levant,* 482–83. They came mostly from Laconia, and the best from Navplion and Thermisi. Contamine gives French reactions to the Stradiots (*War in the Middle Ages,* 128–29). They wore Turkish dress and slept outdoors with their horses. Their shields were small.

72. In Thessaly Xerxes staged a race between his horses and those of the Hellenes. The latter lost badly (*Hist.* 7.196). This scene in the *Innamorato* provided the model for the Atlante-Bradamante battle in Ariosto.

73. Kritoboulos shows Mehmed's use of infantry for mountain warfare. In Albania they twice captured the passes (*History of Mehmed the Conqueror,* 3.95–96, 5.66), formed the van for marches (5.70–71), and could also raid (5.96).

74. Ibid., 5.3–6, also 3.39, 3.83 (for Lesvos and old Patrai); McNeill, *Venice,* 70–71; Lopez, "Il principio della guerra veneto-turca," 53, 64 (for the Morea).

75. Pieri, *Il rinascimento,* 267–68; Mallett, *Mercenaries,* 154–55, 215.

76. Within Boiardo's lifetime Western infantry had likewise become a crucial tactical arm. In France and Italy it had won parity with cavalry, and in the English and German areas, superiority. The English had long won battles with dismounted knights and longbows. More recently, while Boiardo was writing the *Innamorato,* Swiss pikes had defeated the Burgundians in the north and prompted Maximilian to imitate them with the Landsknechten. The armies of Venice and Milan, when successful against the Germans, used northern tactics. At Arbedo (1422) Carmagnola dismounted his horsemen and defeated the Swiss (Pieri, *Il rinascimento,* 305–6 and note; Mallett, *Mercenaries,* 232–33), and the Trivulzios won Ponte di Crevola (1487) with an infantry force (Pieri, *Il rinascimento,* 313–15; Mallett, *Mercenaries,* 234). In Italy itself infantry had been decisive in recent battles. Federico da Montefeltro captured the Florentine camp at Poggio Imperiale by infantry assault (1479), and foot soldiers executed the flanking maneuver that defeated the Neapolitans at Campomorto (1482). See Pieri, *Il rinascimento,* 300–302, 285 and note. The diarist Allegretti gives some interesting statistics in this respect. Carlo da Montone had ten squadrons of horse and ten of foot for his first raid early in the Pazzi War, forty and forty on the second (*Diarj,* 788, entries for 19 May and 7 June 1479). Later the Florentines sent a raiding party of 100 horse and 200 foot (ibid., 791, entry for 30 July), and on August 3 Gastonza di Pesaro took 10 squadrons of horse and 10 of foot to Marmoraja. A squadron does not necessarily mean the same thing in the two branches, but the numbers are suggestive. The Sienese sent to Poggio Imperiale 2,000 foot, 1,000 sappers, and 1,500 horse (ibid., 792–93, entry for 6 September) and the following year they countered a Florentine move with 300 horse and 800 foot (ibid., 798, general entry for January). Duke Ercole, who had commanded the Florentines earlier in the Pazzi War, went home and tried to introduce a militia at Ferrara (1479). See Pieri, *Il rinascimento,* 269 and note. The duke was no doubt moved by the Venetians, who had developed the best trained and

largest of the Italian militia for their Turkish wars (Mallett, *Mercenaries*, 113–14, 119). By the 1470s Italian cavalry and infantry were roughly equal in numbers (ibid., 146). Cavalrymen, while still favored monetarily and supported by tradition and literature (Corvisier, *Armies and Societies*, 183; Mallett, *Mercenaries*, 136–37), were losing their predominance even while Boiardo composed his romance. Vale argues that the importance of heavy cavalry grew in the late fifteenth century (*War and Chivalry*, 101–3). He does not, however, cite examples after the early 1470s.

77. This argument presupposes that Boiardo composed *Orlando innamorato* more or less in the order we have it. He would thus be moving from the traditional romance picture of fighting he gives at Albraca to a more nuanced conception for the war in France.

78. The Kinghts of Rhodes adapted themselves to similar demands, since they had a galley fleet and took part in amphibious operations (Bradford, *Shield and Sword*, 77, 79; Brockman, *Two Sieges of Rhodes*, 53). They used mercenaries as bowmen on the galleys (Brockman, *Two Sieges of Rhodes*, 41–42).

79. Olmstead argues that only three of six land divisions were used (*History of the Persian Empire*, 248, 255–56, 262). He accepts the argument in How and Wells, *Commentary*, app. 19.

80. How and Wells have an analysis, *Commentary*, app. 19.

81. Xerxes had to reconquer Egypt before he could invade Greece (*Hist.* 7.1.3, 7.4–5, 7.7).

82. Ruggieri argues that Pulci likewise believed in the superiority of the Christian world (*L'umanesimo cavalleresco italiano*, 219, 269), though he considered that superiority ethical.

83. See especially the discussion of Nicopolis by Delbrück, *Geschichte*, 3:4.491–96; and Lot, *L'art militaire*, 2:219–22.

84. Pieri, *Il rinascimento*, 227; Corvisier, *Armies and Societies*, 6–7; McNeill, *Venice*, 82–83.

85. Lopez, "Il principio della guerra veneto-turca," 77.

CHAPTER 4: THE SIEGE OF PARIS

1. Croce set the tone for the twentieth-century critics. As Sapegno argues, his notion of harmony isolates the *Furioso* in a zone that is absolutely atemporal ("Ariosto Poeta," 23–24). For the interwar period Saccone (*Il soggetto*, 161) cites Luigi Ambrosini (*Teocrito, Ariosto minori e minimi* [1926], 194), who considered the *Furioso* a third world, outside history and without time. Among later critics Binni (*Metodo e poesia*, 139–40) claims that the *Furioso* exists on a totally fantastic plane, as if another spiritual world; he develops a musical analogy (see p. 149 for an example). Most recently, Donato claims that Ariosto's narrative does not point to an outside world ("'Per selve e boscherecci labirinti'," 58).

2. Some critics have continued to stress Ariosto's realism, but they have been a minority voice. Rajna remarked that Ariosto's own experience of his troubled times helped him compose his military scenes (*Le fonti*, 414). In 1906 Gardner thought of the poem as a mirror held up to a society that was swiftly passing (*King of Court Poets*, 271). In 1919 Bertoni based *L'"Orlando Furioso" e la rinascenza a Ferrara* on such an assumption. As he

said, "Reality—reality, I repeat—continually penetrates the *Furioso* through the golden woof of romance fantasies and manifests itself even where it is least sought" (ibid., 253). The poet filled old material with contemporary life (ibid., 277). In 1963 Greene argued for the importance of historical allusion in the *Furioso;* such allusions "constitute a robust and stiffening element of fact or quasi-fact in the fluid element of poetic fancy" (*Descent from Heaven*, 135). He saw in this effort a rhetorical function: "To attach epic action to history is to attach it, at however great a remove, to the reader's world and thus to render it more imminent, more relevant, and more credible" (ibid., 136). Also in the 1960s Carlo Dionisotti argued that scholars had to relate the *Orlando furioso* to its historical period (La Monica, "Realtà storica," 326). Finally, Wiggins insisted on Ariosto's realistic presentation of character, which he made the thesis of his *Figures in Ariosto's Tapestry* (1986).

3. As scholars have long noted, this new realism has its roots in a generic shift within literature as well as in the drift into history that I discuss. Ariosto and Tasso looked to Virgil, and Ercilla to Lucan. For the latter see Quint, *Epic and Empire*, 157–78.

4. The *Furioso* had been translated into Spanish twice by 1578, and another translation appeared in 1585. The basic translation by the Aragonese Jerónimo de Urrea had gone through eighteen editions by 1588 (Riquer, "Ariosto e España," 322).

5. Gardner, *King of Court Poets*, 122; Bertoni, *L'"Orlando furioso" e la rinascenza a Ferrara*, 137. For the earlier versions I use volume 1 of *"Orlando Furioso" di Ludovico Ariosto secondo le stampe del 1516 e del 1521.*

6. Rajna, *Le fonti*, 414–15. He also remarks that the Saracens are regularly defeated at Paris in Ariosto's Italian sources (420).

7. For Ariosto see Romizi, *Le fonti latine*, 84; Rajna, *Le fonti*, 247. Bertoni shows that Virgil was popular in quattrocento Ferrara (*L'"Orlando furioso" e la rinascenza a Ferrara*, 82–83). Paratore argues that Virgilian influence on Boiardo was limited to warfare ("L'*Orlando innamorato* e l'*Eneide*," 373–74).

8. Bertoni says that Ariosto makes a mosaic of his classical sources for important scenes (*L'"Orlando furioso" e la rinascenza a Ferrara*, 87–88), and he remarks that the poet never does verbal imitation of medieval romance. Virgil is his main classical source, and Bertoni lists the different kinds of things Ariosto borrowed (ibid., 83–85). Romizi (*Le fonti latine*, 44–81, 132–45) and Rajna (*Le fonti*, 246–56) work out the details of Ariosto's borrowings. Romizi claims that there is nothing of warfare in the *Aeneid* that Ariosto does not imitate (*Le fonti latine*, 44). Rajna argues that because so much of the *Furioso* is derived from Latin epic, Ariosto started a new branch of romance, born of an Italian father and a Latin mother. His argument has been remembered by later critics (Gardner, *King of Court Poets*, 266; Saccone, *Il soggetto*, 196). Bertoni makes much the same point (*L'"Orlando furioso" e la rinascenza a Ferrara*, 120). The principal novelty of the *Furioso* is its fusion of classical epic and vernacular romance. Ascoli reminds us that in any one episode Arisoto uses multiple sources (*Ariosto's Bitter Harmony*, 31).

9. The ditch is more than nine meters wide (*OF* 14.130); Rodomonte runs down the old rue de la Harpe (see note 56 below); and 60 percent of the houses in Paris are wooden (*OF* 16.26).

10. The return from the hunt exemplifies the technique. See *Stanze*, 1.60–61. The

translator, Quint, comments on Poliziano's mosaic imitative method (Poliziano, *Stanze*, trans. Quint, xii).

11. Cinzio, *Discorso dei romanzi*, 160.

12. The novella of Fiordespina is an example (*OI* 3.8.53–3.9.25).

13. Segre (*Esperienze ariostesche*, 50) notes Ariosto's stylistic debt both to the classical authors and to Poliziano.

14. Roncaglia, "Nascita," 238, quoting N. Borsellino. Roncaglia says that the romance tradition in Italy was visual as well as literary. He believes it was no accident that Ariosto composed visual poetry in the Ferrara of Tura, Cossa, Ercole de' Roberti, and Dosso Dossi (ibid., 237). Bertoni earlier had shown how Ariosto's art resembled painting (*L'"Orlando furioso" e la rinascenza a Ferrara*, 72, 75) and had argued that the poet's similes either make something palpable and visible or are suggestive (68). See also the remarks of Reynolds in the introduction to her translation of the *Furioso* (Ariosto, *Orlando furioso*, trans. Reynolds, 1981), 1:47, 49.

15. Quint points to a classical source for this kind of presentation (*Epic and Empire*, 150). Before he presents the battle of Pharsalus, Lucan says that he wants future readers to experience the battle as if it were happening while they read (*De bello civili*, 7.207–13).

16. Franceschetti ("Appunti," 116) remarks that seasons come and go in Ariosto but that it is always spring in Boiardo.

17. Armies rarely fought in winter. See Oman's comments concerning quattrocento Italy (*Middle Ages*, 2:302). Bonomo works out a timetable from such references that applies to the whole narrative of the *Furioso*. He limits the war to ten months. Ariosto picks up the war in the fall and concludes it toward the end of the following August (*L'"Orlando furioso" nelle sue fonti*, 168–70).

18. In the high Middle Ages the English favored infantry for sieges (Beeler, *Warfare in Feudal Europe*, 100). Often mercenaries were used because of the length of sieges (castles normally fell only by starvation). See Oman, *Middle Ages*, 2:21. In the *Furioso* Agramante brings infantry to the fosse for his assault (*OF* 14.98).

19. Greene states, "In certain passages portraying Rodomonte, Ariosto most nearly approaches epic intensity and heroic awe" (*Descent from Heaven*, 142).

20. Wiggins notes this comparison (*Figures in Ariosto's Tapestry*, 48).

21. Greene states, "The *terribilitas* of the awesome mass cremation suffered by the Saracens beneath the walls of Paris gains part of its intensity from his [Rodomonte's] gigantic and furious figure dominating the agony" (*Descent from Heaven*, 142). Mirollo has drawn attention to the audio sensations Ariosto creates and has claimed that the poet more often uses them than visual images when he comments on his own art ("Significant Acoustics," 91).

22. *Ae.* 9.691–818; *OI* 1.11.26–46, 1.14.10–19.

23. See Oman, *Sixteenth Century*, 112–14, for the aftermath of Fornovo.

24. Quoted by Hale, *War and Society*, 179.

25. Hale explains that during a siege there was little distinction between soldier and civilian. At Siena, for example, women were the pick-and-shovel brigade (ibid., 191–92). See also Pepper and Adams, *Firearms and Fortifications*, 134–35. In practice the fate of a

fallen town depended on the mood of the army and its commanders, and no distinction was made between a town taken by storm and one that surrendered to terms (Hale, *War and Society,* 194). A sack could also be seen as the peasants' revenge on towns (ibid., 196–97). Oman notes that the Swiss, who normally served as French infantry, took no prisoners, violated terms of surrender given a hostile garrison, and pillaged towns that had capitulated (*Sixteenth Century,* 66).

26. Bertoni, *L'"Orlando furioso" e la rinascenza a Ferrara,* 242. In another place (142) he cites Polidori (Ariosto, *Opere minori,* ed. Polidori, 1:340), who mentions a Latin poem in which the poet talks of his military service, and an epicedium by his brother Gabriele. The extent of that experience is unclear. Henderson discusses the issue in his forthcoming article, "Power Unparalleled." He cites Michele Catalano, *Vita di L. Ariosto;* G. Traversari, "La vita militare di L. Ariosto"; and Robert Finley, "Venice, the Po Expedition, and the End of the League of Cambrai, 1509–10." Branca thinks the poet had had enough experience by 1515 that war was a daily reality for him (*L'"Orlando furioso" e il romanzo cavalleresco medievale,* 103).

27. Marinelli rightly demonstrates that Ariosto shows consciousness of a renewed Turkish threat in the third and final edition of the *Furioso* (1532). See *Ariosto and Boiardo,* 87–88, 90–95. The new sultan, Süleyman, had renewed the war on Christendom, taking Belgrade (1521), Rhodes (1522–23), and finally Hungary (1526).

28. Cephalonia (1500), Santa Maura (1502), and Alessio. Pedro Navarro and the Spaniards gave them aid. See William Miller, *Latins in the Levant,* 498–99; Pieri, *Il rinascimento,* 390n; Lane, *Venice,* 235. A naval war means bowmen and rowers. See McNeill, *Venice,* 70–71.

29. Cisneros's cannon dispersed the Moorish horse and blew through the thin walls of Mars el-Kebir (1505), and Pedro Navarro's fort stymied the Barbarossa brothers' two attempts at Bougie (1514–15). Finally, the Spaniards had put up a fort at Algiers in 1510 and forced the town to pay tribute. See Hess, *Forgotten Frontier,* 37, 61–63.

30. A counterexample in the war of 1499–1503 is Navplion, which defied two Turkish attempts. See Miller, *Latins in the Levant,* 495, 497.

31. By 1532 the situation was very different, for the Imperials had recently captured Genoa, Rome, and Florence.

32. Ariosto, of course, never left Italy and gave up his job rather than accompany Ippolito to Hungary.

33. In strategy, for example, he followed a pattern developed in southern Italy and still valid as late as 1536 for Pizarro, whose forces survived the Inca rebellion in the two cities of Cuzco and Lima. See Hemming, *Conquest of the Incas,* 189–220. In principle an army, either defeated or too small to risk a field engagement, evacuates the countryside and withdraws either to the capital or to a strong point and so forces the enemy to besiege it under difficult circumstances while it awaits reinforcements or a favorable opportunity. For example, the French, badly defeated at Cerignola, withdrew to the seaport of Gaeta. Though Gonsalvo de Cordoba now controlled the whole south, he had to besiege the French there, since Gaeta could serve as a base for a major counterattack. He failed after three weeks (1503). The French had a large garrison, commanded the sea, and threw in

more troops. Meanwhile a relief force was coming from the Papal States, and Gonsalvo eventually had to win the kingdom all over again at the Garigliano. See Oman, *Sixteenth Century,* 115–16; Pieri, *Il rinascimento,* 417–18.

Ariosto inherited from Boiardo a fiction that fit this strategy, and he developed it accordingly. Carlo, routed in the south, withdraws the remnant of his army to Paris and holds out through several assaults, until Agramante must disperse his army to winter quarters (*OF* 2.24–25, 8.69–70, 12.70). Carlo thus forces the Saracens to maintain a siege far to the north with extended supply lines. The poet later has Rodomonte find the Saône full of small boats, bringing food to Agramante's army from many parts (*OF* 27.128–29). Men load supplies onto wagons and send them to Paris under escort. Rodomonte sees the banks filled with cattle brought from various places and the drivers sleeping in huts on the riverbank. Meanwhile Carlo sends Rinaldo to England to raise a new army during the winter so that the Christians can try another field engagement (*OF* 2.25–26). He thus follows the same strategy as the French commanders at Gaeta. So do the Saracens. When Agramante is in turn defeated, his generals recommend a withdrawal to Arles or Narbonne, where he can maintain a long defense and collect a new army. Agramante follows this advice and gets away with 20,000 men to Arles (*OF* 31.83–84).

Ariosto likewise assumes modern tactics. Carlo forms up his army with the infantry at the center and cavalry on the wings (*OF* 18.41), the order used by both sides at Ravenna. For the battle see Pieri, *Il rinascimento,* 491–97; Mallett, *Mercenaries,* 254. Oman notes the change in terminology: *wings* and *battle* (center) for the medieval *van, battle,* and *rear* (*Sixteenth Century,* 34–35). The French infantry, however, often caused problems. The Swiss mercenaries in French service might desert, even change sides, if pay was slow (ibid., 36–37). The French tried to supplement them with Gascons (ibid., 43), and Ariosto alludes to both (*OF* 27.19). The attacking Saracen heroes cause such an uproar in the French camp that many think the Swiss and Gascons are having one of their usual riots. Tactics, like strategy, required no explanations for Ariosto's audience.

34. In the texts of 1516 and 1521 he puts more emphasis on bastions.

35. Pieri, *Il rinascimento,* 276–77; Machiavelli, *Arte della guerra,* 6.474.

36. On his way to besiege Paris in 1465 Charles the Bold constructed just such a bridge downstream from the city. For an eyewitness account, see Philippe de Commynes, *Mémoires,* 1.6.976–77.

37. Castel Nuovo took place after Cerignola. See Pieri, *Il rinascimento,* 278, 417. For Cephalonia, see ibid., 390n.

38. Ibid., 472–75; Hale, "Early Development of the Bastion," 473–77, 489–90. For French parallels see Contamine, *War in the Middle Ages,* 202–5. Pepper and Adams have since modified Hale, pointing to the use of gun towers in Germany and the Venetian colonies (*Firearms and Fortifications,* 22–23) and their continued use in Italy during the 1520s and 1530s. They further claim that gun towers were the rule, not the exception, in northern Europe (ibid., 159–60).

39. Padua itself, however, is an example of a modified medieval concentric fortification. Fra Giocondo added to it a series of round and semicircular bastions (Pepper and Adams, *Firearms and Fortifications,* 20–21).

40. Hale, "Early Development of the Bastion," 477. He cites Machiavelli's "Relazione di una visita fatta per fortificare Firenze." Navarro visited Florence in 1526.

41. Ibid., 489–92. Gian Giacomo Leonardi thought Alfonso invented the use of angle bastions (468), and Hale thinks it might be true for town walls. Biagio Rossetti provided round bastions for Ercole's extension of Ferrara. Pepper and Adams do note some early examples of angle bastions. Antonio da Sangallo the Younger put up the first complete angle-bastioned enceinte around Civitavecchia in 1515. The two authors argue, however, that the angle bastion did not become standard before 1525, and even then Siena ignored the trend (*Firearms and Fortifications,* 6, 28, 45, 172).

42. Mahoney argues that Malory's "great guns" could refer either to cannon or to some older engine of war. She admits, however, that Wynkyn de Worde in his editions of Malory understood the reference to mean cannon. See "Malory's Great Guns," 308 and n. 81.

43. Fornari, *La spositione,* 1:61–63, also 26–27. Fornari says that the poet imitated Pulci.

44. For Gradasso's siege he assumes the French come out of all the city gates for battle (*OI* 1.6.62, 1.7.2–3). The Seine would automatically have made this two separate and autonomous actions. In the second siege the enemy again surrounds Paris (*OI* 3.7.57), but Boiardo presents an assault rather than a field battle. Common to both sieges are the Gate of Saint-Denis and the fictional San Celso. For Gradasso's he adds the fictional Gates of Bourgogna and the Porta Real, and for Agramante's the Market and River Gates (*OI* 1.7.2–3, 3.8.11–12).

45. Bertoni, *L'"Orlando furioso" e la rinascenza a Ferrara,* 267–68. Boiardo's geography for France is vague. Rodamonte lands at Monaco and immediately after the battle enters the Ardennes (*OI* 2.15.18–20). This vagueness contrasts with the precision of the geography for his scenes in the Middle East. See Murrin, *Allegorical Epic,* 75–76. Concerning guidebooks, Bertoni (*L'"Orlando furioso" e la rinascenza a Ferrara,* 267) mentions Guillebert de Metz's *Description de la ville de Paris au xve siècle.* De Lincy (Guillebert de Metz, *Description,* ed. De Lincy, xxxvi–xxxvii) dates the treatise to 1434, but the library lists at Ferrara do not mention it. If Boiardo had been able to read it, he would have learned about the gates in chapters 28–29 (ibid., 76–80). A more likely source would be Antoine Astezan's Latin poem on his French travels, dedicated to the marquis de Montferrat, but I find nothing in the résumé by de Lincy that suggests Boiardo used it (ibid., xviii–xxi).

46. The French had maintained a military presence in Italy for twenty years. They occupied Milan itself from 1500 to 1512 and had just recovered it in 1515. Bertoni gives some details on the connections between the Ferrarese and the French. Ercole asked the orator Bartolomeo dei Cavalieri, who was in Paris, to buy French books for his library (*L'"Orlando furioso" e la rinascenza a Ferrara,* 92), and he called in players and singers from France for his chapel. Josquin des Prés worked for Ippolito, and the cardinal's dance master, Ricciardetto, knew French dances (ibid., 242–44).

47. Gardner provides the evidence. Ariosto went to Milan with Ippolito to meet the French king in 1507, a few months after he had read sections of the *Furioso* to Isabella in Mantua (*King of Court Poets,* 51–52). Chevalier Bayard with a small force of French and

Swiss infantry was in Ferrara in 1510 (ibid., 79). Pigna says the poet tried to learn French and Spanish to read romances (ibid., 263).

48. Bertoni, *L'"Orlando furioso" e la rinascenza a Ferrara*, 267. Pool (*Interpretazione*, 83) says in contrast that at Paris Ariosto draws attention to the unreality of his representation. He cites no evidence, however, and makes no argument.

49. In 1516 and 1521 he has the Seine enter Paris from the south and exit at the north. He dropped the remark in 1532 but still makes the same assumption, since Agramante retires across the river to the west. The river, of course, runs mainly east to west.

50. Hale, *War and Society*, 45.

51. Oman, *Sixteenth Century*, vii.

52. In the late 1520s, the population of Paris was between 350,000 and 500,000. See Thomson, *Renaissance Paris*, 35. The Christian army comes out of all the city gates to fight Gradasso's army (*OI* 1.6.62, 1.7.2–3), and Agramante's army spreads seven leagues around Paris (*OI* 3.7.57), a statement Ariosto echoes (*OF* 8.69). In the most recent attack on Paris—that by Charles the Bold, then the count of Charolois, and his allies (1465)— the besiegers set up camp facing the northeast wall of Paris, with the army deployed between the Seine and the Gate of Saint-Denis. Charles made no attempt to surround the city, and Commynes indicates that no enemy could starve out a city so well supplied by river traffic coming from the east and west (*Mémoires*, 1.6.978, 1.8.983).

53. *OF* 18.159, 31.85. Its earlier depth was nowhere less than about two meters, according to Belloc (*Paris*, 42), and he says there were no fords below Paris.

54. Victory in any quarter, moreover, would not necessarily give him Paris. Christians could defend any of its three parts separately. To an Italian Agramante's whole attempt would have seemed doubtful, and his chances probably less than Maximilian's at Padua.

55. Reynolds provides a map and commentary (*OF* 1.474–77). My principal disagreement concerns the relief force. Reynolds has Rinaldo cross the Seine east of Paris and march past the battling forces on the Left Bank over to the west side of the city, where he attacks. This reading certainly makes the presence of Silence crucial, but two factors make it unacceptable. First, there is the bridge of boats. Rinaldo might not have needed one upstream, where the Seine is shallower, and he could have used the city bridges in any case, since Reynolds assumes he passed north and all around Paris to reach the enemy attacking the west side of the Latin Quarter. Second, by her diagram Rinaldo would not have had to send the baggage under escort by another route to the northern gates of Paris, those of Saint-Denis and Saint-Martin, if he were taking his main force the same way (*OF* 16.29–31). It makes more sense to assume he detached the baggage train west of the city and himself crossed the Seine there and came up behind the Saracens by a direct route (see fig. 14). Carne-Ross says of the war, "It yields some of the best battle poetry ever written, so energetic and professional that we can follow point for point the movement of troops during the Siege and see exactly what both sides are doing" ("One and the Many," 172).

56. Rodomonte runs down one of the most crowded streets of Paris, the one that goes to the old Pont Saint-Michel (*OF* 16.24). This is Rue de la Harpe, the ancient Via Inferior, which then ran from the Seine to the Porte Saint-Michel, which stood at the modern

crossing of Rue Monsieur-le-Prince and Boulevard Saint-Michel. Rue de la Harpe still runs between the Seine and the Hôtel de Cluny. Farther south it has been replaced by the modern Boulevard Saint-Michel. See Hillairet, *Connaissance du vieux Paris,* 2:155, 53–54. The bridge and gate were named after the court chapel of Saint-Michel, adjacent to the Palais de Justice. Reynolds assumes that Rodomonte breaks in at the riverbank and so runs to the Pont Saint-Michel. She does so probably because Ariosto mentions him after he names the leaders fighting near the Seine (*OF* 14.108). The syntax, however, does not connect them, and the poet immediately generalizes about all the Moors in the next stanza. Rodomonte moves with different troops to the walls (*OF* 14.113), not with those the poet puts by the Seine. By Reynolds's diagram Rodomonte would have run along the quay behind the Tour de Nesle, not down a street. See, for example, the map of Truschet and Hoyau that Favier prints (*Paris au xve siècle,* 161).

57. The new defense system was costly, and Pepper and Adams remark that no great European city had a complete, bastioned enceinte even by 1600 (*Firearms and Fortifications,* 29).

58. I use the text of the Pléiade edition (Hugo, *Notre-Dame de Paris, Les travailleurs de la mer,* ed. Seebacher and Gohin, 136). For Stevenson, see his short story, "A Lodging for the Night," in the *New Arabian Nights.*

59. Giocondo returned to Verona in 1506, and the building was complete by 1508 (Belloc, *Paris,* 318–19). Fra Giocondo also gave advice on the Pont Notre-Dame, which received Renaissance features but would still have looked Gothic, with two turrets in the middle of the bridge and the high conical roofs of the houses (ibid., 313–17).

60. Saint-Jacques, of which the tower survives (Belloc, *Paris,* 319–21), Saint-Merri, Saint-Gervais-Saint-Protais, Saint-Etienne du Mont, and Saint-Eustache, which was planned after Notre-Dame. See Bussman, *DuMont Guide to Paris,* 146, 148–50. An exception would be Philibert de l'Orme's chapel for the goldsmiths (ca. 1565). See Thomson, *Renaissance Paris,* 188, 190. One could hazard two reasons for this lingering Gothic. First, Paris had not been the capital for almost a century, and second, the Gothic style continued to be of high quality. Thomson remarks that the surviving decorations of the Hôtel de Gendre help explain why the fashion for classical decoration came in only slowly (ibid., 58). It might be expected that the Ile de France, which invented the Gothic, might go over reluctantly to an art form imported from the south.

61. Hillairet, *Connaissance du vieux Paris,* 1:7, 2:5. Even the new aristocratic hôtels like Sens or Cluny, where one might expect innovation, would not have changed much the general Gothic style. Their square windows would not have deceived an Italian visitor. See Bussman, *DuMont Guide to Paris,* 145; Hillairet, *Connaissance du vieux Paris,* 1:69; 2:38; Thomson, *Renaissance Paris,* 39–40, 43, 47, 49.

62. Hillairet, *Connaissance du vieux Paris,* 1:7. Hillairet notes that Paris still has about thirty such houses, and I have seen some of them. Favier includes a photograph of two in *Paris au xve siècle,* 117. Rue de la Harpe was not one of the streets Philippe Auguste had paved (Hillairet, *Connaissance du vieux Paris,* 1:3).

63. Belloc, *Paris,* 295–300; Hillairet, *Connaissance du vieux Paris,* 2:5.

64. These walls (1356–83) followed the line of the wall of Philippe Auguste on the

Left Bank (Hillairet, *Connaissance du vieux Paris,* 1:2). They had square towers, a small rampart, and a double moat (Belloc, *Paris,* 268). Hugo assumes that Etienne Marcel and King Charles left the old round towers of Philippe's wall in place (*Notre-Dame de Paris,* 124). In 1465 the Milanese ambassador reported that Paris was being fortified, in Italian style, against rebels (Mallett, *Mercenaries,* 171), but this came to nothing. There was, in fact, no modernization until Louis XIII (Hillairet, *Connaissance du vieux Paris,* 1:2).

65. Hillairet reproduces a map of 1570, which shows the water moat (*Connaissance du vieux Paris,* 1:4).

66. *OF* 14.67; Hale, "Early Development of the Bastion," 474–77.

67. The 1516 text lists ladders, matting, bridges, and boats; that of 1521 has ladders, logs, matting, trelliswork, bridges, and boats.

68. Cannon recovered Normandy for the French (1449–50) and blew open the walls of Constantinople (1453). See Oman, *Middle Ages,* 2:226–27; Burne, *Agincourt War,* 310–14, 324–25; Seward, *The 100 Years War,* 240, 248–49, 252–59; and Runciman, *Fall of Constantinople,* 96, 116, 126, 136, but especially 77–78.

69. Like Boiardo, Ariosto did not know of Guillebert de Metz, who would have warned him about the suburbs and in particular about Saint-Germain-des-Prés (Guillebert de Metz, *Description,* ed. de Lincy, 76–77). Hugo describes Saint-Germain (*Notre-Dame de Paris,* 125).

70. Hale, *War and Society,* 191, speaking of Renaissance sieges. Ariosto does have a ruined castle, where duels are arranged (*OF* 27.47), but otherwise he has the tower, where Marfisa takes Brunello (27.93), and a fountain, where Rinaldo and Gradasso agree to duel (31.103). On the other hand, there were and are forests near Paris, so the labyrinthine wood where Cloridano takes refuge has some basis in reality (Hugo, *Notre-Dame de Paris,* 137; Belloc, *Paris,* 54–55).

71. When Rinaldo arrives the second time, Carlo rides out with the paladins (*OF* 31.59). Ariosto forgets that the Saracens had captured the paladins previously (*OF* 27.32).

72. The English were escorting a baggage train. The two gates are at the highest point of the wall (Hugo, *Notre-Dame de Paris,* 117), but Carlo sees people cut up, not just a fire in the distance.

73. The water comes up to the neck of the giant Rodomonte (*OF* 14.119).

74. Romizi (*Le fonti latine,* 81) parallels *Ae.* 2.469–75 and *OF* 17.11, and *Ae.* 9.789–818 and *OF* 18.20–24. See also his tables (ibid., 93–95). Rajna (*Le fonti,* 247–48) adds *Ae.* 2.445–49 and *OF* 17.10, *Ae.* 2.479–90 and *OF* 17.12–13, and calls Ariosto here a translator. He also lists *OF* 18.8 for Turnus; 18.21 as *Ae.* 9.789–92; *OF* 18.22 as *Ae.* 9.792–98, 806–7; and *OF* 18.23–24 as *Ae.* 9.799–801, 815–17.

75. The only courtyard Rodomonte could enter, where he fights a large crowd, must have been within the palace walls. See the map in the Michelin Tourist (or Green) Guide, *Paris* (5th ed., 1985), 62. The king had not lived there since the 1350s. Guillebert de Metz does say that the palace could lodge the twelve peers as well as the king (*Description,* 21.53–54). The miniature for June in the *Très riches heures de duc de Berry* illustrates the palace.

76. Hillairet, *Connaissance du vieux Paris*, 2:1. They were later joined to the Ile de la Cité (1607) and became part of the Place Dauphine and Vert-Galant.

77. At *OF* 27.13 Ariosto makes this romance logic explicit. The devil, seeing Carlo temporarily without heroes, leads all the Saracen champions to Paris. Donato remarks that the heroics of individual knights dominate the battle scenes and the war ends in a duel of six ("'Per selve e boscherecci labirinti'," 42).

78. I pass over the dispute about his lyrical and difficult style. That he wished to convey the illusion of reality is clear enough. In *Discorsi dell'arte poetica*, 1.351, he says: "Dovendo il poeta con la sembianza della verità ingannare i lettori, e non solo persuader loro che le cose da lui trattate sian vere, ma sottoporle in guisa a i lor sensi che credano non di leggerle ma di esser presenti e di vederle e di udirle, è necessitato di guadagnarsi nell'animo loro questa opinion di verità."

79. Virgil provided the epic model for this concern. See Murrin, *Allegorical Epic*, 13–21.

80. Unless otherwise indicated, all citations of the *Gerusalemme liberata* refer to Caretti's edition. The defeat does not impede the Crusader preparations for an assault. The affair is a minor skirmish, as Tasso indicates in a letter to Scipione Gonzaga (5 July 1575; *Lettere*, ed. Guasti, 1:98).

81. The small part of a hill on the southwest provides a distraction rather than a serious danger when Raimondo uses it to assault the town (*GL* 18.54–55).

82. Tasso here ignores Siloe, away on the other side of town, but he knows it exists (*GL* 13.59). It provides the water for Clorinda's baptism (*GL* 12.67).

83. Gray (*History of Jerusalem*, 228, 230) says that the general plan of the Old City still largely conforms to that which it had under the Franks. The walls in fact followed the line of the Byzantine fortifications of the fifth century, which Süleyman maintained when he rebuilt them (1537–42), incorporating older elements that included whole sections of Byzantine and Mamluk work (ibid., 235, 261). See also Finbert, *Israel*, 340–43.

84. Ismeno and Solimano enter the palace by a secret tunnel and find Aladino holding conference there (*GL* 10.34). Tasso draws on *Jewish Antiquities*, 15.11.7.

85. Titus destroyed it in A.D. 70. See Finbert, *Israel*, 355.

86. Letter of 2 June 1575 (*Lettere*, ed. Guasti, 86).

87. Cited by Wiggins, who has recently stressed the importance of Galileo's criticism for Ariosto as well as for Tasso (*Figures in Ariosto's Tapestry*, 6).

88. Tasso would have known that the fortress was so constructed as to overlook and control the temple, which stood on the highest hill. Josephus calls the Antonia a tower (*Jewish Antiquities*, 15.14).

89. Chateaubriand, *Itinéraire de Paris à Jérusalem*, 343–54.

90. Galileo, however, complained that the poet confused the winds of Palestine with those of Lombardy (Wiggins, *Figures in Ariosto's Tapestry*, 6).

91. Tasso goes beyond Homer because he represents the actual siege. Homer, like the later romancers, assumes a siege but shows only open field conflict.

92. The city itself falls in canto 18.

93. Oman, *Sixteenth Century,* 28, 223.

94. Tasso ends canto 3 developing the problem of lumber, and the Crusaders cut timber for the machine used in the first assault (*GL* 3.56, 71, 74–76).

95. *Arte poetica,* 2.367–68. The poet cannot change the final end of his history or events that are too well known.

96. *Arte poetica,* 1.351–52. Of course, he had classical precedent in Lucan and Silius Italicus, and he knew Trissino.

97. Tasso could have used the Venice edition of 1562. I cite from the *Historia rerum in partibus transmarinis gestarum,* ed. Beugnot and Le Prévost. The relevant sections are 8.9–10, 12–13, 18. Guglielminetti in his edition of *Gerusalemme liberata* also notes Robert of Rheims (Robertus Monacus) and the humanists Benedetto Accolti and Paolo Emilio (1:xviii). Chateaubriand translates Robert on the second assault (*Itinéraire,* 355–57).

98. Letter of 2 June 1575 (*Lettere,* ed. Guasti, 84). Tasso argues that Homer allowed excess only to Achilles (ibid., 85).

99. Rinaldo gets Tancredi's skirmish before Jerusalem and slaughter in the Temple area. William of Tyre has him thunder amid the enemy (*HR* 3.14), a metaphor quite apt for the Este hero.

100. See *HR* 8.13–14.

101. Argillano, for example, reflects a contemporary political understanding. See Quint, "Argillano's Revolt," 1:455–64. The Italians serve as *soldati di fortuna,* or adventurers, a cinquecento term that designated warriors who went to war at their own expense. They were much prized by their commanders both for their gallantry and for their cheapness (Hale, *War and Society,* 138). Tasso had a sophisticated sense of changing manners and their effect on poetry, but he never discusses technology. For manners see *Arte poetica,* 1.357–58. He also argued that setting a story in a distant age allows for some fiction (ibid.).

102. These were the war of Siena and the conflict between the pope and Philip II.

103. They would have captured his sister Cornelia except that she lost her way that night. See Solerti, *Vita di Torquato Tasso,* 1:35–36.

104. Tasso also visited France during the period of its religious wars, but he saw Paris in the lull before St. Bartholomew's Day (1570–71).

105. In his *Arauco domado* Pedro de Oña gives 180 (*AD* 4.52, p. 146).

106. Pedro Mariño de Lovera says they also used silver dishes, plus the governor's casks and trays (*Crónica del reino de Chile,* 2.2.199–203). Oña reproduces this detail (*AD* 4.58, p. 148).

107. Najera describes a typical fort of the early seventeenth century (*Desengaño y reparo,* 3.5.2). Oña says the Spaniards built an earthen wall (*AD* 4.61, 5.65, pp. 149, 181).

108. Marmolejo (*Historia de Chile,* 24.109–11) says the Spaniards had six days to themselves, during which they continued to improve the defenses of Penco. He dates the Indian attack at 10 a.m., 15 August 1557. Lovera, however, dates it to 7 September and notes that Mendoza had put six cannon in place, facing the probable direction of attack, only the day before (*Crónica del reino de Chile,* 2.2.199–203). Figueroa (*Hechos,* 1.26–27) also gives six, not eight, cannon. He notes that they faced the level ground,

the obvious sector from which the Indians would attack. Medina (*Vida de Ercilla*, 46) dates the battle to 25 August. Oña has them attack the fort on one side and the other (*AD* 5.66–67, pp. 181–82).

109. Figueroa says they made three assaults at the ditch (*Hechos*, 2.35). He also states that the Indians initially chased the sailors back into the water up to their waists (*Hechos*, 2.36).

110. A previous earthquake (1751) had already caused the Spaniards to change the location of their fort and town, so modern Concepción borders the Biobio and not the bay. One might guess that Mendoza had the fort built where the eighteenth-century fort of La Planchada still stands. It could hold about 200, but it does not fit other details. Ercilla has Tucapel leap from a cliff nearly thirty-seven meters high (*Araucana*, 20.8, p. 325), a side of the hill the Spaniards left unfortified, facing the sea. Bibar (*Crónica*, 131.200) calls it a low, smooth hill with the sea at its back, so Ercilla may have exaggerated the height. Figueroa says the site was accessible only at the front and on the left, the area where the Spaniards dug a wide and deep ditch. On the right, high bushy hills protected it (*Hechos*, 1.26–27). Of course, he never saw Chile, but he was able to use documents of the Mendoza family. The north hill has a precipice but would have been too high for Oña's anecdote about the priest who passed gunpowder from the beach up to the garrison during the fighting (*AD* 6.85–87, pp. 236–37). It does have a slight dip on top, near the sea, which could have served as a basis for a trench. The south hill is also high enough, but its summit is too broad, and any precipice would face inland, toward the northeast, where a dirt road now runs. Medina puts the fort a harquebus shot from old Concepción, citing Juan Gomez, one of the commanders (*Vida de Ercilla*, 45).

111. Medina says they were on the island forty-eight days (*Vida de Ercilla*, 44).

112. Marmolejo, *Historia de Chile*, 24.109–11; Lovera, *Crónica del reino de Chile*, 2.2.200–203; Figueroa, *Hechos*, 1.26–27, 2.31–37. Marmolejo and Lovera were veterans of the Chilean wars. Neither one could have been at the battle, since the land forces had not yet arrived, and the ship brought only troops from Peru. Lovera and Figueroa normally accept Ercilla's accounts and add stray details. Oña used both Ercilla and Lovera.

113. *Araucana*, Prol.xvii. He apologizes for the lack of preparation and the little time he found to write during the war and compares himself to a cook making poor bread. He also tells King Philip he was an eyewitness (*Araucana*, 1.1.5, p. 2), and he indicates where the narrative turns to events he himself witnessed (12.69–72, pp. 205–6). He was present at Galvarino's punishment (*Araucana*, 2.22.45, p. 364), was clubbed in the marsh by the Biobio (2.22.36, p. 362), led an attack to destroy holdouts after Millarapue (26.13–22, pp. 430–32), was a hero at Purén (28.63–71, pp. 466–67), and traveled south to Ancud with Mendoza.

114. Lucan was doubly important in Spain, since he came from Córdoba and formed part of the local literary tradition.

115. See, for example, Sallust's preface to *De coniuratione Catilinae*, 1–3.

116. Figueroa, in fact, claims that Fenistón's death so enraged the Indians that they chased the sailors back into the water (*Hechos*, 2.36). See also Oña, *AD* 6.54–62, pp. 224–27.

117. Bibar says that the fire of harquebus and cannon forced the Indians to flee (*Crónica*, 131.200). Marmolejo agrees on the importance of guns. Only a few Indians penetrated the fort. Harquebus fire kept the rest at a distance, and cannon did them much damage during their retreat (*Historia de Chile*, 24.110–11). Figueroa claims that the Spaniards killed so many that they feared the Indians could cross the ditch, it was so full of corpses. The Spaniards directed the cannon wherever the Indians were massed together. Firepower forced them to withdraw out of range (*Hechos*, 2.34–36). Lovera adds the interesting detail that because munitions were scarce, Mendoza collected what powder he had and chose twenty good harquebusiers, telling them to shoot at the leaders, who could be distinguished by their dress. When the Indians retreated, they left many dead by the bulwark and in other chosen spots (*Crónica del reino de Chile*, 2.2.200–202). Oña likewise has the sharpshooters (*AD* 6.82–91, pp. 235–38) and attributes the victory to harquebuses and cannon (87–93, pp. 237–38).

118. Oña also has guns kill Gracolano and another Indian with Piñol (*AD* 6.43–45, pp. 221–22).

119. Oña has the Indians basically assault the bastions (*AD* 5.78, p. 184).

120. I argue in chapter 8 that firepower made the group, not the individual, heroic. See also Pocock, *Conquest of Chile*, 241.

121. *Araucana*, 1.13.43–14.3, pp. 222–28. The dialogue between Mandricardo and Doralice before his death provides Ercilla with his general model (*OF* 30.31–44).

122. She kills Stefano of Amboise, Clotareo, Bishop Ademaro, and Palamedes and wounds Guglielmo of England and Roberto of Flanders.

123. Solimano is a historical figure, but he was not at the siege of Jerusalem.

124. The sieges of Albraca and Paris, for example, run through much of the *Innamorato* and *Furioso*. It would be more accurate to call the *Iliad* a poem of blockade, since the Achaeans never surround Troy with siege works, cut off access to the city, or assault its walls. They camp by the sea, denying Troy its trade, raid the surrounding area, and fight any armies the Trojans send out against them.

125. Chateaubriand, *Itinéraire de Paris à Jérusalem*, 358.

CHAPTER 5: THE PROBLEMS HISTORY MAKES FOR THE POET

1. Aristotle, *Poetics*, 23.1–4, 1459a–b, in *Aristotle's Theory of Poetry and Fine Art*, trans. S. H. Butcher (1894; reprint, New York: Dover, 1951); Horace, *Ars poetica*, 136–52. For Ercilla see Medina, *Vida de Ercilla*, 22–24.

2. In fact, poets were turning to history before the revival of classical epic.

3. It began in Italy with the *poemetti eroici*, which preceded the revival of Aristotle's *Poetics;* these have been published in an anthology edited by Marina Beer. Spain lacked the theory of and debate over epic that marked Italy, and although its period of peak production (1580–1630) follows the publication of the *Liberata*, the preference for natural order and recent history among Spanish poets points to the influence of Lucan. See Pierce, *Poesía épica*, 21–22, 232, 321.

4. Some events Camões elaborates to such an extent that critics have classed them as

fiction: the Old Man of Belém, the rescue from Mombasa, and the storm. See Pierce's introduction to Camões, *Lusiadas*, xxviii.

5. Tétis's explanation (*Lusiadas*, 10.82).

6. The Nereids, for example, represent the foam caused by the ship's movement (*Lusiadas*, 1.96).

7. Camões himself allegorizes the Isle of Love as Fame (*Lusiadas*, 10.73) and its nymphs as the honor won by the warrior (9.89–92).

8. Lope da Vega similarly put all Spanish history into his *Jerusalén conquistada*. See Pierce, *Poesía épica*, 45, citing René Rapin.

9. Burton, *Camoens*, 3.195. The initial flashback, that at Malindi, alone occupies 333 ottave, stretching from canto 3 to canto 5, this in a poem of only 1,102 ottave.

10. Not to mention Jove's prediction in canto 2 (*Lusiadas*, 2.46–55).

11. He cannot stop looking at the banners (*Lusiadas*, 7.74).

12. Aside from the historical distortion necessary to set up the situation, Camões presents a king who regards himself as a Portuguese subject and wants all their ships to stop in Malindi (*Lusiadas*, 6.4). In fact, mutual suspicion was so great that the two leaders met initially in boats, and da Gama had finally to seize a *fidalgo* to get the pilot he wanted. See Burton, *Camões*, 4.427–29.

13. *Araucana*, Prol. to Reader, pp. 261–62.

14. The other two were the Dutch and Chichimeca Wars.

15. Ercilla had already decided not to let the biography of Caupolicán determine the shape of his poem, a choice that would not have pleased Sismondi. See Pierce, *Poesía épica*, 117–18, citing from J.C.L. Sismondi, *De la littérature du midi de l'Europe* (Paris, 1813).

16. See also *Araucana*, 3.37.70, p. 603; and Medina, *Vida de Ercilla*, 77–80.

17. *Discorsi del poema eroico*, 2.558, in Tasso, *Prose*, ed. Mazzali. Tasso accordingly rejects Lucan and Silius Italicus. Jean Ducamin thought that Lucan had more influence on Ercilla than Ariosto did. See Pierce, *Poesía épica*, 183.

18. Tasso mentions this empty time in a letter to Scipione Gonzaga (letter 29, 14 May 1575; Tasso, *Lettere*, ed. Guasti, 1:76).

19. Books 1 and 2 of the *Siriade* came out in 1582, books 3 and 4 in 1584, books 1–6 in 1585, and the whole twelve-book epic in 1591. See Vivaldi, *Prolegomeni*, 143.

20. Ibid., 119–20. Vivaldi cites letters 29 and 60 ("storico nobilissimo") in Tasso, *Lettere*, ed. Guasti.

21. *Lusiadas*, 1–2, 5–7, and part of 8.

22. Pittorru, *Torquato Tasso*, 23. Quint argues that the *Liberata* celebrates "an Italian nationalism of another kind. A sixteenth-century Italian poet aiming to revive the imperialist formula of Virgilian epic could find in the papacy the only peninsular power with genuinely international claims" (*Epic and Empire*, 230; also 214, 221). I do not as yet see how a papal focus would have provided Tasso with much more material for his *plot*. Quint is not concerned directly with this issue, though he does discuss Argillano's revolt from this perspective.

23. *Discorsi dell' arte poetica*, 2.367–68; and my discussion in chapter 4.

24. For these details Tasso relied on William of Tyre. See Vivaldi, *Prolegomeni,* 93, 95; Vivaldi, *"La Gerusalemme liberata" studiata,* 7–8. Vivaldi speaks of three assaults rather than two, since the second took two days. Tasso composed canto 11 in the early 1570s, after he had written the *Discorsi dell' arte poetica.*

25. As Chateaubriand long ago pointed out in his *Itinéraire de Paris a Jérusalem,* 349.

26. Tasso later inserted this passage on Argante. The addition improves the sense of crisis before God intervenes (*GL* 9.56).

27. In the redaction of an earlier draft of canto 9 (*An*), which Ignazio Angelini first published in 1877 and which Caretti reproduces in his edition of the *Liberata,* he sends Raimondo, a more plausible choice. Tasso substituted Guelfo for dynastic compliment, presumably after he took service with the duke in 1572. For the latter see Pittorru, *Torquato Tasso,* 86, 93. Tasso then inserted Guelfo's heroic deeds (*GL* 9.72–73). As of 2 June 1575, however, he still talks of Raimondo. See letter 32 in Tasso, *Lettere,* ed. Guasti, 1:83.

28. More plausibly named Alimante in *An.* Lesbino is a function word, of the sort common to comedy, and historically the island of Lesbos was Christian until the mid-fifteenth century.

29. See Greene, *Descent from Heaven,* 193–202.

30. Robert of Rheims may have suggested this description to Tasso. At Dorylaeum new troops suddenly appear. Their lances glitter like stars, their helmets and corselets are like the spring dawn, and their armor sounds like thunder (*Historia iherosolimitana,* 3.17.765).

31. Chiappelli, *Il conoscitore del caos,* 34–51.

32. Tasso mentions a Procoldo, count of Rochese, three times in his letters (25, 60, and 82). See Vivaldi, *Prolegomeni,* 81–83). In letter 25, where he talks of this battle, Tasso calls him Rocoldo, count of Prochese, but the *Conquistata* has Procoldo, count of Prochese (1.52). See also Vivaldi, *"La Gerusalemme liberata" studiata,* 150. In his letter of June/July to Orazio Capponi (in Tasso, *Prose,* ed. Mazzali, 798–99), Tasso says that the count asserted that women played an active role in the Crusade and that priests blamed their adversities on the attractions of Saracen women. Vivaldi was never able to find a copy of Procoldo, and Pittorru says that the chronicle is very rare (*Torquato Tasso,* 119). To my knowledge no Tasso scholar has ever used this source, if anyone ever found it.

33. Robert of Rheims, *Historia iherosolimitana,* 9.2.863–64. See also Vivaldi, *Prolegomeni,* 110–11; Vivaldi, *"La Gerusalemme liberata" studiata,* 7. Tasso mentions Robert twice, in letters 52 and 82. See Vivaldi, *Prolegomeni,* 81.

34. In his *Historici clarissimi,* Paolo Emilio covered the First Crusade under the reign of Philippe I; he has this story at 4.83v–84r. He presents different, perhaps muddled tactics. Smail remarks that the twelfth-century Crusader historians, being clerics, lacked experience in war (*Crusading Warfare,* 3). A later compiler, therefore, might produce confused descriptions. Tasso mentions Emilio in letters 47, 82, 532, 707. See Vivaldi, *Prolegomeni,* 81. William covers the incident at *HR* 5.4–6.198–204.

35. His name is Axcianus in William, Casanus in Emilio.

36. Vivaldi, as usual, pointed out the relevance of Dorylaeum to canto 9. See *Prolegomeni,* 111–12.

37. I follow Runciman's analysis here. See *First Crusade,* 183–87, for his complete account.

38. Fulcher of Chartres, *History of the Expedition to Jerusalem,* 1.11.1–2.83–84. Tasso did not read Fulcher, but all his sources insist that Boemondo knew about the impending attack. Robert of Rheims gives the third hour (mid-morning) as the time of the attack, a mistake that Paolo Emilio silently corrects to the third watch of the night. For their accounts see Robert of Rheims, *Historia iherosolimitana,* 3.8.759–18.766; and Emilio, *Historici clarissimi,* 4.76v–77v. For William of Tyre's account, see *HR* 3.13–15.129–34.

39. Here again I follow Runciman on the topography. He personally inspected the site. See *First Crusade,* 186–87n.1.

40. The Turks used an arrow shower to destroy the cohesion of the enemy. The arrows could not harm the men but could hit the horses and provoke an untimely charge. The Turks liked to envelop an enemy, attacking from all sides. See Smail, *Crusading Warfare,* 79–82.

41. This is William's version, which Smail accepts. For his account see *Crusading Warfare,* 168–70, also 117–20, 128. He cites Fulcher, who said that the French were clustered together like frightened sheep. Robert of Rheims reconstructs the battle in favor of Boemondo, though his source, the anonymous *Gesta francorum et aliorum hierosolimitanorum,* does not have these details. In Robert's version Boemondo goes back to camp with infantry, chases off the Turks, and then returns to the front, now near panic, which he and Robert of Normandy restabilize. The chronicler then has to admit, however, that Turks were still in the camp when Goffredo arrived later. Emilio follows Robert.

42. A maneuver Tasso did not know about, since he read neither the *Gesta francorum* nor Raymond of Aguilers. See *Gesta francorum,* 3.9.20; for Raymond of Aguilers, see Runciman, *First Crusade,* 186n.1.

43. The Saracens were originally an Arab tribe living east of Egypt and Palestine. See Hitti, *History of the Arabs,* 44–45. The Agarenes would be the children of Hagar, or Arabs. For the lists see Robert of Rheims, *Historia iherosolimitana,* 3.13.762–63.

44. Robert of Rheims, *Historia iherosolimitana,* 3.16.764–18.766. According to Runciman they were really Syrian Turks (*First Crusade,* 187).

45. Vivaldi says that Tasso made the action grander by transferring the clash with Palestinian Arabs from a patrol to the Crusader camp; he cites letter 82. See *"La Gerusalemme liberata" studiata,* 7.

46. Vivaldi argues that *Ae.* 10 provided Tasso with most of his details in *GL* 9. See *"La Gerusalemme liberata" studiata,* 151–54, 183–85, 187–91, 204–6.

47. *HR* book 9; also 3.17.137, 4.22.188, 5.6.303–4.

48. So Runciman (*First Crusade,* 331–32), but Smail points also to Fulcher of Chartres (*Crusading Warfare,* 110).

49. Albert of Aix is also well informed about Goffredo's march times in the Balkans. See Runciman, *First Crusade,* 331. Vivaldi argues persuasively that Tasso also read Albert of Aix. See *Prolegomeni,* 25, 45, 108–9, 121–22, 283; *"La Gerusalemme liberata" studiata,* 54.

50. Smail, *Crusading Warfare,* 85. Arabs, Berbers, and Sudanese made up the Egyptian army, but it might also include a Turkish contingent, as Tasso imagines.

51. For a description of *An,* see the editions of the *Liberata* by Solerti (95–96) and Caretti (1:660–61). Solerti assigns this form of the canto to 1566, but Caretti prefers a later date, arguing that it is too close to the published version. I incline rather to Solerti's position, since Tasso took over long passages of his original *abbozzo,* or draft, into the vulgate *Liberata* virtually unchanged. The other two MSS with versions of canto 9 are *Mc* (Venice, Biblioteca Nazionale Marciana, Codice Marciano, cl IX, no. CLXVIII), which has many corrections in Tasso's own hand, and *Am* (Milan, Biblioteca Ambrosiana, formerly MS Q.120 sup. and R.99 sup., now Italian No. 4, 169–285, and No. 6, 126–67). *Am* has the first complete version of the canto. It is in a miscellany that belonged to Tasso's friend, G. V. Pinelli, to whom he read the *Liberata* in 1575. See Solerti, *Vita di Torquato Tasso,* 1:201. Solerti describes *Am* in his edition of the *Liberata,* 96–99. He provides a description of *Mc* in "Un nuovo manoscritto," 29–30.

52. I discuss in chapter 6 Tasso's sense that the Crusaders fought differently. In *An,* however, he does say that Solimano had lost his horse (77 = 85).

53. Tasso already had a Solimano in his *abbozzo,* there imagined as king of Egypt and recent tyrant of Judaea (*Gierusalemme* 38–42). At that time, presumably, the poet thought only of a plausible name and not of the historical character. For a nice contrast between the historical Solimano and the fictional Argante, see Giovanni Getto, *Nel mondo della "Gerusalemme,"* 87–128.

54. Letter 25. See Vivaldi, *"La Gerusalemme liberata" studiata,* 150.

55. Vivaldi says that Tasso used only William of Tyre (*HR* 4.20) for Sveno. See *Prolegomeni,* 93; and also his *"La Gerusalemme liberata" studiata,* 7.

56. *HR* 1.5.18–19, 6.23.274. Tasso also probably alludes to contemporary iconoclastic riots in the north, like those of August 1566 in the Netherlands. See Lynch, *Empire and Absolutism,* 279–80.

57. Tasso's sequence in *GL* 20 thus parallels *Siriade* 12 on Antioch. See Vivaldi, *Prolegomeni,* 153.

58. *HR* 6.17–21.271; for the dew fall, 6.19.266.

59. Vivaldi, *"La Gerusalemme liberata" studiata,* 11–12.

60. By the intercepted message the Crusaders learn that the Egyptians will arrive on the fourth or fifth day, so they must assault the city instantly (*GL* 18.49–54).

61. Vivaldi, *"La Gerusalemme liberata" studiata,* 12. At Jerusalem the refugees surrendered the Tower of David on condition of safe passage to Ascalon.

62. Tasso had the family copy of the *Iliad* in Valla's Latin translation. It included Quintus Calaber and had annotations both by Bernardo and Torquato Tasso. See Solerti, *Vita di Torquato Tasso,* 3:Doc.118.

63. Cited by Pierce, *Poesía épica,* 13. Horace gives the scholiasts' conception of the *Iliad.* See Murrin, *Allegorical Epic,* 195.

64. I here elaborate Aristotle's analysis at *Poetics,* 8.3.1451a, 23.3.1459a.

65. Vivaldi, *"La Gerusalemme liberata" studiata,* 1, citing letter 45. Tasso went on to say that his poem resembles the *Odyssey* for the loves of Rinaldo. Tasso named his poem *Gerusalemme liberata,* and not *Gottifredo,* the title he frequently used earlier, indicating that he had based his poem on an event and not a person. See Pittorru, *Torquato Tasso,* 119.

66. In the *Siriade* Angeli, in contrast, covers the whole First Crusade, starting with Peter the Hermit's return to Europe. See Vivaldi, *Prolegomeni,* 144.

67. The *Iliad* has 15,693 lines; *Gerusalemme liberata,* 15,336; the *Aeneid,* 9,896; *Os Lusiadas,* 1,102 ottave or 8,816 lines; and *Paradise Lost,* 10,565 lines.

68. *Poetics,* 10.1–2.1452a, 13.2.1452b, where he discusses tragedy. At 24.2.1459b he contrasts the plots of the *Iliad* and the *Odyssey,* and he summarizes the plot of the *Odyssey* at 17.5.1455b.

69. Vicente Fabricio commented on Homer in Greek at the Monastery of the Holy Cross in Coimbra, where Camões probably studied. See Ramalho, *Portuguese Essays,* 21–22.

70. Tasso provides short background sketches for characters: how Tancredi fell in love with Clorinda (*GL* 1.46–49), how Erminia became enamored of Tancredi (6.56–61), an exploit of Goffredo in Saxony (7.72), and Solimano's political career (9.3–7). For his structure Tasso could have appealed to Trissino, who also imitated the *Iliad,* but the failure of the *Italia liberata* (1547–48) would not have encouraged him, and he did not own a copy of the poem. There is, however, the similarity of titles.

71. In the revised epic Tasso did find room for a retrospective. See *Gerusalemme conquistata* (Pavia, 1594), 2.92–3.51.

72. For the date of the *abbozzo,* see Solerti, *Vita di Torquato Tasso,* 1:51.

73. The Dog River, north of Beirut, marked the boundary between Egyptian territory and the independent principalities of Lebanon and Syria. See Gray, *History of Jerusalem,* 234.

74. *HR* 7.19.305–6; and Vivaldi, *"La Gerusalemme liberata" studiata,* 55–56, 63.

75. Vivaldi notes that Goffredo gives gifts to the ambassadors in Tasso, as he did at Antioch according to Paolo Emilio. See *"La Gerusalemme liberata" studiata,* 72.

76. *GL* 2.65; and *HR* 4.24.191–92.

77. In *Storici Arabi delle Crociate,* 1:6.

78. Letter to Ercole Tasso, studying in Bologna, No. 3 in Tasso, *Prose,* ed. Mazzali, 741.

79. Just which cantos Tasso meant in his letter to Ercole Tasso is unclear. Some scholars, assuming that he composed in chronological order, would argue for the first six, but the numeration then was different, cantos 3–4 in 1566 being the vulgate 4–5. The MSS Solerti ascribed to this period have the vulgate cantos 4–5, 9, 12. Since Tasso had not yet split up the original *abbozzo* into separate cantos, the total would be five, and he would be correct in saying he had reached the "sixth canto," that is, he had started a new one. The vulgate cantos 4–5 introduce Armida, and canto 12 has Clorinda's death.

80. *Discorsi dell' arte poetica,* 2.368, 380. In the first passage Tasso distinguishes the poet and the historian by the way they treat their material. The poet follows verisimilitude and is not bound to the historical order. Tasso does not argue here for fiction directly, but the principle could be extended to it. Angeli reproved Tasso for his love stories and kept them out of his *Siriade.* See Vivaldi, *Prolegomeni,* 150, 157.

81. Of the four MSS that have the material dated to 1566 (*An, Vo, Am,* and *Mc*), two have later material and may be later. *Am* has the complete version of canto 9, and *Mc* has

the intermediate version of canto 12. These two alone of the four have cantos 6, 8, and 15—presumably the one he had begun in 1566 and the two others to which he refers in the memorial he sends to Ercole Rondinelli (letter 5 in Tasso, *Prose*, ed. Mazzali, 743), before his departure for France in October 1570 (Pittorru, *Torquato Tasso*, 73–74). It is hoped that Luigi Palma will clarify these matters when he finishes the new critical text of the *Liberata*. *Vo* (Vatican City, Biblioteca Apostolica, Vaticano-Ottoboniano 1355) has cantos 4 and 5 and is described by both Solerti (1.96) and Caretti (1.661–63) in their editions of the *Liberata*. Caretti reprints its version of canto 4 and uses it with *An* for canto 5.

82. Díaz Rengifo in his much used primer, the *Arte poética española* (Salamanca, 1592), refers to Ercilla as one opposed to love and enchantment. See Pierce, *Poesía épica*, 33.

83. In part 2 he calls his material dry and unpleasing, desert and sterile (*Araucana*, 2.20.3, p. 324).

84. The *novelle* of Tegualda (*Araucana*, 2.20.26–21.12, pp. 328–44), Glaura (2.27.61–28.41, pp. 451–61), and Dido (3.32.51–33.54, pp. 521–42). Already in part 1 he had the dialogue between Lautaro and Guacolda at the end of canto 13 (*Araucana*, 13.43–57, pp. 222–25). Lagos points out that, beginning with Mataquito, the poet alternates battle scenes with love episodes ("El incumplimiento," 174–75).

85. The poet was on guard duty, exhausted, and fighting off sleep, having been fifteen hours in armor (*Araucana*, 2.20.22, 25, p. 328), and he cites Simon Pereira as a witness (20.77, p. 339). It is not implausible that he was able to speak with Tegualda, since she grew up by the Rio Itata in a zone of Spanish control.

86. Her lover, Crepino, ran for the *palio* (*Araucana*, 20.65, p. 336) for the prize of an emerald encircled by enamelwork (20.63, p. 336).

87. Letter of June/July 1576 to Capponi (in Tasso, *Prose*, ed. Mazzali, 798–99). The count asserted that Saracen women caused such a problem that some of the priests attributed their adversities to this fact.

88. Ercilla had already inserted the vignette of Lauca after the battle (*Araucana*, 3.32.32–42, pp. 518–20)—another fictional episode, at least in its presentation, since it ends in a reversal of the Angelica and Medoro episode in Ariosto. The Spaniards squeeze a herbal juice into her wound, which is more large than dangerous (*Araucana*, 3.32.41, p. 519).

89. Cantos 10 and part of 11 present the Indian victory games (*Araucana*, 1.10.11–11.31, pp. 161–79), Fitón's marvels occupy parts of cantos 23 and 26 (23.46–69, pp. 376–81; 26.40–50, pp. 435–37), and the duel of Tucapel and Rengo overlaps cantos 29 and 30 (29.11–30.25, pp. 471–80, 485–90). I do not include in this count what Ercilla sees at Fitón's, since those visions concern history and geography, nor do I include the Indian war councils, which function like the speeches in classical histories, as ways to analyze a real situation and present motives.

CHAPTER 6: NEGATIVE CRITIQUES

1. Hale, "Gunpowder and the Renaissance," 113–44. See also his "War and Public Opinion in Renaissance Italy" and "War and Public Opinion in the Fifteenth and Six-

teenth Centuries." Hale has had the first two essays reprinted in his *Renaissance War Studies.*

2. The angle bastions were built between 1512 and 1518, during which time Ariosto completed the first edition of the *Furioso.* Hale discusses this use of the bastion in "Early Development of the Bastion," 489–90. Hale has reprinted this essay in his *Renaissance War Studies.*

3. Gardner, *King of Court Poets,* 70–71; Ariosto, *Orlando Furioso,* trans. Reynolds, 1.21; also Cipolla, *Guns, Sails and Empires,* 26. The Ferrarese chroniclers considered the duke the best artillery master in Italy and an innovator (Merendoni, "Le 'genti d'arme'," 119, 120–21).

4. Hale, "Gunpowder and the Renaissance," 131–33, for the use of guns in art.

5. The Este had thirty or forty large cannon, thirty *passavolanti,* and thirty falconets (Merendoni, "Le 'genti d'arme'," 120 and n.58).

6. Pieri, *Il rinascimento,* 491–97; Mallett, *Mercenaries,* 254. This revolution in tactics was made possible by the new light artillery, which the French introduced and others soon imitated (Pieri, *Il rinascimento,* 252–53, 281; Cipolla, *Guns, Sails and Empires,* 28). By 1509 Venice had the best Italian artillery (Pieri, *Il rinascimento,* 379, 456, 596). For the guns of Ravenna, see Merendoni, "Le 'genti d'arme'," 121. Henderson in his forthcoming "Power Unparalleled" says that the Ferrarese exaggerated the importance of Alfonso's guns, which were indeed important but at the same time only one of many causes for the French victory. La Monica remarks that the Spanish cavalry refused to take shelter behind barricades, as the infantry had done, so they eventually had to charge ("Realtà storica," 334).

7. Mallett, *Mercenaries,* 160. Field artillery was developed to defend and attack field works.

8. The actual battle of the ancients and the moderns occurred more than a century later and was fought in France and England. Both sides in that battle had their roots, however, in Italian theory of the mid-sixteenth century, when the Ferrarese critics defended vernacular literature against the new Aristotelianism, which became neoclassicism.

9. Hale, "Gunpowder and the Renaissance," 128–30.

10. Pieri, *Il rinascimento,* 491–97; Mallett, *Mercenaries,* 254; Gardner, *King of Court Poets,* 87, 89. Henderson in "Power Unparalleled" puts the death toll at 12,000: 3,000 French, 9,000 Leaguers.

11. Henderson lists other possible references to Ravenna in the *Furioso.* Of particular importance is *OF* 3.55, part of Melissa's prophecy, in which horses swim in blood up to their bellies. In his careful survey of all Ariosto's references to guns in the earlier versions of the *Furioso,* Henderson concludes that Ariosto at that time considered the gun merely a weapon of war, neither unfair nor unchivalric.

12. Ariosto adds that the human inventor of the gun deserves a place in hell with Judas (*OF* 11.28). Since Ariosto normally assumes a Dantesque hell, this would be at the very bottom.

13. Hale, "Gunpowder and the Renaissance," 115–16, 118–20.

14. Gunpowder is already "inferni pulveris usus" in the second of Milton's elegies on

the Gunpowder Plot ("In eandem," 6) and "Tartareo . . . ab igni" in the third ("In eandem," 11). In his little epic, *In quintum novembris,* the pope likewise calls gunpowder
"Tartarean" (161). Thus Milton held to this theory throughout his life.

15. Hale, "Gunpowder and the Renaissance," 115–16, 119–20.

16. Machiavelli, *Arte della guerra,* 7.498–99. Germans supplied Portugal with cannon,
and their gunners were mostly Flemish and German (Cipolla, *Guns, Sails and Empires,*
31–32). The argument applies more aptly to Portugal.

17. One must wonder, however, if the legend of Satan's revolt did not itself determine
a northern location for the invention of gunpowder. Such a location, nevertheless, made
sense because Germans had been leaders in technological innovation during the later
Middle Ages.

18. See Ugaritic Fragment 3A-4viii in Gibson, *Canaanite Myths and Legends,* 46–67.

19. Revard, *War in Heaven,* 34. Origen is commenting on Luke, where Jesus says he
saw Satan fall like lightning from heaven (Luke 10:18). Revard, *War in Heaven,* 141–42,
notes Genesis A.

20. See also Freeman, *Milton and the Martial Muse,* 104–5. The *OED* cites Sir Baltha-
zar Gerbier, *Counsel and Advice to All Builders* (1663), 50, for the first use of *Vandal* as a
term for wanton destruction: "For who would Rob them but Goths and Vandals." The
verb form, *to vandalize,* came into use in the nineteenth century, and the first attested use
of *vandalism* is 1798.

21. Mallett, *Mercenaries,* 156–58. Olimpia's father is killed at a siege.

22. Pepper and Adams, *Firearms and Fortifications,* 15; Henderson, "Power Unparalleled." Modern tests indicate that the late fifteenth-century harquebus was reasonably
accurate and could penetrate armor plate at a range of more than eighteen meters, using
wet-mixed gunpowder and steel bullets (Vale, *War and Chivalry,* 137–38). The French
introduced mounted harquebusiers to Italy in 1494 (Pieri, *Il rinascimento,* 363 and n. 1).
Italians then quickly developed such companies (Garibi, *Armi da fuoco,* 23–24).

23. Henderson, "Power Unparalleled."

24. It was another northern invention, probably at Nürnberg in 1517. Pieri discusses
the new harquebus (*Il rinascimento,* 530 and note, 543–44, also 234, 252).

25. Angelucci argued that the Milanese had squadrons of *schioppettieri* (soldiers with
portable guns) already in the fifteenth century (*Gli schioppettieri,* 33–34), but more recent
historians doubt that they fought by themselves. Contamine notes that the Franc-archers
included a mixture of archers, crossbowmen, pikemen, and handgunners shortly after
1448 (*War in the Middle Ages,* 133), and Pieri indicates that the mounted harquebusiers of
the 1490s were mixed with mounted bowmen (*Il rinascimento,* 363). At Ferrara the horse
guard of the duke in 1506 included crossbowmen and light cavalrymen as well as *schioppettieri* (Merendoni, "Le 'genti d'arme'," 72).

26. Pieri, *Il rinascimento,* 555–63. Many of the casualties, of course, happened at the
center, where pikemen fought each other. See also the remarks of Beer, *Romanzi di cavalleria,* 128, 144. For Paolo Giovio, see La Monica, "Realtà storica," 337.

27. Pieri, *Il rinascimento,* 550–51, 589–90.

28. Ariosto, *Orlando furioso,* trans. Reynolds, 72.

29. Hale, "Gunpowder and the Renaissance," 120–22. For Cervantes, see Don Quijote's remarks in Cervantes, *Don Quijote de la Mancha,* ed. Riquer, 1.38, pp. 393–94. It is normally assumed that the harquebus was behind Cervantes's complaint (Vale, *War and Chivalry,* 129). Samuel Daniel also simply repeats Ariosto's analysis (*CW* 6.39–40). Nemesis says that guns will mar prowess and manhood. Basest cowards from afar will wound the most courageous. Valor, wrapped up in smoke as in the night, shall perish, without witness, without sight. In the mid-seventeenth century Grimmelshausen is still repeating Orlando's criticism: "Aber diese Ursach macht' mich so gross, dass jetziger Zeit der geringste Rossbub den allertapfersten Helden von der Welt totschiessen kann, wäre aber das Pulver noch nit erfunden gewesen, so hätt ich die Pfeife wohl im Sack müssen stecken lassen" (*Simplicissimus,* 3.12.250).

30. Mahoney argues that Mordred's "grete gunnes" were probably some kind of mechanical engines of war or missile-throwing devices, and she points out that *gunne* or *grete gunne* in the fifteenth century could mean any very large missile-throwing device ("Malory's Great Guns," 291, 302–5). She shows that in the *Mort Artu,* Malory's ultimate source, Mordred uses mangonels against the Tower of London (ibid., 301, 307). She does not, however, address the possibility that Malory, following standard practice, would modernize his source, and she has to admit that the illustrations for the 1498 and 1529 editions of the *Morte Darthur* have cannon for this scene (ibid., 308).

31. Hemming, *Conquest of the Incas,* 111. He gives Titu Cusi's description of the Spaniards as gods. For thunder see Mason, *Ancient Civilizations,* 208.

32. Paolo Giovio described *spingards* as minor missile throwers, three cubits long (about one and a half meters), which shoot projectiles the size of large prunes. He was writing about the battle of Riccardina (1467). See *Gli elogi degli uomini illustri,* ed. Meregazzi, 3.6.341. Actually, the English had used cannon as early as Crécy (Contamine, *War in the Middle Ages,* 198–99).

33. Roberts, *Essays in Swedish History,* 66–67, 69–70. The new field artillery was used in the English civil wars but for old-style tactics, defending an entrenched position against a frontal attack (Parker, *Military Revolution,* 33). Gonsalvo de Córdoba had so employed guns at Cerignola (1504).

34. Freeman, *Milton and the Martial Muse,* 173. Revard indicates that Erasmo di Valvasone had already had Satan invent cannon for the heavenly war. See her discussion of the 1590 *Angeleida* (*War in Heaven,* 188–91).

35. Freeman, *Milton and the Martial Muse,* 57–66.

36. Wolper, "Rhetoric of Gunpowder," 596–97.

37. *PL,* 1.645–49, 2.368–76, 10.389–93; *PR,* 1.47–52, 97–99.

38. Cipolla, *Guns, Sails and Empires,* 35n.1, 41–42, 61–62, 153–54.

39. Simile was one of the easiest ways to bring gunpowder into poetry. Boiardo compares Agricane cutting his way through the enemy to a bombard opening enemy ranks (*OI* 1.11.1). Henderson says that powder magazine explosions were common and cites as an example one at Dubrovnik in 1459 ("Power Unparalleled").

40. Gardner, *King of Court Poets,* 64–65. Ariosto knew of this battle by report. There were also the burning gunpowder wagons at Cerignola, which Gonsalvo de Córdoba said

would light their way to victory (Pieri, *Il rinascimento,* 408–16; Mallett, *Mercenaries,* 250–51, for the battle).

41. They had been common since Castelnuovo (1495). See Pieri, *Il rinascimento,* 361–62. Antonio di Settignano probably collaborated with Antonello da Trani. Antonello later helped Pedro Navarro capture Cephalonia in the same way (Pieri, *Il rinascimento,* 390n). See also Pepper and Adams, *Firearms and Fortifications,* 17. Henderson discusses Ariosto's simile and other incidents of explosive mines ("Power Unparalleled").

42. Parker's figures are telling (*Military Revolution,* 69). Even though Henri IV won Coutras (1587) and Ivry (1590) by cavalry charges, heavy cavalry practically disappeared in the same period (1575–1600). In 1494 the French ratio was two horsemen to three soldiers. By Pavia it had dropped to one in five. Afterward cavalry averaged 10 percent of the army.

43. As I argue in chapter 4, the illusionist realism of Ariosto's presentation of combat made the clash between his poem and contemporary warfare all the more acute.

44. Beer accepts Yates's arguments (*Romanzi di cavalleria,* 112) and cites Folengo, whose hero Baldus reads chivalric romance the way Don Quijote will later (24–25). The *Baldus* of Teofilo Folengo dates from the same year (1516) as the first edition of the *Furioso.*

45. John Hughes for his edition of Spenser in 1715, and Richard Hurd, letter 8 in his *Letters on Chivalry and Romance* (1762). See the excerpts in Mueller, ed., *Spenser's Critics,* 18–20, 67–70.

46. See, for example, Malle, *Au revoir, les enfants,* 24–25. In the game of stilts the hero, Julien Quentin, calls himself Bayard, and the bully Laviron identifies himself with Richard Coeur de Lion, so the boys casually mix figures from the twelfth and sixteenth centuries.

47. Parisians continued to model their parish churches on Notre-Dame. See Bussman, *DuMont Guide to Paris,* 146, 148–50.

48. For French cannon making, Cipolla, *Guns, Sails and Empires,* 66–67. For Parma's remark, Oman, *Sixteenth Century,* 517.

49. Cipolla, *Guns, Sails and Empires,* 28–29, 74–75; McNeill, *Pursuit of Power,* 141. The ring bayonet made the pike unnecessary.

50. Trissino had, of course, anticipated Tasso, but his *Italia liberata dei Goti* had no popular impact.

51. Hippolyte Taine, *History of English Literature,* trans. H. Van Laun (New York, 1872), 1:449–50, as quoted by Freeman, *Milton and the Martial Muse,* 13.

52. Freeman, *Milton and the Martial Muse,* 11–12, 70–71, 78, 82–83, 88, 104–5, 212; Fallon, *Captain or Colonel,* 134–35.

53. Also forecast in the letter to Raleigh. West argues effectively that Spenser would not have been a good poet for a military epic. The poet shows no sense of tactics in the Maleger episode ("Spenser's Art of War," 662–63), and the sequence that concerns the Soldan and his chariot reveals an academic use of Vegetius that was impractical and inconsistent (ibid., 673, 675–79). A reader of *The Faerie Queene* could never have learned anything about tactics. West connects Spenser's impractical tactics to Elizabethan court culture (ibid., 696).

CHAPTER 7: POSITIVE EVALUATIONS

1. Though Rufo, of course, did raise these questions, as discussed in chapter 6.

2. To the Reader, *Austriada,* 2:2.

3. Camões, *Lusiadas,* comm. Faria e Sousa, 1.352. He points to *Metamorphoses* 14 for the periphrastic description of the cannon ball. For citations of *Os Lusiadas,* I use Pierce's edition.

4. Longinus, *De sublimitate,* 11–12.

5. He uses the comparison again for the battle of the Maltese flagship (*Austriada,* 23.83, p. 129A). Corte Real twice compares cannon to thunder and mentions the smoky cloud, but he does not develop a comparison to storms. See *FV* 13.267–68, 279–92, p. 176v; 14.5–12, p. 187r.

6. Giovanni Tortelli expresses the modernist view in his *De orthographia dictionum e Graecis tractarum* (ca. 1450), a dictionary of Greek words appearing in Latin. For *horologium* he assembles a list of modern inventions, among them the bombard, which he compares to lightning by its sound, light, and smell. See Keller, "Renaissance Humanist," 348–50; also Wolper, "Rhetoric of Gunpowder," 597, for the later views. Samuel Daniel, like Milton, attacks the comparison. A cannon mocks sky thunder, but he admits it kills more (*Civile Wars,* 6.26–27). As a young man, Milton discussed thunder as a possible topic in poetry (*Ad patrem,* 49). Satan makes the modernist point (*PL* 6.486–91), saying that the loyal angels will fear that the rebels have stolen God's thunderbolt. See also *PL* 6.584–90. It is, of course, God's thunder that wins the war and receives constant mention (*PL* 1.92–93, 171–77, 257–58; 2.64–68, 165–166; 3.392–96; 6.632, 763–64, 835–38, 854, 858; also *PR* 1.89–90). In places the poet equates angels with thunderbolts (*PL* 1.326–29 and especially 844–52). Milton does not, however, equate the heavenly war with a storm, as do many other poets. See Revard, *War in Heaven,* 178–80.

7. Caetani, *Lettere,* 52–53. Veniero agrees that the galleass fire forced the enemy fleet to part and to attack immediately. See Veniero, "Relation of 22 December 1572." See also Medina della Motta del Friuli, *Dialogo,* A3v–4r. Filippo Bragadin, the proveditor-general "di Golfo," said that galleass firepower made the allied victory clear from the start (Mallett and Hale, *Military Organization,* 238–39). A galleass carried eight heavy guns at stem and stern, plus seven or more antipersonnel guns on each side (Parker, *Military Revolution,* 87 and pl. 22). A galleass thus carried almost twice as much artillery as a "light" or regular galley (Tenenti, *Piracy,* 132).

8. Parker, *Military Revolution,* 87. Corte Real notes that the galleass fire forced the Turks to withdraw, but he makes no tactical inferences (*FV* 13.125–40, p. 173v).

9. Veniero, "Relation of 22 December 1572," 312. By 1550 a Venetian light galley carried more than sixty one-pound bronze cannon, as well as two sixteen-pounders and fifteen smaller guns, at prow and poop (Parker, *Military Revolution,* 86). Parker's notes contain a bibliography. Wolper notes that some writers defended the gun with the argument that it helped Christians defeat the Turks ("Rhetoric of Gunpowder," 596).

10. Parker, *Military Revolution,* 128.

11. This factor too could be explained technologically. Paruta argued that the soldiers

wore better armor, were better protected by the *paveses* (wooden shutters that they could open to shoot and close to protect themselves against enemy missiles), and used harquebuses that killed more men than Turkish bows (Mallett and Hale, *Military Organization*, 238).

12. Corte Real, stressing the noise of the initial barrage, likewise points to the end of the world (*FV* 13.291–92, p. 176v).

13. The *San Nicola* of Naples blows away the oars on one side of an enemy galley, leaving it crippled and useless (*FV* 13.321–27, p. 177v); the *Imperial* of Sicily sinks a Turkish galley with a single shot (14.93–112, p. 189r); and Turkish cannon sink the frigate of Ottavio Gonzaga (14.117–32, p. 189v). Corte Real gives an example of antipersonnel usage in the slow-motion death of one soldier hit by an esmeril, or small cannon (*FV* 13.603–28, pp. 183r–v).

14. Captain Rutîa, Virgilio Orsino, Martel and Riniero on the *Florentia*, Angelo Bifôlo, Juan Miranda, and Juan de Cordova (*FV* 13.689–91, p. 185r; 14.70–72, p. 188v; 453–56, p. 196v; 469–72, p. 196v; 539–40, p. 198r; 563–64, p. 198v).

15. Like Camões, Corte Real uses planetary deities and stresses Venus (*FV* 13.533–34, p. 182r), and he has the marine gods greet the victorious fleet on its way home (15.185–312, pp. 209v–12v).

16. Corte Real twice refers briefly to Actium (*FV* 12.201–4, p. 157r; 15.229–36, p. 210v).

17. For the similar location of both battles, see *Austriadis libri duo*, 2.20r; *Austriada*, 22.92–95, pp. 121B–22A; *Araucana*, 2.23.77, p. 383.

18. Vecelli, *Titiani Vecelli equitis . . . ad Sereniss. Venetiarum principem Aloysium Mocenicum oratio*, 2v–3r.

19. Thucydides, however, ascribes more sophisticated tactics to Phormio and the Athenian fleet stationed at Naupactus (Lepanto). See *Historiae*, 2.83–92.

20. For Ariosto, see the discussion in chapter 6. For Monluc, see his *Commentaires*, 34–35. Even the experts on firearms thought they were demonic. See Hale, "Gunpowder and the Renaissance," 119, and especially 124–25, where he discusses Monluc and others who held a split position.

21. Cipolla, in fact, dismisses Mediterranean warfare as an anachronism. See *Guns, Sails and Empires*, 100–101.

22. Bibar, *Crónica*, 135.205–6. Ercilla indicates that he came the night before (*Araucana*, 3.31.33–34, p. 506), and Martin Ruiz de Gamboa in his second testimonial (1569) agrees with him (Ruiz de Gamboa, "Document 13"). According to Gamboa the company consisted of select troops (ibid., 245). Marmolejo and Lovera exaggerate the numbers, giving sixty and eighty respectively (Marmolejo, *Historia de Chile*, 28.128–31; and Lovera, *Crónica del reino de Chile*, 2.11.23.234–35). The Jesuit Bartolomé de Escobar gave Lovera's chronicle its final form. Miguel de Velasco commanded the troops, and Ercilla gave testimony for him, though he does not name him in the *Araucana* account. See *Araucana*, ed. Medina, 2: Doc. xxvii, 39. Velasco himself gave two reports of the battle, in his *Información* of 29 July 1559 (in *Colección . . . Chile*, 10:347–48) and at Lima in 1560 (ibid., 10:391). They had to follow a mountain route because the Araucanians had cut communi-

cations between Cañete and Imperial. See Reinoso's testimony for Velasco (*Colección . . . Chile,* 10: 359–60).

23. Bibar, *Crónica,* 135.205–6; Marmolejo, *Historia de Chile,* 4.28.128–30; Lovera, *Crónica del reino de Chile,* 6.2.11.234; Figueroa, *Hechos,* 5.5.3.64–65.

24. Bibar, *Crónica,* 135.205–6.

25. Marmolejo, *Historia de Chile,* 28.128–30. The Indian tactics are a variant on an earlier attack made on the same fort, then named Tucapel, a surprise assault timed for the siesta. Ercilla describes this earlier fight at *Araucana,* 1.2.67–85, pp. 33–37.

26. In Lovera's chronicle the *yanacona* Baltazar exhorts his compatriots to rebel, meanwhile telling Reinoso everything. The historian does not say that Reinoso set the tactics (*Crónica del reino de Chile,* 2.11.234). Figueroa, as usual, agrees but adds that Baltazar had asked to draw the Indians into an attack. Reinoso had doubted his fidelity, but Baltazar persisted in his request and received permission and a promise of liberty and citizenship. He was excellent in fraud, the chronicler noted (Figueroa, *Hechos,* 5.3.64).

27. He is addressing the Indian senate (*Araucana,* 3.30.40, p. 493) and uses information that is in part erroneous. He assumes that raw troops make up the garrison at Cañete when, in fact, Mendoza left there his elite, seasoned soldiers (*Araucana,* 3.30.30, 41, pp. 491, 493). He also assumes that Mendoza, busy with new conquests, will not aid the garrison. Instead the Spanish general rushes thirty cavalrymen to aid Cañete as soon as he learns that the Indians have broken the truce (*Araucana,* 3.30.32–33, p. 492).

28. With the same rationale (*Araucana,* 3.31.23, p. 504) that the Spaniards sleep incautiously during siesta.

29. See especially the remark (*Araucana,* 3.31.39, p. 507) as Andresillo and Pran, the deceiver and the deceived, enter the fort. Held argues that Cañete is punishment for Caupolicán's use of treachery (*Studien,* 91–92). She also points out that deception marks Araucanian activity earlier. The Indians used the initial peace negotiations to spy out the enemy camp. Colocolo sent Millalauco to talk peace, while the Araucanians prepared for war (ibid., 84–87).

30. Najera, *Desengaño y reparo,* 1.3.3.44, 1.4.2.56.

31. Durand argues persuasively that Ercilla assumes the same honor code for Indians as for Spaniards ("El chapetón," 128–31). Lagos claims that the *Araucana* involves a historical defense of Indian heroism against the other conquest narratives for Chile, especially Valdivia's letters ("El incumplimiento," 161).

32. Here I differ from Lagos, who considers all the Spanish victories unfair and unheroic, beginning with Villagrá's surprise attack on Lautaro ("El incumplimiento," 173–76). She does not distinguish between a surprise attack and fraud. Lautaro had a regular fortified camp, which Villagrá attacked at a changing of the guard. He did not deceive his enemy. Lagos assumes a military code, and such an assumption would require explanation and documentation to be persuasive. She seems to assume that the code for duels and that for war are the same. By her own standards the Indians, whom she calls heroic, would begin the war unheroically, since they try to enter Fort Tucapel disguised as Indians in the Spanish service. By her analysis Ercilla changed his mind during the writing of the

poem. Villagrá's attack on Lautaro's camp would signal this change. One could as well say that the poet's refusal to condemn that attack represented a position he changed later, when he condemned the *Indian* attack on Cañete.

33. Lovera, *Crónica del reino de Chile,* 2.1.192.

34. See chapters 9 and 11. Marmolejo also stresses the impact of cannon on the Indian center at Millarapue (30 November 1557) and says the Indians had faced only small artillery before. They were astonished when a cannonball smashed a great number of upright pikes. Harquebus fire then made a great slaughter (*Historia de Chile,* 26.117–20). Harquebusiers also helped determine the outcome of the conflict by the Bío-Bío (8 September 1557). Lovera attributes the victory to a combination of horse, artillery, and harquebus (*Crónica del reino de Chile,* 2.3.207–8), and both he and Bibar emphasize the kills made by the harquebusiers who shot at the Indians who took refuge in the swamp (Bibar, *Crónica,* 132.201).

35. Faria e Sousa compares the assegai (*azagaya*) to the European dart and says the Arabic word denotes "easily thrown" (Camões, *Lusíadas,* comm. Faria e Sousa, 1.86, p. 348). The shields were of skin (Brasil, *Comentários,* 1:404 [*Lusíadas,* 1.87]).

36. Characteristic of the Portuguese is the fact that no one ordered the charge. Someone leaps onto land, but no one can say who is first (*Lusíadas,* 1.87). On the infantry rush, see Boxer, *Portuguese Seaborne Empire,* 117, 299–300.

37. Faria e Sousa explains that an *almadia* is made from a single tree trunk but is smaller than a *pangayo* (Camões, *Lusíadas,* comm. Faria e Sousa, 1.92, p. 357). Camões describes them (*Lusíadas,* 1.45–46), and Faria e Sousa remarks that their proportions make the boats fast, like the European *saetias* or brigantines. Africans call them *almadias, pangayos,* and *zambucos.*

38. Hemming, *Conquest of the Incas,* 37–43.

39. Brasil glosses the technical terms in this passage (*Comentários,* [*Lusíadas,* 1.67]). *Malhas finas* are chain mail; *laminas,* laminated arms and those made of steel plate. *Pelouros* are stone or metal balls. *Pantazanas* resemble long wooden lances, but each has at its head a double iron knife or a cutting half-moon. *Chuças* are poles ending in sharpened steel, and *bombas de fogo* are metal cannonballs. Finally, *panelas sulfúreas* are pots of sulfur, used to protect a ship. See also ibid., 1:339–40.

40. Some of this Camões read in his sources and simply assumes. Castanheda (*First Booke,* 5.14v) and Barros (Barros and Couto, *Da Asia,* 1.4.4.296) describe the houses.

41. Castanheda, *First Booke,* 7.18v–19r; Barros and Couto, *Da Asia,* 1.4.4.302, for the first incident. Castanheda's source was *Journal of the First Voyage,* 29–30.

42. *Journal of the First Voyage,* 30–31; Castanheda, *First Booke,* 7.19r–v; Barros and Couto, *Da Asia,* 1.4.4.302–4.

43. They carry the weapons Camões assigns them, except that he substitutes poisoned arrows for slingshots.

44. Castanheda, *First Booke,* 7.18v. Faria e Sousa claims that the poet went to Mozambique to paint the inhabitants to life (Camões, *Lusíadas,* comm. Faria e Sousa, 1.47, p. 299). Camões probably wintered there on his way home, according to Pierce (Camões,

Lusiadas, ed. Pierce, xi), citing Camões's first biographer, Pecho de Mariz (in the 1613 edition), and Couto.

45. *Journal of the First Voyage,* 28–29; Castanheda, *First Booke,* 6.16v–17r, 18v; Barros and Couto, *Da Asia,* 1.4.4.302.

46. Da Gama's fleet had up to 170 men, of whom 55 made it back to Portugal. See Diffie and Winius, *Foundations,* 178. Opposed to them were about 2,000 men (Camões, *Lusiadas,* comm. Faria e Sousa, 1.86, p. 348). For a single ship, Hess remarks that Columbus's *Santa Maria* had 40 sailors, while a Venetian galley had 144 rowers plus 30–40 crew and marines (*Forgotten Frontier,* 15–16).

47. The natives fled yet again when the Portuguese returned once more to town and shot a few bombards (Castanheda, *First Booke,* 7.19v). Machiavelli (*Arte,* 4.432) relates how the noise of the Turkish cannon similarly defeated the Persian cavalry (1514) and the Mamluks (1516–17).

48. After da Gama, Portuguese commanders found that showing the gun had mixed results. It impressed the Japanese but outraged the Chinese. See Bitterli, *Cultures in Conflict,* 135, 137, 139. See also Fernão Peres in Cipolla, *Guns, Sails and Empires,* 107–8.

49. Cipolla, *Guns, Sails and Empires,* 141–43. Goa was captured twice (1509, 1510).

50. Quoted in Parker, *Military Revolution,* 93–94.

51. The Turks for their part had 15,000 men on their ships. Cipolla discusses their galleys in the Indian Ocean (*Guns, Sails and Empires,* 101–3). Almeida in effect destroyed the competition, the Arab fleet that plied between Egypt and India (Bitterli, *Cultures in Conflict,* 62).

52. Cipolla, *Guns, Sails and Empires,* 122n, citing C. R. Boxer, *The Great Ship from Amaçon* (Lisbon: Centro de Estudos Históricos Ultramarinos, 1959), 31.

53. Brasil, *Comentários,* 1:367.

54. Ibid., 1:347, 350.

55. *Lusiadas,* 1.101–5; 2.1, 17. The Portuguese stayed a month at Mozambique, so the sheik had time to alert the other towns up the coast (Brasil, *Comentários,* 1:374, 391, 421, also 431, 447). Camões expresses this action mythologically through Bacchus, who intervenes at Mombasa as well as at Mozambique. Thus the king at Mombasa *already* knows who the Portuguese are when they arrive (*Lusiadas,* 1.104).

56. *Lusiadas,* 1.53, 57; Brasil, *Comentários,* 1:290–91.

57. The rejected stanzas are printed in *Lusiadas,* trans. Burton, 2:422–23. They come after 1.80.

58. Camões, *Lusiadas,* comm. Faria e Sousa, 1.86, p. 348, and 1.43, p. 294.

59. Barros and Couto, *Da Asia,* 1.4.4.303. The charge has been reiterated by Nambiar, whom Toussaint mentions (*History of the Indian Ocean,* 112).

60. The charge would occur naturally to Bacchus. Early in his career sailors tried to abduct him from Chios for the slave market, but the god turned his enemies to dolphins. Ovid has the story (*Metamorphoses,* 3.577–691). Faria e Sousa notes Camões's use of a passage from *Metamorphoses,* 5 (Camões, *Lusiadas,* comm. Faria e Sousa, 1.42, p. 292).

61. See, for example, the article on *pirata* in António de Morais Silva (or Moraes e Silva), *Grande dicionário da lingua Portuguesa*, 10th edition.

62. Phillips, *Six Galleons*, 182.

63. Pérotin-Duman, "Pirate and the Emperor," 203, 215.

64. Gentleman Brown, for example, in *Lord Jim*, 38.303–4.

65. There was then and still is no authoritative definition of piracy in international law (Pérotin-Duman, "Pirate and the Emperor," 198, 202; Andrews, *Trade, Plunder and Settlement*, 27).

66. See Parry, *Spanish Seaborne Empire*, 119, 122, 133–35, 253–58.

67. They could not burn the ship because its crew made a desperate resistance (Correa, "Second Voyage," 6.313–15, in Correa, *Three Voyages*).

68. Hawkins, *Observations*, 64.318–19; Pérotin-Duman, "Pirate and the Emperor, 198–99. The people of Malabar were not the Arabs but the indigenous traders, or Mappila, who relentlessly attacked Portuguese shipping during the sixteenth century (ibid., 214). The Portuguese called them corsairs (Curtin, *Cross-Cultural Trade*, 147). They would attack becalmed merchant ships in wolf packs (Parker, *Military Revolution*, 105–6).

69. Chaudhuri, *Trade and Civilization*, 65. Barros and the other historians of the incident involving da Gama and the pilgrim ship presuppose this and not the other situation. They assume that the ship belonged to the Mamluks, with whom there was as yet no state of war, and not to the merchants of Calicut, against whom war had been declared (Correa, "Second Voyage," 6.315–18, n. 1, in Correa, *Three Voyages*).

70. Similarly, the Spaniards called Drake a pirate, but Queen Elizabeth knighted him.

71. Pérotin-Duman, "Pirate and the Emperor," 212. She cites Fernand Braudel, *The Mediterranean and the Mediterranean World in the Age of Philip II*, trans. Siân Reynolds, 2 vols. (New York: Harper Torchbooks, 1975), 2:865–91. She provides her own variant on this thesis and cites for further support C. R. Villar, *Piracy Today: Robbery and Violence at Sea since 1980* (London: Conway Maritime, 1985), 196–97.

72. Tenenti, *Piracy*, 58–59, 61–63.

73. Bitterli, *Cultures in Conflict*, 61–62. In his letter to the rulers of Castile, in which he communicates news of da Gama's voyage, King Manuel is quite explicit about this. The Portuguese will divert the trade now controlled by Muslims in the Indian Ocean (*Documentos sobre os Portugueses*, 1:30–31).

74. Parker lists them all (*Military Revolution*, 105).

75. Chaudhuri, *Trade and Civilization*, 66. The Portuguese developed their system initially for West Africa (Curtin, *Cross-Cultural Trade*, 139).

76. Curtin, *Cross-Cultural Trade*, 137–38.

77. Da Gama sailed on 8 July 1497 (Diffie and Winius, *Foundations*, 176). He sent a ship to explore the islands of Mozambique on 1 March 1498 (Castanheda, *First Booke*, 5.13v).

78. Envy also drove Milton's Satan. See *PL* 5.659–65; and Revard, *War in Heaven*, 67–75, 203–9.

79. The Catual also finds this out by black arts (*Lusiadas*, 7.55–56).

80. Castanheda, *First Booke,* A ii recto–verso. Unlike Camões he argues that the enemy had more guns.

81. The other was the printing press. See Wolper, "Rhetoric of Gunpowder," 590–92; Keller, "Renaissance Humanist," 349–50. Keller reprints Tortelli, who also mentions the lateen sail.

82. On this point Parker (*Military Revolution,* 108 and n.74) cites Simon Digby in *Cambridge Economic History of India,* ed. T. Raychauduri and I. Habib (Cambridge: Cambridge University Press, 1982), 1:150–51.

83. Guns came to the north in the 1440s and to the south in the 1470s (Parker, *Military Revolution,* 128).

84. Ibid., 105, 108. Parker provides a bibliography at 108n.75.

85. Ibid., 131n.51.

86. Parker, "Europe and the Wider World," 175n.33. He refers readers to R. J. de Lima Felner, ed., *Subsídios para a história da India Portuguesa* (Lisbon, 1868), pt. 3, 12. Parker, *Military Revolution,* 128.

87. Cipolla (*Guns, Sails and Empires,* 78–81) contrasts the sailing ship and the galley, which the Turks used.

88. *Journal of the First Voyage,* 22–23, 28; Castanheda, *First Booke,* 5.13v, 5.14v, 7.17v–18r; Barros and Couto, *Da Asia,* 1.4.4.301.

89. In the *Journal of the First Voyage* (25) it is da Gama who asks the sheik initially for pilots. Camões's two sources agree: Castanheda, *First Booke,* 5.14r; Barros and Couto, *Da Asia,* 1.4.3.293.

90. Da Gama explains this to the Moors in the boats initially (Barros and Couto, *Da Asia,* 1.4.3.293–94).

91. *Journal of the First Voyage,* 25; Castanheda, *First Booke,* 6.15r. The Portuguese later traded glass beads for food (*Journal of the First Voyage,* 28).

92. Castanheda (*First Booke,* 6.15v) gives the following description of the sheik: a linen robe, over it another of Mecca velvet, a cap of varicolored silk trimmed with gold, and silk shoes. Camões also does not mention that two Portuguese deserted da Gama to serve Indian rulers at higher wages (Parker, *Military Revolution,* 129). Indians normally bought their experts in this fashion, often from Safavid Iran.

93. Brasil suggests a lion to sheep when he discusses Portuguese armament (*Comentários,* 1: 341 [*Lusiadas,* 1.64–66]).

94. One exception to this technique is the booty the Portuguese take from the boats. It becomes a "rich prize," as befits an epic (*Lusiadas,* 1.93).

95. Rufo refers to Hesiod and Ariosto and also mentions the arms Vulcan forged for Troyano. Earlier he argues that older poets would not have needed fiction, if they had narrated Lepanto (*Austriada,* 21.1–4, p. 111B). By periphrasis he names both epic and lyric poets.

96. Camões argues (*Lusiadas,* 5.86–89) that da Gama saw more than Aeneas or Odysseus ever did. The truth of his topic surpasses all the wonders of Homer and Virgil. Pacheco surpasses the great generals of Greece and Rome (*Lusiadas,* 10.19–21).

97. Rufo admits that he lacks the ability of the classical poets (*Austriada*, 23.1–3, p. 125A).

98. Take *Kim,* for example.

99. Cipolla, *Guns, Sails and Empires,* 134 and notes. He cites Charles Boxer, *Four Centuries of Portuguese Expansion, 1415–1825* (Johannesburg: Witwatersrand University Press, 1961), 20. Cipolla thinks the figure should be much higher. Bitterli, in fact, does give slightly higher numbers: between 12,000 and 14,000 Portuguese from East Africa to China. Half were sailors and soldiers, and half were administrators, traders, and missionaries (*Cultures in Conflict,* 63).

100. Pocock (*Conquest of Chile,* 218) gives Valdivia only forty. In her suggestive essay Lagos argues that technological superiority made the fighting in Chile unheroic. She never considers the odds, and when she gives numbers, she errs. She claims that the Araucanians had *fewer* men than the Spaniards when they assaulted Penco ("El incumplimiento," 175).

CHAPTER 8: THE HEROIC FEW

1. I cite *La Araucana* from the Medina edition. For Ercilla and Villagrá I give canto and stanza, and also page number, following Spanish practice. Ercilla describes the ambush at 2.28.53–71, pp. 464–67. I have added clarifying material from the other early accounts. The first is Bibar's *Crónica;* the original manuscript, which stops at 1558, is now in the Newberry Library and has been edited by Irving A. Leonard. Second is Marmolejo, *Historia de Chile,* 27.124–26. The third is Lovera, *Crónica del reino de Chile,* 2.7.220–24; the Jesuit Bartolomé de Escobar gave this chronicle its final form. Figueroa, *Hechos,* 2.56, has another detail. The rest of his account is drawn from previous sources. Besides the chroniclers there are the testimonials: various participants in the battle gave evidence of their military service with corroborating testimony by others, including the poet. Those concerning Purén were given by Nuño Hernández Salomón (1569; *Colección . . . Chile,* 23: Doc. 14.211–64), Tristán de Silva Campofrío (1571; ibid., 23: Doc. 15.264–83), Martín Ruiz de Gamboa (second testimonial, 1569; ibid., 19: Doc. 13.243–99). In his edition of *La Araucana,* Medina includes biographies of the two commanders, Velasco and Reinoso, and of Martín Ruiz de Gamboa (5:274–79, 287–96, 316–21). He also prints Ercilla's testimony for Velasco and Campofrío (2:37–40, 101–4). Citations of Medina's edition of the *Araucana* that do not refer to Ercilla's text are noted as Ercilla, *Araucana,* ed. Medina, with volume and page number. Medina also discusses the ambush in his *Vida de Ercilla,* 56–58. Ercilla gives no date for this battle, and Lovera has the impossible date of 20 March, which Medina in the *Vida* corrects to 20 January, but it must have occurred before then, since that is the date of Mendoza's departure from Cañete for Imperial. See the chronological index to Bibar, *Crónica,* p. 226. In their herd of 2,000 animals the Spaniards had pigs as well as cattle, as Medina notes in the *Vida* and as Rodrigo Bravo testifies (*Colección . . . Chile,* 23:270). Ercilla does not mention Purén Fort in his account. The Spaniards had evacuated it after Valdivia's death, and the Indians promptly burned it.

2. Martín Ruiz de Gamboa, who was part of his party, gives eight as a total (*Colección . . . Chile,* 19:245).

3. Others were of the opinion that the Spaniards saved most, if not all, the baggage and herds: Bibar, Lorenzo Vaca de Silva (*Colección* . . . *Chile,* 23:273), and Cristóbal Mosquera de Figueroa (Ercilla, *Araucana,* ed. Medina, 4:77).

4. The chroniclers assign Miguel de Velasco, who brought the supplies, thirty or sixty men. Captain Alonso de Reinoso, who led the escort, probably had eighty, the opinion of the majority of the chroniclers and witnesses. Bibar cites native informants for his estimate of 6,000. Lovera exaggerates it at 15,000.

5. Martín Ruiz de Gamboa was one of the eight or eleven who first ascended the ridge. Probably in the second group were Tristán de Silva Campofrío and Nuño Hernández Salomón, for both of whom Ercilla gave testimony. Reinoso ordered the second group up and later gave General Mendoza a list of twenty who reached the heights. Mendoza summarized this report in his testimony for Campofrío. The number could include all those on the heights or only the second group; Medina assumes the latter.

6. Ercilla published part 2 of *La Araucana,* which covers the first four battles, in 1578; in 1589 he published part 3, which describes Cañete.

7. I have used the edition of González Obregón. Volume 1 gives the text of the poem, cited as *NM,* while volume 2 includes four appendices of historical documents, which I cite as *NM* 2: App., with document number and page number. I cite the poem by line number and page number. Here the pages are 61r–63v, 147r–63v.

8. For a modern retelling of the incident, see Belloc, *Eye-Witness,* 76–82.

9. In the epic the Basques became Arabs.

10. *Araucana,* 1.3.17, p. 43. The report sent to Peru by allied Indians who were eyewitnesses gave the Araucanians 13,000. Garcilaso de la Vega, el Inca, who transmits this report, estimates Valdivia's Spanish force at 150 horsemen (*Royal Commentaries,* 1.7.21.451–53, 23.456).

11. Indian numbers at Tucapel grow from chronicler to chronicler. Bibar (*Crónica,* 115.170) and Marmolejo (*Historia de Chile,* 14.61–62) give 50,000; Lovera, 150,000. Lovera agrees with Ercilla on the Spanish numbers (*Crónica del reino de Chile,* 1.3.42.152, 43.154). Bibar gives Valdivia 35 (*Crónica,* 115.170); Espinosa (*Compendium,* 6.19.2001) thought he had 150. Indian oral tradition gave Valdivia 200 and themselves 6,000. See Tureupillan's relation in Bascuñan, *Cautiverio feliz,* 3.19.254. For the 14, Lovera agrees that Caupolicán sent 4,000 to join the Indians already fighting. In his usual fashion he later multiplies this number to 30,000 (*Crónica del reino de Chile,* 1.3.45.161–62). Lovera gives 162 Spanish cavalry for Mareguano (ibid., 1.3.47.166) but says that the Indian army covered hills and valleys for two leagues (ibid., 1.3.48.167–68). Reinoso, the *maese de campo* at the battle, gives the odds at 150 versus 100,000 (Ercilla, *Araucana,* ed. Medina, 5:277). Bibar has 160 (*Crónica,* 119.176). Pocock (*Conquest of Chile,* 227) gives 154 for the Spaniards. In the Ácoma massacre, Horgan (*Great River* 1:201) gives the Indians more than 1,000. He presumably includes women and children in his estimate, since Weber has only 580 men and 800 women and children in Ácoma. Weber gives the Spaniards 72 (*Spanish Frontier,* 86).

12. Pocock, *Conquest of Chile,* 91–92, 114–15; Lovera, *Crónica del reino de Chile,* 1.2.31.111–12; Bolton, *Coronado,* 208.

13. Herodotus, *Historiae,* 7.210–12; How and Wells, *Commentary,* note to 7.211. How

and Wells also suggest that the larger shields of the Greeks made a difference, citing 9.62 and Diodorus Siculus, 11.7.

14. Lovera, *Crónica del reino de Chile*, 1.3.55.188–89. Bibar gives 1,200 Indians versus 70 Spaniards at Mataquito (*Crónica*, 129.196–97). For Coronado, Horgan (*Great River*, 1:127–28) gives 340 Spaniards and nearly 1,000 Mexicans, while Bolton, citing Castañeda, prefers 300 and 800 respectively (*Coronado*, 52). The chroniclers as well as the poets followed the tradition of Cortesian historiography, which ignored Indian allies but stressed the numbers of the Indian enemies (Adorno, "Warrior and the War Community," 239). Held indicates that Ercilla generally followed this tradition (*Studien*, 165).

15. Najera, *Desengaño y reparo*, 4.1.1.200–201, 5.3.4.277–80. Adorno indicates that by this time Indian chroniclers in Mexico were also beginning to correct previous statistics. Fernando de Alva Ixtlilxochitl argued that Cortés's conquest was a war not of the few versus the many but of many versus many, once the allied Indians were included in the count. Ixtlilxochitl's ancestors had, in fact, helped Cortés (Adorno, "Warrior and the War Community," 238).

16. Bolton, *Coronado*, 5.

17. Parry, *Spanish Seaborne Empire*, 94–97.

18. Forbes, *Apache, Navaho, and Spaniard*, 58–59.

19. Beeler, *Warfare in Feudal Europe*, 72, 124.

20. Heavy snow ended the action at Arenal (Bolton, *Coronado*, 212; Horgan, *Great River*, 1:126), and snow provided the Indians at Moho with water for several weeks (Bolton, *Coronado*, 222).

21. For his length of service, see *NM* 2: App. 1, Doc. 2, p. 8. Villagrá mentions hunger and thirst at *NM* 12.85–97, p. 61r; 14.90–99, p. 73r–v; 19.200–204, 220–44, pp. 105v–6v. He speaks of snow at *NM* 19.140–46, p. 105r; 24.208–16, p. 129v.

22. Parry, *Spanish Seaborne Empire*, 325.

23. Purén had ravines and cliffs. For forests see *Araucana*, 2.23.27–32, pp. 373–74, or 26.40–41, p. 435, or the background of the novella of Glaura, 28.21, 23, 30, 33, pp. 457–60. The English traveler W. B. Stevenson wrote of the green woods of Tucapel and described a picnic in the woods: "The spot at which we arrived was enchanting. The branches of a large carib tree extended themselves above our heads, while the beautifully green sward was spread under our feet. A small stream of water worked its way among the pebbles on one side, and in the distance on the other the Pacific Ocean, silvered with the rays of the newly risen sun, heightened in brilliancy by the intervening deep green of the woods, presented itself to our view" (*Twenty Years' Residence*, 1:21; also 1:10–11). In 1882 the Chilean army found an impenetrable wood between the Rio Toltén and Lake Villarrica. Using axes, they had to cut their way through the dense trees, entangled with liana and *colihue*. See Calvo, *Secretos*, 29.

24. Najera, *Desengaño y reparo*, 1.3.4.50, 2.1.86–88, 3.1.3.132–33.

25. Bascuñan, *Cautiverio feliz*, 1.8–9.21. For cold see ibid., 2.3.98, 2.4.100, 2.20.161, 3.1.200. For other references to rainstorms, see ibid., 1.5.19–20, 1.7.26, 1.12.48–49, 1.16.71, 2.13.135, 2.15.143, 2.18.153, 2.21.163, 3.2.204, 3.17.247. For a modern version there is Pablo Neruda's "Primer Viaje" in *Memorial de Isla Negra*. He grew up there.

26. Friar Alonso de Benavides, "Memorial," in *NM* 2: App. 2, p. 12.

27. Coronado, letter to Charles V, cited by Horgan, *Great River,* 1:143.

28. Horgan, *Great River,* 1:229. The exception would be the Franciscans, who stressed the potential mineral wealth of New Mexico to attract Spanish attention. Friar Marcos de Niza and his stories of Cibola are only the most prominent example. There is also Benavides (*NM* 2: App. 2, pp. 15, 51).

29. Najera, *Desengaño y reparo,* 2.1.89–90.

30. The Conchos and Tobosos, who lived nearby, also possessed only bows and arrows. See Friar Juan Gonzalez de Mendoza, "Historia de las cosas mas notables, ritos y costumbres del Gran Reyno de la China," in *NM* 2: App. 3, Doc. 7, pp. 105–6. The Navajos at that time also stuck to the bow and arrow, according to Benavides (ibid., App. 2, p. 37). I assume Villagrá's "Alarabes" were Suma Apaches but cannot identify them with certainty. The modern tribal groupings emerged only in the eighteenth century, when many groups mentioned by the Spaniards had already disappeared. By then the Sumas no longer existed (Gutiérrez, *When Jesus Came,* xxvii, xxix).

31. Ercilla gives a more detailed list at *Araucana,* 1.1.19–20, p. 6, and also names the weapons they brought to the battle at Concepción: spear, pike, mace, ax, and missiles (1.9.43, p. 144). The Araucanians had already learned to intersperse bowmen amid the pikes (*Araucana,* 1.1.23, p. 7). Tucapel and Rengo carry mace and sword for their duel (*Araucana,* 2.29.25, p. 474). The sword would be booty, and Ercilla describes an incident where Tucapel takes and uses a Spanish sword (*Araucana,* 2.25.30, p. 415). He normally uses the *macana,* which Pedro de Oña says is a wooden shaft longer than two arm lengths, the upper end of which is wider and curved. See Oña, *Arauco domado,* ed. Medina, gloss at p. 686. It is a two-handed weapon. For other references consult Bibar, *Crónica,* 104.153–55; *AD* 5.102–3, pp. 191–92 (Penco); Lovera, *Crónica del reino de Chile,* 1.2.31.112 (Andalien), 2.3.208 (Bío-Bío); Najera, *Desengaño y reparo,* 1.1.5–6, 2.2.2.95–96 for a detailed description. At Mareguano the Araucanians used lassoes against horses (Marmolejo, *Historia de Chile,* 16.78). The Dillman Museum near Angol displays some Indian weapons, including the *hachas de mando,* or *clavas,* and the *mapudum,* or mace, which was about the size of a hatchet. The slingshot later was rather like the Argentine *bola.* See Smith, *Araucanians,* 286n. Pocock notes that the Araucanians differed from neighboring tribes, preferring short bows and large clubs (*Conquest of Chile,* 238–39).

32. Earlier the Pueblo Indians lacked spears. The Piros used bow and arrow and *macana,* according to Mendoza (*NM* 2: App. 3, Doc. 8, p. 110; also Forbes, *Apache, Navaho, and Spaniard,* 57), and the Hopi likewise used arrows and maces when Tovar first visited them. See Castañeda de Nájera, *Relación,* 1.11, p. 214. Coronado sent the viceroy a mallet, bow, and some arrows (Bolton, *Coronado,* 145).

33. Juan de Guzman in his *Convite de Oradores* said that Ercilla was a true Homer. See Pierce, *Poesía épica,* 32. In his *Essay on Epic Poetry* Voltaire also compared Ercilla to Homer (Held, *Studien,* 2). The comparison has continued up to the present. See, for example, Ladero in his preface to *La Araucana* (Ercilla, *Araucana,* ed. Ladero, 6). He quotes Menéndez y Pelayo, who argued that Ercilla connected barbarian customs to the old heroism and made *La Araucana* the most Homeric of modern poems.

34. Bascuñan describes some Araucanian games (*Cautiverio feliz,* 1.15.61) and has other references at 3.26.273 and 4.1.304. Stevenson explains *chueca* and *peuca* (*Twenty Years' Residence,* 1.17, 23–24), the rules for wrestling (226), and other sports (319–20). For *chueca* see also Calvo, *Secretos,* 28.

35. See, for example, *Araucana,* 1.3.39, 62, pp. 48, 52; 1.4.42, 49, pp. 68–69; 1.5.6, p. 82; 1.6.4, 13, 26, pp. 94, 96, 98; 1.11.62, 64, p. 186; 1.14.21, 49, pp. 231, 237; 2.19.7, 10, 31, pp. 313, 317; 2.20.12–13, 16–17, pp. 326–27; 2.22.13, 38, 44, pp. 358, 363–64; 2.25.62, 74, pp. 422, 424; 2.28.58, 62, pp. 465–66; 2.29.31, p. 475; 3.32.18, p. 515. This is not a complete list.

36. Examples are *Araucana,* 1.5.41, p. 89; 1.9.71, p. 149; 2.14.24–28, pp. 232–33.

37. The Plains Indians met by Cabeza de Vaca (*NM* 3.52, p. 9v) and Ácomas like Pilco (32.216, p. 167r) and Gicombo (32.324, p. 168v). The poet, of course, did not really know who most of these Indians were. The generic term *Alarabes* masks his ignorance.

38. In Villagrá the Spaniards still rage on occasion. Zapata strikes his enemy six times in blind fury (*NM* 22.341, p. 121v), and Juan de Zaldívar is as angry as a trodden viper (22.156–61, p. 119r). The Spaniards are furious (*NM* 30.222, p. 157v), and Robledo picks himself off the ground furious (31.140, p. 161r). In most of these cases, however, the Spaniard has just been struck or wounded.

39. Marcos A. Morínigo argues that the Indians make the *Araucana* heroic (Held, *Studien,* 170). Quint parallels the Araucanians and European aristocrats, who were losing power (*Epic and Empire,* 174–75).

40. Najera, *Desengaño y reparo,* 2.2.1.93, 2.1.89–90. See also Figueroa, *Hechos,* 1.15–16, 2.35. The Indians agreed with Najera. The Spaniards normally made the first peace overtures. See Ulloa and Ulloa, *Voyage,* 2.76. The Indians called themselves "the never vanquished, always victorious" (Stevenson, *Twenty Years' Residence,* 10).

41. In the end the sergeant major, Vicente de Zaldívar, casually refers to their fury (*NM* 33.376, p. 174v). It is possible that Villagrá considered the Ácomas an exception to the peacefulness of the Pueblos. Castañeda de Najera called Ácoma a robbers' den, and the Indians there threatened the first Spanish visitors (*Relación,* 1.12). Next they skirmished with Espejo's men (Forbes, *Apache, Navaho, and Spaniard,* 62).

42. Ercilla, testimony for Tristan de Silva Campofrío (Ercilla, *Araucana,* ed. Medina, 2:103). Rodrigo Bravo, who also testified, agreed (*Colección . . . Chile,* 23:270), as did the historian Marmolejo (*Historia de Chile,* 14.58).

43. The battles include the assault on the fort, the defeat of Valdivia, and the attack on Cañete (the rebuilt and renamed Tucapel). The war leader need not be the local chief, and he is not in the system Ercilla presumes in his story of Caupolicán's election. Bibar mentions a Chief Tucapel, who participated in Caupolicán's election (*Crónica,* 117.173–74).

44. At Concepción (*Araucana,* 1.9.68–76, pp. 149–50) and Penco (2.19.31–34, pp. 317–18; 51–52, pp. 321–22; 20.7–13, pp. 325–26).

45. He starts another ruckus at the games (*Araucana,* 1.11.17–23, pp. 177–78). In Villagrá Zutacapan similarly attacks old Chumpo during a council at Ácoma (*NM* 21.97–102, p. 115r). For Rodamonte see *OI* 2.1.60–61, 3.20–24.

46. The single exception is the battle at Concepción. The *furioso* Zutacapan leads the Ácomas when they kill Juan de Zaldívar and ten Spaniards, but Villagrá associates him more with the political demagogue and suggests that he is a coward. He tries to surrender later and then hides rather than commit suicide.

47. Medina (*Vida de Ercilla*, 51 and n. 112) shows that the Zuñiga whom Rengo fights must be the poet.

48. *Araucana*, 2.26.25–37, pp. 432–35. Quint analyzes this scene (*Epic and Empire*, 101–2).

49. Forbes, *Apache, Navaho, and Spaniard*, 78. Villagrá does not mention his tactical role.

50. Najera remarks that no Indian would shoot one (*Desengaño y reparo*, 1.1.6) and that they must use fugitives and captives as gunners (2.3.4.120). The Indians lacked spirit to aim while firing (Lovera, *Crónica del reino de Chile*, 2.11.241), and the bravest would tie a harquebus to a tree and pull a rope (Najera, *Desengaño y reparo*, 1.1.6).

51. For example, the battle of Tirua (Bascuñan, *Cautiverio feliz*, 3.29.281–82).

52. Other versions are found in Bibar, *Crónica*, 116.172–73; Marmolejo, *Historia de Chile*, 15.66–71; Lovera, *Crónica del reino de Chile*, 1.3.45.161–63.

53. Valdivia says in his letter of 25 September 1551 that the Indians are very afraid of horses. Graham provides a translation (*Pedro de Valdivia*, 210).

54. The Hopis provide examples of earlier reactions. They had heard of Coronado's fierce men and cannibal animals, which had taken Cibola (Castañeda de Nájera, *Relación*, 1.11.214), and Espejo forty years later gets them to build him a house by saying that the horses threaten to kill Indians and need stables. A great crowd instantly makes a house of stone and mortar (Mendoza in *NM* 2: App. 3, Doc. 10, pp. 115–16).

55. Villagrá's horse falls into a horse trap (*NM* 19.149–75, p. 105r–v). Ercilla describes a more advanced version with stakes (*Araucana*, 1.1.32, p. 9). See also Marmolejo, *Historia de Chile*, 29.134. The Incas had already used pits at Sacsahuaman. See Hemming, *Conquest of the Incas*, 197–98.

56. Najera gives them 2,000 or 3,000 horses to 400 Spanish (*Desengaño y reparo*, 2.3.1.107), and the Indian horses never have to carry baggage (2.3.2.110–11). Their riders are slightly better armed than Lautaro's, but they have not yet had the time to develop into good horsemen (*Desengaño y reparo*, 2.3.3.115–16). He estimates 100 Spanish horse are worth 1,000 Indian (*Desengaño y reparo*, 5.1.4.254–55) and especially praises the Creole cavalry (1.2.10.37). Pineda y Bascuñan, writing a generation later, notes that the Araucanians still choose defensive positions, such as mountains and swamps (*Cautiverio feliz*, 1.3.11).

57. Medina argues that Ercilla served as a lancer in the cavalry (*Vida de Ercilla*, 49, 75). Villagrá lists a harquebus as one of his weapons (*NM* 19.192, p. 105v). For his sponsorship of harquebusiers, see *NM* 2: App. 1, Doc. 3, pp. 17–18.

58. Oman, *Sixteenth Century*, 62. Villagrá, however, describes an old-fashioned cavalry tournament for St. John's Day and notes how well the two Zaldívars handled their lances (*NM* 15.180–95, p. 84r).

59. Hemming, *Conquest of the Incas*, 112–15. Oña lists the weapons used by Mendoza's

expedition (*AD* 1.27, p. 49): *venablos* (short lances), regular lances, pikes, *ginetas,* and guns. Villagrá himself wore a coat, corselet, and helmet, and carried a shield, sword, and dagger, plus his harquebus (*NM* 19.190–93, p. 105v). The soldiers sent to chastise Ácoma have mail, lances of two irons or else bows, and shields, as well as horse armor (*NM* 27.38–55, p.140v). Horgan adds that they also took maces, that all had double-strength mail, and that the soldiers had glaive and halberd. He interprets the lance of two irons as a partisan, a weapon that had pointed sharp leaves facing both ways (*Great River,* 1:204–5). Fifty years earlier Coronado's men had double-edged swords, daggers, lances, maces, and different kinds of helmet. Some wore plate armor, and others had mail coats and breeches (ibid., 1:128).

60. Sepúlveda in *De rebus Hispanorum gestis ad novum orbem Mexicumque* (written between 1553 and 1558) argued that the Indians were as brave as the Spaniards but inferior in their manner of fighting and contrasted "those nearly unarmed fighting against those who were armed; novices or apprentices in the military arts struggling against veteran soldiers; those without horses or cannons opposing those who had them" (7.26, quoted by Adorno, "Warrior and the War Community," 232). Lagos considers this difference sufficient to make the fighting unheroic ("El incumplimiento," 173–74).

61. The historians give us the names of the commanders: Velasco and Reinoso. See note 1 above.

62. At *NM* 29.156, p. 151v, it is a dust storm instead. An outside example of these tactics would be the Indian ambush of Coronado's main army at the Firebrand River. They shoot arrows and are answered by harquebus and lance (Castañeda de Nájera, *Relación,* 1.10.212).

63. Marmolejo says he died by a sword thrust, so his killer would have been an unknown Spaniard (*Historia de Chile,* 22.104). Molina follows Ercilla. The teenage general was killed by a Purumancian dart (Smith, *Araucanians,* 154).

64. Oña says that Mendoza used sharpshooters at Penco to get Indian leaders, who were conspicuous by their ensigns and gestures (*AD* 6.82–83, pp. 235–36), but the consensus of modern historians is that such weapons were not accurate enough to do the job. See Roberts, *Essays in Swedish History,* 57; and Brodie and Brodie, *From Crossbow to H-Bomb,* 55–56.

65. Ercilla gives an explanation for Cañete, saying that none of the great warriors would participate in a surprise attack (*Araucana,* 3.32.21–23, pp. 515–16). More likely, the nature of the conflict did not allow for the traditional kind of heroics he associated with his fictional Indian heroes. Lovera, for example, names a Captain Quapolican plus others who died there (*Crónica del reino de Chile,* 2.11.234).

66. The first is for those who created a diversion while the twelve scaled Ácoma (*NM* 29.184–87, p. 152r; 195–215, p. 152r–v). The second covers some of the thirteen who were trapped next day by the Indians (*NM* 30.158–62, p. 156v).

67. Compare his description of the Spanish panic at the battle of Concepción (*Araucana,* 1.9.83–92, pp. 152–54) or of the Indians at Cañete (3.32.16–19, pp. 514–15). Bibar, citing his own experience, says that the Spaniards regularly became disorganized in retreat. Each man looked after himself, and no one helped another (*Crónica,* 116.17). He is discussing the exploits of the fourteen, who lost no man fighting the enemy but seven in their retreat.

68. *Historiae*, 1.67.5–72.1. See also the dialogue of the Melians and Athenians (*Historiae*, 5.87–111).

69. See, for example, Livy's presentation of a battle between Romans and Lacedaemonians (*Ab urbe condita*, 34.38.4–39.13).

70. See, for example, *De bello civili*, 7.617–37. The individuals the poet stresses are Brutus and Domitius (*De bello civili*, 7.586–616). Lucan uses "quis . . . quis" here rather than the "alii . . . alii" formula and explains that he uses the technique because he does not have time for individuals in a battle in which whole peoples perished.

71. For Cañete he uses "some . . . others" to describe the victims of artillery (*Araucana*, 3.32.8, p. 513). For Lepanto (*Araucana*, 2.24), as for Purén, such units indicate characteristic stages of a naval battle: boarding (50–51, p. 397), skirmishing (54–56, pp. 398–99), people in the water (58–59, p. 399), death (90, p. 405), those escaping to the coast (94, p. 406). For Millarapue he alternates generalized description, name lists, and the detailed heroics of his fictional Indian heroes. He uses the formula of "one . . . one" at *Araucana*, 2.25.20–21, p. 413 (the clash of horse and pike); 43, p. 418; and 2.26.19, p. 431 (forms of death).

72. For other examples of warfare, see Mataquito (*Araucana*, 1.14.12, p. 230), Penco (2.19.37, p. 319; 20.16, p. 326). Then there are the Indians looting the empty town of Concepción (*Araucana*, 1.7.49, p. 115). For overuse there is the lamentation in Concepción (*Araucana*, 1.7.7, p. 107). He also uses it outside the epic. His *Romance* (1586) on Santa Cruz's recent naval victory in the Azores frames its description with the "alii . . . alii" formula. Medina reprints the poem (*Vida de Ercilla*, 132–34).

73. Oña, for example, uses it frequently at first, but his lyrical style and copiousness make the device less obtrusive. Some examples are *AD* 3.9, p. 100 (the arrival at Coquimbo); the storm, where he imitates Ercilla (3.89, 91, p. 124); building a camp (4.36, p. 141; 4.39, p. 142), which is partially modeled on *Ae.* 6.6–7; the sailors' makeshift weapons at Penco (6.55, pp. 224–25); and the lament of the Indian women (6.108, p. 242). He uses the formula rarely later: of the dead at Penco (8.44–45, p. 290), of the fight in the swamp (11.100, p. 405).

74. Much of the preceding analysis applies to Camões as well as to the poets of the Spanish Indies. The Portuguese poet keeps his description of the skirmish at Mozambique on a generalized plane. He even uses the same "one . . . one" formula. He applies it twice to the locals, once to their warlike preparations (*Lusiadas*, 1.86), and once to their flight across the sea channel to the mainland (1.92). The historical formulas frame the battle, presenting the locals before and after the conflict. Camões, moreover, presents both sides as groups and leaves them nameless. With the substitution of ships for horses, the whole incident would fit smoothly into the preceding analysis: the anonymous few with modern equipment scattering an alien enemy, somewhere in a distant colonial zone.

CHAPTER 9: THE OFFICERS TAKE OVER

1. Lane describes the Venetian galley that was the standard before 1540 (*Venetian Ships*, 9–13). Guilmartin (*Gunpowder and Galleys*, 222–24) discusses the later developments and explains why boarding was necessary (59–62, 72, 209–10). Jachino (*Marine italiane*, 18) describes the beak and technical terms.

2. Jachino, *Marine italiane,* 18. Mallett and Hale give 100–120 soldiers per galley as the norm (*Military Organization,* 237).

3. They did so in the galleys of Venice and Barbary and in many galleys of the Ottoman Empire. See Jachino, *Marine italiane,* 18; Guilmartin, *Gunpowder and Galleys,* 111–12, 118; Hess, *Forgotten Frontier,* 91; Spencer, *Algiers,* 116.

4. Lesure, *Lépante,* 63.

5. This is the central thesis of Guilmartin's *Gunpowder and Galleys.*

6. Don Juan had once escorted a convoy from Gibraltar to Cartagena (Jachino, *Marine italiane,* 13). Colonna was limited to the previous year's experience (Lesure, *Lépante,* 34–35, 107), as was also Ali Paşa (ibid., 64), a former Janissary commander. Lesure likewise points to Veniero's naval incompetence (ibid., 36).

7. For Rufo I cite canto and stanza, and page and column number, from the edition of *La Austriada* by Don Cajetano Rosell. The general might ignore warnings about bad weather, as did Requesenes (*Austriada,* 8.10–14, p. 41A) and then Don Juan himself at Corfu (20.93–103, p. 110A–B). This practice was not confined to galley conflicts. Both Medina Sidonia, the commander of the Armada in 1588, and his English counterpart Howard lacked practical naval experience (Martin and Parker, *Spanish Armada,* 23, 59, 147).

8. Rufo notes that the rowers on Spanish galleys were watched constantly (*Austriada,* 9.101, p. 51A). See also Guilmartin, *Gunpowder and Galleys,* 111, 117–18. Veniero complained that Don Juan ruined the rowers before the battle ("Relation of 22 December 1572," 310); see note 36 below.

9. Guilmartin, *Gunpowder and Galleys,* 131–33. Don Garcia de Toledo regarded the Spanish soldiers in the fleet as raw. See his letter to Requesenes of 11 August 1571 in *Colección . . . España,* 3:8.

10. Don Juan, letter to Don Garcia de Toledo, 9 September 1571, in *Colección . . . España,* 18:20. See also the letter of 30 August, ibid., 18:18; and Veniero, "Relation of 22 December 1572," 299–300, which has the estimate of 23 August.

11. Lesure, *Lépante,* 230–31; Guilmartin, *Gunpowder and Galleys,* 250–52.

12. *FV* 15.153–54, 181–82, ff. 209r–v. See also *Austriada,* 24.92–94, p. 135A; Diedo, *Battaglia di Lepanto,* 40–43; report of the Venetian Senate to its ambassador in Madrid, in *Colección . . . España,* 18:349–50; Friar Juan de San Geronimo, table, in ibid., 18:253–57; Hammer-Purgstall, *Geschichte,* 3:596–97; Guilmartin, *Gunpowder and Galleys,* 251; Lesure, *Lépante,* 144–45; and Onorato Caetani, Aurelio Scetti, and others, cited in *Journal de la bataille de Lépante,* 212–13. Modern estimates have the Ottomans losing 200 galleys and 30,000 men (Parker, *Military Revolution,* 88).

13. Belloni gives a long list of Italian poets who wrote on Lepanto (*Il poema epico,* 279). Of interest to students of Tasso would be Danese Cataneo, who began but did not finish his *Vittoria navale,* and Francesco Bolognetti, who composed his *Christiana vittoria marittima ottenuta ai tempi di Pio V* in three books just before he died (ca. 1576). Bolognetti at one time contemplated writing a poem on the First Crusade and corresponded with Tasso.

14. Himself Portuguese, Corte Real wrote in Spanish. Portuguese poets of this period

generally could also write in Spanish, though António Ferreira opposed the practice; see Ramalho, *Portuguese Essays,* 29.

15. For Latino I use *Ad catholicum pariter et invictissimum Philippum . . . de felicissima serenissimi Ferdinandi principis nativitate, epigrammatum liber; deque sanctissimi Pii Quinti . . . rebus, et affectibus erga Philippum regem . . . liber unus; Austrias carmen . . .* (Granada: Hugo de Mena, 1573); for Corte Real I use *Felicissima victoria en el Golfo de Lepanto. En el año de 1572* (Lisbon: Antonio Ribero, 1578).

16. At 4.34, p. 515B in Rosell, *Poemas épicos.* As with Rufo I cite by canto and stanza, and page and column. Virués summarizes Lepanto at 4.27–47, pp. 515A–16A.

17. Lane, talking of Drake (*Venetian Ships,* 27).

18. Hawkins, *Observations,* 59.287–60. 293. He notes that Howard avoided boarding in the battle with the Armada (39.222), and his ship the *Daintie* had a crew of only seventy-seven men when captured. See "Relation of Pedro Valaguer de Salcedo," in Vega, *Dragontea,* 2:140–41, doc. 97. The viceroy had this relation printed (ibid., 2:144–45). All citations from *Dragontea* are from vol. 1 (Burgos: Museo Naval, 1935).

19. Ropp, *War in the Modern World,* 72; Guilmartin, *Gunpowder and Galleys,* 37–38, 162.

20. In particular he refers to the naval battle off Diu (1509), where the Portuguese used cannon to defeat a superior Muslim fleet. See *Lusiadas,* 2.50, 10.35–36. Guilmartin discusses Captain Towerson's skirmish with some Portuguese off Guinea in 1557, which illustrates the new technique (*Gunpowder and Galleys,* 89–93).

21. For Spenser's allusions, see Arthur's battle with Orgoglio and Duessa (*FQ* 1.8), and Arthur and Artegall versus the Soldan (5.8). The Armada inspired Latin odes in Holland and ballads in England, twenty-four of which survive (Martin and Parker, *Spanish Armada,* 261). For Oña I use Medina's edition of *Arauco domado.* I cite by canto and stanza, and page numbers.

22. Veniero, for example, emphasizes the effects of the galleass fire, which forced the enemy to break their line. He argues that the missiles kept the Turks on Ali Paşa's galley from going beyond the poop to the prow of their ship and so gave Don Juan room to board ("Relation of 22 December 1572," 311–12). Modern historians agree that guns were a major reason for the Christian victory. The Western powers had better guns and many more of them: 1,815 to 750 for the Ottomans (Parker, *Military Revolution,* 87–88, 128).

23. *De bello civili,* 7.250–329 (Caesar), 342–82 (Pompey).

24. Probably Don Juan repeated his speech orally in slightly different versions as he went through the fleet. For eyewitness versions, see Crillon in Lesure, *Lépante,* 127, and *Journal de la bataille de Lépante,* 178; Scetti in *Journal de la bataille de Lépante,* 177; and Fray Juan de San Gerónimo in the shorter version in *Colección . . . España,* 18:262. For the poets see *Austriadis libri duo,* 1.10r–v; *Araucana,* 24.7–18, pp. 389–91. Rufo adds the argument that to die in battle wins one heaven (*Austriada,* 23.15–17, p. 125B).

25. The soldiers and sailors were all at the rails applauding (*Journal de la bataille de Lépante,* 177). See also *Araucana,* 24.19, p. 391; *Austriada,* 23.18, p. 125B. Corte Real does not give Don Juan a speech, but he has him respond to the terrifying appearance of the Turkish fleet with confidence and so animate his men (*FV* 12.441–54, f. 162r).

26. Ercilla concludes with a comet simile. Don Juan's small ship in which he visits his fleet raises a white spume in the water like a shining comet, which swiftly breaks the thin air and leaves its mark behind a great while (*Araucana*, 24.20, p. 391).

27. This is the case in *Austriada*, 23.6–12, p. 125A–B; and *Araucana*, 24.27–39, pp. 393–95.

28. *Araucana*, 24.27, 37–39, pp. 393, 395. Quint argues that Ercilla crosses Lucan's pattern. He models the speech of Ali Paşa on that of Caesar and Don Juan's on Pompey's (*Epic and Empire*, 158).

29. Diedo, *Battaglia di Lepanto*, 10–17. Mehmet Bey was the tutor of Ali Paşa's sons. He and Caur Ali are supported by all the Turkish historians: Selâniki, Petchevi, and Hadji Khalifah (Lesure, *Lépante*, 122). Corte Real assumes that Caracossa, who made the scouting report on the Christian fleet when it was anchored at Gumenizze, persuaded Ali Paşa to risk battle (*FV* 12.97–112, ff. 154v–55r; 129–64, ff. 155v–56r).

30. Latino, *Austriadis libri duo*, 2.24r; *Araucana*, 24.89, p. 405; *FV* 14.385–88, f. 195r, 702–12, f. 201v; *Austriada*, 24.31, p. 132A. Among the historians and news reporters are Fray Juan de San Gerónimo, *Colección . . . España*, 18:244–45, and Medina della Motta del Friuli, *Dialogo*, A4r. Lesure in his anthology (*Lépante*, 137) argues that it was the turning point of the battle and says that Ali's death was quickly known in the galleys nearby and that Pertev Paşa, the commander of the land forces, fled. Technically, the Turks had a *capitana* not a *real* in the battle, since the sultan was not present.

31. Corte Real alludes briefly to the beheading. He paraphrases Virgil on the body of Priam. A corpse without a name lies on the ground, headless (*Ae.* 2.557–58; *FV* 14.367–68, f. 194v). He further dignifies the death of the Turkish leader with two extended similes, unique to this section of the poem because he draws them from the physical world. He compares Mars's dart to lightning (*FV* 14.333–40, f. 194r) and confers gigantic size on the fallen body by comparing it to a fallen cedar (14.369–76, f. 194v).

32. *FV* 14.233–36, f. 191v; 259–60, f. 192r. In an elaborate simile Corte Real compares Don Juan to a lion, chasing a flock and tearing to pieces any animal that it reaches (*FV* 14.261–68, f. 192v).

33. Diedo has Don Juan leap onto the enemy galley and cover his sword with enemy blood (*Battaglia di Lepanto*, 32).

34. *Austriada*, 23.33–34, p. 126B; 37–41, pp. 126B–27A; 51–57, p. 127B; 72–74, p. 128B; 99–101, pp. 129B–30A; 108, p. 130A.

35. Even if Philip was only being polite, since he also told Don Juan in the same letter to stay in Sicily and not come home, the form of the praise bespeaks a widely shared attitude. For the latter see Rosell, *Historia . . . de Lepanto*, letter 15, 210.

36. Veniero complains ("Relation of 22 December 1572," 310) that Don Juan ruined the rowers on the night of 3–4 October by making them work, though they had a favorable wind. Don Juan reviewed the fleet both at Messina and at the Gumenizze, shortly before the battle. See his letter to Don Garcia de Toledo of 30 August 1571 in *Colección . . . España*, 18:17–18; or Lesure, *Lépante*, 107 (Messina); and Caetani in *Journal de la bataille de Lépante*, 168 (Gumenizze). In Corte Real's poem Don Juan has battle in mind throughout.

He expresses his desire for battle both in the initial debate on strategy (*FV* 12.17–84, ff. 153r–54v) and at the meeting held just before the actual fight (12.457–88, ff. 162r–63r).

37. See, for example, the two Venetian engravings of G. B. Camocio, which present stages of the battle (reproduced in Oman, *Sixteenth Century*, 730–31, 734–35). More elaborate are the four tapestries woven at Brussels and now in the Doria Pamphili Palace on the Corso in Rome. Michele Coxie's designs show multiple stages of the battle. See *Roma e dintorni*, 163.

38. Other examples are the missile exchange (*Araucana*, 24.54, p. 398), fighting in the water (58–59, p. 399), and the Turks swimming to shore (94, p. 406).

39. Bury, *History of Greece*, 745, 763.

40. Guilmartin, *Gunpowder and Galleys*. See the whole of his chapter on Lepanto (221–52) but especially 240–41, 250. Parker notes that Guilmartin reflects Spanish, not Venetian and Ottoman views (*Military Revolution*, 87n.14). For Venice he refers the reader to M. Morin, "La battaglia di Lepanto: Il determinante apporto dell' artiglieria Veneziana," *Diana: Armi* 9/1 (1975): 54–61; and J. R. Hale, "Men and Weapons: The Fighting Potential of Sixteenth-century Venetian Galleys," in *War and Society: A Yearbook of Military History* I (1975): 1–23. For the Ottomans there is C. J. Heywood's review of Guilmartin in *Bulletin of the School of Oriental and African Studies* 38 (1975): 643–46. It is not surprising that Corte Real's data support Guilmartin's analysis, since the poet draws on Spanish sources. Uluj Ali tries to outflank the Christian right (*FV* 13.393–424, f. 179r–v), and Siroco tries to do the same against the Venetians, or Christian left wing (13.305–8, f. 177r). Oman (*Sixteenth Century*, 729–34) considered Lepanto a messy battle.

41. Veniero ("Relation of 22 December 1572," 312) and Caetani (letter to Cardinal of Sermoneta, 9 October 1571, in *Lettere*, 54) both complain that others took their prizes.

42. They barely mention the Venetians. Veniero, the Venetian commander, provides a contrast ("Relation of 22 December 1572," 311–14). He mentions only Venetians, except when he wishes to criticize others. In contrast to Rufo, Ercilla uses his list of officers to survey the fortunes of the battle just before its climax (*Araucana*, 24.80–86, pp. 403–4).

43. In his dedicatory poem Ludovico Franco says that Corte Real knows the names of all the Iberian leaders, and an endless list makes the catalogue of ships in canto 12 dull reading. For Rufo see *Austriada*, 22.119–38, pp. 123A–24A. For his catalogue and for names in the narrative, see *Austriada*, 23.76–79, p. 128B, and especially 24.51–58, p. 133A–B.

44. *Austriada*, 23.79, p. 128B. Corte Real likewise focuses on Cardona for the same action (*FV* 14.137–208, ff. 189v–91r).

45. Keegan, *Face of Battle*, 62–73. He points especially to Caesar's *Commentaries*. One thinks also of the many documentary paintings that put the commander in the foreground and show his battle dispositions in the distance.

46. Hawkins notes that the Spaniards gave up trying to board the *Daintie* at the end of the first day and went over to artillery (*Observations*, 59.284). For a modern account see Spake, *Spanish Lake*, 287–88.

47. Oña sets the battle in the bay of Tucámez, but Atacamez (in the modern spelling) was a general term applied to that stretch of coast and not simply to the bay of the modern

maps. Hawkins places the fight near the mouth of the Rio Esmeraldas, and his editor puts it just east of the river (*Observations*, 53.267–69 and notes).

48. Medina in his edition of *Arauco domado* notes phrases borrowed from the "Relation of Balaguer de Salcedo" (19.30, p. 656.10n).

49. *AD* 18.40, 69–70, pp. 623, 632–33. Of these three galleons the *almirante*, or second in command, became the *capitana* after the storm off Chincha and went north to fight Hawkins (*AD* 19.65–67, pp. 667–68). As late as the 1620s thirty guns would be a standard complement for a galleon. Phillips cites the *San Felipe* with thirty gunports (*Six Galleons*, 69).

50. Figueroa, *Hechos*, 9.15, 60; Means, *Spanish Main*, 81. *Galizabras* and *pataches* made up the communications squadron of the Armada. Martin and Parker say they were mostly pinnaces and caravels, lateen-rigged and equipped with oars (*Spanish Armada*, 43–44). Phillips, however, calls a *galizabra* a small galleon (*Six Galleons*, 81).

51. He dropped one-third of his original force, which the poet says numbered 420 (three companies of 100 each [*AD* 18.48, pp. 625–26] and 120 volunteers [18.72–73, pp. 633–34]). Infantry companies of 100 per galleon were standard (Phillips, *Six Galleons*, 146). The two ships that survived the battle of Esmeraldas had a slightly higher average of men per ship, since the *galizabra* was a smaller ship, but still within standard limits. The war fleet that sailed in 1629 averaged 126 men per ship (ibid., 112).

52. Lope exaggerates its tonnage at 500 tons and says it had castles fore and aft and sides proof against bombard (*Dragontea*, 3.173). Hawkins gives 300–400 tons for the *Daintie* (*Observations*, 1.89). It was a new ship, built after the Armada. At that battle the English had the old-style large warships (Parker, *Military Revolution*, 92–93; Martin and Parker, *Spanish Armada*, 195), and the effect of that conflict was to perpetuate this tradition through the Jacobean period (Parker, *Military Revolution*, 96, 99).

53. Phillips defines *pinnace* as a light vessel using sail and oar (*Six Galleons*, 67).

54. In the "Relation of Balaguer de Salcedo" (in Vega, *Dragontea*, 2: doc. 97) the *Daintie* makes one shot from its *amura*, near the prow, and the Spanish ship, to windward, answers with two culverins. The *Daintie* passes the prow of the Spanish *capitana*, shooting from one part and the other. Oña agrees, adding that the prows almost touch, as the *Daintie* doubles on the port side. Hawkins briefly makes the same point. The *Daintie* shot and was answered two for one from the Spanish ship in the windward position. The "Relation" then has the *capitana* turn before the *Daintie* reaches its middle, and the two ships join, prow to prow and stern to stern. Oña specifies that the *capitana* turns into the wind and says that the two ships almost scrape. Hawkins merely says that the enemy came to leeward of him, but the *Daintie* had only one gun working on that side. The *capitana* fell off and kept windward, cannonading.

55. A *pedreñal* is a small harquebus or pistol, shot by flint, and most often used by bandits.

56. Spanish artillery gunners came from the sailors, not from the soldiers on board (Phillips, *Six Galleons*, 144).

57. Spake calls him a thoughtful seaman but too permissive as a commander (*Spanish Lake*, 286).

58. The "Relation" notes that Hawkins acted out of confidence, trusting his ship (in Vega, *Dragontea*, 2:132). He himself explains that Spanish crews are bad. The men are few, serve as slaves to the soldiers and gunners, must sleep on deck, lack arms, and usually suffer the first casualties. All this follows from the error of making land captains officers (*Observations*, 58.280–81). Spake concurs (*Spanish Lake*, 287). Hawkins's father had converted the English to Portuguese-style tactics of bombardment when he was treasurer of the navy in 1578 (Martin and Parker, *Spanish Armada*, 52, 56). The Spaniards, including King Philip, knew before the Armada sailed that the English would fight in this fashion (ibid., 152–53, 158), and they did (ibid., 165–66; Parker, *Military Revolution*, 92–93).

59. The Spaniards built the ships of their Pacific fleet to tack windward (*Observations*, 49.259–60), and Hawkins regularly failed to catch them. An example is his pursuit at Paytoc (ibid., 50.262), where he did not catch a ship after a chase of a night and a day. For the problems of a ship to leeward, see Martin and Parker, *Spanish Armada*, 158, 209.

60. *Observations*, 53.271. The "Relation" notes that the Spaniards shot 255 balls to 100 for the English in the three-day battle (in Vega, *Dragontea*, 2:142–43). Oña lists the Spanish artillery by types (*AD* 18.97, p. 642): *pedreros* (rock throwers), *esmeriles* (small pieces), culverins with chain shot and sharpened or pointed balls (*navaja*). For a further discussion of the Spanish guns, see the introduction.

61. Hawkins, *Observations*, 61.300; Guilmartin, *Gunpowder and Galleys*, 170–73, 175. The poet also did not know about the difficulties Hawkins lists (*Observations*, 53.271–72). All the English stern pieces and those to leeward were not primed except for a demi-cannon in the quarterdeck. The chief gunner had no cartridges prepared, so they had to use a ladle for the powder. Martin and Parker argue that the length of the barrel made no difference in the range of a gun (*Spanish Armada*, 197), but they do note that Don Juan de Acuña Vela, Philip's captain general of artillery, was arguing for short gun barrels on 25 July 1587 (210–11). They also indicate that in the Armada battles the English had weightier shot (ibid., 197).

62. The English had compact, four-wheeled truck carriages for their guns by the 1540s (Parker, *Military Revolution*, 95–96). They could reload much more easily than the Spaniards, who had the long two-wheeled carriages used on land. Bobadilla, Philip's general for the soldiers on the Armada, reported to the king afterward that the English ships had the advantage in design, guns, gunners, and crews (Martin and Parker, *Spanish Armada*, 265). Petruccio Ubaldino, a Florentine artist and historian who wrote an account of the Armada battles for Drake, also noted that the English could use their guns more easily because their decks were not crowded with useless soldiers (ibid., 214).

63. Hawkins, *Observations*, 61.303–4; Phillips, *Six Galleons*, 148.

64. See *NM* 10.109–13, p. 51r; 12.311–14, p. 64r; 22.172–80, p. 119v.

65. Hawkins, *Observations*, 58.281; *AD* 18.78, pp. 635–36. Don Beltram had commanded 20,000 soldiers, though he was only twenty-two at the time. For the Spanish ratio of soldiers to sailors, see Phillips, *Six Galleons*, 124, 140, 220.

66. Martin and Parker, *Spanish Armada*, 24.

67. Parker, *Military Revolution*, 93–94, 96, 105 and n. 56; Martin and Parker, *Spanish Armada*, 35, 95, 158, 210.

68. Phillips, *Six Galleons,* 216. At Matanzas thirty-two Dutch ships cornered four Spanish galleons and eleven merchant ships (ibid., 4). Off the Downs Tromp had odds of five to one (ibid., 216–17).

69. I have been unable to directly consult Scetti's text, which was published in *Rivista marittima* 10–11 (1884). Lesure, *Lépante,* and *Journal de la bataille de Lépante* include excerpts and some of his drawings.

70. Charrière prints Romegas's letter in *Collection de documents inédits sur l'histoire de France,* 3:185–90. Rosell has Don Juan's "Relation" at pp. 216–23. He also prints the letter of Francisco de Murillo to Antonio Perez (224–26). As an example of the poets' reliance on Spanish sources, Corte Real, for example, says little about the Venetians in the battle.

71. For Balaguer de Salcedo, see note 48. Hawkins argues that two acts, which he opposed, ruined the English chances: they showed themselves first at Valparaiso instead of Peru and so alerted the whole coast, and they delayed at Atacames and Esmeraldas and so were caught by the pursuit fleet (*Observations,* 42.231–32, 53.267).

72. Francisco de Borja, Prologue, *Dragontea,* p. 16. Canto 3, which includes the battle at Esmeraldas, reads like chronicle history.

73. V. B. Spratlin, "Juan Latino: Slave and Humanist," *The Crisis* 39 (1932): 283.

74. *FV* Prologue, *3v; 12.701–12, f. 167v. Corte Real's praise of Santa Cruz, however, did not help him in Lisbon. When typhus took Santa Cruz in early 1588, only four people were willing to accompany his coffin to his tomb, and a Lisbon chronicler claimed that "his death was regretted by no one" (Martin and Parker, *Spanish Armada,* 146).

75. In his dedicatory poem Francesco Cabero says Don Juan gave charge of his fame to his faithful *criado,* Juan Rufo, whose soft and elevated song brings the golden age to the world. The poet dedicates the epic to Don Juan's sister, the dowager empress of Rome.

76. Hawkins notes that Peruvian ships were built for the fair weather that generally prevailed there (*Observations,* 49.259–60). The sudden storm nearly wrecked Don Beltram's ships. Similarly, King Philip had no seasoned troops in Spain when the Moriscos rebelled. Veniero provides a further example. He argues that if his council had accepted his advice, the Venetians might have saved Famagusta ("Relation of 22 December 1572," 291–92).

77. Malory, *Works,* ed. Vinaver, 1.16. I give the Caxton numbers, which Vinaver preserves. In this section, however, the northerners in general are praised, not only their kings.

78. Corte Real has him killed with a dart (*FV* Argument to canto 14, f. 186r).

79. Murrin, *Allegorical Epic,* 103–5, 107.

80. Ercilla begins his account with the remark that both battles occurred in the same place (*Araucana,* 23.77, p. 383). Latino argues that Cleopatra's flight makes Actium inferior to Lepanto (*Austriadis libri duo,* 1.2v, 2.20r). Corte Real twice refers to Actium (*FV* 12.201–4, f. 157r; 15.229–36, f. 210v). For the *Austriada* Gongora alludes to Actium in his dedicatory poem. Rufo himself argues that the technology that made artillery possible elevates Lepanto above any older battle (*Austriada,* 23.4–5, p. 125A). He refers to Actium (*Austriada,* 22.92–95, pp. 121B–22A). Virues juxtaposes the two battles (*Monserrate,* 4.18–42,

pp. 514B–16A) and makes the same point. Artillery makes Lepanto the greater battle. The idea was commonplace. See, for example, Vecello, *Titiani Vecelli equitis . . . oratio,* 2v–3r.

81. A Roman knight said that he could not look on Augustus because he could not bear the thunder of his eyes. For Servius I have used *Servii Grammatici qui feruntur in Vergilii carmina commentarii,* ed. Thilo and Hagen.

82. In one sense, however, Tasso does suggest something like an epiphany. When Goffredo quells the mutiny, the common soldiers see in his visible presence a supernatural power (*GL* 8.84). Allegorical theory, of course, does not require consistency, and many allegorical poets vary their application of symbols. See Murrin, *Veil of Allegory,* 135–46. Some poets, however, had a tendency toward consistency, encouraged by the mythographical dictionaries. See Murrin, *Allegorical Epic,* 7–8. Tasso was one of these. For a discussion of example, see Wallace, "Examples," 275–90.

83. An idea Sidney attacks in the *Apology,* when he argues that a reader can derive both good and bad examples from history. See Smith, *Elizabethan Critical Essays,* 1:169–71.

CHAPTER 10: ARE THERE LIMITS TO VIOLENCE?

1. The phrase was not new. In the war between the dukes of Burgundy and Liège (1465–68) the aldermen *(échevins)* of Antwerp were told to write to their troops so that "ilz feissent guerre aux Liègois de feu et de sang." See Vale, *War and Chivalry,* 160 and n. 72. He cites from the *Journal de Jehan Aubrion, bourgeois de Metz, 1465–1512,* ed. L. Larchey (Metz, 1857), 27.

2. Frenzy drives Aeneas initially to battle (*Ae.* 2.314–17). Venus later refers to this fury (*Ae.* 2.594–95), and in the rejected scene with Helen it is frenzy that makes him want to kill her (2.575–76, 588).

3. Aeneas's killing of Turnus caused considerable discussion among those who analyzed honor in the sixteenth century. For some opinions see Seem, "Limits of Chivalry," 116–18.

4. Johnson, *Darkness Visible,* 122–28, 148.

5. *Eyrbyggja Saga,* 25, p. 86.

6. See the discussion in Saccone, "Osservazioni," 31–60.

7. Gradasso burns his way through Spain (*OI* 1.4.8–9, 24). At Monaco Rodamonte routs the various Christian forces, killing indiscriminately (*OI* 2.6.35–7.30, 14.15–15.17). He goes berserk once the Lombards overturn his banner (*OI* 2.7.30, 14.21–23).

8. Oman, *Middle Ages* 2:307–8; Mallett, *Mercenaries,* 197–200; Treppo, "Gli aspetti organizzativi," 273–75. Treppo studied Micheletto's company of 512 soldiers, which suffered 15 deaths in battle in 25 years. Pieri points, however, to some bloody battles in the Pazzi War (*Il rinascimento,* 304), and Mallett notes that Machiavelli distorted his figures. He gave one dead for Anghiari, but 900 actually died.

9. Runciman, *Fall of Constantinople,* 146, 150. The Venetian colony was Negroponte (Chalkis). See Babinger, *Mehmed der Eroberer,* 300–303; Lane, *Venice,* 358–59. Greeks went as slaves to Istanbul.

10. Babinger, *Mehmed der Eroberer,* 339.

11. Keen, *Chivalry*, 228; Corvisier, *Armies and Societies*, 98; Oman, *Middle Ages*, 2:410–11.

12. Vale, *War and Chivalry*, 157, 160–61; Keen, *Chivalry*, 221.

13. Oman, *Sixteenth Century*, 66.

14. Ibid., 91, 111–12; Pieri, *Il rinascimento*, 337 and n.; Mallett, *Mercenaries*, 240.

15. Pieri, *Il rinascimento*, 337–38, 380–81.

16. Hale, "War and Public Opinion in Renaissance Italy," 111–12.

17. At the same time he tacitly acknowledges the strategy behind terror. Ravenna should have taken warning from the sack of Brescia, just as Rimini and Faenza did from that of Ravenna, surrendering without resistance (*OF* 14.9). As cities became the focus of war, atrocities of this kind became common for the Spanish army. See Hale, "The Art of War and Renaissance England," 2. Parker (*Army of Flanders*, 179) remarks that the Spanish army in Flanders was brutal. Alba encouraged sack and massacre at Malines, Utrecht, Zütphen, and Naarden (1572). The sack of Antwerp took 7,000 lives (1576), and in the storming of Maastricht (1579) the Spaniards killed one-third of the people immediately. See Hale, *War and Society*, 185, 195.

18. Adorno points out that the nature of a war was determined by the characterization that the protagonist made of the enemy ("Warrior and the War Community," 227). During the reign of Charles V, Spaniards distinguished sharply between the French and the Muslim enemy. The former had chivalry, courage, liberality, and perseverance, but the latter showed cowardice, treachery, and inertia. The latter stereotype was based on Castilians' experience with their declining and now vanquished Moorish enemy in the Iberian peninsula rather than on their new contacts with the Ottoman Turks (ibid., 240).

19. Fulcher of Chartres, *Historia hierosolymitana*, 1.27.13, 28.1, 33.19. Jerusalem fell on 15 July 1099, but Fulcher says the corpses still made a smell in December. His chronicle was published in 1611. Fulcher assumes the soldiers killed 10,000 in the Aqṣā Mosque (Gray, *History of Jerusalem*, 237). William of Tyre, drawing ultimately on eyewitness testimony, accepts this figure and says a similar number died elsewhere, so 20,000 in all. See Peters, *Jerusalem*, 287. Muslim estimates are much higher but do not derive from eyewitness evidence. Ibn al-Athir and al-Maqrizi say 70,000 were killed in the Aqṣā Mosque alone (Mustafa A. Hiyari, "Crusader Jerusalem, 1099–1187 A.D.," in *Jerusalem in History*, ed. Asali, 138n.50).

20. *HR* 1.1.8.19–20. See also Runciman, *First Crusade*, 286–87.

21. Runciman, *First Crusade*, 234–35, 287. Peters, however, argues that both Muslims and Jews largely ignored the capture of Jerusalem. It was the fourth time in less than thirty years (*Jerusalem*, 288–90).

22. *Discorsi dell'arte poetica*, 1.351, 2.367–68, in Tasso, *Prose*, ed. Mazzali.

23. Letter to Luca Scalabrino, 2 June 1575, in Tasso, *Lettere*, ed. Guasti, 1:84–85. It was Tancredi who captured the Aqṣā Mosque. See Runciman, *First Crusade*, 286–87.

24. For Ácoma it was the commanders who stood trial afterward.

25. Canto 18 still did not exist at the stage represented by *Br₁* (Vatican City, Biblioteca Apostolica Vaticana, Barberiniana, Segn. XLV. 146, old numeration 3248). *Br₁* represents

the primitive redaction of the *Liberata* and runs through 16.62, minus cantos 11 and 13. See Solerti's bibliography in his edition of the *Liberata*, 1:121–25.

26. He was elected king historically *after* the fall of Jerusalem and never commanded more than his own men during the campaign. Tasso had made this change already in the *Gierusalemme* (1559–60).

27. Held, *Studien*, 66, 73, 97. She shows that Ercilla also adopted this position.

28. Donadoni complained about this idealization of Goffredo (*Torquato Tasso*, 1:341–42).

29. Petrocchi devotes a chapter to Virgil's influence (*I fantasmi*, 83–99).

30. Seem, "Limits of Chivalry," 118.

31. Heinze (*Virgils epische Technik*, 18) so interprets Laocoon's sacrifice to Neptune. Panthus likewise speaks of the "ineluctabile tempus" (*Ae.* 2.324).

32. Heinze, *Virgils epische Technik*, 7, 28, 54; Johnson, *Darkness Visible*, 55. Sophocles composed a *Sinon* and also a *Laocoon*, though in the latter he has Aeneas leave Troy before it falls.

33. See especially *GL* 18.100, where nature rejoices as Goffredo plants his standard on the walls.

34. Donadoni, characteristically, praises this contradiction (*Torquato Tasso*, 1.306).

35. *GL* 19.31; *HR* 8.20: "Verum et ipsos victores a planta pedis usque ad verticem cruore madentes periculosum erat conspicere, et horrorem quemdam inferebant occurrentibus."

36. For Tancredi, see *HR* 8.20. Seem argues that in addition to dropping Virgil's scene between Priam and Pyrrhus, Tasso also mutes Virgil's ending. He has Goffredo spare, not kill, Altamoro ("Limits of Chivalry," 124). Such softening of his model might also suggest that Tasso felt uncomfortable with this notion of war, but nowhere in the poem does he express such a view directly.

37. Qilij Arslan (Solimano) was still alive in 1107, and al-Afdal (Emireno), the Egyptian commander, controlled Egypt until his assassination in 1121. See Smail, *Crusading Warfare*, 68, 84.

38. *HR* 8.20: "Justoque Dei judicio id certum est accidisse, ut qui superstitiosis ritibus Domini sanctuarium profanaverant et fidelibus populis rediderant alienum, id proprii cruoris luerent dispendio, et, morte interveniente, piaculare solverent flagitium."

39. Hale, *War and Society*, 186, 191–92; Pepper and Adams, *Firearms and Fortifications*, 135.

40. Hale, *War and Society*, 194. Plunder, including slaves and prisoners held for ransom, had traditionally formed part of a warrior's income. Though Renaissance governments tried to pay their soldiers, the money often came irregularly and late. Plunder provided an immediate reward, and it was difficult to restrain killing during a sack.

41. *GL* 2.54–55; Runciman, *First Crusade*, 279–80, 287.

42. Alba regarded townspeople as rebels and gallows material, so atrocities marked his captures of Mechlin, Zütphen, and Naarden. When Haarlem surrendered (12 July 1573), he executed 2,300 prisoners. See Oman, *Sixteenth Century*, 560–61.

43. Rufo also records the experiences of a villager who saw and heard the tumult in his village (*Austriada*, 3.49–58, pp. 17B–18A). He found bodies everywhere, with ugly wounds. The church was ruined, and priests had the sign of the cross cut into their faces and breasts. He could barely recognize the faces of his own children for all the wounds. Rufo's reports may have exaggerated, yet specific details mark them, and the war was very bitter.

44. For the preliminaries to this battle, see chapter 7.

45. Lovera and Figueroa mention only harquebuses. For the latter's account, see Figueroa, *Hechos,* 3.64–65. Marmolejo lists cannon as well, as does Ercilla (*Araucana*, 31.44, p. 508: "la gruesa artilleria"). Medina assumes Reinoso set up cannon at the two entrances of the fort and put the harquebuses in the loopholes of the wall. For his account of the battle, see his *Vida de Ercilla,* 59–61.

46. In Bibar's account the Indian commander, Teopolican, seeing the trap, orders a retreat. For his account see Bibar, *Crónica,* 2.135.205–7. Lovera and Figueroa both agree that the Indians kept a kind of order in their flight.

47. He elegantly uses the first passage to end a canto.

48. Lagos calls the battle a martyrdom of the Indians ("El incumplimiento," 183). She also argues that Ercilla inserts a love episode whenever he considers the fighting unheroic, so he follows Cañete with the story of Dido (ibid., 174–75).

49. Bibar alone gives a figure, listing 300 dead. Marmolejo says that the *yanaconas* (Indians in Spanish service) and blacks killed many. Ercilla expresses the views of the *chapetón*, or newcomer, while Bibar and Marmolejo were *baquianos,* or veterans of the colonial wars (Durand, "El chapetón," 113–14). The poet's ideas fit those of other newcomers, critical of colonial practices in Peru (ibid., 117–21). Critics such as Roberto Mesa and Augustín Cueva put Ercilla in an anticolonialist position, while Ciriaco Pérez Bustamente lines up the poet with Las Casas. For a bibliography and summary of these arguments, see Held, *Studien,* 6–7. According to Held, Las Casas attacked not the right of the Spaniards to the New World but their methods (ibid., 33). At Penco the Dominican Gil González de San Nicolás criticized the killing there. He was probably a student of Vitoria but influenced by Las Casas and, unlike Ercilla, would have held the individual soldier responsible for his actions (ibid., 42–43).

50. *Araucana*, 3.32.20, p. 515. Marmolejo alone among the chroniclers mentions executions and describes the terror that followed. The Indians made hidden pits on the road between Cañete and Imperial, which they filled with sharpened stakes and covered over. In this manner they killed many horses. In response, captured Indians were impaled in these pits (*Historia de Chile,* 29.134).

51. *Araucana*, 3.34.19–30, pp. 555–57. Six bowmen then shot him to death. Bibar (*Crónica,* 136.207) and Marmolejo (*Historia de Chile,* 28.132) also describe the death.

52. After Penco, Mendoza delivered a speech to his troops in which he exhorted them to fight in a restrained fashion and to spare the defeated (*Araucana*, 2.21.56, p. 352). His later policy, however, does not fit this statement of principles.

53. *Araucana*, 2.22.45–54, pp. 364–66. Ercilla also considers this punishment unjust (*Araucana*, 2.26.30, p. 433). See Held, *Studien,* 89–90.

54. Quint argues that characters like Galbarino, by their refusal to admit permanent defeat, project resistance into the future (*Epic and Empire*, 104), and indeed the Araucanians stopped all attempts at conquest until the 1880s. Galbarino and figures modeled on him, such as Cotumbo and Tempal in the *Historia de la Nueva Mexico*, function as "the bad conscience of the poem that simultaneously writes them in and out of its fiction" (ibid., 99). At the same time, however, Quint points out that such defiance justifies Spanish severity (ibid., 105) and so creates a closed circle of violence, each side justifying its harshness by the actions of the other side.

55. August J. Aquila, "*La Araucana:* A Sixteenth-Century View of War and Its Effects on Men" (dissertation, Indiana University, 1973), stresses Ercilla's dependence on scholasticism. See Held, *Studien*, 6.

56. Held, *Studien*, 67, 69–70, 97. She cites Vitoria and shows that Ercilla held to the theory of the just war throughout the *Araucana*. Adorno cites Sepúlveda, who similarly justifies war as a means to peace, citing Augustine, Aquinas, and Vitoria ("Warrior and the War Community," 227).

57. Astolfo defeats Gradasso with an enchanted lance (*OI* 1.7.49–71). At Albraca the Turks and Mamluks finally capture the castle, only to find the princess gone and no one there (*OI* 2.18.6–18).

CHAPTER 11: ÁCOMA

1. Friar Alonso de Benavides in his *Memorial* (Madrid, 1630) assumes they had Indian auxiliaries, when he refers to the previous massacre and this assault (*NM* 2: App. 2, 23). There is no information about their numbers. Oñate's contract and the two reviews held of his army while still in Mexico say nothing about them.

2. Vargas attacked Ácoma without success on 15 August 1696. See White, *Ácoma Indians*, 28. Other members of Oñate's expedition agreed with Villagrá. Juan de Olague said he had never seen a place so difficult of access (*OD* 1.443), and the compiler of the "Expedition to the South Sea and the Salines" considered Ácoma practically impregnable (*OD* 1.394). Sergeant Zapata and Juan Blásquez de Cabanillas noted that it was a league in circumference at the base (*OD* 1.441, 447), or nearly five kilometers—a size that would make a siege impracticable. Earlier a member of Coronado's party remarked that if the Indians had stayed above, the Spaniards could not in the least have disturbed them. See Bolton, *Coronado*, 183.

3. Actually it is 110 meters high, but the cliffs overhang. See Sedgwick, *Ácoma, the Sky City*, 17–18.

4. Villagrá gives the maximum width. At points the walls of the crevasse almost meet. See Villagrá, *History of New Mexico*, trans. Espinosa, intro. and notes by Hodge, 29.236n.7.

5. Garcia-Mason assumes that the present gridiron pattern also characterized the sixteenth-century town ("Acoma Pueblo," 459), yet Villagrá suggests a place more like present-day Taos pueblo. It was the Spaniards who used gridiron patterns for their towns. In a letter written after the battle (2 March 1599, to the viceroy), Oñate talks like Villagrá. The pueblos have rectangular plazas but no streets, though the larger ones have narrow

passages between buildings (*OD* 1.483). For Ácoma, Tabora and Cabanillas speak of two small plazas and some narrow streets (*OD* 1.434, 446).

6. On the water supply see Sedgwick, *Acoma, the Sky City,* 25–26; White, *Acoma Indians,* 29. The reservoir on the North Mesa sufficed for daily use. That on the south never ran dry and always had cold, clear water. If the Indians massacred the Spaniards in December because they were worried about their food supply, as has been argued, Villagrá's guess of six years seems wild. On numbers the poet claims 500 for the ambush alone (30.21–22, p. 155r). Sedgwick, in contrast, assumes a total force at Ácoma of 300 plus some Navajos (*Acoma, the Sky City,* 79). Population estimates for Ácoma in the sixteenth century vary widely. Espejo and Villagrá give 6,000; Oñate, 3,000; and Benavides, 2,000. The later range varies considerably but never rises above 960. Simmons, though he presents the large figures in his table, later admits that the Spaniards exaggerated their figures (in Ortiz, *Southwest,* 185, 192). See also Sedgwick, *Acoma, the Sky City,* 292; White, *Acoma Indians,* 23–24.

7. Coronado had earlier fought the Tiguex War through the winter. In Europe winter campaigns were rare.

8. All modern writers agree that the Spaniards scaled the South Mesa: Sedgwick, *Acoma, the Sky City,* 82; White, *Acoma Indians,* 27; and Garcia-Mason, "Acoma Pueblo," 457. Testimony at the Indian trial afterward indicates that they captured a point near the North Mesa (Carabajal, Medel, and Figueroa, in *OD* 1.472, 474–75).

9. Zaldívar did not attack until 3 P.M., so he reduced to less than two hours the time the twelve had to fight. See the testimony of Zaldívar, Villagrá, and Carabajal (*OD* 1.461, 470, 472). The sun sets early in winter. Witnesses said the fighting next day ended at 5 P.M. (for example, Zaldívar, at *OD* 1.462).

10. Villagrá calls the openings "windows."

11. In fact, the Spaniards started fires, trying to smoke resisters out of the *estufas,* or kivas (Medel and Figueroa, in *OD* 1.474, 476). At this point Zaldívar had the houses and even the provisions fired (Zaldívar and Villagrá, in *OD* 1.462, 471).

12. Eyewitnesses list 500–600 prisoners. Zaldívar and Figueroa have 500 (*OD* 1.462, 476). Villagrá also gives 600 in his prose testimony, enumerating 70 men, 300 women, and some children (*OD* 1.471). Carabajal gives 70–80 men and 500 women and children (*OD* 1.473). Among the modern historians Schroeder opts for lower figures (in Ortiz, *Southwest,* 246). He has 800 dead, 70–80 captive men, and 350–500 women and children.

13. Zaldívar confirms Villagrá's account. The sergeant major ordered the women and children arrested to prevent the warriors from killing them (*OD* 1.462). Weber lists 500 men dead, and 300 women and children (*Spanish Frontier,* 86).

14. He is called from Apache lands by Gicombo (*NM* 26.27–33, p. 135v), which at Ácoma would probably mean Navajo. Though he is married, his wife does not live in Ácoma (*NM* 33.50–53, p. 170r). Ramón Gutiérrez indicates that modern tribal categories arose only in the eighteenth century (*When Jesus Came,* xxvii), so we must be cautious about such identifications. Fray Alonso de Benavides in 1630, however, knew about the Navajo and explained the name. *Nabaju,* he said, meant "large, cultivated fields"; the Navajo farmed more than other Apache or Athapaskans. In the seventeenth century

the Acomas, as well as the Indians of Taos, Jemez, and Zuñi, took refuge among the Apache and Navajo when necessary (Gutiérrez, *When Jesus Came*, xxviii).

15. In a speech shared by Bempol.

16. Jonestown is a recent example, but the Japanese civilians who committed suicide on 11–12 July 1944 on Saipan provide a closer parallel. See Morison, *New Guinea*, 338–39; Toland, *Rising Sun*, 2:638–50.

17. Appian, *Iberica*, 96–97, in *Historia romana;* and Florus, *Epitome*, 1.34.18.

18. Bibar, *Crónica*, 122.184–85. Eight hundred Indians died, and Pedro Villagrá had the captives mutilated.

19. *OD* 1.464. Caoma was probably Coomo, one of the three chiefs who gave Ácoma's submission before the December massacre (*OD* 1.354–56). He would most likely be one of the three war or outside chiefs but not the first (White, *Acoma Indians*, 45). In historical times the war chiefs were elected and installed annually in December or January, and Villagrá has Gicombo so elected in January. The office, however, was originally a lifetime, hereditary appointment (White, *Acoma Indians*, 67, 146), and I suspect that annual elections reflect Spanish influence. Gutiérrez says that the War Chief in myth had two assistants, who represented the Twin War Gods of the pueblo, but later he says the Twin War Gods themselves were the outside chiefs (*When Jesus Came*, 6, 25–26).

20. See also the testimony of Excasi and Caucachi, in *OD* 1.467, and Cat-ticati, at 1.465.

21. *OD* 1.466. The Spaniards assumed that the old men ran a pueblo (Gutiérrez, *When Jesus Came*, 13), so they could force the war on the rest.

22. He comes from a family below the rest of the crowd (*NM* 18.15–24, 22.21–24, pp. 97r, 117v). Outside this family, however, Villagrá prefers the romance pattern familiar since Boiardo. Zutacapan creates a clique of young warriors (*NM* 18.185–93, p. 99v) and opposes the aged Chumpo, another king of Garamanta (18.136–64, p. 99r).

23. Villagrá develops the tension effectively through two debates, which precede the December massacre. The peace party wins the first debate, an affair of set speeches (*NM* 18.165–68, p. 99r). The second dramatizes a complete breakdown. No one can finish a speech, and the debate ends in a riot (*NM* 21.14–152, pp. 113v–15v).

24. Villagrá had a good education and would have known Virgil. He got a degree at Salamanca, and it was this that recommended him as a judge assessor to Friar Alonso Martínez (*NM* 2: App. 1, Doc. v, 24–25).

25. The latter reference picks up *Il.* 22.74–76, where Priam imagines his own death.

26. Villagrá alludes to the scene where Laocoon throws a spear into the wooden horse (*Ae.* 2.50–53).

27. Villagrá constantly associates the two. They participate in the December massacre, Tempal killing Pereira (*NM* 22.193–206, p. 119v), and give joint speeches at the council, where Cotumbo sounds like Boiardo's Rodamonte (26.137–45, p. 137r). At the beginning of the battle the two appear with Zutacapan (*NM* 28.96–99, 29.189, pp. 146r, 152r). Villagrá was present at the Indian trial in February, leaving for Mexico in March. See Horgan, *Great River*, 1:211.

28. *NM* 34.245–388, pp. 179r–81r. Quint shows the extensive literary imitation involved in this episode, particularly of Ercilla (*Epic and Empire*, 100–102).

29. After the war Indian testimony pointed to requisitions as a major cause of the war. Caoma told Oñate that the Spaniards demanded too much maize, flour, and blankets, though in December the incident that started the war concerned turkeys. Other charges involved rape and murder. Recent historians accept the Indian analysis (Weber, *Spanish Frontier,* 85; Gutiérrez, *When Jesus Came,* 53). I am somewhat more skeptical. Weber relies on Oñate's enemies, such as Velasco, who was not present. It is true, however, that the Spaniards did not solve the problem of requisitions until Vargas and the reconquest (Bannon, *Spanish Borderlands,* 90–91).

30. The dying Cotumbo and Tempal call themselves luckless (*NM* 34.357, p. 180v). Quint notes that the defeated in epic regularly blame fate, fortune, or chance, thus denying superiority to the victor (*Epic and Empire,* 103).

31. He also exemplifies "miserable fate" (*NM* 33.28, p. 170r). Earlier Villagrá speaks of fortune's enmity (*NM* 19.1–14, p. 103r), says that the December massacre shows it (24.20–34, p. 127r), and has Zutancalpo express typical Renaissance sentiments during the third debate (26.172–80, p. 137v): How many, enthroned on high, have we seen fall with unhappy ruin! Before the battle the youth again fears that fortune will spin her wheel (*NM* 28.107–13, p. 146r). Villagrá later draws the standard moral: good fortune is unstable, but evil is certain (*NM* 32.157–64, p. 166r).

32. Gicombo and Bempol (*NM* 32.295–302, p. 168r), Chumpo (33.224–25, 252–55, pp. 172v–73r).

33. The charges were formulated between 1606 and 1609. See Forbes, *Apache, Navaho, and Spaniard,* 111.

34. *OD* 1.Intro.35. Hodge gives the list of the modern historians who accepted Villagrá's story in Villagrá, *History of New Mexico,* trans. Espinosa, intro. and notes by Hodge, 19–25. They include Adolph Bandelier, Hubert Howe Bancroft, and Herbert E. Bolton. Hodge himself concurs: "There is no reason to doubt the poet's account of the bloody battle of the Ácoma *peñol*. . ." (ibid., 28). Among the students of Ácoma pueblo, White, the most important, also accepts Villagrá, though he finds details of his personal adventures before the battle absurd (*Acoma Indians,* 26). Among the revisionists Garcia-Mason accepts Villagrá's facts but reinterprets them according to Jack Forbes ("Acoma Pueblo," 456–57). It is well to note that the poet could have understood the Ácomas through interpreters. See the report of Las Casas on the December massacre (*OD* 1.438). The Spaniards acquired two interpreters at Santo Domingo, a Keresan pueblo like Ácoma ("Itinerary," in *OD* 1.319). One of the two, Tomás, presented Zaldívar's peace offer to the Ácomas at the end of the second day of fighting, and Villagrá guarded him (Zaldívar and Villagrá, in *OD* 1.462, 471).

35. Horgan, *Great River,* 1:216; Forbes, *Apache, Navaho, and Spaniard,* 97–98. See Friar Juan de Escalona's letter of 1 October 1601, in *OD* 2.697–99.

36. *OD* 2.693; Forbes, *Apache, Navaho, and Spaniard,* 97.

37. *NM* 33.328–413, pp. 174r–75r. Oñate had originally intended to lead the expedition, but Vicente de Zaldívar claimed the post. Some Spaniards believed he had the right

to avenge his brother's loss (according to the testimony of Alonso Sanchez, in *OD* 1.427). See also Villagrá, *Historia de la Nueva Mexico,* ed. and trans. Encinias, Rodríguez, and Sánchez, xxxvii.

38. *OD* 1.455–56. For Oñate's instructions to the sergeant major, see ibid., 456–59. Powell (*Soldiers, Indians, and Silver,* 109) notes how frontiersmen arranged documentary evidence by using each other as witnesses. The viceregal court presumably judged the public meeting in this light.

39. *OD* 1.458–59 (given 11 January 1599).

40. *OD* 1.471, 473–74, 476 (Carabajal, Medel, and Figueroa).

41. *OD* 1.462, 471, 473–74, 476 (Zaldívar, Villagrá, Medel, Figueroa, and Carabajal).

42. He has those who incited the December massacre hide like cowards in caves (*NM* 31.260–64, p. 162v).

43. In his appeal of 1617 Oñate specifies the details of the charge (*OD* 2.1127–28).

44. He has 60, not 70, men for the Spanish side and gives the kills at 600, a low figure (see note 12 above). He also lists the prisoners at 600 and may have confused the two. For the Indian trial he says that those under twenty were put under a surveillance of twenty years and those over twenty were enslaved. In fact, all males older than twelve had to do twenty years of personal servitude (*OD* 1.477–78, 2.614–15). Weber uses this suspect source for his reconstruction of the December incident (*Spanish Frontier,* 85 and n. 108).

45. No one else mentions blankets except Cat-ticati, an Indian absent from the scene (*OD* 1.465, 2.614).

46. Villagrá escorted him north. They left Mexico in September 1600 and arrived at San Gabriel on Christmas (*OD* 1.Intro.24). Escalona claims that he interviewed friars, captains, and soldiers (*OD* 2.693). He mentions blankets in connection with the December massacre, so he probably had talked with Velasco.

47. The friar was not, of course, among the few who scaled the rock by ladder on the first day, and on the second Salado had to descend the rock to receive confession (*NM* 30.273–318, pp. 158r–59r).

48. Forbes accepts Velasco's report and calls Ácoma a planned murder, a massacre spread over several days (*Apache, Navaho, and Spaniard,* 89–90). He later calls Zaldívar the butcher of Ácoma (ibid., 94). For the assault and for the December massacre Forbes regularly follows Velasco and the Franciscans (ibid., 87–88). He selects his evidence to fit his hypothesis that the Spaniards and not the Apache were the enemies of native culture in New Mexico (ibid., 284). For Oñate he accepts the Franciscan versions, but since his thesis requires him to judge all Spaniards negatively, he attacks the Franciscans as well. He does not realize that he thereby undercuts the authority of his evidence. If the Franciscans are bad, why trust what they say?

49. Powell, *Soldiers, Indians, and Silver,* 50–51. He is my authority for the Chichimeca War throughout.

50. Ibid., 90, 109. Viceroy Martín Enríquez (1568–80) instituted "guerra a fuego y sangre" (Naylor and Polzer, *Presidio and Militia,* 36–37).

51. *OD* 1.65; Powell, *Soldiers, Indians, and Silver,* 113–14, 117–18, 221. Viceroy Gastón de Peralta (1566–68) first instituted the office of lieutenant captain general. Its holder

supervised warfare and defense in the Gran Chichimeca and set up forts and fortified towns (Naylor and Polzer, *Presidio and Militia,* 46 and n. 6).

52. Villagrá, *Justificación,* 6r; Powell, *Soldiers, Indians, and Silver,* 9, 11, 14 (talking of Cristóbal de Oñate, a hero of the Mixtón War, who had administered Coronado's province during his visit to New Mexico). See *OD* 2.1145–46, 1151–52; also Bolton, *Coronado,* 55, 407.

53. Simmons remarks that Spanish reactions initially reflected previous experience. For example, they called the Pueblo dances *mitotes,* a term they used for the frenzied war dances of the Chichimecas (in Ortiz, *Southwest,* 179). *Chichimeca* itself was a Spanish term for the wild tribes beyond the area of the old Aztec Empire (Bannon, *Spanish Borderlands,* 5).

54. Villagrá, *Justificación,* 1r, 2r–v, 4r. In the margin he cites Thomas Aquinas and Roman law to support his position (ibid., 2r).

55. Villagrá mentions eleven deaths in his epic narrative. At the Indian trial Oñate adds two servants and so gets thirteen (*OD* 1.429–30). In the *Justificación* Villagrá lists ten deaths (5v).

56. Jones, *Pueblo Warriors,* 12. He is talking of the eighteenth century. New Mexico was still farther in 1599. Estimates of the distance vary. Bannon has 1,000 miles, or 1,609 kilometers (*Spanish Borderlands,* 38); Weber, 800 miles, or 1,287 kilometers (*Spanish Frontier,* 80). These differences probably depend on where one sets the frontier. Weber has it at Santa Barbara near the Rio Conchos, the last Spanish town Oñate visited on his trek. The supply line from Mexico City was more than 2,400 kilometers long, and the round trip took eighteen months (Bannon, *Spanish Borderlands,* 80).

57. *OD* 1.435. Márquez stated previously that the other Indians were watching to see what the Spaniards would do (ibid., 433). Las Casas thought they had to make the pueblo permanently uninhabitable (ibid., 438–39); Olague, another survivor, said, "If they did not have such a stronghold, they would not dare to rebel" (ibid., 443).

58. *OD* 1.445. The first Spaniards to visit Ácoma called it a robbers' citadel, feared by the whole country (see Garcia-Mason, "Acoma Pueblo," 455; Sedgwick, *Acoma, the Sky City,* 58).

59. Oñate instructed Zaldívar to fight a war without quarter if the Indians refused to surrender those responsible for the December massacre (Villagrá, *Historia de la Nueva Mexico,* ed. and trans. Encinias, Rodríguez, and Sánchez, xxxvii). Although the Indians made peace overtures at the end of the second day of fighting, they never agreed to this condition.

60. *OD* 1.477–78. They each lost a foot. Men and women over twelve were sentenced to twenty years of personal servitude, though most soon ran away. Children were distributed to monasteries and convents. The aged who had been disabled in the war were freed. Two Hopi Indians lost their right hands and were sent home. Velasco says that twenty-four Indians lost a foot (*OD* 2.615).

61. Villagrá, *Justificación,* 2r; Weber, *Spanish Frontier,* 86.

62. Villagrá, *Justificación,* 5v. He overlooks the war with the Saline pueblos in the following year, but otherwise his point applies.

63. Simmons, in Ortiz, *Southwest*, 184. In 1650 Jemez revolted, and a Tewa uprising was forestalled. Before, there had been incidents involving friars at Zuñi (1632) and Taos (1639). Modern historians accept Villagrá's assessment and agree that the terror worked. See Bannon, *Spanish Borderlands*, 37–38; Gutiérrez, *When Jesus Came*, 54.

64. He mentions only Chile but assumes the Chichimeca experience and refers to it on the same page.

65. Forbes, who argues against the Spaniards, nevertheless allows that some evidence indicated that the Pueblo Indians were planning to unite and throw out the invaders. The swift capture of Ácoma cowed them all (*Apache, Navaho, and Spaniard*, 108).

66. Powell (*Soldiers, Indians, and Silver*, 124–25) gives the pay scale. A soldier was allowed to enslave unbelievers or apostates in a just war, and Gonzalo de las Casas, who provided the intellectual defense for the harsh war in the Gran Chichimeca, drew on this tradition. The stockmen of the area in their petition to the viceroy (1582) similarly asked for the right to enslave the Chichimecas, and slaving as well as higher salaries provided the incentives to attract more and better soldiers to this frontier war (Naylor and Polzer, *Presidio and Militia*, 36–38, 48n.15).

67. Powell, *Soldiers, Indians, and Silver*, 137. Powell also lists many other charges, all of which derive from the low salaries given soldiers. See ibid., 182, 186–87. For Chile, Najera notes that the most bellicose Indians live nearest the Spanish frontier (*Desengaño y reparo*), 5.1.5.257.

68. *OD* 2.692. The Council of the Indies had already worried about this in 1596, and Philip had suspended the expedition temporarily (*OD* 1.89–91).

69. Powell, *Soldiers, Indians, and Silver*, 204. It became a characteristic Spanish practice to transplant Christian Indians north to help stabilize the frontier (Bolton, *Rim of Christendom*, 9; Bannon, *Spanish Borderlands*, 6). In Mexico the former lieutenant captain general for the Chichimeca War, Juan Bautista de Orozco, had already suggested the use of Tlaxcalans for this purpose in 1576, and King Philip picked up the suggestion. The Tlaxcalans moved north in 1591 (Naylor and Polzer, *Presidio and Militia*, 40, 42–43, 50 and n. 22, 54n.32). I cite from the English text because it has the annotations.

70. Arguing as a military commander, Orozco anticipated this clerical analysis by some years. In his letter to Philip II of 25 November 1576 he described slave raids during the Chichimeca War that could take one to four months and brought in mostly women and children (Naylor and Polzer, *Presidio and Militia*, 46). Such raids would only antagonize the Indian warriors.

71. Ibid., 182, also 93–94, 133, 187–89, 193–96, 212, 218–19.

72. Ibid., 159, 189–90, 199, 201.

73. Villagrá, *Historia de la Nueva Mexico*, ed. and trans. Encinias, Rodríguez, and Sánchez, xvii.

74. *NM* 2: App. 1, Docs. xvii–xviii, xx–xxi, xxviii.

75. Molina, *Chili*, 2.249–54.

76. Villagrá, *Justificación*, 5v–6r.

77. Ibid., 5r.

78. C. R. Friedrichs (in Parker, *Thirty Years' War*, 210–11, 214–15) calls it an unprece-

dented catastrophe and estimates that Germany lost 15–20 percent of its population, up to 50 percent in the war zones.

CHAPTER 12: THE ENGLISH

1. In his notes Smith argued for the former position (Sidney, *Defence,* in Smith, *Elizabethan Critical Essays,* vol. 1). Levao has recently made a persuasive argument for the skeptical line in his *Renaissance Minds,* 134–56. He relates his analysis to the *New Arcadia* in a later chapter (212–49).

2. For the publication see the headnote to Grosart's edition (Daniel, *Civile Wars,* ed. Grosart).

3. Daniel glosses the claim in his Dedicatory Epistle (*CW* 6). He has followed the truth of history, not adding or subtracting from the generally received opinion. It is impious to depart from it or to introduce fictions.

4. *Defence,* 153. The poet also discusses history in his letter to Robert Sidney of 18 October 1580. The historian becomes an orator in his orations and like a poet paints the effects, notions, and whisperings of the people. If the facts were not so, it is enough that they *might* have been so. See Sidney, *Prose Works,* 3:131.

5. Drayton writes historical epic but does not talk about it in his *Barons Warres.*

6. He began to revise the *Old Arcadia* between 1582 and 1584 but died in 1586 with book 3 unfinished. See Sidney, *Arcadia,* ed. Evans, 12–13. He reprints the 1593 version plus the bridge passage by Sir William Alexander (1621), which connects the *New Arcadia* to the *Old Arcadia.* The changes made by Mary Sidney do not affect the passages we will consider.

7. Buxton reprints the 1619 version. See Drayton, *Barons Warres,* ed. Buxton, 707–8.

8. Grosart reproduces the 1623 quarto, which came from the same type setting as the 1609 quarto.

9. The only other depictions that concern this siege are the two days of fighting caused by Anaxius's intervention (*NA* 3.15) and the skirmish on the island (18.542–44), but there is also the fighting with the helots (1.6).

10. In an earlier, undramatized battle—between the Lycians and Armenians—Sidney informs us that the horse had to rescue the foot (*NA* 2.3.303). The fighting in *NA* 1.6, being inside town, is on foot.

11. Hotspur also acts like a cavalryman. Led by fury into the midst of spears and swords, he dies surrounded (*CW* 4.54). This description would not fit the close-ranked advance of dismounted knights characteristic of the period. At Towton Daniel says that Yorkist arrows stampeded the Lancastrian horse (*CW* 8.15–16), though, in fact, the Lancastrians charged successfully. See Goodman, *Wars of the Roses,* 50–52. For Castillon Daniel does assume infantry fighting in one place (*CW* 6.90).

12. He is specific at *Mortimeriados,* 372, less clear in *Barons Warres,* though the word *charge* normally suggests cavalry (*BW* 2.33, 42). For Borough Bridge he mentions the light horse Andrew Herckley brought (*BW* 2.49, 56).

13. *Defence,* 156, 154. Levao remarks that the "only access to reality is through fiction

and conjecture" ("Sidney's Feigned Apology," 229). Weiner argues that this conception is the other side of the Calvinist view of human corruption (*Sidney and Poetics*, 9–11).

14. Oman, *Sixteenth Century*, 405, 401.

15. Ibid., 359, 364–65, 367.

16. West, "Spenser's Art of War," 658. Spenser provides a literary example when he has Arthur and Guyon chase Maleger's rabble away from the gate of Alma's castle (*FQ* 661–62).

17. Oman, *Sixteenth Century*, 373.

18. Ibid., 373, 403.

19. West remarks of Spenser: "The guerilla warfare of the Irish marches made possible military anachronism that would have proved grotesquely out of place in the increasingly mathematical siege warfare of the Lowlands. Spenser's nostalgia for the mounted knight obliquely reflects the essential backwardness of Elizabethan armies, among the last in Europe to abandon the lance" ("Spenser's Art of War," 658–59). West later observes that cavalry fighting in Ireland allowed Spenser to gloss over the tension between the old-style need for personal prowess in battle and the new military mode, dominated by massed infantry, gunpowder, and siege tactics (680).

20. Ariosto and Tasso, for example, also use images and details effectively, but they keep in view the general disposition of the combatants and make the tactics clear to their readers. The *exclusive* reliance on images and stray details creates the lyric or impressionistic effect that characterizes these English presentations.

21. Sidney here casts Amphialus in the role of Turnus in book 12 of the *Aeneid*.

22. In the *Mortimeriados* the barons meet this charge (449–55), and Drayton simply announces their flight later (491–92).

23. Arthur then wins Bedgrayne, and Charlemagne would have won Montealbano but for the still later appearance of the African army on the field. For Bedgrayne, see chapter 2; for Montealbano there are occasional remarks in chapter 1.

24. In the *Mortimeriados*, 374, he observes that the barons had to divide their force to meet an enemy coming from two directions.

25. He never clarifies the tactics for Shrewsbury or Towton either, though he stresses the effect of the initial arrow shower by the Yorkists in the latter battle (*CW* 8.15–16).

26. Nashe writes a fine parody of this mode, when he describes the tournament Surrey held at Florence. All the knights come in allegorical armor, and Surrey himself makes his horse look like an ostrich. The jousters, of course, are quite inept—all but Surrey himself (*UT* 316–23).

27. Among the many studies of chivalric tournaments one can cite Arthur Ferguson, *The Indian Summer of English Chivalry* and *The Chivalric Tradition in Renaissance England*; Huizinga, *Waning of the Middle Ages*; Keen, *Chivalry*; McCoy, *Rites of Knighthood*; and Yates, *Astraea*.

28. A standard example of anachronism would be the military formation assumed by the shepherds who represent reason and passion (*NA* 2.Ec.407): a square with wings, and a van. This suggests Spanish practice.

29. The use of a series of forts replaced the old lines of circumvallation by mid-century (Pepper and Adams, *Firearms and Fortifications,* 108). West notes that Spenser similarly muddles the siege of Alma's castle. The defenders dare not open the gates until Arthur and Guyon chase off Maleger's rabble. Then, however, they open the gates before entrenched artillery, and the besiegers never think to rush the gate ("Spenser's Art of War," 663–64).

30. See the comparisons in the duel of Amphialus and Argalus (*NA* 3.12.505) and in Amphialus's poem (3.9.477), which originally was in the Fourth Eclogue of the *Old Arcadia.* See Sidney, *Arcadia,* ed. Evans, 475n. The helots in book 1 provide the exception. They have shot in town (*NA* 1.6.97).

31. In book 1 galley slaves are promised freedom if they fight well (*NA* 1.8.107). Sidney later contrasts the fighting styles of Amphialus and Musidorus as that between a sailing ship and a galley (*NA* 3.18.541).

32. Shrewsbury involves the actions of Douglas and Hotspur (*CW* 4.47, 49–56); for Towton he stresses Falconbridge and Northumberland (8.15–16, 19).

33. For modern accounts of Castillon, see Burne, *Agincourt War,* 331–45; Seward, *The 100 Years War,* 259–62; Jacob, *Fifteenth Century,* 505–6; and Goodman, *Wars of the Roses,* 165.

34. On fortified camps see Goodman, *Wars of the Roses,* 21–22, 30, 167, 214; Pieri, *Il rinascimento,* 276–77; Mallett, *Mercenaries,* 147, 160–61, 168–71, 177.

35. See, for example, Erona, who banished the statues of Cupid from Lycia and then fell in love with a commoner who later betrayed her (*NA* 2.13.302, 14.306, 29.398–99).

36. Chateaubriand, *Itinéraire,* 358.

37. For details of the battle see the references in note 33 above.

38. *NA* 1.6, 3.7–8, 15, 18. The representations of war take up no more than 6.5 percent of the whole work.

39. *Defence,* 188–89. At 179 he tacitly includes prose romance in the epic category.

40. The eight wars are the Thessalian, Macedonian, Phrygian, Pontine, Paphlagonian or Galatian (the geographical terminology is inconsistent), the Lycian, Bithynian, and Trapezuntine. The siege of Cecropia's castle covers chapters 4–19 of the twenty-nine–chapter fragment.

41. Jonson, *Conversations with William Drummond,* 599.

42. Castillon is eight stanzas but twenty-seven with preliminaries, Shrewsbury has twelve, and Towton has twenty-two.

43. West analyzes the instances: Calidore and the brigands, Arthur and Guyon versus Maleger's rabble (659–65), Artegall and 100 of the Soldan's knights (669), Talus and the Amazons and then the Irish ("Spenser's Art of War," 667–68).

44. West, who discusses anything related to warfare in *The Faerie Queene,* remarks that single combat is the norm ("Spenser's Art of War," 659). Even scenes where a knight fights a crowd actually revert to the old tactics of romance. Artegall defeating the Soldan's knights or Talus chasing crowds recall similar incidents involving Orlando and Rinaldo in the *Innamorato.* See, for example, *OI* 1.17.23–32, 2.3.53–59.

45. West, discussing the *Muiopotmos,* makes a remark that could just as well apply to

The Faerie Queene: "At the core of Spenser's little mock-heroic is thus a paradoxical vision where epic poetry somehow sustains itself gaily without war, and military victory becomes artistic triumph. The fragility of this integrative vision is evident" ("Spenser's Art of War," 693).

46. Contamine, *War in the Middle Ages,* 124–25.

47. Oman, *Sixteenth Century,* 373–74. Soldiers in expeditionary forces normally received their training abroad.

48. Ibid., 374, 388. Already in 1523 the English troops in Picardy were undisciplined (327).

49. Lope de Vega served on the Azores campaign and in the Armada, where he lost a brother. See Morel-Fatio and Fitzmaurice-Kelly, "Vega, Lope de." We have no evidence for military service of Juan Rufo, although as a resident of Córdoba he lived near the war zone during the Morisco Revolt, which takes up most of the narration in his *Austriada.*

50. West provides a summary of the evidence for and against Spenser's possible military experience ("Spenser's Art of War," 656–57 and n. 7). His own analysis of Calidore and the brigands indicates that the poet had no sense for fighting on foot (ibid., 660–61), and West adds that "massed human bodies have only fitful military reality for him" (661). West similarly points out the bizarre behavior of armies in book 5 of the *Faerie Queene.* For example, Geryoneo brings an army with him against Arthur, but we never hear about it again (ibid., 670). Spenser's friend, Gabriel Harvey, did not understand the military authors he read (ibid., 699).

51. Milton does give a military muster: Jesus sees the Parthians going out to war (*PR* 3.298–344).

52. For Italy see Corvisier, *Armies and Societies,* 13, 95–96.

53. *BW* 2.45–46; *CW* 4.55, 8.6–7, 22–24. Raphael, speaking for the victorious side in another civil war, leaves the deeds of the fallen angels in oblivion (*PL* 6.373–85).

54. Dropped at *CW* 4.44. It was in the 1595 edition.

55. There had, of course, been a theoretical link between the two genres ever since Plato and Aristotle.

56. *Discorsi dell'arte poetica,* 2:380.

57. Ercilla is the exception. Though he has scenes with leaders and dramatizes conferences, especially on the Indian side, he also presents the Araucanian war from the viewpoint of a volunteer soldier and stresses group activity on the Spanish side.

58. See, for example, *UT* 255–57, 262–63, 270–71, 277–79. Nashe also begins his narrative by parodying the old oral formulas of earlier romances (*UT* 255). For a discussion of *The Unfortunate Traveller* as picaresque, see the introduction, 30.

59. Grimmelshausen, *Simplicissimus,* 1.1.7–10.

60. He never traveled outside England and lived mostly in London (*UT,* introduction, 14–16).

61. *UT* 276–77. The description of the carnage, however, is famous, especially that of François I, his face splattered with the brains of his own men.

62. *UT* 370. Jack Wilton is probably seventeen in 1513 but has aged only a year by 1520 (*UT* 256, 348).

63. He and Surrey meet Erasmus and More in Rotterdam, where they never were together (*UT* 290), and are helped by Aretino, who has just received the pension from Henry VIII, which he did not get until 1542 (309 and n. 209).

64. In his dream Simplicius defines mercenaries by a verse: "Gewalttat, Unge-rechtigkeit, / Treiben wir Landsknecht allezeit" (Grimmelshausen, *Simplicissimus*, 1.16.46) The naive farm boy, surrounded by heavy cavalry, thinks them the wolves his foster father talked about (ibid., 1.3.14). In general, the author gives one a clear sense of the war between peasant and soldier. Simplicius's foster mother sings that the soldier's trade brings great loss and harm to peasants (ibid., 1.3.13–14). Simplicius later sees soldiers burning the nearby village, but the peasants come from the forest and drive off the horsemen (ibid., 1.13.38–39). In Hanau the soldiers overeat and drink at a great feast, despite the famine in town and several hundred homeless peasants at the door (ibid., 1.30.88). Peasants of the Black Forest regularly kill soldiers (ibid., 4.23.374). Many of these soldiers, of course, came from the same peasant stock.

65. Grimmelshausen, *Simplicissimus*, 1.4.17, 2.11.129, 5.20.463. He also makes careful distinctions. *Marauders,* for example, are soldiers who cannot keep up with the regular army, for various reasons (ibid., 4.13.344–45).

66. Cervantes similarly avoids war, despite his own extensive military experience in the Cyprus War, in which he lost an arm at Lepanto and was taken prisoner at Tunis, and despite the fact that *Don Quijote* takes a comic look at romance and epic.

67. Grimmelshausen, *Simplicissimus*, 2.21.469–72, 2.27.184–85, 5.21.469–72. Parker summarizes the battle of Wittstock briefly in *Thirty Years' War,* 163. In the bibliographical essay he discusses Grimmelshausen and his use of Sidney (ibid., 299–300).

68. Parker, *Military Revolution,* 1.

69. For the late medieval period, see Contamine, *War in the Middle Ages,* 123, 125.

70. Grimmelshausen says very early that his story requires him to show the cruelties of the German war (*Simplicissimus*, 1.4.15). He constantly emphasizes the land made bar-ren by the fighting. The countryside by Dorsten in the north lacks loot, having been ravaged (ibid., 3.7.231), and that of Lorraine is almost deserted (ibid., 4.9.332). Simplicius later thinks that one could not find a cat or dog in the empty villages of the plain (ibid., 5.7.411). He then sees his own mountain refuge ravaged (ibid., 5.20.461). Peaceful Switzer-land provides a striking contrast, and its prosperous countryside seems to Simplicius an earthly paradise (ibid., 5.1.391).

71. See especially Auerbach, *Mimesis,* 400–404.

72. See, for example, the author's remarks (*Le rouge et le noir,* 1.15–16.297).

73. See, for example, ibid., 1.7.254, 11.277–78.

74. Stendhal, *La chartreuse de Parme,* 1.2–4.52–91.

APPENDIX 1: MALORY AND THE *SUITE DU MERLIN*

1. The first editor of the *Suite,* Gaston Paris, dated the work between 1225 and 1230 (*Merlin,* lxix). Bogdanow prefers 1230–40 (*Romance of the Grail,* 10–13).

2. For a summary of the evidence, see Vinaver's notes (Malory, *Works,* ed. Vinaver), and Bogdanow, *Romance of the Grail,* 24–25. Malory got his peculiar spellings from the

Cambridge *Suite:* Igrayne for Igerna, Hector for Antor (Vulgate *Merlin*) or Auctor (Huth *Merlin*), Arthur's foster father. The Cambridge *Suite* also has the King of the Hundred Knights, not Lot, receive the dream that warns the kings of Arthur's night ambush (*Suite*, 218v).

3. The Spanish translation, the *Baladro del sabio Merlin*, does not include the war (Bogdanow, *Romance of the Grail*, 12, 31).

4. An example of this development is the description of a night with brilliant moonlight. The shorter Vulgate mentions it once, to explain how Arthur's army can travel to the ambush and keep formation (Vulgate *Merlin*, 113). The expanded Vulgate adds a night ride of the three kings from Logres to Bedigran (111). In the Cambridge *Suite* the Breton army likewise rides by moonlight (*Suite*, 215v). Normally the expansion is by stock phrase, which does not alter the sense of the original.

5. The catalogue gives 39,000 (*Suite*, 216r), and after the first ambush 20,000 rally and 20,000 dead and wounded are left on the field (219r–v).

6. Arthur invades France with 60,000 (*Morte*, 20.19.1211).

APPENDIX 3: *ARAUCANA* I

1. Both go back ultimately to the dialogue of Hector and Andromache at *Il.* 6.390–502. In all three the hero leaves his wife to die, though in Villagrá Gicombo kills his wife first.

2. Lagos thinks the Spanish attack violated the norms for a just war ("El incumplimiento," 173, 176), but Held sees it as divine punishment for Araucanian aggression (*Studien*, 81–83).

3. Medina, *Vida de Ercilla*, 82.

4. Critics have also emphasized the importance of the avarice of Valdivia and his conquistadores. See Durand, "El chapetón," 115–16; Held, *Studien*, 74–76.

5. He does not go as far as the Dominicans, who decided that the Chichimeca War was unjust. At Viceroy Enríquez's second assembly in Mexico City (1574), the Dominicans disagreed both with their previous opinion and with that of the other orders and said that the Spaniards could not fight the Chichimecas, since they had been the aggressors. The case parallels that of Valdivia, only in Mexico it was silver rather than gold. See Powell, *Soldiers, Indians, and Silver*, 106. Critics generally agree that Ercilla thought the Spaniards fought a just war in Araucania. Durand says that Ercilla had reservations but did not consider the conquest illegitimate ("El chapetón," 119). The poet, therefore, assumed that the Indian rebellion was unjustified (ibid., 133). Held agrees. Ercilla thought the Spaniards had a right to wide rule because of the missions (*Studien*, 48–49, 53–55, 58) and believed, therefore, that they had objective right on their side (77). Held gives multiple citations to show that the poet regarded the Indians as rebels (ibid., 47), though with qualifications (49, 77–78). Even Lagos in her "deconstructive" reading of the *Araucana* allows that the narrator-poet initially considered the war just ("El incumplimiento," 163).

6. Held shows that Ercilla carried the theme of avarice throughout the poem (*Studien*, 85, 88, 132–33).

BIBLIOGRAPHY

Since the system of reference to classical texts is standardized, this list includes only nonstandardized texts and editions of classical works.

Adorno, Rolena. "The Warrior and the War Community: Constructions of the Civil Order in Mexican Conquest History." *Dispositio* 14 (1989): 225–46.

Allegretti, Allegretto. *Diarj.* Ed. L. A. Muratori. Vol. 23 of *Rerum italicarum scriptores ab anno aerae Christianae quingentesimo ad millesimum quingentesimum.* Milan: Societas Palatina, 1733.

Alliterative *Morte Arthure.* See Benson, D. Larry, ed., *King Arthur's Death.*

Anceschi, Guiseppe, ed. *Il Boiardo e la critica contemporanea.* Florence: L. S. Olschki, 1970.

Andrews, Kenneth R. *Trade, Plunder and Settlement: Maritime Enterprise and the Genesis of the British Empire, 1480–1630.* Cambridge: Cambridge University Press, 1984.

Angelucci, Angelo. *Gli schioppettieri Milanesi nel xv secolo.* Milan, 1865.

Appian, *Historia romana.* Ed. P. Vidreck and A. G. Roos. Leipzig: Teubner, 1939.

Ariosto, Ludovico. *Opere di Ludovico Ariosto.* Ed. Adriano Seroni. 1961. Reprint. Milan: Ugo Mursia, 1966.

———. *Opere minori in verso e in prosa di Lodovico Ariosto.* Ed. Filippo-Luigi Polidori. Florence, 1894.

———. *Orlando furioso.* Trans. Barbara Reynolds. 2 vols. 1975. Reprint. New York: Penguin, 1981.

———. *"Orlando furioso" di Ludovico Ariosto secondo le stampe del 1516, 1521, 1532.* Ed. Filippo Ermini. 3 vols. Vol. 1. Milan: G. Pirotta, 1909.

Asali, K. J., ed. *Jerusalem in History.* Brooklyn, N.Y.: Olive Branch, 1990.

Ascoli, Albert. *Ariosto's Bitter Harmony: Crisis and Evasion in the Italian Renaissance.* Princeton, N.J.: Princeton University Press, 1987.

Atil, Esin. *Art of the Mamluks.* Washington, D.C.: Smithsonian Institution Press, 1984.

Aubigné, Agrippa d'. *Les tragiques.* In *Oeuvres,* ed. Henri Weber with Jacques Bailbé and Marguerite Soulié, 1–243. Bibliothèque de la Pléiade. Paris: Gallimard, 1969.

Auerbach, Erich. *Mimesis.* Trans. Willard Trask. 1953. Reprint. Garden City: Doubleday Anchor, n.d.

Austria, Don Juan of. Letter to Don Garcia of Toledo, 9 September 1571. In *Colección de documentos inéditos para la historia de España,* ed. Don Martin Fernandez Navarrete, Don Miguel Salvá, Don Pedro Sainz de Baranda, Marques de Pidal, Marques de Miraflores, Marques de la Fuensanta del Valle, José Sancho Rayón, and Francisco de Zabálburu, 3:20–21. 112 vols. Madrid, 1843–95.

Babinger, Franz. *Mehmed der Eroberer und seine Zeit.* Munich: F. Bruckmann, 1953.

Bannon, John Francis. *The Spanish Borderlands Frontier, 1513–1821.* 1970. Reprint. Albuquerque: University of New Mexico Press, 1974.

Barros, João de, and Diogo de Couto. *Da Asia.* 1778. Reprint. Lisbon: Livraria S. Carlos, 1973.

Bascuñan, Nuñez de Pineda y. *Cautiverio feliz.* Vol. 3 of *Historiadores de Chile.* Santiago de Chile, 1863.

Beazley, C. Raymond. *Prince Henry the Navigator.* 1895. Reprint. New York: Burt Franklin, 1968.

Beeler, John. *Warfare in Feudal Europe, 730–1200.* Ithaca, N.Y.: Cornell University Press, 1972.

Beer, Marina. *Romanzi di cavalleria: Il "Furioso" e il romanzo italiano del primo cinquecento.* Rome: Bulzoni, 1987.

Belloc, Hilaire. *The Eye-Witness.* 1908. Reprint. London: J. M. Dent, 1949.

———. *Paris.* London: Methuen, 1902.

Belloni, Antonio. *Il poema epico e mitologico.* In *Storia dei generi letterari italiani.* Milan: F. Vallardi, 1912.

Bennett, Jack Arthur Walter, ed. *Essays on Malory by Walter Oakeshott (and Others).* Oxford: Clarendon Press, 1963.

Benson, D. Larry, ed. *King Arthur's Death.* Indianapolis and New York: Bobbs-Merrill, 1974.

———. *Malory's "Morte Darthur."* Cambridge, Mass.: Harvard University Press, 1976.

Benvenuti, Antonia Tissoni. "Il mondo cavalleresco e la corte estense." In *I libri di "Orlando innamorato,"* 13–33. Ferrara: Panini, 1987.

Beowulf and the Fight at Finnsburg. Ed. F. Klaeber. 1922. Reprint. Boston: D. C. Heath, 1950.

Bertoni, Guilio. *La biblioteca Estense e la coltura ferrarese.* Turin: E. Loescher, 1903.

———. *L'"Orlando furioso" e la rinascenza a Ferrara.* Modena, 1919.

Bibar, Gerónimo de. *Crónica y relación copiosa y verdadera de los reynos de Chile.* Ed. Irving A. Leonard. Santiago de Chile: Fondo Histórico y Bibliográfico José Toribio Medina, 1966.

Binni, Walter. *Metodo e poesia di Ludovico Ariosto.* Messina and Florence: G. d'Anna, 1961.

Bitterli, Urs. *Cultures in Conflict: Encounters between European and Non-European Cultures, 1492–1800.* Trans. Ritchie Robertson. Stanford, Calif.: Stanford University Press, 1989.

Bogdanow, Fanni. *The Romance of the Grail: A Study of the Structure and Genesis of a Thirteenth-Century Arthurian Prose Romance.* New York: Barnes and Noble, 1966.

Boiardo, Matteo Maria. *Orlando innamorato.* Ed. Luigi Garbato. 4 vols. Milan: Marzorati, 1970.

———. *Orlando innamorato*. Trans. Charles Stanley Ross. Berkeley: University of California Press, 1989.

Bolton, H. E. *Coronado, Knight of Pueblos and Plains. (Coronado on the Turquoise Trail, Knight of Pueblos and Plains.)* Albuquerque and New York: University of New Mexico Press and Whittlesey House/McGraw-Hill, 1949.

———. *Rim of Christendom: A Biography of Eusebio Francisco Kino, Pacific Coast Pioneer*. 1936. Reprint. Tucson: University of Arizona Press, 1984.

Bonomo, Dario. *L'"Orlando furioso" nelle sue fonti*. Rocca San Casciano: Cappelli, 1953.

Bornstein, Diane. "Military Manuals in Fifteenth-Century England." *Mediaeval Studies* 37 (1975): 469–77.

———. "Military Strategy in Malory and Vegetius' *De re militari.*" *Comparative Literature Studies* 9 (1972): 123–29.

Boulanger, Robert. *Greece*. Trans. M. N. Clark and J. S. Hardman. 1964. Reprint. Paris: Hachette, 1973.

Boxer, Charles R. *The Portuguese Seaborne Empire, 1415–1825*. New York: Alfred A. Knopf, 1969.

Bradford, Ernle. *The Shield and the Sword: The Knights of St. John, Jerusalem, Rhodes and Malta*. New York: E. P. Dutton, 1973.

Branca, Daniela Delcorno. *L'"Orlando furioso" e il romanzo cavalleresco medievale*. Florence: L. S. Olschki, 1973.

Brasil, Reis [José Gomes Bras]. *"Os Lusíadas," comentários e estudo crítico*. 10 vols. Vol. 1. Lisbon: Editorial Minerva, 1960.

Bravo, Rodrigo. Testimony concerning Tristán de Silva Campofrío, 8 February 1571. In *Colección de documentos inéditos para la historia de Chile*, ed. J. T. Medina, 23:268–71. Santiago de Chile, 1900.

Brockman, Eric. *The Two Sieges of Rhodes, 1480–1522*. London: J. Murray, 1969.

Brodie, Bernard, and Fawn Brodie. *From Crossbow to H-Bomb*. Bloomington: Indiana University Press, 1973.

Brute, or the Chronicles of England. Ed. Friedrick W. D. Brie. 2 vols. London: K. Paul, Trench, Trübner, 1908.

Bueil, Jean de. *Le jouvencel*. Ed. C. Favre and L. Lecestre. 2 vols. Paris: Librairie Renouaud H. Laurens, 1887–89.

Burne, Alfred H. *The Agincourt War*. London: Eyre and Spottiswoode, 1956.

Burton, Sir Richard. *Camoens: His Life and His Lusiads*. 2 vols. London, 1881.

Bury, J. B. *A History of Greece*. 1900, rev. ed. 1913. Reprint. New York: Random House, n.d.

Bussman, Klaus. *DuMont Guide to Paris and the Ile de France*. Trans. Russell Stockman. New York: Stewart, Tabori, and Chang, 1984.

Caetani, Onorato. *Lettere di Onorato Caetani*. Ed. G. B. Carinci. Rome: Salviucci, 1870.

Calvo, Mayo. *Secretos y tradiciones mapuches*. 1968. Reprint. Santiago de Chile: Bello, 1983.

Camões, Luis de. *Os Lusiadas*. Ed. Frank Pierce. 1973. Reprint. Oxford: Clarendon Press, 1981.

———. *"Lusiadas" de Luis de Camoens*. Commentary by Manuel de Faria e Sousa. 2 vols. Vol. 1. Madrid: Juan Sanchez, 1639.

————. *Os Lusiadas (The Lusiads)*. Trans. Richard Burton, ed. Isabel Burton. 2 vols. Vol. 2. London: Bernard Quaritch, 1880.

Campofrío, Tristán de Silva. Información de méritos y servicios de Tristán de Silva Campofrío. In *Colección de documentos inéditos para la historia de Chile*, ed J. T. Medina, 23:264–67. Santiago de Chile, 1900.

Carne-Ross, D. S. "The One and the Many: A Reading of the *Orlando furioso*." *Arion*, n.s. 3 (1976): 146–219.

Castañeda de Nájera, Pedro de. *Relación de la Jornada de Cíbola*. In *Narratives of the Coronado Expedition, 1540–1542*, ed. George P. Hammond and Agapito Rey, 191–283. Albuquerque: University of New Mexico Press, 1940.

Castanheda, Fernão Lopes de. *The First Booke of the Historie of the Discoverie and Conquest of the East Indies*. Trans. N. L. London, 1582.

Cervantes, Miguel de. *Don Quijote de la Mancha*. Ed. Martín de Riquer. 1955. 2 vols. Barcelona: Editorial Juventud, 1979.

Chanson de Roland, La. Ed. Joseph Bédier. 1922. Reprint. Paris: L'Edition d'Art H. Piazza, 1966.

Charrière, E. *Collection de documents inédits sur l'histoire de France*. Vol. 3: *Négociations de la France dans le Levant*. Paris, 1853.

Chateaubriand, François-Auguste-René de. *Itinéraire de Paris à Jérusalem*. Introd. Jean Mourot. 1811. Reprint. Paris: Garnier-Flammarion, 1968.

————. *Mémoires d'outre-tombe*. Ed. Maurice Lavaillant and Georges Moulinier. 2 vols. Bibliothèque de la Pléiade. 1951. Reprint. Paris: Gallimard, 1972.

Chaucer, Geoffrey. *The Works of Geoffrey Chaucer*. Ed. F. N. Robinson. 1933. Reprint. Boston: Houghton Mifflin, 1957.

Chaudhuri, K. N. *Trade and Civilization in the Indian Ocean: An Economic History from the Rise of Islam to 1750*. Cambridge: Cambridge University Press, 1985.

Chiappelli, Fredi. *Il conoscitore del caos*. Rome: Bulzoni, 1981.

Chiericati, Chiereghino. See Zorzi, Giangiorgio.

Christine de Pisan. *The Book of Fayttes of Armes and of Chyvalrye*. Trans. William Caxton. Ed. A. T. P. Byles. Early English Text Society, o.s. 189. London: Oxford University Press, 1932.

Cinzio, G. G. Giraldi. *Discorso dei romanzi*. In *Scritti critici*, ed. Camillo Guerrieri Crocetti, 35–167. Milan: Marzorati, 1973.

Cipolla, Carlo. *Guns, Sails and Empires*. New York: Pantheon, 1965.

Colección de documentos inéditos para la historia de Chile. Ed. J. T. Medina. 30 vols. in 15. Santiago de Chile, 1888–1902.

Colección de documentos inéditos para la historia de España. Ed. Don Martin Fernandez Navarrete, Don Miguel Salvá, Don Pedro Sainz de Baranda, Marques de Pidal, Marques de Miraflores, Marques de la Fuensanta del Valle, José Sancho Rayón, and Francisco de Zabálburu. 112 vols. Madrid, 1843–95.

Commynes, Philippe de. *Mémoires*. In *Historiens et chroniqueurs du moyen âge: Robert de Clari, Villehardouin, Joinville, Froissart, Commynes*, ed. Albert Pauphilet and Edmond Pognon. Bibliothèque de la Pléiade. Paris: Gallimard, 1952.

Conrad, Joseph. *Lord Jim.* Ed. Cedric Watts and Robert Hampson. 1949. Reprint. New York: Viking Penguin, 1987.

Contamine, Philippe. *War in the Middle Ages.* Trans. Michael Jones. 1984. Reprint. New York: Basil Blackwell, 1986.

Correa, Gaspar. *The Three Voyages of Vasco da Gama and His Viceroyalty.* Trans. from *Lendas da India* by Henry E. J. Stanley. 1869. Hakluyt Society, 42. New York: Burt Franklin, n.d.

Corte Real, Hieronymo (Jerónimo). *Felicissima victoria concedida del cielo al señor don Juan d'Austria, en el golfo de Lepánto de la poderosa armada Othomana. En el año de nuestra salvacion de 1572.* Lisbon: Antonio Ribero, 1578.

Corvisier, André. *Armies and Societies in Europe, 1494–1789.* Trans. Abigail T. Siddall. Bloomington: Indiana University Press, 1979.

Curtin, Philip D. *Cross-Cultural Trade in World History.* 1984. Reprint. Cambridge: Cambridge University Press, 1985.

Daniel, Samuel. *The Civile Wars between the Two Houses of Lancaster and Yorke.* Vol. 2 of *The Complete Works in Verse and Prose of Samuel Daniel.* Ed. Alexander B. Grosart. London and Aylesbury: Hazell, Watson, and Viney, 1885.

Davis, Walter R., and Richard A. Lanham. *Sidney's Arcadia.* New Haven: Yale University Press, 1965.

Delbrück, Hans. *Geschichte der Kriegskunst in Rahmen der politischen Geschichte.* 7 vols. Vol. 3. Berlin: G. Stilke, 1907.

———. *Medieval Warfare.* Vol. 3 of *History of the Art of War.* Trans. Walter J. Renfroe, Jr. 2d ed. 1923 (German), 1982 (English). Reprint. Lincoln: University of Nebraska Press, 1990.

Dictys Cretensis. *Ephemeridos belli Troiani libri.* Ed. Werner Eisenhut. 1958. 2d ed. Leipzig: B. G. Teubner, 1973.

Diedo, Gerolamo. *La battaglia di Lepanto e la dispersione della invincibile Armata di Filippo II.* Milan, 1863.

Diffie, Bailey W., and George D. Winius. *Foundations of the Portuguese Empire, 1415–1580.* Minneapolis: University of Minnesota Press, 1977.

Documentos sobre os Portugueses em Moçambique e na Africa Central, 1497–1840/Documents on the Portuguese in Mozambique and Central Africa, 1497–1840. 2 vols. Vol. 1. Lisbon: Centro de Estudos Históricos Ultramarinos/National Archives of Rhodesia and Nyasaland, 1962.

Donadoni, Eugenio. *Torquato Tasso.* 2 vols. Florence: L. Battistelli, 1920.

Donato, Eugenio. "'Per selve e boscherecci labirinti': Desire and Narrative Structure in Ariosto's *Orlando furioso.*" In *Literary Theory/Renaissance Texts,* ed. Patricia Parker and David Quint, 33–62. Baltimore: Johns Hopkins University Press, 1986.

Drayton, Michael. *The Barons Warres.* Vol. 2 of *Poems of Michael Drayton.* Ed. John Buxton. 1950. Reprint. Cambridge, Mass.: Harvard University Press, 1967.

———. *Mortimeriados. The Lamentable Civell Warres of Edward the Second and the Barrons.* Vol. 1 of *The Works of Michael Drayton.* Ed. J. William Hebel. Oxford, 1931.

Durand, José. "El chapetón Ercilla y la honra Araucana." *Filologia* 10 (1964): 113–34.

Duri, Abdul Aziz. "Jerusalem in the Early Islamic Period, 7th–11th Centuries A.D." In *Jerusalem in History,* ed. K. J. Asali, 105–29. Brooklyn: Olive Branch, 1990.

Emilio, Paolo. *Historici clarissimi de rebus gestis Francorum . . . De regibus item Francorum chronicon.* 1529. Reprint. Paris, 1550.

Ercilla y Zuñiga, Don Alonso de. *La Araucana.* Pref. L. S. Ladero. Barcelona: Ramón Sapena, 1972.

———. *La Araucana.* Ed. J. T. Medina. 5 vols. Vol 1. Santiago de Chile: Imprenta Elzeviriana, 1910.

Espinosa, Antonio Vázquez de. *Compendium and Description of the West Indies.* Trans. Charles Upson Clark. Smithsonian Miscellaneous Collections, 102. Washington, D.C.: Smithsonian Institution, 1942.

Estoire de Merlin, L'. Vol. 2 of *The Vulgate Version of the Arthurian Romances,* ed. H. Oskar Sommer. Washington, D.C.: Carnegie Institution of Washington, 1908.

Eyrbyggja Saga. Trans. Hermann Pálsson and Paul Edwards. Toronto: University of Toronto Press, 1973.

Fallon, Robert Thomas. *Captain or Colonel: The Soldier in Milton's Life and Art.* Columbia, Mo.: University of Missouri Press, 1984.

Favier, Jean. *Paris au xve siècle, 1380–1500.* Nouvelle histoire de Paris. Paris: Association pour la Publication d'une Histoire de Paris (distributed by Hachette), 1974.

Ferguson, Arthur. *The Indian Summer of English Chivalry.* Durham, N.C.: Duke University Press, 1960.

Figueroa, Suarez de. *Hechos de don Garcia Hurtado de Mendoza, cuarto marques de Cañete.* Vol. 5 of *Historiadores de Chile.* Santiago de Chile: Ferrocarril, 1864.

Finbert, Elian-J. *Israel.* Paris: Hachette, 1956.

Florus, Lucius Annaeus. *Epitome of Roman History.* With trans. by Edward Seymour Forster. In *Florus and Cornelius Nepos,* 2–351. Loeb Library, 231. New York: G. P. Putnam, 1929.

Forbes, Jack D. *Apache, Navaho, and Spaniard.* 1960. Reprint. Norman: University of Oklahoma Press, 1984.

Fornari, Simon. *La spositione di M. Simon Fornari da Rheggio sopra l'"Orlando furioso" di M. Ludovico Ariosto.* 2 vols. Florence, 1549.

Franceschetti, Antonio. "Appunti sull'Ariosto lettore dell'*Innamorato.*" In *Ludovico Ariosto,* 103–17. Rome: Accademia Nazionale dei Lincei, 1975.

Freeman, James A. *Milton and the Martial Muse.* Princeton, N.J.: Princeton University Press, 1980.

Frontinus. *The Stratagems and The Aqueducts of Rome.* Trans. Charles E. Bennett (trans. of *The Aqueducts* revised from trans. of Clemens Herschel). Ed. Mary B. McElwain. Loeb Library, 174. Cambridge, Mass.: Harvard University Press; London: William Heinemann, 1969.

Fulcher of Chartres. *Historia hierosolymitana, 1095–1127.* Ed. Heinrich Hagenmeyer. Heidelberg: C. Winter, 1913.

———. *A History of the Expedition to Jerusalem, 1095–1127.* Trans. Frances Rita Ryan, ed. Harold S. Fink. Knoxville: University of Tennessee Press, 1969.

Gamboa, Martín Ruiz de. Segundo información de servicios del general Martín Ruiz de Gamboa, 28 July 1569. In *Colección de documentos inéditos para la historia de Chile,* ed. J. T. Medina, 19:243–56. Santiago de Chile, 1899.

Garcia-Mason, Velma. "Acoma Pueblo." In *Southwest,* ed. Alfonso Ortiz, vol. 9 of *Handbook of North American Indians,* 450–66. Washington, D.C.: Smithsonian Institution, 1979.

Gardner, Edmund. *The King of Court Poets: A Study of the Work, Life, and Times of Lodovico Ariosto.* 1906. Reprint. New York: Greenwood, 1968.

Garibi, A. *Le armi da fuoco portatili italiane dalle origini al Risorgimento.* New ed. Milan: Bramante, 1968.

Geoffrey of Monmouth. *Historia regum Britanniae.* Vol. 3 of *La légende arthurienne.* Ed. Edmond Faral. Paris: H. Champion, 1929.

Gesta Francorum et aliorum Hierosolimitanorum. Ed. Rosalind Hill. London: T. Nelson, 1962.

Getto, Giovanni. *Nel mondo della "Gerusalemme."* Florence: Vallecchi, 1968.

Gianni, Angelo. *Pulci uno e due.* Florence: Nuova Italia, 1967.

Gibson, J. C. L. *Canaanite Myths and Legends.* Edinburgh: Clark, 1978.

Giovio, Paolo. *Gli elogi degli uomini illustri.* Ed. Renzo Meregazzi. Rome: Istituto Poligrafico dello Stato, 1972.

Göller, Karl Heinz. "Arthurian Chivalry and War in the Fourteenth and Fifteenth Centuries: History and Fiction." In *Spätmittelalterliche Artusliteratur,* ed. Karl Heinz Göller, 53–68. Paderborn: Ferdinand Schöningh, 1984.

Goodman, Anthony. *The Wars of the Roses: Military Activity and English Society, 1452–97.* London: Routledge and Kegan, 1981.

Goodman, J. R. "Malory and Caxton's Chivalric Series, 1481–1485." In *Studies in Malory,* ed. James W. Spisak, 257–74. Kalamazoo: Medieval Institute Publications, 1985.

Graham, R. B. Cunninghame. *Pedro de Valdivia.* New York: Harper and Brothers, 1927.

Gray, John. *A History of Jerusalem.* London: Hale, 1969.

Greenblatt, Stephen. *Renaissance Self-Fashioning, from More to Shakespeare.* Chicago: University of Chicago Press, 1980.

Greene, Thomas. *The Descent from Heaven, a Study in Epic Continuity.* New Haven: Yale University Press, 1963.

Grimmelshausen, Hans Jacob Christoffel von. *Der Abenteuerliche Simplicissimus.* Afterword by Alfred Kelletat. Munich: Winkler-Verlag, 1956.

Guillebert de Metz. *Description de la ville de Paris au xve siècle.* Ed. Le Roux de Lincy. Paris: Auguste Aubry, 1855.

Guilmartin, John Francis. *Gunpowder and Galleys: Changing Technology and Mediterranean Warfare at Sea in the Sixteenth Century.* London: Cambridge University Press, 1974.

Gutiérrez, Ramón A. *When Jesus Came, the Corn Mothers Went Away: Marriage, Sexuality, and Power in New Mexico, 1500–1846.* Stanford, Calif.: Stanford University, 1991.

Hale, J. R. "The Art of War and Renaissance England." Washington, D.C.: Folger Shakespeare Library, 1961.

———. "The Early Development of the Bastion: An Italian Chronology, c. 1450–c. 1534." In *Europe in the Late Middle Ages*, ed. J. R. Hale, J. R. L. Highfield, and B. Smalley, 466–94. London: Faber, 1965. Reprinted in *Renaissance War Studies*, 1–29. London: Hambledon, 1983.

———. "Gunpowder and the Renaissance: An Essay in the History of Ideas." In *From the Renaissance to the Counter-Reformation*, ed. Charles H. Carter, 113–44. New York: Random House, 1965. Reprinted in *Renaissance War Studies*, 389–420. London: Hambledon, 1983.

———. *Renaissance War Studies*. London: Hambledon, 1983.

———. "War and Public Opinion in Renaissance Italy." In *Italian Renaissance Studies*, ed. E. F. Jacob, 94–122. London: Faber, 1960. Reprinted in *Renaissance War Studies*, 359–87. London: Hambledon, 1983.

———. "War and Public Opinion in the Fifteenth and Sixteenth Centuries." *Past and Present* 22 (1962): 18–35.

———. *War and Society in Renaissance Europe, 1450–1620*. Baltimore: Johns Hopkins University Press, 1985.

Hamilton, A. C. *Sir Philip Sidney*. Cambridge: Cambridge University Press, 1977.

Hammer-Purgstall, Joseph von. Vol. 3 of *Geschichte des Osmanischen Reiches*. 10 vols. Pest, 1827–35.

Hammond, George P., and Agapito Rey, eds. *Don Juan de Oñate, Colonizer of New Mexico, 1595–1628*. Albuquerque: University of New Mexico Press, 1953.

Hardin, Richard F. *Michael Drayton and the Passing of Elizabethan England*. Lawrence: University Press of Kansas, 1973.

Hathaway, Baxter. *The Age of Criticism: The Late Renaissance in Italy*. Ithaca: Cornell University Press, 1962.

Hawkins, Sir Richard. *The Observations of Sir Richard Hawkins, Knight, in his Voyage into the South Sea*, A.D. 1593. In *The Hawkins' Voyages during the Reigns of Henry VIII, Queen Elizabeth, and James I*, ed. Clements R. Markham, 83–329. Hakluyt Society First Ser., 57. 1878. Reprint. New York: Burt Franklin, 1970.

Heinze, Richard. *Virgils epische Technik*. 3d ed., rev. Leipzig: B. G. Teubner, 1915.

Held, Barbara. *Studien zur "Araucana" des don Alonso de Ercilla*. Frankurt am Main: Haag and Herchen, 1983.

Hemming, John. *The Conquest of the Incas*. New York: Harcourt Brace, 1970.

Henderson, David. "Power Unparalleled: Gunpowder, Firearms, and the Early *Furioso*." *Schifanoia* 13 (1993). Forthcoming.

Herodotus. *Historiae*. Trans. Lorenzo Valla. Paris: Ioannis Parvus, 1510.

———. *Storie*. Trans. M. M. Boiardo. Venice: Marchio, 1533.

Hess, Andrew C. *The Forgotten Frontier*. Chicago: University of Chicago Press, 1978.

Hillairet, Jacques. *Connaissance du vieux Paris*. 3 vols. in 1. Paris: Éditions Princesse or Metro Éditions Internationales, 1956.

Hitti, Philip K. *History of the Arabs*. London: Macmillan, 1937.

Hiyari, Mustafa A. "Crusader Jerusalem, 1099–1187 A.D." In *Jerusalem in History*, ed. K. J. Asali, 130–76. Brooklyn: Olive Branch, 1990.

Horgan, Paul. *Great River: The Rio Grande in North American History.* 2 vols. New York: Rinehart, 1954.

How, W. W.. and J. Wells. *A Commentary on Herodotus.* 1928. Reprint. 2 vols. Oxford: Oxford University Press, 1975.

Hugo, Victor. *Notre-Dame de Paris, Les travailleurs de la mer.* Ed. Jacques Seebacher [*Notre-Dame*] and Yves Gohin. Bibliothèque de la Pléiade. Paris: Gallimard, 1975.

Huizinga, Johan. *The Waning of the Middle Ages.* Trans. F. Hopman. 1924. Reprint. Garden City: Doubleday Anchor, 1954.

Jachino, Angelo. *Le marine italiane nella battaglia di Lepanto.* Rome: Accademia Nazionale dei Lincei, 1971.

Jacob, E. F. *The Fifteenth Century, 1399–1485.* Oxford: Clarendon Press, 1961.

Johnson, W. R. *Darkness Visible.* Berkeley: University of California Press, 1976.

Jones, Oakah L., Jr. *Pueblo Warriors and Spanish Conquest.* Norman: University of Oklahoma Press, 1966.

Jonson, Ben. *Conversations with William Drummond of Hawthornden.* In *Ben Jonson,* ed. Ian Donaldson, 595–611. Oxford: Oxford University Press, 1985.

Jordan, Constance. *Pulci's "Morgante": Poetry and History in Fifteenth-Century Florence.* Washington, D.C.: Folger Shakespeare Library; London: Associated Presses, 1986.

Journal de la bataille de Lépante. Ed. François Garnier. Paris: Editions de Paris, 1956.

Journal of the First Voyage of Vasco da Gama, 1497–1499. Ed. and trans. E. G. Ravenstein. Hakluyt Society 99. New York: Burt Franklin, n.d.

Kamal, Prince Youssouf. *Monumenta cartographica Africae et Aegyptii.* 5 vols. Cairo, 1926–51.

Keegan, John. *The Face of Battle.* New York: Viking, 1976.

Keen, Maurice. *Chivalry.* New Haven: Yale University Press, 1984.

Keller, Alexander. "A Renaissance Humanist Looks at 'New' Inventions: The Article 'Horologium' in Giovanni Tortelli's *De orthographia.*" *Technology and Culture* 11 (1970): 345–65.

Kennedy, Beverly. *Knighthood in the "Morte Darthur".* Cambridge: D. S. Brewer, 1985.

Kirk, Elizabeth. "'Clerkes, Poetes and Historiographs': The *Morte Darthur* and Caxton's 'Poetics' of Fiction." In *Studies in Malory,* ed. James W. Spisak, 275–95. Kalamazoo: Medieval Institute Publications, 1985.

Knight, Stephen. *Arthurian Literature and Society.* New York: St. Martin's, 1983.

Kollias, Elias. *The City of Rhodes and the Palace of the Grand Master.* Trans. William Phelps. Athens: Ministry of Culture, 1988.

Kritoboulos. *History of Mehmed the Conqueror.* Trans. Charles T. Riggs. Princeton, N.J.: Princeton University Press, 1954.

Lagos, Ramona. "El incumplimiento de la programación épica en *La Araucana.*" *Cuadernos Americanos* 40 (1981): 157–91.

La Monica, Stefano. "Realtà storica e immaginario bellico ariostesco." *Rassegna della Letteratura Italiana* 89 (1985): 326–58.

Lancelot. Ed. Alexandre Micha. 9 vols. Geneva: Droz, 1978–83.

Lane, Frederic C. *Venetian Ships and Shipbuilders of the Renaissance.* Baltimore: Johns Hopkins University Press, 1934.

———. *Venice.* Baltimore: Johns Hopkins University Press, 1973.

Latino, Juan. *Austriadis libri duo.* In *Ad catholicum pariter et invictissimum Philippum . . . de felicissima serenissimi Ferdinandi principis nativitate, epigrammatum liber; deque sanctissimi Pii Quinti . . . rebus, et affectibus erga Philippum regem . . . liber unus; Austrias carmen. . . .* Granada: Hugo de Mena, 1573.

Lefebvre, Georges. *Napoleon: From 18 Brumaire to Tilsit, 1799–1807.* Trans. Henry F. Stockhold. New York: Columbia University Press, 1969.

Lestoire de Merlin. Vol. 2 of *The Vulgate Version of the Arthurian Romances.* Ed. H. Oskar Sommer. Washington, D.C.: Carnegie Institution of Washington, 1908.

Lesure, Michel. *Lépante: La crise de l'empire ottoman.* Mesnil-sur-l'Estrée: Julliard, 1972.

Levao, Ronald. *Renaissance Minds and Their Fictions.* Berkeley: University of California Press, 1985.

———. "Sidney's Feigned Apology." *Publications of the Modern Language Association* 94 (1974): 223–33.

Lopez, Roberto S. "Il principio della guerra veneto-turca nel 1463." *Archivio Veneto,* ser. 5, 29–30 (1934): 45–131.

Lot, Ferdinand. *L'art militaire et les armées au moyen âge.* 2 vols. Vol. 2. Paris: Payot, 1946.

Lovera, Pedro Mariño de. *Crónica del reino de Chile.* Vol. 6 of *Colección de historiadores de Chile y documentos relativos a la historia nacional.* Santiago de Chile: Imprenta del Ferrocarril, 1865.

Ludovico Ariosto. Rome: Accademia Nazionale dei Lincei, 1975.

Lynch, John. *Empire and Absolutism, 1516–1598.* Vol. 1 of *Spain under the Habsburgs.* 1964. Reprint. New York: New York University Press, 1965.

Machiavelli, Niccolò. *Arte della guerra e scritti politici minori.* Ed. Sergio Bertelli. Milan: Feltrinelli, 1961.

Mahoney, Dhira B. "Malory's Great Guns." *Viator* 20 (1989): 291–310.

Malle, Louis. *Au revoir, les enfants.* Paris: Gallimard, 1987.

Mallett, Michael. *Mercenaries and Their Masters.* Totowa, N.J.: Rowman and Littlefield, 1974.

Mallett, Michael, and J. R. Hale. *The Military Organization of a Renaissance State: Venice, c. 1400 to 1617.* Cambridge: Cambridge University Press, 1984.

Malory, Sir Thomas. *La Morte Darthur.* Ed. H. Oskar Sommer. London: D. Nutt, 1889–91.

———. *The Works of Sir Thomas Malory.* 3 vols. Ed. Eugène Vinaver. 1947. Reprint. Oxford: Clarendon Press, 1967.

Marinelli, Peter V. *Ariosto and Boiardo.* Columbia: University of Missouri Press, 1987.

Marmolejo, Captain Alonso de Góngora. *Historia de Chile desde su descubrimiento hasta el año de 1575.* Vol. 4 of *Memorial historico español: Colección de documentos, opúsculos y antigüedades que publica la Real Academia de la Historia.* Madrid: Real Academia de la Historia, 1852.

Martin, Colin, and Geoffrey Parker. *The Spanish Armada*. New York: W. W. Norton, 1988.

Martorell, Joanot, and Martí Joan de Galba. *Tirant lo blanc*. Ed. Martín de Riquer. Barcelona: Editorial Selecta, 1947.

———. *Tirant lo blanc*. Trans. David H. Rosenthal. New York: Shocken, 1984.

Mason, J. A. *The Ancient Civilizations of Peru*. 1968. Rev. ed. New York: Penguin, 1979.

McCarthy, Terence. "Order of Composition in the *Morte Darthur*." *Yearbook of English Studies* 1 (1971): 18–29.

———. "The Sequence of Malory's Tales." In *Aspects of Malory*, ed. Toshiyuki Takamiya and Derek Brewer, 107–24. Totowa, N.J.: Rowman and Littlefield, 1981.

McCoy, Richard C. *The Rites of Knighthood: The Literature and Politics of Elizabethan Chivalry*. Berkeley: University of California Press, 1989.

———. *Sir Philip Sidney: Rebellion in Arcadia*. New Brunswick, N.J.: Rutgers University Press, 1979.

McNeill, William H. *The Pursuit of Power*. Chicago: University of Chicago Press, 1982.

———. *Venice, the Hinge of Europe, 1089–1797*. Chicago: University of Chicago Press, 1974.

Means, P. A. *The Spanish Main, Focus of Envy, 1492–1700*. New York: Scribner's, 1935.

Medina, J. T. *Vida de Ercilla*. 1916. Reprint. Mexico City: Fondo de Cultura Económica, 1948.

Medina della Motta del Friuli, Fray Bartolomeo. *Dialogo sopra la miracolosa vittoria ottenuta dell' armata della santissima lega Christiana, contra la Turchesca*. Venice, 1572.

Merendoni, Antonio. "Le 'genti d'arme' dei duchi d'Este (1465–1598): Storia e notizie sulle armi e il costume." *Schifanoia* 9 (1990): 67–138.

Merlin. Ed. Gaston Paris and Jacob Ulrich. 2 vols. Paris: Firmin Didot, 1886.

Miller, William. *The Latins in the Levant*. 1908. Reprint. Cambridge: Speculum Historiale; New York: Barnes and Noble, 1964.

Milton, John. *Complete Poems and Major Prose*. Ed. Merritt Y. Hughes. Indianapolis: Bobbs-Merrill, 1957.

Mirollo, James. "On the Significant Acoustics of Ariosto's Noisy Poem." *Modern Language Notes* 103 (1988): 87–112.

Molina, Abbé Don J. Ignazio. *The Geographical, National, and Civil History of Chili*. London, 1809.

Monluc, Blaise de. *Commentaires, 1521–1576*. Ed. Paul Courteault. Bibliothèque de la Pléiade. Paris: Gallimard, 1981.

Monmarché, Marcel. *Pyrénées*. Guides bleus. Paris: Hachette, 1921.

Morel-Fatio, Alfred, and James Fitzmaurice-Kelly. "Vega, Lope de." In *Encyclopedia Britannica*. 11th. ed. New York: Encyclopaedia Britannica, 1911.

Morison, Samuel Eliot. *New Guinea and the Marianas, March 1944–August 1944*. Vol. 8 of *History of United States Naval Operations in World War II*. 15 vols. 1953. Reprint. Boston: Little, Brown, 1984.

Morocco. 2d ed. Geneva: Nagel, 1969.

Mort le roi Artu. Ed. Jean Frappier. Geneva: Droz; Paris: Minard, 1964.

Mueller, William R., ed. *Spenser's Critics.* Syracuse: Syracuse University Press, 1959.

Murrin, Michael. *The Allegorical Epic: Essays in Its Rise and Decline.* Chicago: University of Chicago Press, 1980.

———. *The Veil of Allegory.* Chicago: University of Chicago Press, 1969.

Myrick, Kenneth. *Sir Philip Sidney as a Literary Craftsman.* 1935. Reprint. Lincoln: University of Nebraska Press, 1965.

Nájera, Alonso González de. *Desengaño y reparo de la guerra del reino de Chile.* Ed. J. T. Medina. Santiago de Chile: Impresión de la Viuda de Calero, 1886.

Nashe, Thomas. *The Unfortunate Traveller and Other Works.* Ed. J. B. Steane. 1972. Reprint. New York: Viking Penguin, 1985.

Naylor, Thomas H., and Charles W. Polzer, S. J., eds. *The Presidio and Militia on the Northern Frontier of New Spain: A Documentary History.* Vol. 1: *1570–1700.* Tucson: University of Arizona Press, 1986.

Nelson, William. *Fact or Fiction: The Dilemma of the Renaissance Storyteller.* Cambridge, Mass.: Harvard University Press, 1973.

Neruda, Pablo. *Memorial de Isla Negra.* Bogota: Oveja Negra, 1982.

Olmstead, A. T.. *History of the Persian Empire.* 1948. Reprint. Chicago: University of Chicago Press, 1978.

Oman, Sir Charles. *A History of the Art of War in the Middle Ages.* 2 vols. 2d. ed. Boston: Houghton Mifflin, 1923.

———. *A History of the Art of War in the Sixteenth Century.* London: Methuen, 1937.

Oña, Pedro de. *Arauco domado.* Ed. J. T. Medina. Vol. 1 of *Obras completas de Pedro de Oña.* Santiago de Chile: Imprenta Universitaria, 1917.

Ortiz, Alfonso. *Handbook of North American Indians.* Vol. 9: *Southwest.* Washington, D.C.: Smithsonian Institution, 1979.

Orvieto, Paolo. *Pulci medievale.* Rome: Salerno, 1978.

Paratore, Ettore. "L'*Orlando innamorato* e l'*Eneide.*" In *Il Boiardo e la critica contemporanea,* ed. Giuseppe Anceschi, 347–75. Florence: L. S. Olschki, 1970.

Parker, Geoffrey. *The Army of Flanders and the Spanish Road, 1567–1659.* Cambridge: Cambridge University Press, 1972.

———. "Europe and the Wider World, 1500–1750: The Military Balance." In *The Political Economy of Merchant Empires,* ed. James D. Tracy, 161–95. Cambridge: Cambridge University Press, 1991.

———. *The Military Revolution: Military Innovation and the Rise of the West, 1500–1800.* Cambridge: Cambridge University Press, 1988.

———. *The Thirty Years' War.* London: Routledge and Kegan Paul, 1984.

Parry, J. H. *The Spanish Seaborne Empire.* 1966. Reprint. New York: Alfred A. Knopf, 1970.

Pepper, Simon, and Nicholas Adams. *Firearms and Fortifications: Military Architecture and Siege Warfare in Sixteenth-Century Siena.* Chicago: University of Chicago Press, 1986.

Pérotin-Duman, Anne. "The Pirate and the Emperor: Power and the Law on the Seas,

1450–1850." In *The Political Economy of Merchant Empires,* ed. James D. Tracy, 196–227. Cambridge: Cambridge University Press, 1991.

Peters, F. E. *Jerusalem: The Holy City in the Eyes of Chroniclers, Visitors, Pilgrims, and Prophets from the Days of Abraham to the Beginnings of Modern Times.* Princeton, N.J.: Princeton University Press, 1985.

Petrocchi, Georgio. *I fantasmi di Tancredi.* Caltanissetta: S. Sciascia, 1972.

Phillips, Carla Rahn. *Six Galleons for the King of Spain: Imperial Defense in the Early Seventeenth Century.* Baltimore: Johns Hopkins University Press, 1986.

Pierce, Frank. *La poesía épica del siglo de oro.* Trans. J. C. Cayol de Bethencourt. 1961. Rev. ed. Madrid: Editorial Credos, 1968.

Pieri, Piero, ed. "Il 'Governo et exercitio de la militia' di Orso degli Orsini e i 'Memoriali' di Diomede Carafa." *Archivio storico per le provincie napoletane,* new ser., 19 (1933): 99–212.

———. *Il rinascimento e la crisi militare italiana.* Turin: Einaudi, 1952.

Pittorru, Fabio. *Torquato Tasso: L'uomo, il poeta, il cortigiano.* Milan: Bompiani, 1982.

Pochoda, Elizabeth T. *Arthurian Propaganda: "Le Morte Darthur" as an Historical Ideal of Life.* Chapel Hill: University of North Carolina Press, 1971.

Pocock, H. R. *The Conquest of Chile.* New York: Stein and Day, 1967.

Poliziano, Angelo. *The Stanze.* Trans. David Quint. Amherst: University of Massachusetts Press, 1979.

Ponte, Giovanni. "L'*Orlando innamorato* nella civiltà letteraria del Quattrocento." In *Il Boiardo e la critica contemporanea,* ed. Giuseppe Anceschi, 407–25. Florence: Leo S. Olshki, 1970.

———. *La personalità e l'opera del Boiardo.* Genoa: Tilgher, 1972.

Pool, Franco. *Interpretazione dell'"Orlando furioso".* Florence: La Nuova Italia, 1968.

Powell, Wayne. *Soldiers, Indians, and Silver.* Berkeley: University of California Press, 1952.

Pulci, Luigi. *Lettere di Luigi Pulci a Lorenzo il Magnifico e ad altri.* Ed. Salvatore Bongi. Lucca: Giusti, 1886.

———. *Morgante.* Ed. Franca Ageno. Milan: Riccardo Ricciardi, 1955.

———. *Morgante.* 2 vols. Ed. George B. Weston. Bari: Laterza, 1930.

Quint, David. "Argillano's Revolt and the Politics of the *Gerusalemme Liberata*." In *Renaissance Studies in Honor of Craig Hugh Smyth,* ed. Morrogh, Gioffredi, Morselli, and Borsook, 1:455–64. 2 vols. Florence: Giunti Barbèra, 1985.

———. *Epic and Empire.* Princeton, N.J.: Princeton University Press, 1993.

Rajna, Pio. *Le fonti dell'"Orlando furioso".* Rev. ed. Florence: G. C. Sansoni, 1900.

Ramalho, Américo da Costa. *Portuguese Essays.* Lisbon: National Secretariat for Information, 1968.

Reichenbach, Giulio. *L'"Orlando innamorato" di M. M. Boiardo.* Florence: La Nuova Italia, 1936.

Revard, Stella Purce. *The War in Heaven.* Ithaca: Cornell University Press, 1980.

Riquer, Martín de. "Ariosto e España." In *Ludovico Ariosto,* 319–29. Rome: Accademia Nazionale dei Lincei, 1975.

————. *Cavalleria fra realtà e letteratura nel quattrocento.* Trans. M. Rostaing and V. Minervini. Bari: Adriatica, 1971.

Robert of Rheims [Robertus Monacus]. *Historia iherosolimitana.* Ed. D. Bongarsius. In *Recueil des historiens des Croisades: Historiens occidentaux,* 3:717–882. Paris: Imprimerie Impériale, 1866.

Roberts, Michael. *Essays in Swedish History.* Minneapolis: University of Minnesota Press, 1967.

Roma e dintorni. Guida d'Italia. 1962. Reprint. Milan: Touring Club Italiano, 1965.

Romizi, A. *Le fonti latine dell'"Orlando furioso".* Turin: G. B. Paravia, 1896.

Roncaglia, Aurelio. "Nascita e sviluppo delle narrativa cavalleresca nella Francia medievale." In *Ludovico Ariosto,* 229–50. Rome: Accademia Nazionale dei Lincei, 1975.

Ropp, Theodore. *War in the Modern World.* Rev. ed. New York: Collier Books, 1962.

Rosell y Lopez, Don Cayetano. *Historia del combate naval de Lepanto.* Madrid: Real Academia de la Historia, 1853.

Rosell y Lopez, Don Cayetano, ed. *Poemas épicos.* Biblioteca de Autores Españoles 17. Madrid, 1866.

Rossignol, Gilles. *Pierre d'Aubusson: "Le bouclier de la chrétienté".* Besançon: Editions la Manufacture, 1991.

Roteiro da primeira viagem de Vasco da Gama (1497–1499). Ed. A. Fontoura da Costa. 3d ed. Lisbon: Agência-Geral do Ultramar, 1969.

Rufo, Juan. *La Austriada.* In *Poemas épicos,* ed. Don Cajetano Rosell, 2:1–136. Biblioteca de Autores Españoles 29. Madrid, 1854.

Ruggieri, Ruggero, M. *L'umanesimo cavalleresco italiano da Dante all'Ariosto.* Rev. ed. Naples: Fratelli Conte, 1967.

Ruiz de Gamboa, Martín. "Document 13." In *Colección de documentos inéditos para la historia de Chile,* ed. J. T. Medina, 19:243–99. Santiago de Chile, 1899.

Runciman, Sir Steven. *The Fall of Constantinople, 1453.* 1965. Reprint. Cambridge: Cambridge University Press, 1969.

————. *The First Crusade and the Foundation of the Kingdom of Jerusalem.* Vol. 1 of *A History of the Crusades.* Cambridge: Cambridge University Press, 1951.

Saccone, Eduardo. "Osservazioni su alcuni luoghi dell'*Innamorato.*" *Modern Language Notes* 86 (1971): 31–60.

————. *Il soggetto del "Furioso".* Naples: Liguori, 1974.

Salomón, Nuño Hernández. Información de los servicios de Nuño Hernández Salomón, 1 July 1569. In *Colección de Documentos Inéditos para la Historia de Chile,* ed. J. T. Medina, 23:211–17. Santiago de Chile, 1900.

Sapegno, Natalino. "Ariosto poeta." In *Ludovico Ariosto,* 23–31. Rome: Accademia Nazionale dei Lincei, 1975.

Sedgwick, Mrs. William T. *Acoma, the Sky City.* Cambridge, Mass.: Harvard University Press, 1927.

Seem, Lauren Scancarelli. "The Limits of Chivalry: Tasso and the End of the *Aeneid.*" *Comparative Literature* 42 (1990): 116–25.

Segre, Cesare. *Esperienze ariostesche.* Pisa: Nistri-Lischi, 1966.

Servius. *Servii Grammatici qui feruntur in Vergilii carmina commentarii.* Ed. Georg Thilo and Hermann Hagen. 1884. Reprint. 3 vols. Hildesheim: George Olms, 1961.

Seward, Desmond. *The 100 Years War.* 1978. Reprint. New York: Atheneum, 1982.

Sidney, Sir Philip. *The Countess of Pembroke's Arcadia.* Ed. Maurice Evans. 1977. Reprint. New York: Viking Penguin, 1987.

———. *The Defence of Poesie, or An Apologie for Poetrie.* In *Elizabethan Critical Essays,* ed. G. Gregory Smith, 1:148–207. 2 vols. 1904. Reprint. London: Oxford University Press, 1964.

———. *The Prose Works of Sir Philip Sidney.* Ed. Albert Feuillerat. 4 vols. 1912. Reprint. Cambridge: Cambridge University Press, 1963.

Smail, R. C. *Crusading Warfare, 1097–1193.* 1956. Reprint. Cambridge: Cambridge University Press, 1972, 1978.

Smith, E. R. *The Araucanians or, Notes of a Tour among the Indian Tribes of Southern Chili.* New York, 1855.

Smith, G. Gregory, ed. *Elizabethan Critical Essays.* 2 vols. 1904. Reprint. Oxford: Oxford University Press, 1964.

Solerti, Angelo. "Un nuovo manoscritto della *Gerusalemme* con correzioni autografe." *Rivista delle Biblioteche e degli Archivi* 10 (1899): 29–30.

———. *Vita di Torquato Tasso.* 3 vols. Turin: E. Loescher, 1895.

Spake, O. H. K. *The Spanish Lake.* Minneapolis: University of Minnesota Press, 1979.

Spencer, William. *Algiers in the Age of the Corsairs.* Norman: University of Oklahoma Press, 1976.

Spisak, James W. "Introduction: Recent Trends in Malory Studies." In *Studies in Malory,* ed. James W. Spisak, 1–12. Kalamazoo: Medieval Institute Publications, 1985.

Stanzaic *Morte darthur.* See Benson, D. Larry, ed., *King Arthur's Death.*

Stendhal. *Romans et nouvelles.* Ed. Henri Martineau. 2 vols. Bibliothèque de la Pléiade. Paris: Gallimard, 1947.

Stevenson, W. B. *A Historical and Descriptive Narrative of Twenty Years' Residence in South America.* 3 vols. London, 1825.

Storici arabi delle Crociate. Ed. and trans. Francesco Gabrieli. Turin: Einaudi, 1973.

Suite du Merlin. Cambridge University Library, Additional MS 7071, fols. 202v–343v.

Tasso, Torquato. *Gerusalemme liberata.* In *Tutte le poesie di Torquato Tasso,* ed. Lanfranco Caretti. Verona: Mondadori, 1957.

———. *Gerusalemme liberata.* Ed. Marziano Guglielminetti. 2 vols. Milan: Garzanti, 1974.

———. *Gerusalemme liberata.* Ed. Angelo Solerti and others. Florence, 1896.

———. *Le lettere di Torquato Tasso.* Ed. Cesare Guasti. 5 vols. Florence: F. le Monnier, 1853.

———. *Prose.* Ed. Ettore Mazzali. Milan: Riccardo Ricciardi, 1959.

Tenenti, Alberto. *Piracy and the Decline of Venice, 1580–1615.* Trans. Janet Pullan and Brian Pullan. Berkeley: University of California Press, 1967.

Thomson, David. *Renaissance Paris.* Berkeley: University of California Press, 1984.

Toland, John. *The Rising Sun.* 2 vols. New York: Random House, 1970.

Toledo, Don Garcia de. Letter to Requesenes, 1 August 1571. In *Colección de documentos inéditos para la historia de España*, ed. Don Martin Fernandez Navarrete, Don Miguel Salvá, Don Pedro Sainz de Baranda, Marques de Pidal, Marques de Miraflores, Marques de la Fuensanta del Valle, José Sancho Rayón, and Francisco de Zabálburu, 3:7–10. 112 vols. Madrid, 1843–95.

Toussaint, Auguste. *History of the Indian Ocean*. Trans. June Guicharnaud. Chicago: University of Chicago Press, 1966.

Tracy, James D., ed. *The Political Economy of Merchant Empires*. Cambridge: Cambridge University Press, 1991.

Treppo, Mario del. "Gli aspetti organizzativi economici e sociali di una compagnia di ventura italiana." *Rivista Storica Italiana* 85 (June 1973): 253–75.

Ulloa, Jorge Juan, and Antonio de Ulloa. *A Voyage to South America*. Trans. John Adams. 2d ed. London, 1760.

Vale, M. G. A. *War and Chivalry: Warfare and Aristocratic Culture in England, France and Burgundy at the End of the Middle Ages*. Athens: University of Georgia Press, 1981.

Vecello, Tiziano. *Titiani Vecelli equitis pro Cadubriensibus ad Sereniss. Venetiarum principem Aloysium Mocenicum oratio*. Venice, 1571.

Vega, Garcilaso de la [El Inca]. *Royal Commentaries of the Incas and General History of Peru*. Trans. Harold V. Livermore, foreword by Arnold J. Toynbee. 2 vols. 1966. Reprint. Austin: University of Texas Press, 1970.

Vega, Lope de. *Dragontea*. 2 vols. Burgos: Museo Naval, 1935. Vol. 1: text; vol. 2: related documents.

Veniero, Sebastiano. "Relation of 22 December 1572." In Pompeo Molmenti, *Sebastiano Veniero e la battaglia di Lepanto*, app. doc. 5. Florence, 1899.

Vico, Giambattista. *Principj di scienza nuova*. Ed. Fausto Nicolini. 3 vols. 1953. Reprint. Turin: Einaudi, 1976.

Villagrá, Captain Gaspar Pérez de. *El Capitan Gaspar de Villagrá para justificación de las muertes, justicias, y castigos que el Adelantado don Juan de Oñate dizen que hizo en la Nueva Mexico, como uno de sus soldados, y por lo que le deve, por aver diso su Capitan general, suplica humilmente a V. Señoria, se note, y advierta lo que en este memorial por el se pone, como por persona que supo, vio, y entendio tanto de las cosas que los foragidos le imputan, y de lo que por aquellas tierras y entrada passaron*. Madrid, 1612.

———. *Historia de la Nueva Mexico*. Ed. and trans. Miguel Encinias, Alfred Rodríguez, and Joseph P. Sánchez. Albuquerque: University of New Mexico Press, 1992.

———. *Historia de la Nueva Mexico*. Ed. L. González Obregón. 2 vols. Mexico City: Impr. del Museo Nacional, 1900.

———. *History of New Mexico by Gaspar Pérez de Villagrá*. Trans. Gilberto Espinosa. Foreword and notes by F. W. Hodge. Los Angeles: The Quivira Society, 1933.

Virues, Cristóbal de. *Historia de Monserrate*. In *Poemas épicos*, ed. Don Cayetano Rosell y Lopez, vol. 1 in the Biblioteca de Autores Españoles, 17. Madrid, 1854.

Visconti, Carlo E., ed. "Ordine dell' esercito ducale Sforzesco, 1472–1474." *Archivio Storico Lombardo* 3 (1876): 448–513.

Vivaldi, Vincenzo. *"La Gerusalemme liberata" studiata nelle sue fonti: Azione principale del poema*. Trani: Vecchi, 1901.

———. *Prolegomeni ad uno studio completo sulle fonti della "Gerusalemme liberata"*. Trani: Vecchi, 1904.

Wallace, John. "Examples Are Best Precepts." *Critical Inquiry* 1 (1984): 275–90.

Weber, David J. *The Spanish Frontier in North America*. New Haven, Conn.: Yale University Press, 1992.

Weinberg, Bernard. *A History of Literary Criticism in the Italian Renaissance*. 2 vols. 1961. Reprint. Chicago: University of Chicago Press, 1963.

Weiner, Andrew. *Sir Philip Sidney and the Poetics of Protestantism: A Study of Contexts*. Minneapolis: University of Minnesota Press, 1978.

West, Michael. "Spenser's Art of War: Chivalric Allegory, Military Technology, and the Elizabethan Mock-Heroic Sensibility." *Renaissance Quarterly* 41 (1988): 654–704.

Whitaker, Muriel. *Arthur's Kingdom of Adventure: The World of Malory's "Morte Darthur"*. Cambridge: D. S. Brewer; Totowa, N.J.: Barnes and Noble, 1984.

White, Leslie A. *The Acoma Indians*. 1929. Reprint. Glorieta, N.M.: Rio Grande Press, 1974.

Wiggins, Peter DeSa. *Figures in Ariosto's Tapestry*. Baltimore: Johns Hopkins University Press, 1986.

Wilkins, Ernest H. "On the Dates of Composition of the *Morgante* of Luigi Pulci." *Publications of the Modern Language Association* 66 (March 1951): 244–50.

William of Tyre. *Historia rerum in partibus transmarinis gestarum*. Ed. A. Beugnot and A. Le Prévost. Vol. 1 of *Recueil des historiens des Croisades: Historiens occidentaux*. Paris: Imprimerie royale, 1844.

Wolper, Roy S. "The Rhetoric of Gunpowder and the Idea of Progress." *Journal of the History of Ideas* 31 (1970): 589–98.

Yates, Frances A. *Astraea: The Imperial Theme in the Sixteenth Century*. London: Routledge, 1975.

Zorzi, Giangiorgio. "Un vicentino alla corte di Paolo Secondo (Chiereghino Chiericati e il suo trattatello della milizia)." *Nuovo Archivio Veneto*, n.s. 30 (1915): 369–434.

INDEX